Scientific C++

Building Numerical Libraries the Object-Oriented Way

Guido Buzzi-Ferraris

Polytechnic of Milan

ADDISON-WESLEY
PUBLISHING
COMPANY

Wokingham, England · Reading, Massachusetts · Menlo Park, California · New York
Don Mills, Ontario · Amsterdam · Bonn · Sydney · Singapore
Tokyo · Madrid · San Juan · Milan · Paris · Mexico City · Seoul · Taipei

Cover designed by Chris Eley
incorporating photographs supplied by Tony Stone Images (main photograph)
and the National Motor Museum Beaulieu (other images)
and printed by the Riverside Printing Co. (Reading) Ltd.
Translated and typeset by Logotechnics C.P.C. Ltd., Sheffield
Printed and bound in Great Britain at the University Press, Cambridge

First printed 1993.

British Library Cataloguing-in-Publication Data
A catalogue record for this book is available from the British Library.

Library of Congress Cataloging-in-Publication Data
Buzzi-Ferraris, G. (Guido)
    Scientific C++ : building numerical libraries the object-oriented
    way / G. Buzzi-Ferraris.
        p.   cm.
    Includes bibliographical references and index.
    ISBN 0-201-63192-X
    1. Object-oriented programming.   2. C++ (Computer program language)
    I. Title
QA76.64.B89   1993
519.4'0285'5133--dc20   93-15310
                                                              CIP

Scientific
C++

**Building Numerical Libraries
the Object-Oriented Way**

To my wife, Luisella,
who introduced me to Wookie algebra whereby
ONE + ONE = ONES

Contents

Introduction

Qui si convien lasciare ogni sospetto;
ogni viltà convien che qui sia morta.

Now here you must leave all distrust behind
let all your cowardice die on this spot.

Dante, *Inferno*, III

Aim of the Book

The last few years have seen the coming of age of a powerful programming language, C, and of a new programming technique: object-oriented programming. This revolutionary type of programming is proving far superior to the traditional so-called procedural one, because it allows production of much safer and easier to use code which is, moreover, easily extendible and reusable according to varying circumstances. C++ stems from the need to exploit the efficiency of the C language in object-oriented programming. As a result of the synergy generated by this union, C++ has become a language with exceptional features.

Owing to a number of circumstances which I shall try to explain, the number crunching world has been bypassed by this evolution.

The main reason for this is the fact that numerical problems have always been solved using FORTRAN: it should not be overlooked, actually, that FORTRAN was born with this specific aim. As a consequence, all numerical program libraries currently available are written in this language.

This has created a vicious circle. Anyone involved in numerical problems believes FORTRAN to be particularly suited to the task and does not feel the need to change language. On the other hand, those who are beginning to tackle numerical problems are virtually obliged to use it, even though well aware of FORTRAN's considerable limitations, in order to work with existing program libraries.

In order to escape from this impasse, two things are necessary. The first is to show FORTRAN's limitations against the advantages of a language such as C++ and of object-oriented programming in the specific field of numerical computing. The second consists in creating program libraries for solving numerical problems written in C++.

Unfortunately the few texts dealing with numerical problems in C++ are often inadequate: the techniques they use may be effective in other sectors but not in this field. If one wants to write efficient code, it is not enough to transcribe formulae found in books of numerical analysis; neither it is possible to translate a program literally from FORTRAN for a number of reasons, some of which would not be understood by users unfamiliar with C++. For instance, in FORTRAN matrices are stored by column, while in C++ they are stored by row. A program is more or less efficient according to how loops are arranged in order to access the matrix coefficients. Some implementations show much more serious deficiencies. For instance, it is possible, when using object-oriented programming, to assign one matrix to another using the statement:

```
A = B;
```

Now, it is obvious to anybody with a minimum knowledge of numerical analysis that this symbol is aimed at generating a matrix A, initially equal to B but at the same time independent of B. If both matrices have common data, this would be a real source of errors. And yet, some of the available implementations propound this very solution.

In my view the books presenting C++ are inadequate in two respects: they are not suitable for those interested in solving numerical problems because they deal with problems of a different nature; and they do not try to build a bridge from FORTRAN (to date the most used language in solving scientific problems) to C++, because they are written for users familiar with C or Pascal.

Vice versa, all books dealing with numerical analysis have an algorithmic, not object-oriented, set-up.

Therefore the aim of this book is to try to explain, gradually, a new language, C++, and a new way of programming, object-oriented programming, to users interested in numerical problem solving, especially those used to FORTRAN.

This book does *not* aim to teach numerical analysis methods or algorithms.

Our Approach

There are various techniques which can be used to explain a programming language.

(1) Reference manual technique. This approach is fundamental if the aim of the book is to supply a language manual to be consulted in case of doubt. This technique is not suitable for a teaching book.

(2)   Ready-made programs technique. This approach is the most used, since it is the easiest and fun to write (at least for the author): instead of writing a book on the language one gives plenty of examples, which means writing lots of programs. This approach is important if the aim of the book is to supply the user with ready-made programs. It is also useful didactically, since it allows for verification of possible solutions to a problem.

In my opinion, however, this technique shows two serious flaws when used on its own: it requires the reader to have a good knowledge of the language and, above all, it does not allow the author to focus on the single item of information that he wants to highlight: key points are scattered and become obscured amidst less important items.

(3)   One information at a time technique. Here the language features are introduced not in a full program but by means of a list of few and essential statements. In this way teaching can be graded, starting from the basic through to the advanced notions, yet trying each time to isolate and highlight a particular feature of the language.

In this book I am going to use the third technique in order to introduce both the new C++ language and the new object-oriented programming method gradually.

The book will also present complete applications pertinent to numerical problems. To this end, some chapters (8,12,13,15) will be devoted to the analysis of the possibility of creating a program library of numerical methods using C++ with an object-oriented approach. The full list of the programs shown in these chapters is found in the enclosed diskette.

Finally, so that the reader can assess his own level of understanding, the various chapters include questions on the issues discussed.

Conventions

In order to make the one information at a time technique more effective I have introduced some conventional symbols (or icons) which help to highlight the features of the various issues discussed.

Of all the icons, one I believe to be of significant importance:

 When this icon appears it means that there is a *new way to tackle an old problem.*

When a new way of solving a problem needs to be explained, we encounter an all too often overlooked didactical snag: many words and concepts previously used change their meaning.

Take for instance the following statement:

It is the sun that moves, the earth stands still.

The meaning of the concept of movement changes substantially according to who has uttered or utters the statement. Aristotle, Galileo, Einstein or the man in the street simply using his common sense would give totally different meanings to the expression.

In these situations, correct communication depends entirely on in-depth comprehension of the meaning that the speaker attributes to the various concepts at play.

The function of the above mentioned icon is to warn the reader that there is some change in the way a problem is tackled and that consequently some concepts change their meaning. In such cases I will also try to make the reader experience the shift from the old to the new attitude and to show the reasons for it by highlighting differences, merits and flaws.

I have deliberately chosen the symbol of a stylized sun in memory of Kant's famous Copernican revolution in the domain of knowledge:

> This is exactly the same as it was for Copernicus' first idea; who, realizing that he couldn't explain the heavenly movements without conceding that the entire army of stars was rotating around the observer, tried to see whether he could achieve more by making the observer go round instead and leaving the stars at rest (Kant, *Critique of Pure Reason*).

Similarly for knowledge:

> If intuition must adjust itself to the nature of the objects, I do not see how one could have a priori knowledge of anything; if, on the other hand, the object (as object of the senses) adjusts itself to the nature of our intuitive faculty, I can easily perceive this possibility... We can only have a priori knowledge of what we ourselves put into objects (*idem*).

The lesson we learn from Kant's theory of knowledge is this: the background of theoretical knowledge has a powerful and indispensable rule-making function, which addresses and guides our observations, our intuitions, our language. This rule-making function is an obstacle as well, because it makes it difficult to observe known fact in a different way, which is an indispensable condition for any scientific discovery and, coming back to us, for any conceptual change.

Carefully observe the following picture.

It is not difficult to recognize the face of an old and ugly woman. It is more difficult, instead, to be able to see the face of a young and pretty woman in the same picture. Moreover, once the face of an old woman has been seen, it is almost impossible to see the young one. It is a truism to say that when we observe something, as well as when we tackle a problem, we remain bound to a precise point of view which is essentially dependent on past knowledge and experience.

For instance, when we find in this book an expression written in FORTRAN such as:

```
FUNC(A,M,N)
```

which uses a matrix, A, and we compare it with one written in C++:

```
Func(A);
```

we need to make a mental effort in order to see the second statement's matrix from the point of view of object-oriented programming rather than from the usual one typical of FORTRAN.

A second icon is also particularly important:

 When this icon appears it means that I am indicating some style choices I have adopted in the language. In order to write easy-to-manage programs it is indispensable to maintain a serious stylistic coherence. In this way I will try to provide those indications which, in my opinion, are useful to achieve such stylistic coherence.

The meaning of the other icons used in the text are as follows.

 The icon indicates explicitly that there is something to remember. It will be used when a feature is shown or a specially important concept is explained.

 This icon is used when, in the presentation of an algorithm or of some language peculiarity, the positive aspects are underlined.

 If, on the contrary, some negative aspects of an algorithm or of the language are underlined, this will be highlighted by this icon.

 There are limitations of some sort. For instance, a problem which could be interesting is not examined.

We are in the presence of a specially brilliant idea, ingenious, almost a stroke of magic.

This icon indicates an exceptionally elegant method to solve a problem; it is more than simply brilliant.

A bomb indicates danger. It highlights the danger of errors which are not easily perceived.

I will use this icon when I believe that an algorithm or some language aspect is obsolete. The argument has only historical interest.

There are various possible alternatives to solve a problem; those marked with this symbol are *not* better than others.

A method of solving a problem with maximum efficiency in terms of computing time.

I will use this icon when an algorithm is particularly slow, even if it has some value.

Indicates tests which check the level of understanding of the argument discussed.

As you are reading, you will often encounter two characters: the user and the programmer. It is obvious that a user can also be a programmer and vice versa. I will use the user to spotlight the advantages and disadvantages which can be found in programs written by someone else, and the programmer to highlight some programming peculiarity.

Why C++

E stupor m'eran le cose non conte.

My mind was stunned by what it did not know.

Dante, *Purgatorio*, XV

1.1   Procedural Programming

Functions Abstraction

Traditional languages, such as FORTRAN, C or Pascal, are based on a very important concept which is fundamental in building efficient programs: *the abstraction of computing modules.*

A computing module, which depending on the language used is called either a subroutine, a function or a procedure and which for simplicity's sake I will just call a function, is used to solve a given problem. If the same problem reappears, it is not necessary to write that portion of the program again. This leads to codes which are easier to write and to interpret.

Within this setting the data needed by the functions are separate entities flowing from one function to the other; each function processes and gives back the data. The name of data processor, which is sometimes given to the computer, stems from the relationship between functions and data which is peculiar to this setting.

The programming model, on the other hand, is called procedural in order to indicate the pre-eminence of the computing modules (procedures) over data.

Operating on these principles, skilled programmers have taken those main algorithms which were formulated at theoretical level by expert mathematicians and implemented them as efficient functions.

Unfortunately, the chosen language for the field of sciences has been FORTRAN. I say unfortunately because FORTRAN itself, as well as programs written in FORTRAN, is not easily extendible to meet other needs brought about by the development of programming concepts. On the other hand, programmers who have been used to this programming language for years do not feel the need to change to more efficient languages because they are not aware of the possible advantages from which they could benefit. They only see the disadvantages, which are undoubtedly real: the first being to abandon a well known and easy language for a still mysterious and much more complex one; the second and more important being the fact that those mathematical structures indispensable for the development of complex programs have not yet been built in languages other than FORTRAN. Beside these more than sound reasons there is another subconscious one which, in my opinion, is even more limiting: that is, FORTRAN is a very easy language to learn, but a program written in FORTRAN is not easy to use and to read; those who have struggled to learn to use a particular code perceive themselves almost like guardians of a mysterious knowledge which somehow makes them indispensable to those without the will or the time to study that same code.

Even if we want to stay with procedural programming, where the concepts which we shall soon see are not developed, FORTRAN is deficient in many aspects, all of which are decisive for producing efficient programs.

For instance, think of the following deficiencies.

(1)   Lack of support for dynamic use of memory (that is, the possibility of introducing, during any phase of computing, a vector or a matrix of exactly the required size and of using such memory for the required time only). This deficiency involves both the over-configuration of generic programs (in order to ensure maximum generality) and the transfer of working vectors, so mysterious to the user, to functions (in order to reuse the same portion of memory in several SUBROUTINES).

(2)   Lack of pointers, with the consequential inefficiency in matrix computing, the impossibility of generating effective techniques for storing structured matrices and so on.

(3)   Impossibility of creating 'blocks' in which variables are hidden (with the ensuing possibility of conflicting definitions) and lack of control of variable visibility among different functions.

1.2   Object-Oriented Programming

Data Abstraction

As the problems tackled by computer have increased in complexity, another need has been developing alongside the idea of separate computing modules: to be able to use data associations different from the standard ones supplied by the compiler.

This is a first step towards what is defined as *data abstraction* which is in turn the basis of *object-oriented programming*.

Since we are now moving away from FORTRAN's capabilities, let's look more closely at this first phase.

In FORTRAN, as in all procedural languages, there are standard variables on which a program can operate. They are differently defined in the various languages, but their features and scope do not change.

So we have floating point variables with simple or double precision, integer variables and character variables. There can be vectors or matrices of each of these. The matrices are variables derived from the basic type and they are the only derived variables in FORTRAN. Other procedural languages, such as C and Pascal, go further (and therefore are more powerful and more flexible). In particular, C can have *pointers* (which will be discussed later) and *structures*. The latter generalize the vector and matrix concept, but with an important variation. While vectors and matrices must be made up of variables of the same type (integer, for example), this is no longer necessary for structures: a structure can group together under the same name different types (for example, character type, double precision type and so on). It can contain other structures and can also have vectors and matrices, just like basic variables. It is worth underlining that with structures it is possible for the programmer to define to some extent variables for his own use.

This possibility has greatly helped the programmer in solving graphics and Database problems.

Let us consider a simple Database problem: students' addresses. Name, surname, address, age and so on, are all needed for each person. Each of these items may belong to a different basic type. Therefore, in FORTRAN we would use different vectors for different items and link them by an index. This is not a very good procedure and it could, moreover, lead to errors.

It is much more natural to group all data under one label so that they are naturally associated.

Example:

```
struct Students
    {
    char *name;
    char *surname;
    char *address;
    int age;
    ....
    };
```

In scientific computing this need is felt less. After all what are really needed are floating point vectors and matrices with simple or double precision, together with basic variables. FORTRAN 77, the version in use today, shows such deficiencies that it would be better to use a language such as C or Pascal. The brand new FORTRAN 90 has added some functions which bring its efficiency closer to C and Pascal, but to the detriment of its ease of use. The switch from FORTRAN 77 to FORTRAN 90 is even more traumatic than that from FORTRAN 77 to C! For this reason, and also because some of FORTRAN's deficiencies cannot be eliminated if compatibility with previous versions is to be maintained, I do not think it worth going over to FORTRAN 90. If one has to make the jump, it is better to make it wisely. From now on, in any case, when talking about FORTRAN I will refer to the currently used version FORTRAN 77.

The crucial point is that, in the context of scientific computing, if one wants to stay with a procedural language it is difficult to justify leaving FORTRAN 77 for more advanced languages. However, all procedural languages have a basic problem in the connection between data and functions: data, even if more advanced, diversified and customizable structures are used, remains something which is separate from the functions which use it. C and Pascal are themselves procedural languages in which data is passed from the user to the required function, examined and possibly modified, transferred to another function and so on. In all these transfers, the user is responsible for passing data to a function correctly. The function itself cannot do anything or know anything about its suitability until it is too late, that is, when it is transmitted. On the other hand the user does not know exactly how the function works, because he or she did not program it. The user is, however, forced somehow to study how it works in order to avoid the risk of wrongly manipulating data during transfer from one function to another.

All this can be avoided through a powerful new concept: *data abstraction*.

> Data abstraction consists of encapsulating in a single container (the object) both data and functions manipulating that data.
>
> The object programmer supplies the user with interfaces to access both functions and object-related data. Now every time the user uses the object's data or functions, that object knows it and can take the appropriate decisions. Data abstraction allows not only data and their manipulating functions to be used together, but also the same operators as used for basic variables (for example +, -, *, /) to be used for this new abstract data, with modalities defined by the programmer. Therefore, abstract data becomes to all intents and purposes new data to work on.

Try to write a program in FORTRAN to solve a simple problem like this: find the product of two matrices A and B of dimensions M,N and N,K and then put the result in matrix A; that is, do the operation:

A = AB

Now, of course, the dimensions of the new matrix **A** are M,K.
It would be nice to be able to write:

    A = A*B;

or even better (using a typical C operator):

```
A *= B;
```

where the operator used automatically verifies the matrix size congruence, whether there is a need to size matrix **A** in a different way, the possible freeing of the memory where matrix **A** was positioned should the new one have a different size, the choice of the most effective computing method for the different instances (square **A** and **B**, **A** equal to **B**, different dimensions), all in less computing time than required in FORTRAN.

This is possible with C++.

I have obtained the following times for multiplying two 60×60 matrices on a PC 386: FORTRAN 4.4 s, C 2.7 s and C++ 2.4 s.

It is important to point out some facts about the comparison of computing times between two programs.

Computing time is heavily dependent upon some obvious factors, such as the computer and the algorithm used.

Computing time is also dependent upon other less obvious factors, such as the compiler used, the method of implementing the algorithm and others. For instance, different compilers can produce executables of the same code with computing times with a ratio of two or more; just by changing the order of execution of operation loops, one obtains a very different level of efficiency.

Therefore, it can appear absurd to compare two languages without analysing all the associated conditions. This is very true in the sense that it is undoubtedly easy to demonstrate that one language, algorithm or computer is more efficient than another.

What can be stated, though, is that C++ is intrinsically more efficient than FORTRAN for three (and a half) reasons.

(1)   Because it can use pointers (see Chapter 3).
(2)   Because it can build data structures (see Chapter 4).
(3)   Because it can treat data structures as objects (see Chapter 12). (This last reason makes C++ more efficient than C in the previous example of the multiplication of matrices.)

The half reason which I have added is due to the fact that most of the modern operating systems (first of all UNIX, but also the Macintosh System 7) are mainly written in C; it is rather logical, therefore, that C and its offspring C++ are privileged languages on these systems.

It is useless to try and understand fully the meaning of encapsulating functions and data in an object at this point, because it would be impossible. It is important, though, to remember from now on that an object is not a variable or a function, but a new entity containing both variables and functions.

From FORTRAN to C++

Habit is habit, and not to be flung out of the window by any man, but coaxed downstairs one step at a time.

Mark Twain, *Pudd'nhead Wilson.*

2.1 Introduction

FORTRAN is a very poor language which really represents only a small portion of what it is possible to do with C; in turn, C represents a subset of C++ (with small variations in the common parts).

In this chapter we are going to analyse the main differences between C++ and FORTRAN, with specific reference to what can be written in FORTRAN. For the moment, we are not looking to write a program in C or C++ style, but rather to do a literal translation between the two languages.

In this way we can highlight the differences between the two languages and we can then see that switching over to C++, if you do not want to use it at its maximum potential but rather at FORTRAN level, does not give rise to special problems.

6

2.2   Statements

In order for a computer language to be used in practice, it must permit the user to obtain new values from a combination of known variables.

Definition: *Expression*
An expression is a consistent combination of variables, operators and functions, which produces a result.

For example, the following are valid expressions in C++:

```
a
3.14
a+2.*(b-3.*c)
y < 15.
x = y + sin(z)
```

Definition: *Statement*
A statement is the smallest executable unit within a language. A program is a sequence of statements.

For example, in FORTRAN, if you want to calculate the sum of two variables A and B, putting the outcome in the variable C, you would write the following statement:

```
C = A + B
```

The same statement in C++ becomes:

```
C = A + B;
```

> FORTRAN suffers from being born at a time when programs were written on punch cards. This is why it is necessary to have statements which start from the seventh column and which cannot exceed 72 columns. Also, this is why it used to be convenient to reduce the lengths of variable names. The outcome is that listings are not immediately readable for an external user (as well as for the program's author).

A statement in C++ shows important differences when compared with the FORTRAN equivalent.

The main differences between C++ and FORTRAN statements are the following.
In C++:

(1)   a statement always ends with a semicolon (;);
(2)   a statement can be placed anywhere on the line;
(3)   all space symbols (blank, tab) and paragraph symbols (new line) are ignored by the compiler;
(4)   there are no numbered statements.

Furthermore in C++ it is important to make a conceptual distinction between an *expression* and a *statement*. The former gives a numerical result, whereas the latter completes an operation.

Examples of permitted statements in C++:

```
a=b+c; a=3.*f; a=(expression);
;
i++;
```

As can be seen, you can put several statements on the same line, and you can use a statement which has no outcome because it is made up of only ; and a statement which does not explicitly use the assignment operator =.

The most frequent error in the first C++ programs, for somebody who comes from a FORTRAN background, is to forget to put ; at the end of each statement.

The character ; is used as a terminator in C++. Without ; this would only be an expression.

C++ is a free format language. Provided a statement is syntactically correct, it does not matter where it is written or how long it is.

Initially, C++'s greater flexibility and lack of any reference to numerical labels can be embarrassing for someone who is used to FORTRAN. This, coupled with the presence of a large number of symbols (especially the curly brackets{ }), can appear to make the code less readable and more disorganized. Once you have got used to this, you will realize that quite the opposite is true.

It is extremely important to select one writing style for a program and use it for all program components.

2.3   Program Structure

The structure for a program written in C++ is much more articulate than for a program written in FORTRAN. Since at this introductory stage we are only considering a literal translation from a program written in FORTRAN to one written in C++, I shall keep the analysis to a minimum. For a more in-depth treatment, see Chapter 6.

> Specifically, our hypothesis will be to write a brief program which can fit into one file.

A C++ program is usually made up of several functions.

> Unlike FORTRAN, C++ does not differentiate between SUBROUTINE and FUNCTION. C++ has only *functions*. One of these functions must *always* be present and must be named `main`.
> Therefore, `main` *is itself a function* and its name *is not arbitrary*.
> There is *only one* `main` for each program.

A basic concept for C++ is the *block*.

Definition: *Block*
A part of a program between two curly brackets, { . . . }, is a block.

In order to make a program easily readable, it is helpful to adopt a standard convention to determine where to place the start and the end of a block, so that it will be instantly recognizable.
Two conventions are used.

(1)   Position the start of the block, {, on the same line as the expression where the block starts, and all the statements which make up the block, including the block end, }, indented slightly to the right.

(2)   Position the start of the block, {, on the following line and align it with the other statements in the block.

Example of the first style:

```
for(i=0;i<10;i++){
    statements;
    }
```

Example of the second style:

```
for(i=0;i<10;i++)
  {
  statements;
  }
```

The first style allows you to save one line. The second style, however, is ultimately more effective, in my opinion.

 The second style will always be adopted when defining a block: the two curly brackets, {}, which define a block will be aligned with the statements which make up the block.

 Every function must contain at least one block: this defines the start and the end of the function.

Since `main` is a function, the simplest program you can write, which does not execute any statement, will be:

```
void main()
{
}
```

Let us not for the moment concern ourselves with the word `void` in front of `main`.

You put the relevant statements which make up the program inside the block.

 Let us assume for the time being that you do not have to use any other function apart from `main`.

2.4 Identifiers

In every language, in order to be able to use a variable or a function (or a SUBROUTINE), you need to give it a name, so that it may be identified.

 In FORTRAN 77 there are two very heavy constraints, when choosing an identifier.

(1) The difference between small and capital letters is not recognized.
(2) You can use a maximum of 6 characters.

This has two very negative consequences.

(1)   The author of the program is forced to do some juggling in order to give a comprehensible meaning to the variable, while still remaining within the 6 characters limit.

(2)   The person reading the program is at a loss when faced with a sequence of characters which have no apparent meaning and which can only be understood by using relevant decoding tools.

This is immediately obvious if you look at any program library.

For example, in the IMSL library, the following SUBROUTINES are used in order to solve linear systems in simple precision using the Gauss factoring method: LSARG, LSLRG, LFCRG, LFTRG, LFSRG, LFIRG, LFDRG, LINRG. Each of these subroutines is specialized to execute a certain task; many are linked and are to be used in sequence, but their names are not immediately comprehensible.

In C++:

(1)   an identifier can be of any length (and is recognized even when its last letter is the only difference between it and another identifier);
(2)   small and capital letters are perceived as different;
(3)   you can use characters, numbers and underscores.

The following constraints apply when selecting an identifier.

(1)   The first character must be a letter or an underscore.
(2)   The identifiers used by the language are forbidden (see Table 2.1).

Table 2.1 shows the keywords for C++. Such keywords *cannot be used as identifiers.*

Table 2.1   Keywords for C++.

asm	delete	if	return	try
auto	do	inline	short	typedef
break	double	int	signed	union
case	else	long	sizeof	unsigned
catch	enum	new	static	virtual
char	extern	operator	struct	void
class	float	private	switch	volatile
const	for	protected	template	while
continue	friend	public	this	
default	goto	register	throw	

Here are some valid identifiers:

```
viscosity, dynamic_viscosity, DynamicViscosity,
tax_payable, TaxPayable, Matrix, vector, _pinco.
```

Conversely the following are not valid as identifiers:

`%zxy`	% invalid character
`z(xas`	(illegal within identifier
`-vava`	- illegal; do not confuse with _
`auto`	illegal identifier because `auto` is a keyword
`8Value`	cannot begin with a number

As well as keywords which are present in every C++ compiler, there are also other terms specific to each individual compiler. These identifiers can only be used for the purpose for which they are defined.

> There are currently several working environments (DOS, UNIX, OS/2, Macintosh and others) and, for each one of them, several compilers. In the rest of the book, for the examples which are working environment and compiler related, I shall refer to DOS and to Turbo C++ respectively.

For example, when using Turbo C++ in the MS-DOS environment, the identifiers `_cs`, `_ds`, `_es`, `_export`, `far`, `huge`, `_loadds`, `near`, `pascal`, `_regparam`, `_saveregs`, `_seg`, `_ss` cannot be used.

> In order to make a program more easily readable, it is better to use a constant style when choosing identifiers.

It is useful to make a primary distinction in connection with the various items that identifiers relate to. For example, it is important to make a distinction between common variables and functions.

A widespread convention is to use:

(1)   for the variables: identifiers beginning with a small letter;

(2)   for the functions: identifiers beginning with a capital letter.

Example:

```
tax, taxPayable, tax_payable  are variables.
Tax, TaxPayable, Tax_payable  are functions.
```

If one identifier is made up of several words, they should be easily recognizable. For example, if you want to indicate dynamic viscosity you do not have to write `dynamicviscosity`. In this case there are two conventions, both widespread and reasonable:

(1)   using a capital letter to separate words;
Example: `TaxPayable,taxPayable`

(2)   using the underline symbol, _, between words.
Example: `tax_payable, may_be_used`

In general, I shall adopt the following convention.

> (1)   No identifier begins with _. This choice is due to the fact that many predefined dimensions in some C++ compilers begin with _ and it is desirable not to have definition conflicts.
> E.g. `_bla_bla,_astrid` must be avoided as identifiers.
> (2)   The constant identifiers are made up of capital letters only. They must never be made up of one character only (better if one uses four or more characters).
> E.g. `EPSILON, TOLERANCE` are valid; `Pi, T, Epsilon` should be avoided.
> If the constant is made up of more than one word, the words must be separated with _.
> E.g. `MACH_EPS, ERR_FUNCTION`.
> (3)   Function identifiers and identifiers of a new type of variable which I have defined always begin with a capital letter. The identifier must always include one or more small letters. If the function identifier or the identifier of a new type of variable is made up of several words, this is shown by a capital letter.
> E.g. `Matrix, MatrixRight, TransposeSolve, AddRow` are identifiers which refer either to functions or to the definition of new type variables. You should avoid using identifiers for this purpose:
> `Addrow:` r must be capital;
> `Add_row:` it is better not to use the divider _;
> `ADDROW:` at least one letter must be small;
> `A:` as above; identifiers formed by one character are therefore not allowed;
> `addRow:` must begin with a capital letter.
> (4)   The actual variables (standard variables or variables defined by derived variables) have an identifier beginning with a *small letter*, unless it is made up of a single letter. In this case, the letter can be capital. If the identifier is made up of more than one word, the following words are shown by a capital letter. There are cases when it is more convenient to show a variable using a single capital letter
>
> *cont.*

> *cont.*
>
> identifier: matrices are a typical case, so it might be useful to write
> `x=A*b;` x and b being `Vector` type variables and A a `Matrix` type
> variable.
> Valid examples:
> `errMatrix, viscosity, dynamicViscosity, A, x`
> Invalid examples:
> `AB, dynamic_viscosity, ErrMatrix`
> (5)   The identifiers for labels referred to by a `goto` (see further on) are
> always made up of more than one word shown by the underscore
> symbols, _, and with all small characters.
> Example of label names :
> `name_nonexistent, variable_xy_out_of_range`

2.5   Comments

Comments in FORTRAN are identified by the characters C or c or *, and are put in
the first column of each line that you want to be treated as a comment.

Example:

```
C This is a comment
C and this is another comment
```

> In C++ there are two possibilities.
>
> (1)   Everything included between the pair of symbols `/*` and `*/` is taken
> as a comment.
> (2)   If the comment is on one line, it is sufficient to put a double bar `//` in
> front of the comment.

The following are examples of comments in C++:

```
/*
Construction of
a structure
and example of a comment
of the first type
*/
struct pinco     // comment of the second type
{
int aaaa;
```

```
float bbbb;        // another comment
double cccc;       // yet another
};
```

> Comments in C++ are much more flexible and effective.
> Comments of the first type are very similar to those in FORTRAN with the added advantage that you do not have to repeat the C symbol on every line. These are useful for long comments.
> Comments of the second type are particularly effective because they can be placed alongside the expression you want to comment.

> Comments of the first type cannot be encapsulated within each other. One cannot, therefore, write:
>
> ```
> /*blabla...../* blabla  */  blabla    */
> ```
>
> Inside a comment of the first type you can have both // and /*. You cannot have */.

This comment produces a compilation error:

```
/* bla bla
// bla and again bla
/* yet again bla */
*/
```

This comment is acceptable:

```
/* bla bla
// bla and again bla
/* yet again bla
*/
```

> If you want to cut part of a program temporarily, a convenient and efficient way would be to enclose the whole part between /* and */.
> Careful though: if within the section there is a comment of the first type:
>
> ```
> /* comment */
> ```
>
> you get an error during compilation. If you want to use this method, you cannot use comments of the first type.

Use only comments of the second type. Save the use of comments of the first type for when you need to solve the problem of temporarily hiding part of a program. If you really want to use comments of the first type as well, do it only if they are particularly long. In any case comments of the first type must be positioned in visible places, such as at the beginning of functions. *You must never use comments of the first type inside functions mixed with statements.*

Example of a correct style (in my opinion):

```
//      =====================
//      initial comments
//      others
//      others
//      others
//      others
//      ===================
struct pinco     // comment
    {
    int aaaa;
    float bbbb;        // another comment
    double cccc;       // yet another
    };
```

Avoid this style:

```
struct pinco     /* comment */
    {
    int aaaa;
    float bbbb;        /* another comment */
    double cccc;       /* yet another */
    };
```

This style is also not advisable:

```
/*
===========================
    initial comments
    others
    others
    others
others
===========================
*/
```

```
struct pinco      // comment
   {
   int aaaa;
   float bbbb;        // another comment
   double cccc;       // yet another comment
   };
```

It is very important to have consistent rules for the use of comments when writing a program.
The following rules are to be adopted.

(1) At the beginning of each of the files into which the program is subdivided, you should insert some comments describing the content of the file itself.

(2) At the beginning of each function, you should provide a brief description of the function itself.

(3) Each introduced variable must be justified with a comment in order to clarify its use (unless this is perfectly obvious).

(4) When a numerical algorithm is used, it is useful to quote a text where that particular algorithm is described.

2.6 Variables

In C++ every variable, constant and function belongs to a specific type. The type determines the quantity of memory occupied and the features of the operations which involve that item.

C++ is an extremely rigorous language as far as the control of the type of variable is concerned. If a variable of a certain type is passed on to a function which expects to receive a different type of variable and for which a translation procedure has not been given, a compilation error appears. This control on type is extremely useful, because it prevents errors, which would otherwise be very difficult to spot, occurring during execution.
Further on in the book we shall see what other advantages are offered by such close control on type.

There are two categories of type: the *basic type* and the *derived type*.

Basic Types in C++

In C++ there are four predefined basic types: `char`, `int`, `float`, `double`. A variable is declared to be of a certain type when it is *defined*.

> In C++ it is necessary to define all the variables which are used, explicitly stating the type of variable they refer to.
> Defining has the following syntax:
>
> <type of variable> <identifier>;

The following are definitions of variables belonging to the four basic types :

```
char c;      // c variable type char
int i;       // i variable type int
float f;     // f variable type float
double d;    // d variable type double
```

In their turn these types can be further subdivided by using *modifiers*: signed or unsigned, short or long. A combination does not always generate a truly different type and not all combinations are possible.

A type modified with unsigned (applicable only to char or int) takes into account only the positive values of the variable. Thus the possible values are doubled, with the same memory space taken up.

The modifiers short and long, too, do not apply to all types. When they apply, the former reduces and the latter increases the available memory, with an ensuing variation in the possibilities of representing a number.

> The possible combinations and the limits are dependent on the working environment and the compiler used. It is therefore prudent, in order to make a program transportable, not to base your work on the dimensions which can be realized with a particular compiler.
> The C++ manual provides information on what C++ guarantees and on what is machine dependent.
> We shall see what provisions should be made in order to avoid problems.

Table 2.2 shows all the main types present in Turbo C++ and, in general, in the compilers in the MS-DOS environment.

Table 2.2 Main types in Turbo C++.

Type	Byte	Range
signed char, char	1	from −128 to 127
unsigned char	1	from 0 to 255
short, int, short int, signed short int, signed int	2	from −32768 to 32767

Table 2.2   *cont.*

unsigned short, unsigned short int, unsigned int	2	from 0 to 65535
long, long int, signed long, signed long int	4	from −2147483648 to 2147483647
unsigned long, unsigned long int	4	from 0 to 4294967295
float	4	from 3.4E−38 to 3.4E+38
double	8	from 1.7E−308 to 1.7E+308
long double	10	from 3.4E−4932 to 3.4E+4932

There is a close correspondence between the following FORTRAN and C++ types:

FORTRAN	**C++**
CHARACTER	char
INTEGER	int
REAL	float
DOUBLE	double

For the scientific problems to which FORTRAN is dedicated and which we will be dealing with, the most interesting types are numerical (int, float, double).

In FORTRAN it is *not* compulsory to define the type of variable before using it.
In C++, leaving a variable undefined would cause a compilation error, that is if you do not state explicitly to which type of item an identifier belongs.

Therefore, if an old FORTRAN user (such as myself) was used to using, automatically, all the identifiers beginning with i, j, k, l, m, n as integers, he or she will receive error messages if he or she continues to do this in C++.

Let us now see part of a FORTRAN and a C++ program, which executes a sum.
In FORTRAN:

```
REAL WGHT1,WGHT2,TOTAL
WGHT1=10.
WGHT2=20.
TOTAL= WGHT1+WGHT2
```

In C++:

```
float weight1,weight2,total;
weight1=10.;
weight2=20.;
total=weight1+weight2;
```

Derived Types

Starting with the main types in C++, you can obtain the following derived types.

(1)   Pointers.

(2)   References.

(3)   Array (vectors and matrices).

(4)   Type `enum`.

(5)   Type `struct`.

(6)   Type `union`.

(7)   Type `class`.

Apart from array, none of these derived types are available in FORTRAN. With the derived type array it is possible, in FORTRAN and in C++, to represent vectors and matrices which are the fundamentals for all numerical calculations and for scientific calculations.

The representational differences between the two languages for such derived types cause one of the major difficulties encountered by a FORTRAN user in C++ (and in C). One initial problem is linked to the fact that in C++ two different ways to use and define a vector or a matrix are already provided by the language (and which C++ has inherited). (In Chapter 12 we shall see how it is possible, in C++, to define new types of vector and matrix, which are much easier to use for scientific problems than the two embedded in the language). One way is, for the user, fairly similar to the FORTRAN representation, even though conceptually the two representations are very different. The other way, which is more efficient in terms of speed of calculation and sizing of required memory, is completely alien to FORTRAN and, therefore, more difficult to understand. Since this approach is linked to the pointer concept, we shall not consider it now, but leave it to Chapter 3.

We shall now analyse the differences in use, not in the essence, of the first way of representing a vector and a matrix in C++, comparing it with the representation in FORTRAN.

In FORTRAN:

```
         REAL WEIGHT,TOTAL
         DIMENSION WEIGHT(10)
         INTEGER I
         DO 100 I=1,10
         READ (*,*) WEIGHT(I)
         TOTAL=TOTAL+WEIGHT(I)
100      CONTINUE
```

In C++:

```
float weight[10],total;
int i;
for(i=0;i<10;i=i+1)    // same as DO in FORTRAN
    {      // beginning of the iterative cycle
    (read weight[i])    // for the moment we are not
                        // interested in how
    total=total+weight[i];
    } // end of the iterative cycle
```

In the *representation* and *use* of a vector there are two *formal* differences between the two languages (other more substantial differences are in Chapter 3).

(1)   A vector is defined and used by means of *round* brackets in FORTRAN and *square* ones in C++.
(2)   The index to scan the vector goes from 1 to the maximum value (in this case 10) in FORTRAN and from 0 to the maximum value −1 in C++.

A frequent error for a C++ (and C) user coming from FORTRAN is to forget that if a vector has been defined to contain n terms, the nth term *will not* be part of that vector, which is only defined between 0 and n−1.

Example:

```
float y[100];
y[100] = 5.; // dangerous error when executing!
```

The same applies to matrices.
In FORTRAN:

```
REAL MATRIX
DIMENSION MATRIX(10,20)
INTEGER I,J
.......
MATRIX(I,J)=....
.......
```

In C++:

```
float matrix[10][20];
int i,j;
......
matrix[i][j]=....;
.......
```

In the representation and use of matrices with m rows and n columns there are the following *formal* differences between the two languages.

(1)   A FORTRAN matrix is defined and used by means of round brackets with dimensions separated by commas. C++ uses a *pair of square brackets* for any dimension.

(2)   The index to scan the rows and columns goes from 1 to the maximum value in FORTRAN and from 0 to the maximum value −1 in C++.

(3)   The matrix is *stored* by *column* in FORTRAN and by *rows* in C++.

Other more substantial differences can be seen in Chapter 3.

Given the importance in calculus of both matrices and vectors we shall return to this issue later on, when we shall get into in-depth programming in C++.

It must be noted that C++ does not allow the sizing of a matrix between two arbitrary indices (for example, between −100 and 500), which FORTRAN 77 can do.

Naturally, if you want, you can define a new matrix type which allows this. However, this does not become immediately valid with the variables defined by C++.

In FORTRAN 77 it is possible to define:

```
DIMENSION VARVEC(-20:20)
```

The vector VARVEC(I) can now vary by I between −20 and 20.

In C++ this is not possible so directly. One method consists of adding one constant, an offset, to the index.

```
float varvec[41]    // between -20 and 20 there are 41
elements
int offset = 20;
    for(int i = -20;i <= 20;i++)
    {
    varvec[i + offset]=.....
    }
```

2.7   Constants Without Identifiers

A constant without an identifier is equally associated to one type.

> There are four types of constant without an identifier.
>
> (1)   Integers.
> (2)   Floating point numbers.
> (3)   Characters.
> (4)   Strings.

Example:

```
153 // integer
3.14 // floating point number
'A' // character
"Viva Zapata" // string
```

Constants too have modifiers which extend the possibilities.

In particular, for integers, if you put the symbol u or U after the numerical value the constant becomes unsigned int, if you put l or L it becomes long. The two modifiers can be used together. If 0 (zero) is put before an integer, the number becomes *octal*, if 0x is used then it becomes *hexadecimal*.

Example:

```
123U  // unsigned int
123L  // long
123UL // unsigned long
0123  // octal
0x123 // hexadecimal
```

> For floating point numbers the default is double. It can be changed with f of F to make it a float and with l or L to make it a long double.

Example:

```
3.14      // double
3.14F     // float
3.14L     // long double
1.2e+12   // double
1.2e+12L  // long double
```

A constant character is a character which is enclosed between two quotes.

Example:

```
'h' // char
```

Some characters cannot be printed. For these C++ uses one construct, adopted from C, called an *escape sequence* in which the character symbol is preceded by the symbol \ (*backslash*).

Example:

```
'\a' // bell
'\n' // line feed
'\r' // carriage return
'\t' // tab
'\b' // space
'\f' // formfeed
'\v' // vertical tab
'\'' // apostrophe
'\"' // double quote
'\?' // question mark
'\\' // backslash
```

Strings are sequences of characters enclosed between double quotes (").

C++ has inherited from C the method for storing a string: it is made up of a sequence of characters to which the special character '\0' is added. Therefore a *string always has one more character* than actually appears.

Example:

```
"AbraCadabra" // 11+1=12 char string
"0123456789"  // 10+1=11 char string
```

The string may have characters generated by the escape sequence.

Example:

```
"\nThe result is :" // use of \n in the string
```

2.8   Constants With Identifiers

In some situations it is useful to provide an identifier for a quantity, even though you know in advance that it will remain constant throughout the course of the program.

> The definition of one constant with identifier is exactly the same as when dealing with a variable, apart from the fact that the modifier `const` must precede the definition. It is essential to initialize the constant (that is, provide the value in the statement where the constant is defined). It is not possible to define the constant, or to provide a value for it, afterwards (for obvious reasons).

Example of definitions for constants with identifier:

```
const float PI = 3.14;
const char TRUE = 1;
```

> The advantages obtained by providing a constant with an identifier are the following.
>
> (1)   If one wishes to change the value of the constant, the change is placed in the identifier initialization. It is not necessary to search for all occurrences of that constant in the program.
> (2)   The identifier provides information about the meaning of that constant. For example, TOLERANCE is more meaningful than .0001.
> (3)   If you had used a variable, you would run the risk of changing it inadvertently in the course of the program. This becomes impossible, once the magnitude has been defined using the `const` modifier.

2.9   Operators

In order to build an expression beyond variables and constants, operators are also needed.

Definition: *Operators*
By operators we mean those symbols, reserved by the language, which are dedicated to the execution of various operations and to the formation of meaningful expressions.

C++ is rich in operators, which allow the execution of many more operations than those permitted by FORTRAN.

In C++ almost all the operators can be redefined by the user in order to operate specifically on the new variables which have been defined by the user himself.

Definition: *Assignment operator*
The assignment operator allows a value, taken from a certain expression, to be assigned to a variable. It has the same symbol used by FORTRAN, symbol =.
In C++, in order to assign a numerical value to the variable V, we write:

```
V = (expression);
```

Definition: *Initialization*
A variable can also be assigned a numerical value in the statement in which it is defined. This provides an initialization.

Example:

```
float a = 15.; // definition and initialization
float b; // definition
b = a; // assignment
```

There are always two values associated with a variable identifier.

(1)   The value of the variable.

(2)   The address where such value is stored.

Definition: *rvalue*
The *value* of a variable or the *result of one expression* is called *rvalue*, because it must be to the right of an assignment (*rvalue* from *right value*).

Definition: *lvalue*
Anything which denotes the *content of a memory address* is called *lvalue*, because it can be placed on the left of an assignment (*lvalue* from *left value*).

Example:

```
int i = 3; // i is an lvalue
int j = i; // i is an rvalue
```

An identifier can be an lvalue and an rvalue within the same statement.
Example:

```
i = i + 4;
```

The identifier i, to the right of the assignment operator, is used as an rvalue (its value is used) whilst, when on the left, it receives the value of the operation: it is an lvalue.

> After the assignment operator, we shall consider only a few more operators, namely those which allow the execution of some calculations and those which allow the comparison of some numerical values or some expressions between themselves.

Addition, subtraction, division and multiplication operators are the same as in FORTRAN; therefore they are, in sequence, +, -, /, *.

The operator % applied to int type variables provides the remainder in division between integers.

Example:

```
21%7  // result 0
20%6  // result  2
15.5%3 // error: % cannot be used with float
```

Definition: *Arity*

The number of variables on which an operator acts is called arity. If an operator acts on only one variable, it is called *unary*. If it acts on two variables, it is a *binary* operator. If it acts on three variables, it is a *ternary* operator.

The operators +, -, /, *, % are binary operators when they are between two expressions.

In order to change the sign of the value of the result of an expression, the operator -, placed in front of the expression, is used.

The operator +, placed in front of an expression, does not alter its sign; it is only used to make an expression more legible. The operators + and -, when they are applied before an expression and have no expression to their left, are examples of unary operators.

Example:

```
x = -y;  // unary operator -
x = + y; // equivalent to x = y;
```

Furthermore, C++ has some special operators to be used when the variable to the left of the operator = is also on the right.

These are +=, -=, /=, *=, %=.

Definition: *Combined assignment*

The operators which carry out an assignment and, at the same time, execute a specific operation, are called combined assignment operators.

These are equivalent to the following operations:

```
a += expression;   // a=a+(expression);
a -= expression;   // a=a-(expression);
a /= expression;   // a=a/(expression);
a *= expression;   // a=a*(expression);
a %= expression;   // a=a%(expression);
```

These operators are useful whenever access to a variable is time consuming. Specifically, whilst in normal operations access is carried out *twice*, with these operators access is only carried out once. They may well also avoid possible confusion.
In fact the relation:

```
x = x + 10.
```

is mathematically different from the actually executed operation.
There is a third reason too which will only become clear in Chapter 10: in this way one avoids having to use a copy-initializer constructor, that is to say, you avoid having to copy the object resulting from the operation. If the object is large (for example, a matrix), there is a saving in calculation time and memory.

Whenever possible, it is better to favour the combined assignment form.

Other operators which are often used and which have no equivalent counterpart in FORTRAN are the operators ++ and --. Such operators can be applied to the right or left of a variable. If applied to the right, the operation where that variable is involved is executed first, then the variable will be increased by one with ++ and decreased by one with --. If, on the other hand, the operators are applied to the left, the variable will firstly be increased (with ++) or decreased (with --) and then the operation is executed.

```
float s=v=0.,r=1.,h;
h = s++ * r;   // h=0
               // equivalent to:
               // h = s*r; s = s + 1.;

h = ++v * r;   // h=1
               // equivalent to:
               // v = v + 1.; h = v*r;
```

Typically such operators are used in iterative cycles:

```
for(i=0;i<n;i++)
```

> C++ does not have any default operator for executing a power with integer exponent. FORTRAN has the operator $**$.

If a user needs to execute such an operation several times, he or she can define his or her own function. For example, for the square you can write:

```
float Square(float a)
   {
   return a*a;
   }
```

It is possible to write a function which raises a variable to an nth power, for any integer n, even though it is not an easy task.

The operators which allow a comparison between variables are listed in Table 2.3 with their FORTRAN counterparts.

Table 2.3   Operators to compare expressions.

!	.NOT.
==	.EQ.
!=	.NE.
>	.GT.
<	.LT.
>=	.GE.
<=	.LE.
&&	.AND.
||	.OR.

As in FORTRAN you can carry out several comparisons at the same time. Examples in C++:

```
(a > b && x <= z*y)
(a+b/2. <= y || i != 3)
```

> The result of these operators is 1 or 0 according to whether the expression is true or false. From a numerical point of view you must remember that in C++ *true* means not equal to zero and *false* means equal to zero.

An easy mistake to make is to forget one of the two = when creating the test for the equality of the two terms. For example, writing:

```
if(a = b) instead of if(a == b).
```

A good compiler usually sends a warning when you use = instead of == in a test. Please note that this is not necessarily a mistake.

Example:

```
if(i = Func())
    {
    statements;
    }
```

Here it cannot be a mistake: the value calculated by the function `Func` is assigned to the variable `i`. If this value is equal to zero, the test is false; otherwise, the test is true.

It is useful to try to make a program as legible as possible, avoiding excessive simplifications.

In the previous example it is better to make explicit the test you want to carry out:

```
if((i = Func()) != 0)
    {
    statements;
    }
```

C++ optimizes the use of multiple comparisons in the sense that it does not necessarily execute all the operations in the complete expression if it can come up with a true or false from an intermediate position. Specifically:

(1) if the expression contains `&&`, it is sufficient that one of the terms to the right or to the left is false, in order to make the whole expression false;

(2) if the expression contains `||`, it is sufficient that one of the terms is true, in order to make the whole expression true.

Therefore, do not put functions which must be calculated in the expression in a test. The test could come to an end without calculating that function.

In the example:

```
if(x > 0 && c=Func())
```

c does not necessarily receive its value from `Func()`!

Definition: *Operator priority*
As in FORTRAN there is a clear priority for operators. Table 2.4 shows all C++ operators and their priorities.

For the operators considered so far, the priority in decreasing order is:

```
++, --, !, +, - unary
*, /, %
+, - binary
<, <=, >, >=
==, !=
&&
||
=, +=, -=, *=, /=, %=
```

Priorities for common operators are the same as for FORTRAN.
In the example:

```
a = b*c + b/2.;
```

multiplication and division are carried out before the addition.

Obviously, if you wish to alter the order of priority, you can use brackets. Therefore if:

```
a = b*(c + b)/2.;
```

the addition is executed first. Let us suppose that we have the following expression:

```
a = b + c + d;
```

In this case, the operators involved have the same priority. It is therefore necessary to know whether they associate to the right or to the left, to be able to know the order of execution of the operations.

Definition: *Associativity*
The associativity (to the right or to left) of an operator determines which operation is executed first *if the operators have the same priority*.

Since the binary operator **+** associates to the left, in the previous case the sum between **b** and **c** is executed first and **d** is added later. Table 2.4 shows the type of associativity for all operators. For the operators so far examined, associativity is as follows:

```
++, --                           right
+, - unary                       right
*, /, %                          left
+, - binary                      left
<, <=, >, >=                      left
==, !=                           left
&&                               left
||                               left
=, +=, -=, *=, /=, %=            right
```

Table 2.4 shows all the operators used in C++ with their relative priority, P; the type of associativity, As (L if left, R if right); the arity, Ar (1 if unary, 2 if binary); and the possibility of overlap, Ov (Y if it can, N if it can't).

Table 2.4   C++ operators.

Symbol	P	As	Ar	Ov	Meaning
::	17	R	1	N	Global scope
::	17	L	2	N	Class scope
->	16	L	2	Y	Selection of member using pointer
.	16	L	2	N	Selection of member using object
[]	16	L	1	Y	Array index
()	16	L	1	Y	Function call
()	16	L	1	Y	Type conversion
sizeof	16	L	1	N	Size in byte
++, --	15	R	1	Y	Increase, decrease
~	15	R	1	Y	Bitwise NOT
!	15	R	1	Y	Logical NOT
-,+	15	R	1	Y	Unary minus, plus
*	15	R	1	Y	Content of
&	15	R	1	Y	Address of
new	15	R	1	Y	Creates room in memory
delete	15	R	1	Y	Regenerates occupied space
()	15	R	1	Y	Typecasting
->*	14	L	2	Y	Member pointer using pointer
.*	14	L	2	N	Member pointer using object
*,/,%	13	L	2	Y	Product, division, rest
+,-	12	L	2	Y	Sum, subtraction
<<, >>	11	L	2	Y	Shift to left and right
<,<=,>,>=	10	L	2	Y	Relational operator
== , !=	9	L	2	Y	Same, different
&	8	L	2	Y	Bitwise AND

Table 2.4 *cont.*

Symbol	P	As	Ar	Ov	Meaning
^	7	L	2	Y	Bitwise XOR
|	6	L	2	Y	OR at bit level
&&	5	L	2	Y	Logical AND
||	4	L	2	Y	Logical OR
?:	3	L	3	N	Arithmetic IF
=,*=,/=,					
%=,-=,+=,					
<<=,>>=,&=,					
^=,|=	2	R	2	Y	Assignment s
,	1	L	2	Y	Comma operator

It is not important for the moment to understand the meaning of all these operators.

> It must be noted that many operators use the same symbol. In this case they should not have the same arity. For example, the symbol * is used for both multiplication and other purposes; however it is a binary operator in multiplication.

Other Operators

Table 2.4 shows all C++ operators. Up to now we have only dealt with those which intervene directly in numerical calculations. Let us now look at operators of a different nature.

sizeof

The operator sizeof is used to give the byte size of a variable of any type or of an expression.

The syntax is:

```
sizeof (type of variable);
sizeof expression;
```

Example:

```
int k = sizeof (int);
float x;
int k = sizeof x;
```

> A trick that C and C++ programmers often use is to exploit the operator sizeof to make the compiler calculate the number of elements in a vector.

In the example:

```
float x[] = {3.,6.,4.};
int n = sizeof x / sizeof x[0];
n = sizeof x / sizeof(float); // equivalent
```

sizeof x provides the total number of *bytes* taken up by the x vector, sizeof x[0] and sizeof(float) provide the number of *bytes* taken up by one element of the vector; therefore their ratio provides the number of elements in the vector.

> The operator sizeof is very important because it allows you to write transportable codes. C++ does not guarantee the actual sizes of the various types of variables, but only their minimum sizes and, therefore, one variable can be represented differently on two different computers. When, in some operations, it is necessary to know the actual size of a type of variable, it is better to write the program using the sizeof operator instead of providing the sizes used by an individual compiler.

Conversion Operator (Cast)

When, in the argument of a function (or of an operator), a variable of a type which is different from that expected by the function is put through, C++, as a first step, checks whether a way to convert the variable into a type required by the function has been defined.

For basic variables many conversions are defined by the compiler and implicitly applied.

Example:

```
int i = 3.14; // double 3.14 is converted into int 3
```

In some cases (namely exploiting the void pointers, which we shall discuss in Chapter 3) it is important to be able to tell the compiler explicitly that you wish to carry out a conversion from one type to the other. In such a case you would use the conversion operator. Two equivalent syntax forms can be used:

```
(type)expression;
type(expression);
```

Example:

```
int i = (int)3.14;
int j = int(3.14);
```

Avoid, as far as possible, using variables of a different type in operations, and calling functions with variables of a type which does not correspond to the actual one. This may generate errors which are difficult to place. Should such a case arise, you need to avoid an *implicit conversion*, by using the conversion operator *explicitly*, so that it is clear what you are doing.

Bitwise Operators

C++ has inherited from C the ability to carry out several operations at the level of a single bit of a variable.

The ability to access and operate at the level of a single bit considerably enhances C++ (and C) possibilities, allowing it to carry out operations which were previously only possible in machine language.

Table 2.5 shows operators which work at bit level.

Table 2.5   Bit-level operators.

Operator	Function	Use
~	bitwise NOT	~expression
<<	shift to the left	expr1 << expr2
>>	shift to the right	expr1 >> expr2
&	bitwise AND	expr1 & expr2
^	bitwise XOR	expr1 ^ expr2
|	bitwise OR	expr1 | expr2

I shall not describe these operators, because they are relatively little used in normal numerical calculations.

2.10 Iterative Cycles

As in FORTRAN there is the ability to repeat a sequence of statements cyclically.

In C++ there are three ways to carry out iterative cycles: `for`, `while` and `do while`.

Iterative Construct `for`

The iterative cycle structure executed with `for` is as follows:

```
for(Initial Conditions;Test;Modification)
    {
    statements;
    }
```

The Initial Conditions can be made up of one or more expressions separated by a comma (*comma* operator). It is thus possible to assign an initial value to several variables before beginning the iterative cycle.

> The Initial Conditions *must* terminate with ; so that they are separated from the Test. The Initial Conditions together constitute one single statement.

Example:

```
for(i = 0;......)
for(i = 0, j = 1, k = 120,x = Func();......)
for(;.....)
for(int i = 0;......)
for(float x = 0.;.....)
```

> It should be noted that for variables initialized in the Initial Conditions statement, and therefore defined in that statement (such as in the last two examples), the definition is equivalent to a definition placed immediately *before* for.

Therefore:

```
for(int i=0;......)
```

is equivalent to:

```
int i;
for(i=0;......)
```

We shall see that this means that the variable i is also defined when the for iterative cycle is over.

> The Initial Conditions can also be made up of only ;. This is possible when no variable must be initialized.

The Test must be single and must terminate with ;. If the Test result is true (different from zero) the iterative cycle continues. If it is false (equal to zero) the control goes to the first statement after the for block.

Example:

```
for(i=0;i<10;......)
for(i=0,j=1,k=120;k>=30;......)
for(int i=0;x+y<z;......)

for(float x=0.,int i=1;x>10.|| y<3; .....)
for(i=0;;....)
for(;;....)
```

The `Test` can also be made up of only `;`. In this case, the iterative cycle continues without the limits imposed by `for`. In order not to get into an endless cycle it is necessary that there should be a `break` within the `for` block.

Example:

```
for(i = 0;;i++)// potentially infinite cycle
    {
    ...
    if(i > 100)break;
    ...
    }
```

The `Modification` can be made up of one or more expressions separated by a comma. Very often the initialized variables or the variables under `Test` are increased or decreased in this position.

The `Modification` can be made up of any expression, even a complex one, but the expression must *not* be a statement: *it must not terminate with a semicolon* `;`.

Example:

```
for(i=0;i<10;i++)
for(i=0,j=1,k=120;k>=30;kñ,i++,j++)
for(int i=0;x+y<z;i+=10)
for(float x=0.,int i=1;x>10.|| y<3;a=f-h*u)
for(;;)
```

As you can see, the `for` is much more flexible and has many more possibilities than the corresponding DO in FORTRAN. Furthermore, it is also more reliable, because there are no equivocations about the numerical value of the index on which you iterate.

Example

```
     DO 100 I=1,M
     .....
100    CONTINUE
```

What is the value of I when exiting from DO? M or M+1? The language does not help with this information.

On the other hand:

```
for(i=1;i < M;i++)
    {
    statements;
    }
```

the value of i when exiting from for is certainly equal to M (unless there is a break within for).

> If there are several statements on which you are carrying out the iterative cycle, the brackets {} are required to enclose them all. In such a case variables can be defined within the block.

Example:

```
for(i=0;i<10;i++)
    {
    int j = 2*i;   // definition of j
    a[i]=b[j];
    c[j]=a[i]+2.;
    }
```

If only one statement is available on which to carry out the iterative cycle, the brackets {} are not required around the statement.
Example:

```
for(i=0;i<10;i++)
    a[i]=b[i];
```

> It must be noted that the two forms:
>
> ```
>  for(i=0;i<10;i++)
>  for(i=0;i<10;++i)
> ```
>
> are equivalent.

The following are some possible errors.

(1) Using a ; after the `Modification` expression:
```
for(i=0;i<10;i++;)  // wrong ; after i++
```
(2) Using a ; after the `for` bracket:
```
for(i=0;i<10;i++); // does not execute anything
```
(3) Not separating the initializer from the `Test` with ;
```
for(i=0,i<10;i++) // you need ; and not,
```
(4) Not separating the `Test` from the increment with ;
```
for(i=0;i<10,i++)  // you need ; and not,
```
(5) Forgetting the block brackets {} when there are several statements:
```
for(i=0;i<10;i++)
a[i]=b[i];//only this is in the for cycle
c[i]=a[i]+2.;
```

Iterative Construct `while`

The structure of the iterative cycle executed with `while` is as follows:

```
while(Test)
    {
    statements;
    }
```

The statements contained between the brackets are repeated until the `Test` is true (different from zero). When the `Test` is false (equal to 0) the iterative cycle gets interrupted.

The block brackets are needed when there are several statements. They are not needed when there is only one statement.

Example:

```
while(x<y && i>1)
    {
    statements;
    }
while(x+y >= z)
    statement;
while(1)        // always true: infinite cycle
    {
    statements;
    if(x>y)break;
    statements;
    }
```

The two expressions:

```
while(1){statements}
for(;;){statements}
```

are equivalent and are used as an alternative when you want to carry out a potentially endless iterative cycle. The control must be placed within the block in order to avoid an effectively endless iterative cycle.

You may wonder when it is convenient to use a for type iterative cycle and when to use a while type. In most cases it is really just a question of habit.

If the condition of interruption of the iterative cycle is not known in advance, but it happens interactively, it is better to use while. Otherwise using for is almost always clearer.

Example:

```
while(getchar() != 'q')
    {
    statements;
    }
```

The library function getchar() reads a character keyed in from the keyboard. The iterative cycle is repeated until the character q is keyed in.

Iterative Construct do while

The structure of the iterative cycle executed with do while is as follows:

```
do
    {
    statements;
    }while(Test);
```

The statements between the two brackets are repeated until the Test is true. When the Test is false (equal to 0) the iterative cycle gets interrupted.

The iterative cycle do while is useful when you want the statements in the iterative cycle to be carried out at least once. In fact, and this is one difference from the while iterative cycle, the Test is carried out at the end of the sequence of statements which are, therefore, executed at least once.

Example:

```
do
    {
    statements;  // are executed anyway
    }while(getchar() != 'q');
```

 A possible error is to forget the `;` after `while(Test)` at the end of the `do while` structure.

Nested Iterative Cycles

The various types of iterative cycles can be placed inside each other as in FORTRAN. In C++ an iterative cycle cannot intersect another iterative cycle. The difference from FORTRAN is that the error made is not picked up by the compiler. In fact in FORTRAN the compiler can realize that the numbered label in an iterative cycle is internal to another iterative cycle positioned in an incompatible way.

Example in FORTRAN with compilation error:

```
DO 100 I=1,10
DO 200 J=1,20
...
100     CONTINUE
200     CONTINUE
```

Conversely in C++ the compiler has no way of understanding the programmer's intentions:

```
while(Test1)
    {
    while(Test2)
        {
    }  // this is the end of the internal block
        }// and this is the end of the external block
```

 One must remember that the more or less indented position of the curly brackets and the statements is only used to enhance the legibility of the program. For C++ the blank spaces and the tabulations are invisible. For C++, syntax is the only thing that counts.
In the previous example the first bracket `}` completes the internal cycle, not the external one.

Attention: it is an error to initialize a variable in the `Initial Conditions` statement of a `for` which is internal to another one, without using the block brackets.

Example:

```
for(int i=0; i<10;i++)
    for(int j=0;j<20;j++) // error int j=0
```

In this case you must either define j before both `for`s or put curly brackets around the second `for`.

Modification of the Iterative Cycles with break and continue

The keywords `break` and `continue` allow you to alter the statement flow within an iterative cycle.

 The statement `break;` interrupts the iterative cycle where it is located and shifts control to the first statement immediately following the cycle.
The statement `continue;` interrupts the iteration of an iterative cycle and shifts control to the statement where the `Test` is executed.

Example:

```
for(i=0;i<10;i++)
    {
    statements;
    if(x>y) break;  // interrupts the cycle
                    // and executes a=..;
    statements; // only if x<=y
    }
a=...;
```

Example:

```
for(i=0;i<10;i++)
    {
    statements;
    if(x>y) continue;  // interrupts the iteration i
    statements; // only if x<=y
    }
a=...;// is executed only when i==10
```

Example:

```
while(z == 10)
    {
    statements;
    if(x>y)continue; // interrupts the cycle
                     // and controls z == 10
    statements; // only if x<=y
    }
a=...; // is only executed when z != 10
```

The statement continue will not be used because it can generate confusion, especially for users who are familiar with FORTRAN.

2.11 Decisions

As in FORTRAN, the keywords if and else are used to make decisions.

Decision with Simple if

The simplest decision can be taken with the following statement:

```
if(Test)
    {
    statements; // True Test
    }
```

If the Test results in true (different from zero), the statements in the block are executed. If false, they are skipped. In the specific case of a single statement internal to the block, curly brackets are not needed.

Example:

```
if(x>=y)
    a=b;  // a is given equal to b only if x>=y
```

Please note that, contrary to FORTRAN, in C++ you should not put then at the end of the expression which contains if! The compiler would show an error.

You can put several ifs inside each other. Just like for iterative cycles, when a block terminates with }, the closed block is the one with the *nearest* { and *not* the block with the bracket { on the same column as the bracket }. The compiler does not close the block according to the alignment of the brackets!

Example:

```
if(Test1)
   {
   ....
   if(Test2)
      {
      a=b;
      } // this closes the Test2 block
   } //this closes the Test1 block
```

> When there are several blocks inside one another my advice is to keep the arrangement of the whole of the internal block aligned (including the curly brackets {}) indented to the right.

Example:

```
if(Test1)
   {
   statements; // Test1 true
   if(Test2)
      {
      statements; // Test1 true Test2 true
      }
   statements;
   }
```

> When an if has a single statement, the curly brackets {} can be eliminated even when the statement is actually another if.

Example:

```
if(Test1)
   if(Test2)
      {
      statements; // Test1 true Test2 true
      }
```

Else:

```
if(Test1)
   if(Test2)
      statement; // Test1 true Test2 true
```

which is equivalent to:

```
if(Test1 && Test2)
    statement; // Test1 true Test2 true
```

The if else Construct

The if else construct is conceptually similar to the equivalent one in FORTRAN:

```
if(Test1)
    {
    statements; // Test1 true
    }
else
    {
    statements; // Test1 false (0)
    }
```

If Test1 is true, the if block is executed, otherwise the else block is executed.

 An easy error to make is to attribute the else to the wrong if when there are if else structures inside one another (especially if one is not forced to use the curly brackets {}).

Example:

```
if(Test1)
    if(Test2)
        a=b;
else
    x=c;
```

When will the statement a=b be executed and when x=c?

 It must be remembered that, unless you use the curly brackets to change priorities, the statement else belongs to the nearest if.

Therefore in the previous example you must not be sent off course by the (wrong) position of the else aligned with the first if. It forms a pair together with the second. If you want to use this as an alternative to the first if, you must introduce the brackets {}:

```
if(Test1)
   {
   if(Test2)
      a=b; // Test1 true Test2 true
   }
else
   x=c; // Test1 false
```

The else if Construct

When there is a sequence of an if else followed by another if, the construct else if is used:

```
if(Test1)
   {
   statements; // Test1 true
   }
else if(Test2)
   {
   statements; // Test1 false Test2 true
   }
else // goes with the second if
   {
   statements; // Test1 false Test2 false
   }
```

 Too many linked if else if must be avoided. They can lead to errors in the attribution of an else to the wrong if and make the program difficult to read.

The ?: Construct

In C++ there is only one *ternary operator*: the ?: construct. This is made up of one Test and two expressions according to the following syntax:

```
Test ? expression1 : expression2
```

If the Test is true, then the result is the one given by expression1, if it is false the result is the one given by expression2. For example, the following statement is used to assign the c variable the maximum value between a and b:

```
c = a > b ? a : b;
```

The switch Construct

This construct is the equivalent of the GO TO (1,2,3,...), J, in FORTRAN.

It is made up as follows:

```
switch(j) // switch type int
  {
  case 1:
      statements; // if j == 1
      break;
  case 2:
      statements; // if j == 2
      break;
  default:
      statements; // in other cases
      break;
  }
```

else:

```
switch(ch) // switch type char
  {
  case 'a':
      statements; // if ch == 'a'
      break;
  case 'b':
      statements; // if ch == 'b'
      break;
  default:
      statements; // in other cases
      break;
  }
```

> In object-oriented programming, the switch tends to be eliminated. In a way it is the main victim of this type of programming, just as GO TO was the victim in structured programming. Chapter 14 will provide the reason for this.

The goto Construct

In C++ it is possible to move control to one *label* using the keyword goto (it must be only one word!). The label is not a numbered statement as in FORTRAN, in C++ there are no numbered statements. It must be an identifier just like that of any variable, followed by : (colon).

Within a function the labels must each have a different identifier. In different
functions labels with the same identifier can be used without experiencing
incompatibility problems. Remember to put : after the label identifier!

Example:

```
    if(Test1)goto pinco;
    first statement block; // Test1 false
pinco:
    other statement block;
```

In this case the following version is preferable. It is equivalent to the previous
one, but is easier to read:

```
if(!Test1)
    {
    first statement block; // Test1 false
    }
other statement block;
```

Unlike FORTRAN, where the number of the statement to which the GO TO
transfers is unnamed, in C++ the goto transfers to a label whose identifier
can have an easily comprehensible meaning.

Example:

```
variable_x_too_large:
```

Generally speaking it is better to avoid the indiscriminate use of the goto
construct, because it leads to programs which are difficult to read. It is
almost always possible to write a better alternative version. However, you
should not let yourself be too influenced by supporters of structured
programming, who believe you should avoid the goto at all costs.
There are situations where the goto can make a program more readable;
specifically, when there are several iterative cycles, one inside the other, and
you want to get out of them all. Furthermore, as previously stated, it is
possible in C++ to use an identifier with an easily comprehensible meaning.
I shall use the following style:

(1)   All the statements for one function, including the curly brackets {} at
      the beginning and at the end of a function, are three characters to the
      right.

cont.

> *cont.*
>
> (2) The function identifier and the labels to which the `goto` may transfer control are the only statements which begin in the first column. In this way the labels are easily traceable.
>
> (3) The identifier for a label is always made up of more than one word in lower case and separated by the underscore sign _. I shall follow such a style only for label identifiers.
>
> (4) The `goto` will be used for the following purpose: to get out of a series of several iterative cycles.

2.12 Questions

Given the variables x, y, z, r of the `float` type, state whether the following statement is correct:

```
x = y +
    3.*z -
    r;
```

Yes. In C++ a statement follows a free format and can be positioned over several lines.

State which of the following identifiers cannot be used to define a variable and why:

```
xyz, (xy), -z, _uuu, old, new
```

(xy) because it uses brackets;
new because it is a keyword;
-z because the - minus sign is used instead of the underlining;
_uuu is in fact valid, but it is more prudent never to use an identifier beginning with _.

Is the variable x an lvalue or an rvalue ?

```
x = 3.;
```

It is an *lvalue* because it is placed to the left of an assignment.

Give the result of the following square operation:

```
float x = 3.;
float y = x**2;   // y = ?
```

There is a compiling error. C++ does not have the operator **.

Give the value of k at the end of the following program fragment:

```
int  i=0,j=1,k=2;
if(i)
    if(j)
        k=0;
else
    k=1;
```

The position of else should not create confusion: it is associated with the if(j).

Since if(i) is false (being i = 0) all the other statements are out and the value of k is still 2.

Give the value of z at the end of the following program fragment:

```
int x=0,y=0,z;
if(x=y)
    z=1;
else
z=2;
```

Since we have put = and not == in the if, the Test is false (x = y = 0). Therefore z = 2.

Give the value of z at the end of the following program fragment:

```
float x=0.,z;
for(int i=0;i < 100; i++);
    {
    x = x + 5.;
    }
z = x;
```

The value of z is 5 because for does not act on the block in brackets {}. A ; which excludes the block, has been used in error.

The compiler does not show an error, but the program contains a potentially serious danger. Which danger?

```
float v[10];
v[5] = 5.;
v[10] = 10.;
v[1] = v[5] + v[10];
```

v[10] is outside the definition range of v, which is defined between v[0] and v[9].

2.13 Examples

In our first applications, let us try to translate some program fragments literally from FORTRAN to C++. Such translations are *not* the best implementations available in C++.

Sum of Vectors

Given two vectors, calculate their sum and place the result in a third vector.

If we call the sizes of the two vectors n, the required statements are:

```
for(int i=0;i < n;i++)
    x[i] = a[i] + b[i];
```

Please note, once again, that in C++ vectors are defined between 0 and n-1.

Let us now suppose that we want to execute the sum in such a way that the result replaces vector a[1].

In this case, we can write:

```
for(int i=0;i < n;i++)
    a[i] += b[i];
```

By using the += compound assignment operator you need to access vector a's element only once; the code is more efficient.

Product of Vectors

Let us now write a code to execute the scalar product between two vectors:

$$c = \mathbf{x}^{\mathrm{T}}\mathbf{y}$$

There are no special difficulties:

```
double c = 0.;
for(int i = 0; i < n; i++)
    c += x[i]*y[i];
```

Please note that the sum of products is executed with double precision. This does not create problems in C++ because calculations are executed in `double` by default.

Please note that for such an operation it is convenient to use the combined assignment operator `+=`.

The First Complete Program in C++

Let us calculate the computer precision, `macheps`, when working in simple precision. This is a very important issue for any numerical calculation. It is obvious that the best implementation will be the one which allows the calculation to be made when needed; we will therefore need to construct a separate function for the purpose.

For now we will only implement the algorithm in the `main`.

Algorithmically, the problem is solved as follows.

Algorithm to calculate machine precision
| ```
macheps=1
for i=1,2,...
        macheps=macheps/2.
        eps=macheps+1.
        if(eps=1)
                macheps = 2.*macheps
                quit
``` |

In FORTRAN we can write:

```
        REAL MCHPS
        MCHPS=1.
10      CONTINUE
        IF(1.+MCHPS.GT.1.)THEN
        MCHPS=MCHPS/2.
        GO TO 10
        END IF
        MCHPS=2.*MCHPS
        WRITE(*,*)MCHPS
        STOP
        END
```
```

In C++ we could also write:

```
#include <iostream.h>
main()
    {
    float macheps=1.;//macheps defined and initialized
    while((1. + macheps) != 1.)macheps/=2.;
    macheps *=2.;
    cout << macheps;  // print macheps
    return 0;
    }.
```

Some points about this little program:

(1)   As we can see, before the main definition there is a rather mysterious (at least for the moment) expression. This is part of the structure of a program in C++ which, as I was saying earlier, is more articulated than for programs in FORTRAN. All we need to know for the time being is that this tells the compiler that operator << is being used to write the macheps value on screen.

> In order to read from the keyboard or to write on screen, we simply need to remember the following points, at least for now.
>
> (1)   Put at the beginning of the file:
>
>   #include <iostream.h>
>
> (2)   For reading, use the statement:
>
>   cin >> identifier;
>
> (3)   For writing, use the statement:
>
>   cout << identifier
>
> where identifier means the identifier of any type of variables.

(2)   The compound assignments /= and *= are used.
(3)   If the results are printed in FORTRAN you get macheps = $1.19 \times 10-7$ whilst in C++ you would get $1.0842\ 10\ -19$.

Why such higher precision in C++?
The point is that in C and in C++ the operations in floating point are carried out, by default, in double rather than in simple precision. Therefore, if this scheme of

calculation is used, you obtain double precision `macheps`. If you want simple precision `machepss` you need to execute the operations in simple precision. The following program could be used:

```
#include <iostream.h>
main()
    {
    float macheps=1.,eps=2.;
    while(eps != 1.)
        {
        macheps /=2.;
        eps = 1.+macheps; //eps in simple precision
        }
    macheps *=2.;
    cout << macheps;
    return 0;
    }
```

3 Derived Types: Pointers, References, Arrays

Ora incomincian le dolenti note.

And now the notes of anguish start to play.

Dante, *Inferno, V*

3.1 Introduction

Pointers are the main pillars of C and C++, owing to the essential part they play in providing power and flexibility in these languages.

They are, however, not easy to use and incorrect use could even lead to loss of important data or programs.

Whoever comes from a FORTRAN 77 background must, at this point, be prepared to consider variables, functions and constants in a new light.
I shall now try to give a brief description of pointers and their advantages. This will be discussed in more depth further on in this chapter.
All the quantities which are used in a calculation program (variables, constants, functions, vectors, etc.) must be stored somewhere; they must, in other words, have an address. Pointers allow you to use and manipulate these addresses. Pointers must also be resident in memory and therefore also

cont.

> *cont.*
> have an address. It is possible to use new pointers which use the previous
> pointer's address and so on.
> You may ask yourself: what are the advantages in using addresses, that is,
> pointers?
> Programs become more efficient and it is often possible to resolve problems
> which would otherwise be impossible to solve.

Let us first of all consider the problem of accessing a matrix coefficient. Since,
in FORTRAN, matrix coefficients are stored by columns, in order to identify a matrix
coefficient the following operation is necessary: (index column − 1)*(number of rows)
+ index row. The product shows the first coefficient of the column; then a number of
elements equal to the index row is added. If we were working in C or in C++ with a
matrix defined as:

```
float A[10][20];
```

things would be similar, apart from the fact that in C or in C++ coefficients are stored
by row and start from 0 and not 1.

In both cases, in order to access a matrix coefficient a product and a sum must
be carried out. Pointers allow for this step to be avoided. If we are aware of the start
address for each row we can go directly to that position, without having to carry out a
product. You can move from here (with a sum) along the row, up to the desired
coefficient.

Let us consider another problem: let's say that a function uses two matrices so
that when the function is over, the identifier of one of the two can no longer be used,
whereas the other one can (examples of this can be found in Chapter 12).
Unfortunately the matrix that we want to save is the one which will be deleted. What
could be done if there weren't any pointers? If the matrices have an equal number of
columns and rows, the coefficients of one matrix can be recopied, one by one, into the
coefficients of the other. If the dimensions are different, the problem is not solvable.

With pointers the solution is simple but very effective: all you have to do is
swap the addresses of the two matrices. The matrix which is deleted is the same one,
but with the coefficients of the other one. This procedure will be further explained in
Chapter 12. For now, all that we need to know is that, by using pointers, a simple
exchange of addresses is all that is needed, rather than the complete exchange of all
the coefficients of the matrices.

References are a new derived type which were not previously present in C.
Their introduction was necessary in order to efficiently use standard operators (for
example, *, +, -, and so on) for user-defined variables. These also allow programs to
be more easily read and less subject to error when they are used as an alternative to
pointers for certain uses (for example, for passing addresses to a function).

Finally, *arrays* are the starting point for vector and matrix construction, and
are, therefore, extremely important in the scientific field. We shall see that this derived
type is very closely linked to pointers.

3.2 Pointers

A variable or a function or any object which is defined by the programmer resides in an assigned position in memory. In many cases it is important to know the address of this position. It is at this point that pointers come into play.

Let us remember that for fundamental types there are three different situations.

(1)   There are *numerical constants without identifiers*.

For example, if 3.14 appears within a statement, it is to be considered as a numerical constant without identifier.

```
c = 3.14*d; // 3.14 constant without identifier
```

(2)   There are *numerical constants with identifiers*. In other words, they are items which even if they are similar in appearance to variables, cannot change in value.

Example:

```
const float PI = 3.14;
    // PI cannot be modified
```

(3)   There are *variables*, or objects which can be modified.

Example:

```
float x=3.14; // x can be modified
x=15.; // and here I am modifying it
```

> For memory addresses there may be the following situations.
>
> (1)   An address is a numerical constant without identifier.
> (2)   An identifier has been assigned to an address, it contains the numerical value of that address, but this identifier cannot be manipulated, it is a constant. In the case of constant addresses with identifiers there are two situations depending on whether the identifier has been automatically assigned by the compiler or has been chosen by the user.
> (3)   An identifier has been given the value of an address. While the program is running, if it is so required, the value of another address can be assigned to that identifier: the identifier is thus a *variable*.

Addresses as a Constant without Identifier

Particular memory addresses, which depend on the system used and which allow you to do special operations, can be very useful.

For example, if the memory address of a particular screen position is known, a character can be written directly in that position so that the character appears directly on screen. In these cases we are dealing with a constant address, which we cannot manipulate and which doesn't have an identifier, but knowing the address allows us to do certain operations.

Constant Pointers Defined by the Compiler

How do you find out the address of a variable, that is the position in which a variable has been stored? For this purpose the unary operator `&` is applied to the variable.

> **Definition:** *Operator address:* `&(Expression)`
> This operator can be read as: *Address of* `(Expression)`. In the case where the expression is simply a variable, its address can be obtained.

Example:

```
float viscosity;
```

`&viscosity` is the address of the variable `viscosity`. The `&viscosity` address is a constant which cannot be modified.

The same procedure applies to both basic variables and user-defined variables.

Let us suppose we have constructed a new type of variable, called `Matrix`. Let `A` be a variable of this type defined by:

```
Matrix A;
```

The address of variable `A` will be `&A`.

> The identifier of a basic or derived variable preceded by the unary operator `&` is the *identifier of a constant address*. Since an identifier's address is called a *pointer*, it is known as a constant pointer.

Once the address of the variable is known, it can be accessed indirectly, as soon as its position in memory is known. We shall see later how this procedure comes about and why it can often be very advantageous.

> In the case of arrays (vectors and matrices) and functions, the identifier is *the identifier of the memory address*. An array's or a function's identifier is therefore a constant pointer.
> The address of an array type variable is given by the identifier itself: it is not necessary to use the address operator `&`.
> Similarly, a function's identifier is its address.

Example:

```
float a[10],B[100][20];
```

The address of vector a is a and of matrix B is B. There is an identity between a and &a as well as between B and &B. Both a and B are constant addresses: these are the addresses where the compiler has placed the beginning of vector a and of matrix B. Knowing the starting address of the vector and the matrix it is possible to modify the values contained by the vector or by the matrix in an indirect manner, as can be seen by the following.

Similarly if the function is called Func() the name Func is the address of the function.

Variable Pointers

> A pointer points to the memory position where the required information is stored. A variable pointer is a derived type, which allows for operations on addresses.

As with every basic and derived type, a variable pointer needs an *identifier*, a *definition* and an *assignment* or an *initialization*.

As far as the identifier is concerned, the same rules apply to all identifiers of any type. Just by looking at the identifier it is not possible, therefore, to recognize whether it is a variable pointer or another object, nor is it obvious what it is pointing to.

> In order to show that a particular identifier is a pointer, the unary operator * is used when defining it.

Example:

```
float *ptf;
int *ptin;
Matrix *ptmat;
```

The effect of these definitions is that ptf is defined as a variable pointer to a variable of type float, ptin as a variable pointer to a variable of type int and ptmat as a variable pointer to a variable of type Matrix.

> If more than one pointer of the same type is defined in the same statement, each identifier must be given a *.

Example:

```
float *x,*y;      // both are pointers
float *w,z;       // beware: z is not a pointer
```

I will adopt this style (* next to the identifier):

```
float *x;
```

and avoid this style (* next to the type):

```
float* x;
```

in order to avoid the possibility of making the above error.

A variable pointer, as for example ptf, which indeed is a variable, must be allocated to some part of the memory. In order to find out the address where it is, all you need to do is use the unary operator & and apply it to its identifier.

Example:

```
float *ptf;
// &ptf address of ptf
```

The unary operator * is also known as an *indirect value operator*.

Definition: *Indirect value operator*: * (.....)
This operator can be read as: *in the contents of* (.....), where (.....) represents an address at which information has been stored.

The indirect value unary operator, *, is used in conjunction with pointers to achieve three aims.

(1)   We have already seen the first aim: it is used to *define* a pointer.

```
float *ptf;    // ptf is a pointer
               // to a float type variable
```

It is important not to confuse the meaning of the operator * when it is used within definitions.
In the definition:

```
float *ptf;
```

the variable ptf is being defined and *not* the variable *ptf.
From a memory point of view the definition reminds us that the contents of ptf, that is *ptf, are a variable of the float type.

(2)   The second aim is to *use the value* of the variable at which the variable pointer is pointing.

```
x=*ptf+2.;     // use of *ptf
```

The meaning of this statement is as follows: the variable x is the result of the sum of the value contained in the memory position to which ptf points and 2.

Please note that, where ptf is a pointer, *ptf is the value of a variable and, therefore, is an *rvalue* and may be placed to the right of an assignment (see Chapter 2).

(3)   The third aim is to *assign a value* to a variable to which a variable pointer is pointing.

```
*ptf=15.; // assigns a new value to *ptf (that is to the
          // variable to which ptf is pointing)
```

Please note that, where ptf is a pointer, *ptf is the content of an address and, therefore, is an lvalue and may be placed to the left of an assignment (see Chapter 2).

Initialization of Variable Pointers

Once a variable pointer has been defined, an address must be assigned to it before it can be used.

One of the most serious mistakes which can be made while using C++ is to use a pointer without first having made enough room in order to accommodate the variable to which it is pointing.
You must remember that a pointer cannot be used without first having assigned a valid address to it.

Example:

```
float *ptf;    // ptf is a variable pointer
               // to a float type variable
*ptf=15.; // NO !!! you must first assign the
          // value of an address to ptf
```

> Given the pointer, ptf, it is important not to confuse the address at which the pointer is stored, &ptf, which is automatically assigned by the compiler, with the address to which the pointer is pointing, which must be assigned to ptf by the programmer.

There are two methods of assigning a valid address to a variable pointer.

(1)   The first method consists in assigning to the pointer either the address of a pre-defined variable *of the same type* as the variable to which the pointer points or a pointer to a variable of the same type which has already been initialized.

Example:

```
float fx; // definition of float type variable
float *ptfl; // definition of float pointer
ptfl=&fx; // assignment to ptfl of fx address
float *pt2 = ptfl; // assignment to pt2 of address
                   // to which ptfl points
int i;
ptfl=&i; // NO: it must be of the same type
```

Example:

```
Matrix A; // definition of Matrix type variable
Matrix *ptmat; // definition of Matrix pointer
ptmat=&A; // assignment to ptmat of A address
```

> One possible area of confusion could be when initializing a pointer at the time of its definition.

Example:

```
float fl;
float *ptf=&fl;          // ptf is defined and initialized
                         // *ptf and fl are not initialized
```

Example:

```
float fl=5.;
float *ptf=&fl;          // ptf is initialized
                         // *ptf and fl are intialized to 5.
```

 0 (or NULL) can be assigned to any pointer of any type in order to show that the pointer is currently not pointing to any object. It is a practice which is very widespread and quite useful.

Example:

```
float *ptf = 0;          // ptf is initialized to 0
```

(2)   The second way of assigning a valid address to a variable pointer consists in using functions or operators which allow for dynamic management of memory. The functions, which have been inherited from C, are: malloc, calloc, realloc, free. In C++ it is preferable to use the operators new and delete.

In the case of a variable of any type, the syntax of the operator new is as follows:

```
                    //initialization
<type> *<identifier> = new <type>;
```

or:

```
<type> *<identifier>; // definition
<identifier> = new <type> // assignment
```

Example:

```
float *ptf = new float; // initialization
Matrix *A = new Matrix; // initialization
int *ptri; // definition
ptri = new int; // assignment
```

If the operator new is not able to assign a valid address, it gives the pointer a zero value. It is always good to check the validity of an assigned address. This checking might seem unnecessary (and it normally is) in the case where memory is being allocated for a small variable. It is different, however, when the operator is used to allocate memory for a vector or a large object.
Example:

```
float *ptrf = new float;
if(!ptrf) Error(....);
```

In order to free memory created with `new` the operator `delete` is used with the following syntax:

```
delete <identifier>;
```

Example:

```
Matrix *A = new Matrix;
........
delete A;
```

> The operator `delete` *is applied only to pointers which have been initialized with the operator* `new` *or intialized to zero.* If the opposite occurred unforeseeable errors could arise.

Example:

```
float fx;
float *pt1 = &fx,*pt2 = 0;
........
delete pt1; // NO: danger!!
delete pt2; // OK
```

A character pointer can be initialized by a string.
Example:

```
char *ptrc = "This is a string"; //initialization
```

Alternatively, a string may be assigned to it.
Example:

```
char *ptrc; // definition
ptrc = "This is a string"; // assignment
```

> *Beware*: when a pointer is initialized with a string or when a string is assigned to it, copying does *not* occur! Quite simply, the address of the *first character of the string*, stored by the compiler (see Chapter 2) as a sequence of characters followed by '\0' (even constants have an address!), is assigned to the pointer.

In the preceding example *both* `ptrc` *and* `*ptrc` are initialized. The address stored in `ptrc` is that of the first character of the string. Therefore its content, `*ptrc`, is 'T'.

We shall shortly see that `ptrc`, being a variable pointer which points to the first character of the string, can be used both with the vectors' and the pointers' algebra in order to move along the string itself.

Example:

```
char c1 = ptrc[1]; // c1 = 'h';
char c5 = *(ptrc + 5); // c5 = 'i';
```

 It is necessary to use the library function `strcpy` to physically copy a string. Be careful, though, because it is possible to forget to create the space necessary to contain the string which has been copied.

For example, the following portion of code is wrong:

```
char *pts,*ptnew;
pts= "This is a string"; // OK
strcpy(ptnew,pts); // NO!! ptnew has not got
                   // the space needed
```

The error is that `ptnew` hasn't got enough room for the string: it only has enough to store one character.

The correct method of copying a string is to give `ptnew` enough space, equivalent to the length of the string +1 (remember that a string ends with the character '\0'):

```
char *pts,*ptnew;
pts = "This is a string";
ptnew = new char [strlen(pts)+1];
strcpy(ptnew,pts);
```

The library function `strlen` is used to calculate the number of characters in a string (excluding '\0').

We shall see further on that through the following statement:

```
ptnew = new char [strlen(pts)+1];
```

the space for a vector with the identifier `ptnew` is dynamically created.

User Defined Constant Pointers

In order to define a constant pointer the modifier `const` is used with the following syntax:

<type> * `const` <identifier> = <address>;

Example:

```
float fl;
float *const ptrf = &fl;
```

 Particular attention must be paid to where the modifier `const` is placed, because, depending on its position, the result may change completely.

If it is written:

```
const float *ptf;
```

what *cannot* be modified is the *content* to which `ptf` points (that is, `*ptf`), whereas `ptf` can be modified. Please note that, in this case, the modification of the contents of `ptf` is not allowed by means of `*ptf`. Modification of the contents is not wholly excluded!

Example:

```
const int *ptc;
const int c;
ptc=&c; // OK, I assign an address to ptc
int j;
ptc=&j; // OK, I can alter the value of ptc
        // j is not necessarily const
j=4;    // OK, I change the contents indirectly
        // at which ptc is pointing
*ptc=4; // NO, error during compilation
```

If instead you write:

```
float *const ptf;
```

it is the *pointer* `ptf` which cannot be modified, whereas the *content* `*ptf` may be modified.

Example:

```
int c=3.;
int *const ptc=&c; // OK
*ptc=0; // OK, I modify the contents
int j=4;
ptc=&j; // NO, error in compilation
```

If, to conclude, you write:

```
const float *const ptf;
```

neither the *pointer* ptf nor the *content* *ptf can be modified.

Example:

```
int c=3.;
int *const ptc=&c; // OK
*ptc=0; // NO, error in compilation
int j=4;
ptc=&j; // NO, error in compilation
```

> If a variable has been defined by const, it cannot be used as an address for a pointer, unless it too has been defined with const placed before the type specification.

Example:

```
const int c=3;
int *pta=&c; // NO, error in compilation
int *const ptb=&c; // NO, error in compilation
const int *ptc=&c; // OK
const int *const ptd=&c; // OK
```

> Whatever the object defined by const, it can only be given a value in the definition statement: it can only be *initialized*. It is not possible to first give the definition and then assign a value to it afterwards.

Example:

```
float fx;
float *const ptf = &fx; // OK: initialization
float *const pt; // definition;
pt = &fx; // NO: assignment
```

Arithmetic of Variable Pointers

A variable pointer, because it is variable, may take on different values during the course of the program from that with which it was initialized.

Example:

```
float fl,v[10];
float *ptf=&fl; // ptf points to fl
.........
ptf=v; // now points to the start of vector v
```

> The conceptual difference between a constant pointer, such as the name of an array, v, and a variable pointer, ptf, is that v *cannot be modified for the entire duration* of v whereas other addresses may be assigned to ptf.

A variable pointer allows you to do some operations.

> It is possible to add to or subtract from a variable pointer, an integer or a pointer of the *same* type.

The following are examples of valid operations:

```
float *ptfl,fl;
ptfl=&fl;      // I assign fl address to ptfl
ptfl++;        // I increment the address by one
ptfl=&fl+15;   // I assign fl address to ptfl

               // incremented by 15
ptfl=ptfl-3;   // I decrease this value by 3
```

> Whatever the object the pointer is pointing to, the compiler automatically adjusts the scale during addition and subtraction, so that it can adjust itself to the memory requirements of the object.
> Remember also that in defining a pointer it must be explicitly defined to which object it is pointing; thus when a pointer is modified by a quantity n, the address to which it points is modified by n multiplied by the size of the object to which it is pointing.

For example, pti, ptf, ptmat are three variable pointers to int, float and Matrix respectively. Let us consider the operations:

```
pti++;         // increment address by one
ptf++;         // increment address by one
ptmat++;       // increment address by one
```

In these cases the pointer moves by a quantity equal to the number of bytes required for storage of an int, a float and a Matrix respectively.

This characteristic is extremely useful in vectors and in matrices made up of objects of any size, as we shall shortly see.

> If a pointer is a *variable* pointer, it can be *modified* by either subtraction or addition.
> If a pointer is a *constant* pointer, this is not possible.
> An integer may be added to or subtracted from to a *variable* or *constant* pointer.

Example:

```
float *pf,v[10];
pf=v;
pf=pf+3; // OK (but see next danger)
pf=v+2;  // OK (but see next danger)
v=v+3;   // NO, v constant pointer
```

When a constant is added to or subtracted from a pointer, C++ does not guarantee that the obtained address is a valid one. It is up to the user to make sure that this happens!

Example:

```
float *pf,v[10];
pf=v; // v is the start address of the vector v[10]
pf=pf+3; // OK, because it is in the range of v[10];
pf=v-100; // DANGER!!
          // It may be a non-valid address
```

It is important to note that, if ptf is a pointer, the following statements are equivalent:

```
ptf[i];
*(ptf+i);
```

Therefore if a pointer points to the beginning of a vector, the pointer itself can be used with the same syntax as a vector to access elements of a starting vector.

Example:

```
float *pf,v[10];
pf = v;
pf[3] = 5.; // modifies v[3];
```

Beware: for vectors initialized with a vector's address, what applies to pointers to characters initialized with a string also applies: copying does *not* take place, instead the variable pointer is positioned at the beginning of the vector.

Example:

```
float *pf,v[10];
pf = v; // pf has not got its own copy of the data
```

Pointer pf shares vector v's data, it does not possess its own data.

Void Pointers

In some situations it is not known to what type of variable a pointer points. For this purpose a special type of pointer has been introduced, void *, which guarantees compatibility with any type of pointer.

An address of any type can be assigned to a pointer defined as void *.
Example:

```
void *ptvoid;
float varfloat;
int *ptint,varint;
ptint = &varint;
ptvoid = &varfloat;
ptvoid = &varint;
ptvoid = ptint;
```

It can also be *initialized* with any type of address.
Example:

```
double vardouble;
void *ptvoid = &vardouble;
```

> The possibility of using a pointer of generic type allows for writing and using general functions which are valid for any type of variable (see Chapter 7).

> It is not possible, however, to do the opposite: assign to a *non* void * type a void * type pointer *unless an explicit cast is used*. This should, however, be avoided because it is fraught with danger.

Example:

```
double *ptdouble;
float varfloat;
void *ptvoid = &varfloat; // OK
ptdouble = ptvoid; // error in compilation
ptdouble = (double *)ptvoid; // allowed but dangerous
```

3.3 References

References are a new derived type, which were introduced to C++ in order to make reading programs easier. They are, in a certain sense, a halfway house between normal variables and pointers. In fact, their trademark is that they can be used with the same syntax as normal variables, whilst behaving as pointers.

References are useful in the following circumstances.

(1) To redefine operators for new types of variables (see Chapter 11).
(2) To transmit variables and objects via the argument of a function (see Chapter 7).
(3) To return objects and variables through the return of a function (see Chapter 10).

It is possible to explicitly define a reference and use it every time that a variable could be used. This *must be avoided* because indiscriminate use of this could cause confusion and lead to mistakes.

The use of references *must*, therefore, *be limited to the three above mentioned circumstances.*

Bearing in mind all that has been said, let us see how a reference is defined.

A reference is *defined* using the unary operator &. A reference cannot be given a value by assignment: consequently it *must* be initialized and you *cannot* change the object with which it has been initialized. If a multiple definition is made, the operator & must be repeated for each reference.

Example:

```
float var=10.,fip=5.;
float &ref1=var; // OK: defined and initialized
float &ref2;  // error: not initialized

&ref1=fip; // error: it cannot be assigned
                // to another object
float &rere=var,rere2=var; // only rere is a
                // reference
float &re=var,&re2=var; // re and re2 are
                // references
float &refco=155.; //OK
```

The last definition is a slight anomaly in the sense that `refco` is defined as a reference to a constant without identifier. C++ interprets this definition in the following manner: a hidden variable is created to which the value 155. is assigned; `refco` is defined as a reference to the hidden variable. Therefore, by modifying `refco` the hidden variable is modified and not the constant.

> A reference can be thought of as an alternative name for the variable it was initialized with. Every operation performed on the reference is as though it were being performed on the variable to which it refers.

Example:

```
float var=10.;
float &ref1=var; // ref1 defined and initialized
ref1=20.;     // var has become equal to 20
float zz=ref1; // zz is initialized to 20.
```

> Note that, if `ref1` is a reference to a variable, it could be used as an lvalue (since `ref1` is the address content):
>
> ```
>  ref1=20.;     // var has become equal to 20
> ```
>
> as well as an rvalue (since `ref1` gives the value of a variable):
>
> ```
>  float zz=ref1; // zz is initialized to 20.
> ```
>
> (See Chapter 2 for the significance of rvalue and lvalue.)

> I will never use references except in the three situations where they are really useful. In fact, using references as a copy of a variable is pointless and can create confusion and mistakes in so much as both variables refer to the same data.

3.4 Array

As we have already seen in Chapter 2, vectors and matrices are constructed by the derived type *array*. In Chapter 2 we began to examine the main differences in relation to FORTRAN. We shall now examine this more closely. For simplicity we shall start by taking a look at vectors.

Vectors

In order to define a vector the following syntax is necessary:

```
<type> identifier [number of elements];
```

The number of elements must be an expression whose result is an integer *which can be calculated on a compiling level* and *greater than zero*. Specifically, it could be *a constant integer* (with or without identifier).

Example:

```
const int N=10;
float vet[N*(N + 1)], y[45]; // OK
int n = 10;
float x[n]; //NO: n is not known at compiler level
const int M=0;
double z[M]; // NO: M=0
```

To understand how a vector is handled in C++ consider the following definition:

```
const int N=100;
float vet[N];
```

The *identifier* of a vector is the address of element 0 of the vector itself.

```
vet // address of vet[0]
```

Since this address cannot be modified, the vector's identifier is a *constant pointer*.
The *content* of the i-nth element of a vector can be accessed either by using the operator [ ] or using the unary operator * and the pointers' algebra.

```
vet[0]     // content of element 0
*vet       // content of element 0
vet[i]     // content of element i-nth
*(vet + i) // content of element i-nth
```

The *address* of the generic term i can be obtained either by applying the unary operator & to the generic element of the vector, or by using the pointers' algebra.

cont.

```
cont.
    &vet[0]      // address of element 0
    vet          // address of element 0
    &vet         // address of element 0
    &vet[i]      // address of element i-nth
    vet + i      // address of element i-nth
    &vet + i     // address of element i-nth
```

It is vital to insert brackets `*(vet+i)` in order to extract the content of the i-nth element, because the unary operator `*` takes precedence over the binary operator `+` (see Table 2.4).

Example:

```
float f1=*(vet+1);    // f1 = vet[1]
float f2=*vet+1;      // f2 = vet[0] + 1
```

 It is worth repeating that in the C++ language, vectors (and matrices) have indices which go from 0 to N-1. This could cause confusion when referring to a vector element, for instance, the first element. It must be clear in the expression whether the first element is being referred to (that is element 0) or we are considering the element with index 1 (that is the second element).

A vector may be initialized during definition but only if this occurs outside any `{}` block and, therefore, outside of any function (including `main`) or by using the modifier `static`. We shall see why this is so later on.

 For now it is enough to know that if a vector is initialized whilst defining it these are the two consequences.

(1) The vector is *initialized before executing the program* and not when the statement is met during the run. If, therefore, it is modified during the execution of the program the vector is *not* reinitialized.
(2) The vector takes up the memory assigned to it for the whole of the program running time.

Examples of vector initialization during definition:

```
float z[5]={1.,2.,3.,4.,5.}; // outside blocks
main()
    {  // inside block with static
    static float v[5]={1.,2.,3.,4.,5.};
    }
```

The following remarks are important.

(1)　If the size of the vector is not given, it is assigned automatically during compiling and made equal to the number of assigned terms.
(2)　If fewer data than those which correspond to the size of the vector are supplied, the compiler makes the remaining coefficients equal zero.
(3)　If more data than those which correspond to the size of the vector are supplied, the compiler returns an error.

Example:

```
float w[]={1.,2.,3.}; // equivalent to w[3]={1.,2.,3.};
float x[5]={1.,2.}; // x[2]=x[3]=x[4]=0
float y[2]={1.,2.,3.}; // error in compiling
```

Matrices

Bear in mind that the following syntax is used to define a two-dimensional matrix:

<type> identifier [number of rows][number of columns];

As far as the number of columns and rows is concerned the rules are the same as for the size of vectors: it must be an expression whose result is an integer which can be calculated on the compiling level and be greater than zero. Specifically, it can be a constant integer (with or without identifier).

In order to understand how a matrix is handled in C++ consider the following definition:

```
const int M=10,N=20;
float matr[M][N];
```

This definition can be seen in three ways (see Chapter 6):

(1)　`matr` is the identifier of a vector sized as `M`. Each element of this vector is made up of a vector of `N` dimensions which is made of `float` type elements;
(2)　`matr[i]` is the identifier of the `i`-nth vector sized as `N` made up of `float` type elements; thus there are `M` identifiers, `matr[i]` (`i=0,1,...M-1`), of elements sized as `N` of `float` type elements;
(3)　`matr[i][j]` is the identifier of a `float` type element. Therefore, there are identifiers `MxN matr[i][j]` of `float` type variables.

cont.

cont.
Therefore

(1)   `matr` is a constant pointer and the address of the beginning of the first vector, `matr[0]` (sized as `M`);
(2)   `matr+i` is the address of the `i`-nth element of this vector; the pointer's algebra automatically remembers that each element of this vector is made up by `N` `float`;
(3)   the content of address `matr+i` is `*(matr+i)` or `matr[i]`;
(4)   `matr[i]` being the identifier of a vector, it is also a constant pointer: it is the address of the beginning of the vector whose name it is, that is of the `i`-nth vector sized as `N`;
(5)   `matr[i]+j` or `*(matr+i)+j` is the address of the `j`-nth element of this vector (sized as `N`). In this case, the pointers' algebra automatically remembers that each element of the vector is made up of `float` type elements;
(6)   the content of the address `*(matr+i)+j` is `*(*(matr+i)+j)` or `*(matr[i]+j)` or `matr[i][j]` and is the value of the `float` type variable which corresponds to the indices `i,j`.

N.B.:

`&matr[0][0]`, `matr[0]`, `&matr[0]` and `matr` have the same value: the address of the start of the matrix, *but they have different meanings and different properties.* So to recap:

`matr[0][0]` is the identifier of a `float`;
`matr[0]` is the identifier of a vector made up by `N` `float`;
`matr` is the identifier of a vector made up by vectors.

Therefore:

`&matr[0][0] +1` is equal to `&matr[0][1]`;
`matr[0] +1` is equal to `*matr+1` and thus to `&matr[0][1]`;
`&matr[0] +1` is equal to `matr+1`;
`matr+1` is equal to `&matr[1]` and thus to `&matr[1][0]`.

This procedure also applies in the case of matrices which have more than two indices.
Example:

```
float xyx[M][N][K];
xyz[i][j][k]=3.;           // access using indices
*(*(*(xyz+i)+j)+k)=3.;     // access using pointers
```

Matrices can also be initialized during definition. The same remarks as for vectors also apply to them.

Example of a matrix with two rows and three columns:

```
float xy[2][3]=
                {
                {1.,2.,3.}, // first row
                {4.,5.,6.} // second row
                };
```

When initializing a matrix during definition the brackets {} used in order to highlight the different rows can be omitted.

Equivalent example to the above:

```
float xy[2][3]=
                {1.,2.,3.,4.,5.,6.};
```

If some of the rows are not complete, the omitted coefficients are initialized to zero:

```
float xy[2][3]=
                {
                {1.}, // xy[0][1]=xy[0][2]=0.
                {4.,5.}      // xy[1][2]=0.
                };
```

If brace brackets {} differentiating rows are omitted and if the number of coefficients is less than is necessary, the remaining coefficients, which are taken as though the matrix were just one row, are equalized to zero.

```
float xy[2][3]=
                {
                1.,
                4.,5. // xy[1][0]=xy[1][1]=xy[1][2]=0.
                };
```

Note the different behaviour in the last two examples.

> Since matrix initialization during definition only makes sense for small matrices (it is otherwise preferable to use a dynamic memory allocation) I advocate always to use the form of initialization which divides the rows into blocks. This is easier to read and limits the chance of errors.

Dynamically Allocated Vectors and Matrices

Vectors and matrices which are defined in the manner we have so far seen:

```
double vect[M];
float matr[M][N];
```

present inconveniences which affect their efficiency, specifically in general functions, where the dimensions M and N are not known in advance, but may vary from one problem to another.

Imagine, for example, to have to write a function or a SUBROUTINE which uses a matrix of M and N dimensions which are changeable from problem to problem. If the values of M and N must be determined before compiling the program, the following dilemma arises: if I choose M and N to be large, the program will end up being too big for the majority of problems; if I make them small, the program has to be recompiled when there is a problem with bigger dimensions than foreseen.

In FORTRAN variables are static for the length of the program (see Chapter 6). If a matrix is only needed in a SUBROUTINE another problem arises: when it is no longer in use, that portion of memory is wasted and could be used for other purposes. In these cases a working vector is created, sized according to requirements, into which memories which are needed only occasionally can be placed from time to time.

If vectors and matrices take up memory *statically*, the following problems, amongst others (see Chapter 12), can occur.

(1) A possible oversizing or, even worse, undersizing in general-purpose functions or SUBROUTINES occurs.

(2) The need for introducing working vectors, which are a mystery for the user, and which make using general-purpose functions or SUBROUTINES more complicated than necessary.

One of the characteristics which makes FORTRAN 77 obsolete in comparison to other languages, even those with a procedural approach (as for example, C), is the inability to manage memory dynamically when dealing with vectors and matrices.

C and C++ have a different way of dealing with vectors and matrices, which allows for dynamic allocation and de-allocation of required memory.

Specifically, C++ uses the operators new and delete for this purpose, which are better (we shall see why in Chapter 10) compared to the functions alloc and free used by C.

What makes C++ particularly efficient is that it allows you to allocate memory of the correct size dynamically when required and to free the memory when it is no longer being used. This is vital when dealing with vectors or matrices or with large objects.

Let us now consider vectors.

The syntax to be used with the `new` operator to request the necessary memory space for a vector is:

<type> *<identifier> = n e w <type>[number of elements];

Note that the number of elements may not be known at the compiling stage: it could very well not be a constant!
To free the used memory space use the following syntax:

`delete` <identifier>;

Let's suppose that we want to use a vector sized to N of the `float` type:

```
int N = 10; // may be a variable (not a constant)
float *x = new float[N]; // I allocate memory for x
if(!x)Error(....); // insufficient memory
.......// I use x[i]
delete x; // I free memory
```

The second statement defines the variable pointer x and assigns the required memory to it: N variables of the `float` type.

If the operator `new` sees that there is insufficient memory, it assigns the value 0 to x. This makes a verification test possible. In the program extract above, if there is insufficient memory an error function is invoked. In other cases, more complicated decisions can be made, for example, freeing up unused memory.

If, conversely, there is sufficient memory, the pointer x may be used as though it had been defined by:

```
float x[N];
```

When the vector to which x is pointing is no longer needed, the operator `delete` can be used to free memory. This memory can, therefore, be used for other purposes.

There are substantial differences between the two vectors, one being defined dynamically, the other as an array:

```
float *x = new float [N};
float y[N];
```

(1) x is a *variable* pointer whilst y is a *constant* pointer.
(2) The number of elements N, of an array must be a known constant before executing the program.
(3) The address of x, &x, is not the address of the beginning of the vector, whilst y equals &y.
(4) The memory occupation to which x points is dynamically managed by the user; y's memory occupation is automatically managed by the compiler.

Let us consider the case of matrices. Here, a vector of pointers is created whose elements point to the beginning of each row of the matrix. Each row of the matrix, in turn, is made up of a vector which contains as many elements as there are columns in the matrix.

The syntax for requesting memory for a vector of pointers is:

<type> **<identifier> = new <type> *[number of elements];

Let us say, for example, that you want to define dynamically a matrix A[M][N] with float type elements.

The first step is to define a variable which has an a identifier with the same name as the matrix, A, and which is a pointer for pointers to float type variables:

```
float **A;
```

The second step is to create memory for the vector of M pointers by using the operator new:

```
A = new float *[M];
if(!A)Error(...); // insufficient memory
```

Having placed the unary operator * in front of the required sizes, the operator new creates memory for a vector of pointers to float.

The final step is to create memory for the rows of the matrix. The identifiers for this vector are A[i] and thus:

```
for(i=0;i<M;i++)
   {
   A[i]= new float [N];
   if(!A[i])Error(...); // insufficient memory
   }
```

At this point I can use the matrix A[i][j] as though it had been defined by:

```
float A[M][N];
```

To de-allocate memory I must use the procedure in reverse.
First of all, the vectors which contain the rows must be de-allocated:

```
for(i=0;i<M;i++)
   delete A[i];
```

and then the vector of pointers:

```
delete A;
```

You may well ask whether it is worth complicating matters like this. What advantages does it represent?

A matrix treated as a pointer to pointers has the following advantages.

(1)   Access to single elements is faster: in the traditional way a multiplication and a sum are needed; by using pointers you go directly to the address of the row you want and then to the address of the row's element.

(2)   The matrix is dynamically sized. It can, therefore, be sized without waste and cannot be undersized which is even worse. When memory is no longer required it can be freed and, therefore, reused for other purposes.

(3)   The names of rows are the names of variable pointers and not constant pointers. This leads to various advantages. Specifically, if you want to swap over two rows you don't have to physically swap all the separate elements. All you have to do is to swap over the pointers, giving one's address to the other.

(4)   One matrix can be transferred from one function to another without knowing its size beforehand.

(5)   It is possible to resize matrices which have different sizes to the standard 0...M-1, 0...N-1. Specifically, it is possible to have matrices sized to 1...M, 1...N without problems and just by adding two variables (see Chapter 12).

cont.

cont.

(6) Matrices with rows of different sizes can be dealt with without wasting memory. Triangular matrices in particular can be easily handled. Indeed, it is very easy to store each row with the minimum requested memory.

We shall come back to these points later, particularly to further expand on the latter points.

In order to obtain these advantages a vector with auxiliary pointers sized as the rows in the matrix must be used.

A further disadvantage, which isn't too important in general purpose programs, is that it isn't possible to initialize a matrix on definition.

This sort of procedure for dealing with matrices has been handed down from C.

Both with declaring vectors and matrices by means of an explicit declaration and by means of pointers, the user must take care not to overstep the field in which the matrix or vector are defined.
Example:

```
float v[10];
v[100]=3.; // serious danger
```

The error is not picked up because there is no check on the validity of the *range*. On the other hand, however, accessing vector and matrix coefficients is more efficient, because all checks have been eliminated.

In C++ it is possible to personalize the use of vectors and matrices to make them more adept at scientific calculations. We shall see this in the next few chapters.

3.5 Questions

Given the definition:

```
float *ptf;
```

which of the following items is of the `float` type?

cont.

> *cont.*
> (1)   `ptf.`
> (2)   The variable to which `ptf` points.
> (3)   The address of `ptf`.
> (4)   `*ptf.`

The variable to which `ptf` points which is also `*ptf`.

> Given the pointer to `float`, `ptr`, write a statement in which `*ptr` is both an lvalue and an rvalue.

For example:

```
*ptr = *ptr + 5.;
```

> In the following program extract there is a serious mistake.
>
> ```
> float *ptrvar,var=5.;
> *ptrvar = var;
> ```
>
> What is it?

The pointer `ptrvar` has not been initialized. A statement of the following type must be inserted:

```
ptrvar = new float;
```

before:

```
*ptrvar = var;
```

> Find the mistake in the following statement:
>
> ```
> float *pt1=new float,pt2=new float;
> ```

Only `pt1` is a pointer. The correct statement is:

```
float *pt1=new float,*pt2=new float;
```

> Given the definition:
>
> ```
> float *pt = 0;
> ```
>
> what will be defined and what will be initialized?

pt is defined and initialized to 0 (NULL).

> Given that:
>
> ```
> char *p = "Hurrah";
> ```
>
> what do p[1] and p[6] contain?

p[1]='u' and p[6]='\0' (last term in the string).

> Are there any mistakes in the following extract?
>
> ```
> float x=3.;
> float *px = &x;
> float *p = px;
> float *pt = x;
> int *ip = &x;
> ```

Yes, there are two mistakes:

```
float *pt = x;
```

A pointer must be intialized with an address and not with the value of a variable.

```
int *ip = &x;
```

A pointer must be initialized with the address of a variable of the same type.

> The compiler presents an error in the following extract:
>
> ```
> float x = 3.;
> float *p = &x;
> float y;
> y = p;
> ```
>
> Why?

A variable cannot be assigned the address of another variable. The final statement should have been:

```
y = *p;
```

Given the definitions:

```
int x=0;
int *p = &x;
```

explain the significance of the following operations:

```
x = x + 1;
*p = *p + 1;
p = p + 1;
```

The first increments x by 1. The second increments by 1 the contents of the address to which p is pointing, that is x. The last one increments the pointer p by 1. Now p no longer points to x, but to a new address which has been shifted, compared to the preceding one, by the amount necessary to store an integer. Using this could be quite dangerous!

 Given that:

```
float v[10];
float *w=v;
```

explain what happens to vector v after the following statements:

```
*w++ = 10.;
*++w = 10.;
```

```
*w++ = 10.;
```

This means that the value 10 is assigned to the contents of the variable to which w is pointing. Therefore v[0] = 10. The pointer is subsequently incremented by1. It now points to v[1].

```
*++w = 10.;
```

The pointer w is again incremented by 1. The value 10 is assigned to the contents of the variable to which w is pointing. Now v[2] = 10.

Note the exchange of precedence with the operator ++ applied to the right and the left. Please refer to Table 2.4 for precedence between the unary operators * and ++.

Will the following code:

```
const float PI = 3.14;
float *pi = &PI;
```

cause problems or not?

The address of a constant with identifier cannot be assigned to a pointer which has not been defined with a constant content; we should have written:

```
const float *pi = &PI;
```

Given the definitions:

```
float *v = new float [10];
float w[10];
```

which amongst the following statements:

```
*v = 5.;
*w = 5.;
*(v+1) = *(w+1);
*(w+1) = *(v+1);
v = w;
w = v;
v++;
w++;
```

are not accepted by the compiler?

w = v and w++ are wrong, because w is a constant pointer.

The compiler shows an error:

```
int M=10,N=5;
float matr[M][N];
```

Why?

M and N are not constants which are recognized at compiling level.

3.6   Examples

Swapping the Rows of a Matrix

If a matrix has been defined as a pointer of pointers to float:

```
int m=5,n=10;
float **A;
A = new float *[m];
if(!A)Error(...); // insufficient memory
for(int i=0;i<m;i++)
    {
    A[i]= new float [n];
    if(!A[i])Error(...); // insufficient memory
    }
```

two rows can be swapped over without having to physically swap all the coefficients.

Indeed, you can swap two rows, k and j, simply by swapping their pointers A[k] and A[j]:

```
float *temp = A[k];
A[k] = A[j];
A[j] = temp;
```

Left Triangular Matrices

A *left* triangular matrix, also known as *lower*, is a squared matrix characterized by mull coefficients above its main diagonal. Since we know that all those coefficients are null beforehand, it is not necessary to waste that portion of memory.

In a language such as FORTRAN, where pointers do not exist, the trick is to store the matrix in a single vector of appropriate size and to create an auxiliary index, which enables an element in the matrix to be traced to its corresponding position in the vector.

Marking the index of the vector with k and the indices of the rows and columns of the matrix with i and j, the relationship between the indices is:

$$k = \frac{i(i + 1)}{2} - i + j$$

For example, if i = 5, j = 3 then k = 13.

This sort of implementation is penalized by the fact that it requires a decoding process for the indices, with the result of slowing down access to the coefficients of a matrix. The use of pointers allows us to solve the problem very easily. The matrix can either be stored as a single row or one row at a time. In Chapter 12 we shall see how to implement the former alternative, let us see the latter:

```
int m=n=10;
float **A;
A = new float *[m];
if(!A)Error(...); // insufficient memory
for(int i=0;i<m;i++)
    {
    A[i]= new float [i+1];
    if(!A[i])Error(...); // insufficient memory
    }
.......
// I free memory when it is no longer needed
for(i=0;i<m;i++)
    delete A[i];
delete A;
```

As you can see, the only difference when compared to a normal matrix is the statement:

```
A[i]= new float [i+1];
```

which allows you to assign the correct memory size to each row.

4 Derived Types: `class, struct, union, enum`

Poca favilla gran fiamma seconda.

A great flame follows a little spark.

Dante, *Paradiso, V*

4.1 Introduction

As we have already seen in Chapter 1, the first step towards data abstraction is to bring together variables of different sorts into a single user-defined variable.

This was possible in C by means of the derived type `struct`. C++ will accept any `struct` you can define in C; however C++ expands the definition of a `struct` so that it is very similar to a `class` (not present in C). In C++ both the type `struct` and the type `class` are needed as a starting point for defining objects: these constructs, in fact, lead to the completion of data abstraction, because they allow for *encapsulation* of *data* and *functions which use that data* into a single object.

Definition: *Class*
The constructs `class`, `struct` and `union` are often referred to with the generic term class.

For the time being let us look closely at the derived type `struct` in the case where functions are *not* present. By so doing we are taking the first step in data abstraction.

> Whoever comes from a FORTRAN background must, at this level of data abstraction, review the concept of variable.

In FORTRAN it is the norm to treat variables as independent items, apart from vectors and matrices which must be collections of variables of the same type. With the construct `struct` we have to get used to considering the idea of including more variables, even of different types, into a single variable. The advantages this brings can only be understood a few at a time, by analysing their applications.

As a first example let us suppose we want to interpolate a function of which N points y_i in relation to x_i are known. In FORTRAN the N values of y_i and the N values of x_i must be stored in two different vectors whose elements are pairs. It is preferable to create a single vector of a new variable of values, x_i and y_i, since they are intrinsically linked to one another.

As a further example, let us suppose that we want to create a vector dynamically. An integer type variable is needed to store sizes, as well as a `float` pointer to store the coefficients of the vector. In this case too, the variables are closely linked to one another and it is best to bring them together into a single variable.

4.2   The `struct` Type without Encapsulated Functions

The derived type `struct` differs from the ones dealt with in the previous chapter in that it allows us to make a new type of variable. It also requires, therefore, the new type of variable to be defined.

Definition of a New Type of Variable with `struct`

In order to define a new type of variable with `struct` the following construct should be used:

```
struct NameNewTypeOfVariable
   {
   list of variables;
   };   // remember the ;
```

Example:

```
struct Point
   {
   float x,y;
   };
```

`Point` is the name for a new type of variable made up of two `float` type elements.

Example:

```
struct Vector
   {
   float *vector;
   int dimensions;
   };
```

Vector is the name for a new type of variable made up of a float pointer and an int; the integer could be needed to store the size of the vector whose address is to be dynamically inserted into the pointer vector.

Example:

```
struct PointVector
   {
   Point p;
   Vector v;
   };
```

It can be seen from this example that a struct can be made with other struct variables.

Definition: *Member*

The elements (variables or functions) specified in a new type of variable definition are called *members* of that class.

> Variables which are members of a class cannot be initialized, i.e. they cannot be given a numerical value during definition of that class.

Example:

```
struct Point
   {
   float x=1.,y=5.; // NO: error
   };
```

> Identifiers of the new variable type which I define by using the constructs struct or class *always start with a capital and have at least one small letter*. If the identifier is made up of more than one word, the leaders of all the words are *capitals*.

Example:

```
Vector, MatrixRight
```

Access to the Data of a `struct`

`Point`, `Vector` and `PointVector` are identifiers of a new type of variable. Once a new type of variable has been defined, variables of that type can be defined. A defined variable of a certain type can also be referred to as an *instance* of that type.

> Let us remember that a variable, of whatever type, needs an *identifier*, a *definition* and an *initialization* or an *assignment*.

The same rules apply to identifiers of variables which are instances of a new type of variable as for basic type variables, rules which we have already seen.

Definition is also quite similar to that for basic type variables.

Examples of definitions of variables and pointers of the `Point`, `Vector` and `PointVector` type:

```
Point xy,*pt;
Vector x,*y;
PointVector px,*pv;
```

In order to use a variable it is necessary for it to have a valid value; it must, therefore, have been initialized or it must have been assigned a value.

> It is important to note that in C++ a distinction must be made between two operations which are interchangeable in other languages: *initialization* and *assignment*.
> *Initialization occurs in the statement which defines a variable.*
> *Assignment can only occur for a variable which has been previously defined elsewhere.*

Example:

```
float x=3.;   // definition and initialization
x=15.;        // assignment
```

This distinction, which will be explained later, arises from the fact that a different operator is used in the two statements and, therefore, different effects can be produced.

We have already seen that this distinction is important in the case of identifiers defined as `const`: these may only be initialized.

We shall deal with all the notions relating to operations of initialization or assignment of a variable of `struct`, `class` or `union` type in Chapter 10.

Let us now see how we can access the single components of a variable, that is, its *members*.

Definition: *Access to members of* struct, class *and* union

To access the members of struct, class or union type the operator . is used if there is a class variable or reference; the operator -> is used (made from the two symbols minus, -, and greater than, >) if a pointer to a class variable is present.

Example of access to members of the variable xy of Point type:

```
Point xy; // definition of xy of Point type
xy.x=3.;  // assign value 3 to x of xy object.
xy.y=5.;
float prod=(xy.x)*(xy.y); //use of x,y of xy
```

Example of access to members of the variable pt Point pointer:

```
Point *pt = new Point; // definition of pt pointer
              // to Point and initialization of pt
              // by means of the operator new
pt->x=3.; // assignment of x of the object *pt
pt->y=5.;
float prod=(pt->x)*(pt->y); // use of x,y
```

To access the member of a class, by means of a pointer to a class variable, it is also possible to use *, *contents of* (see Chapter 3).

```
Point *pt = new Point;
(*pt).x=3.; // assignment of x of the object *pt
(*pt).y=5.;
float prod=((*pt).x)*((*pt).y); // use of x,y
```

The brackets are necessary to alter precedence between the operators . and *.

 The operator -> is the most commonly used alternative and the one I would most recommend, because it is easier and less likely to generate errors.

The same technique can be applied to the members of a structure which is a member of another structure.

Example:

```
struct PointVector
   {
   Point p;
   Vector v;
   }
```

```
PointVector pv,*ptv=&pv;
pv.p.x=10.;   //access to the member x of Point
int i=ptv->v.dimensions; // access to member
                         // dimensions of Vector
```

> In order to decode an expression of the following type:
>
> ```
> int i=ptv->v.dimensions;
> ```
>
> it is best to work from right to left:
> the variable `dimensions`
> is a member of the object `v` (`.` is used)
> which belongs to an object to which `ptv` points (`->` is used).

We have seen that once a new type of variable has been defined, it is possible to define instances of the same type and pointers to variables of the same type.

> It is also possible to define an *array* (vector or matrix) of `struct` type variables. This gives the language a tremendous flexibility, particularly when dealing with database problems. Moreover, the operators `new` and `delete` may be used to define vectors and matrices of `struct` dynamically.

Example:

```
Point vet[10],mat[5][5];
Point *ptp = new Point [100];
.....
delete [100] ptp;  // note sizes [100]
```

To access variable `x` of `Point` with one of the elements of `vet` or `ptp`, either use the array indices or the pointer arithmetic. The following are all valid expressions:

```
vet[1].x = 3.;
(*(vet +1)).x = 3.;
(vet + 1)->x = 3.;
ptp[1].x = 3.;
(*(ptp +1)).x = 3.;
(ptp + 1)->x = 3.;
```

Note the different use of `delete` in the preceding example compared to the uses we have seen so far: the number of elements to be deleted is also shown:

```
delete [100] ptp;  // note the sizes [100]
```

When delete is used for a struct or class type pointer, it is always safer and on occasion, vital, to state exactly how many elements should be deleted. The reason for this is due to the presence of constructors and destructors, of which more later (see Chapter 10).

Note the position of the sizes to be deleted: they are in square brackets between delete and the pointer's identifier. The same construct can be used for pointers to basic types as well.

I will be applying this style when using delete: for basic types I will *never* place sizes in delete; for pointers to struct or to class objects I will *always* place the sizes even in cases where it is not strictly necessary to do so.

Example:

```
int n = 20;  // does not have to be constant
float *pt = new float[n];
Point *ptPoint= new Point[n];
.......
delete pt;
delete [n] ptPoint;
```

One attribute which has made C (and consequently C++) an incredibly versatile language is that it allows you to define, as a member of a structure, a pointer to an object of the same structure.

Example:

```
struct Demo
   {
   Demo *ptrDemo;
   ...
   };
```

Definition: *Autoreference*
When a member of a struct or of a class is a pointer to an object of its class, this is called an autoreference.

The capabilities an autoreference has allows you to link elements of the same structure in order to form elaborate data structures. These are incredibly useful in advanced applications: simple lists, double lists, queues, stacks, binary trees, generic trees, etc.

> Being able to create structures which are conceptually very different from the usual vectors and matrices allows you to handle data which are interconnected in a totally new manner, *which is as yet scarcely explored in the field of numerical applications*. The reason for this has been mentioned more than once: numerical methods were developed in FORTRAN and in FORTRAN data can only be structured as vectors and matrices.

For the purposes of offering an example let us see how to construct a simple list made up of `float` variables.

We define an element of the list with a `struct`:

```
struct Element
    {
    float element;
    Element *next;
    };
```

By so doing a numerical value and the address of the subsequent element is assigned to each element. Intermediate elements are identified using the chain of addresses `next`, starting from the first one. The last element is usually recognized by assigning a null value to the pointer `next`.

There are various possible methods for defining the first element of a list. For example, by means of a special `struct`:

```
struct HeadElement
    {
    int numElement;
    Element *first;
    };
```

In the object which will be defined as an instance of this `struct`, the number of elements in the list and the address of the first element will be assigned.

Such a structure has its advantages, in certain situations, compared to the usual array. We are not yet in a position to see how it is possible to implement the necessary functions to manage this type of data structure and thereby appreciate its versatility. For now it is enough to know that elements can be added or removed dynamically without the difficulties associated with the array type. It is, however, useful to see how it is possible to scan the elements of a list as though they belonged to a vector. Let us suppose that the beginning of the list is defined in the variable `head` of `HeadElement` type. The elements of the list are scanned according to the following statements:

```
Element *elem; // pointer to Element
for(elem = head.first;elem != 0;elem = elem->next)
    {
    cout << elem->element;
    }
```

Firstly, the pointer elem is set to the value of the address of the first element, stored in head.first. In order to progress to the next element, the expression elem = elem->next is used. The end of the loop occurs when elem equals zero, at the point when the last element in the list is reached.

The basic concept of simple lists can be developed further in two directions.

(1) More pointers can be introduced inside a structure. In this way, one can construct either lists which can be scrolled in both directions or *trees*, in other words branched lists can be made.

(2) The elements which make up the structure do not necessarily have to be basic type variables, such as the float variables used in the example. It is possible to have complex elements for example structures, or better still, pointers to structures.

In Chapter 13 we shall see a practical application to deal with sparse matrices.

4.3   The class Type

Both type struct and type class allow functions as well as data to be defined as members. It is now possible to complete the task of data abstraction.

An example will reveal the problems inherent in a procedural language, even an advanced language like C which has the facility to create new types of data.

Let us look at the new type Vector:

```
struct Vector
{
int dimensions;
float *vector;
};
```

Let us suppose that we have implemented some functions which use this type. For example: SetDimensions, SetValue and GetValue (for the moment it is not important to know *how* they are implemented), the first of which sizes the vector, the second assigns a value to a coefficient of the vector and the third gives its value in a given position.

The problem is as follows: even though these functions are needed to handle or use a Vector type variable, there is no obvious link between functions and data. There is no way of forcing a user to use functions in a correct order. If a user forgets to size a vector and uses the function SetValue, major complications can arise. Worse still: a user can handle data directly without necessarily using these functions.

For example, the dimensions of vector v can be modified by:

```
Vector v;
.....
v.dimensions=150;
```

`Vector v` can now be of a size which does not correspond to that which was previously defined for it, with disastrous consequences.

Let us now see how these problems can be avoided by using the construct `class`. Type `Vector` can now be defined in the following manner:

```
class Vector
    {
    int dimensions;
    float *vector;
. . . . . . . . . . . .
public:
    void SetValue(int i,float value);
    float GetValue(int i);
. . . . . . . . . . . .
    };
```

With the `class` type it is necessary to change the way we think about variables of certain type and, little by little, try to get used to object-oriented programming terminology (OOP).

A `class` type variable becomes an *object*. Instead of viewing functions as modifying data, we must think of them as a means of exchanging messages.

Definition: *Object*
In C++ an object is a variable which is an instance of a `class` type.

We must make a very clear distinction between *objects* and *classes*.
A *class* denotes a type; an *object* is an instance of a particular type (of a particular class). There can be many objects of the same class, which is still a single class. Operations defined within a class apply to its objects, and not to the class itself. A class can only exist through its objects.

For example:

`Vector v, w, y;`

defines objects `v`, `w` and `y` of type `Vector`. In order to access the members of an object, such as `v`, be they functions or data, the same technique used with `struct` applies. There is, however, a basic difference: *not* all members of a `class` are *accessible* to the user. For example, in the case of type `Vector` the user cannot access either `dimensions` directly or the values stored in the variable `vector`.

If we want to find out the value of a vector's coefficient in conjunction with a specified index, i, we must go through an interface implemented by the programmer who set up the `class Vector`:

`float value = v.GetValue(i);`

Object v tells us the desired value by means of GetValue. If we want to modify data within that object, we must again go through an interface implemented by the programmer who set up the class. By so doing, the object is always aware of the changes which its own members undergo and it is able to accept those which are valid and reject those which are not. If, for example, we now want to alter the size of the object, we can do so without any problems: indeed, in the first instance, this request may only occur in conformance with the methods established by the programmer who implemented the class (for example, by means of a request to set v equal to another vector, which can be sized in a different way). Secondly, if the request for resizing is made in the correct manner, not only is the value of dimensions changed, but the amount of storage required by the vector also changes. Let us be satisfied with such a brief introduction to the type class, as further information is necessary in order to delve deeper into the subject.

Let us remember the following two features peculiar to object oriented programming.

(1) *Encapsulation*: functions and data are encapsulated together in the construct class in order to make up an object.
(2) *Data hiding*: certain data and functions of an object can be made inaccessible to the user.

In C++, type struct is similar to type class (and therefore is very different from the corresponding type in C). The only difference between type struct and type class lies in the different defaults they have for their members: in struct these are accessible to the user, whereas in class they are not. Since it is possible to select which members are accessible and which are not, there is in practice no difference between the two.

I will employ the following distinction between the struct type and the class type.
The struct type is only made up of data; it does not contain functions, namely constructors and destructors. Its purpose is similar to its purpose in C. It is used, therefore, to define *grouping of variables, and not objects*. Conversely, the class type is used to define *objects* and is, therefore, made up of member data or member functions and, as is the case with member data only, certain data can be inaccessible to the user.

4.4   The union Type

Type union is also a special kind of class. It is used to save memory when certain variables can only be used as alternatives.

Its definition is similar to that of struct and class.

Example:

```
union GenericValue
    {
    char charValue;
    float floatValue
    double doubleValue;
    long longValue;
    int intValue;
    };
```

Each member of a `union` has the same address in the memory. The largest relocated member is the one which determines the amount of storage. Only one member at a time can be used.

> It is easy to become confused as to which member is active when using type `union`. I will only use this type when it is a type defined by others.

4.5 The `enum` Type

The type `enum` was created to allow a program to be read more easily.
Example:

```
switch(i)
    {
    case 1:
        statements;
        break;
    case 2:
        statements;
        break;
    case 3:
        statements;
        break;
    default:
        break;
    }
```

It is not immediately obvious from this example what the various choices mean. The following code is easier to read:

```
enum Direction // make a type enum
               // with identifier Direction
   {
   NORTH,EAST,SOUTH,WEST // names of enumerators
   };
Direction direction; //direction variable
                     //of type Direction
direction = NORTH; // assign the value NORTH
                   // to direction
......
switch(direction)
   {
   default:
   case NORTH:
      statements;
      break;
   case EAST:
      statements;
      break;
   case SOUTH:
      statements;
      break;
   case WEST:
      statements;
      break;
   }
```

The following remarks are important.

(1) Members of **enum** are *not* variables of any sort. Neither **int** nor **float** nor the name of any other type is used in their definition; they are thus different from the members of a class (**struct, class, union**).

(2) They are to all intents and purposes constants with identifiers of **int** type. The names of the enumerators (in the example NORTH, EAST, SOUTH and WEST) must *not* be treated as variable identifiers.

(3) Their numerical value is given by default: 0 for the first name, 1 for the second and so on. It is only possible to initialize them during definition. This is another way in which they are different from class members.

(4) The value of enumerators is not necessarily unique.

Example:

```
enum Test
   {
   ERROR = -1, NOT_OK, NOT_ACCEPTABLE=0,
   OK_ACCEPTABLE, EXCEPTION = 99
   };
```

If an enumerator is not explicitly initialized (for example, `NOT_OK`), it is assigned the value, which is increased by one, of the enumerator which precedes it. In the example, therefore, `NOT_OK` equals zero, just like `NOT_ACCEPTABLE`, whereas `OK_ACCEPTABLE` equals one.

As we have just seen in the preceding example, it is possible to assign one of the enumerators to an `enum` type variable:

```
direction = NORTH;
```

We cannot assign a numerical value to an `enum` type variable. For example, even though we know that `NORTH` equals zero, the following statement would give an error:

```
direction = 0; // error
```

Enumerators can be defined without defining a name for type `enum`. In this case we refer to `enum` as *anonymous*. Anonymous enumerators can be used in a `Test` or in a `switch`. Since there is no type identifier for an anonymous `enum`, an `int` type variable should be defined.

```
enum
   {
   UP, DOWN, RIGHT, LEFT
   } ;
int move=UP
....
switch(move)
   {
   .......
   }
```

Note that the variable `move` can have a different value from those which are present in the anonymous `enum`.

The same rules which apply to `class` type identifiers also apply to an `enum` type identifier: capital letter leader and at least one small letter. If it is made of more than one word, each of these must start with a capital letter.
Valid examples:

```
Name, Color, Direction.
```

I shall avoid using anonymous enums because they are more susceptible to error.
Since enumerators are constants, we shall use the same criteria used for constants: all letters are capitals. Names must be made up of at least two letters (three or more is better). If the identifier is made up of more than one word, we make a distinction between them by inserting _.
Valid examples:

```
BLUE, RED, UP, DOWN, OK_ACCEPTABLE.
```

4.6   Questions

 What does not work in the following definition?

```
struct Demo
    {
    int iDemo = 0;
    float xDemo = 0.;
    }
```

Members of a `class` cannot be initialized and the ; is missing at the end of the definition.

 Given the definitions:

```
struct Demo
    {
    int iDemo;
    };
....
Demo objDemo;
Demo *ptrDemo = &objDemo;
```

cont.

cont.
which of the following expressions allows access to `iDemo`?

```
1. objDemo.iDemo
2. (*objDemo).iDemo
3. objDemo->iDemo
4. ptrDemo.iDemo
5. (*ptrDemo).iDemo
6. ptrDemo->iDemo
```

Expressions 1, 5 and 6.

Given the definition:

```
enum Direction
    {
    NORTH,EAST,SOUTH,WEST
    };
```

is the following assignment possible?

```
NORTH = -1;
```

No. The enumerators are not variables: they are constants with identifiers. As is the case with all constants with identifiers, they can be given a value only when initialization occurs.

Introduction to Functions

Divide et impera.

Divide and rule.

Attributed to King Philip of Macedon

5.1   Introduction

Programs written in languages like C or FORTRAN consist of a set of functions. In C++, functions have a dual role. The first is similar to that of procedural languages, of which C++ is one. The second role, which makes it distinctly different from C and which is a characteristic feature of object-oriented languages, is to encapsulate functions and data in a single object.

> In this chapter, we will introduce functions only as they are used in the first role, i.e. as units which are isolated from context and which are used to process data and produce results.

A secondary difference between C++ and FORTRAN is that there are only *functions* in C++ and no SUBROUTINES.

5.2   **Definition of a Function**

A function consists of four components.

(1)   The identifier, that is, its name.

(2)   The body of the function, contained in a block {}, which consists of statements.

(3)   The list of variables in its argument.

(4)   The type of variable that the function passes back using `return`.

Example:

```
int First(float var,int i)
    {
    statements;
    }
```

Identifier: `First`. Argument: (`float var, int i`). `return` variable of type `int`.
Example:

```
float Second(double x)
    {
    statements;
    }
```

Identifier: `Second`. Argument: (`double x`). `return` variable of type `float`.

> As can be seen, functions in C++ do not need to be declared as FUNCTIONS or SUBROUTINES, as they do in FORTRAN. The compiler realizes that they are functions by the presence of operators ( ).

Let's have a look at the four components.
The identifier follows the same rules as all identifiers.

> I will follow the convention of always giving functions a name which begins with a capital letter and with at least one small letter. Initials are shown as capitals, if the identifier consists of several words.

The following are (in the proposed style) examples of valid identifiers:

`Pinco, SetPoint, MinimumOfFunctions`

By contrast, the following are to be discouraged:

`pinco, setPoint, M, MIN, Minimum_of_functions`

Function identifiers are *constant pointers*: they represent the function's address, that is, the beginning of that function's code.
Remember that:

(1) A function's name, if followed by parentheses containing whatever arguments there may be within them, ensures that the function is calculated.

(2) If it has no parentheses, it represents a pointer to the function itself, that is, its address.

A function's body is made up of a list of statements.

The other two components, the list of variables in the argument and the return, exchange information between the function and the rest of the program. In the next chapter, we shall see that it is possible in C++ to define variables which can be accessed at various levels by various functions. The highest level of accessibility is the *global* level. Any functions can use and modify a global variable. So this type of variable can be a means of swapping information between functions.

Example:

```
float x = 15.;  // x global variable
int Func(float var)
    {
    var = x;  // x can be accessed
    .......

    x = 35.;  // and can be modified
    .........
    }
```

One of C's basic principles is to make a function's content opaque to the rest of the program, to avoid unwanted side-effects. In C++, this principle is reinforced by making objects, which can only be accessed across interfaces.

Global variables should be used as little as possible, both to avoid interference and to avoid taking up storage throughout the program.

Usually, information is exchanged with a function by using argument variables and the function return. Here, too, C++ has much greater potential than FORTRAN.

5.3 Function Argument

Definition: *Actual argument*
A function argument, when it is *used*, is called an actual argument.

Example:

```
i=Func(ff); // ff actual argument
```

Definition: *Formal argument*
A function argument, when it is *defined*, is called a formal argument.

Example:

```
int Func(float var) // (float var) formal argument
   {
   statements;
   }
```

C and C++ do not pass the variable in the actual argument to the called function, only its value, in order to maintain the basic principle of isolating the function. The corresponding variable, which is defined in the formal argument of the called function, is initialized with the value passed to it by the calling function. So, even if there is a variable identifier in the calling function, a new variable is created in the called function.

Example:

```
   {
   float ff =10.;
   .......
   int i=Func(ff)
   ......
   }
int Func(float var)
   {
   var = 33.;
   .....
   }
```

Even if the argument variable inside the function Func has been modified, this only has an effect inside Func: the variable ff is not modified.

As only a numerical value is being passed, there is no need for a variable in the calling function; there could equally be a constant or an expression.

Example:

```
{
float ff =10.;
.......
int i=Func(10.);
int k=Func(2.*ff);
.......
}
```

If a variable's *address* is passed, instead of a variable, the function constructs a new variable pointer, and the value of the address which has been passed is assigned to it. So the variable can be accessed by means of its address.

Example:

```
{
float ff =10.;
.......
int i=Func1(&ff); // passes the address of ff
......
}
int Func1(float *var) // var is a new pointer
        // variable which is set equal to &ff
        // and which therefore points at ff
    {
*var = 33.; //modifies the content of var and ff
.......
}
```

In C++, you can pass arguments by reference. The result is very similar to passing an address using a pointer – only the syntax changes.

Example:

```
{
float ff =10.;
.......
int i=Func2(ff);  // & should not be used
......
}
int Func2(float &var) // var is a reference
    {
var = 33.; // * should not be used
    // modifies the content of var and thus ff
.......
}
```

Using a pointer or a reference, instead of a variable, as a function argument has the following two aims.

(1) To enable the value of a variable to be modified.
(2) To pass only one address, instead of a variable's value. There are no substantial differences in efficiency, if the variable is a basic type. But if the variable is a struct or class type, and an object is passed, all the members which form that variable type must be recopied (using a copy-initializer constructor, see Chapter 9) and passed to the function. So, in cases like this, it is better to pass just the address.

On some occasions, you may want to use the second characteristic, so that the first is not used – not even inadvertently.

If you want to pass an address, but want the function to be prevented from modifying the variable, all you have to do is make the content of the address const.

Example:

```
{
float ff =10.;
.......
int i=Func1(&ff); // passes the address of ff
i=Func2(ff); // & should not be used
......
}
int Func1(const float *var) // *var is const
{
*var = 33.; // compilation error
.......
}
int Func2(const float &var) //var is a reference
{
var = 33.; // compilation error
.......
}
```

Passing a reference has advantages over using a pointer. The whole program remains identical to what would have been written by passing a variable, except that the operator & is placed inside the function's formal argument, before the variable itself. When using a pointer, you must remember to use the operator & in the function call, and the operator * in the function, so that the variable's value can be accessed.

On the other hand, using the reference may be confusing to the user, precisely because it is indistinguishable from passing the variable (unless the function definition is checked).

I will use the following style, which appears to me to offer all the advantages, but none of the pitfalls.

(1)   If the variable does not have to be modified by the function:
  (a)   with basic variables, the *value* is passed;
  (b)   with `struct` or `class` variables, the *reference* `const` is passed.
(2)   If the variable must or can be modified by the function, a *pointer* is *always* used.

Example:

```
SetValue(float *x)          // x is modified
                            // use: SetValue(&x)
GetValue(int i)             // i is not modified
                            // use: GetValue(i)
Solve(const Vector &b)      // b is not modified
                            // use: Solve(b)

Solve(Vector *b)            // b is modified
                            // use: Solve(&b)
Transpose(Matrix *A) // A is modified
                            // use: Transpose(&A)
```

5.4   void Argument

If a function has no variables in its argument it can use the keyword `void` in its formal argument.
  Example:

```
float Func(void);
```

When the function has no variables in its argument, it is allowed not to use `void` as a formal argument. But this can be a source of confusion. The likelihood of confusion is increased by the fact that a defined function with no variables in the formal argument means something completely different in C – 'unspecified number of variables'.

For example, the definition:

```
float Func()
    {...}
```

is equivalent in C++ to:

```
float Func(void){...}
```

whereas, in C, it means: an unspecified number of terms can be assigned in the function `Func`.

> `void`, as the formal argument of a function with no argument, should *always* be made *explicit*.

Example:

```
float Func(void); // OK
float Func(); // must be avoided
```

5.5   Vectors and Matrices as Function Arguments

In C and in C++, when an array (vector or matrix) has to be transferred from one function to another, only the array's address is passed. This sidesteps the need to copy all the array's coefficients, and conforms with the aim of lending maximum calculating efficiency to programs.

> For vectors and matrices, there is a *transparency* between calling and called functions, so great care must be taken.

As vectors and matrices can occur in two different ways we must look at both. Let's begin with defined vectors and their sizes.
Example:

```
float vect[100];
```

Remember that the `vect` identifier is a *constant* pointer, which points to the beginning of the vector. Using the function call:

```
Func(vect);
```

the address of the beginning of the vector is passed to `Func`. In the function `Func`:

```
int Func(float *vv)
   {
   statements;
   }
```

`vv` is a variable pointer which has the same initial value as `vect`.

> It is important to note that `vect`, the name of the vector in the calling function, is a *constant pointer*, whereas the pointer in the called function, `vv`, is a *variable pointer*. `vv` can thus be modified (`vv++`, for example) without modifying `vect`. But, by modifying `*vv`, `*(vv+i)`, or `vv[i]` the content of `vect` is modified, that is, `*vect`, `*(vect+i)`, or `vect[i]`.

Now let's look at a matrix defined as:

```
float mat[10][20];
```

It should be remembered (see Chapter 3) that the identifier `mat` identifies an array with the size 10. Each element of this array is a 20 `float` array. So `mat` is not an array of `float` pointers, but an array of 20 `float` arrays.

Using the function call:

```
FuncMat(mat);
```

the address of mat is passed to `FuncMat`.

In function `FuncMat`, a pointer to a `float` pointer cannot be used in the formal argument:

```
int FuncMat(float **mm) // wrong
   {....}
```

The function `FuncMat` must be aware of the vector's dimensions, to which `mat` is pointing. Its formal argument must be equivalent to `mat`. The following argument is also incorrect:

```
int FuncMat(float *mm[20]) //this is also wrong
   {....}
```

Indeed, in this case, `mm` is a vector with 20 elements, which consists of pointers to `float`: it is not a pointer to a vector with 20 `float` type elements. The reason for this is linked to the fact that the operator `[]` has precedence over the unary operator `*`.

Thus, the correct formal argument is:

```
int FuncMat(float (*mm)[20]) // correct
    {....}
```

Apart from having to remember to place the pointer in parentheses, to modify the order of precedence, this approach has the serious disadvantage of requiring prior knowledge of the matrix's second index, so that the function can be defined.

FORTRAN shares the same drawback. If the function is to be used in programs of a general nature, either the matrix becomes over-dimensioned or the risk is run of having to recompile the function when it is under-dimensioned.

Now let's look at the second way of dealing with vectors and matrices – by using variable and dynamically dimensioned pointers.

For vectors, it would be:

```
float *vect = new float [N];
```

The identifier vect is now a *variable pointer* which points to the vector's beginning. The vector's N dimensions vary according to the problem; they must *not*, therefore, be fixed at the moment of compilation. The function call and use of the pointer vv inside the function Func are identical to the previous case. For matrices, a pointer to a float pointer (see Chapter 3) needs to be defined:

```
float **mat;
mat = new float *[M];
if(!mat)Error(...); // insufficient memory
for(i=0;i<M;i++)
    {
    mat[i]= new float [N];
    if(!mat[i])Error(...); // insufficient memory
    }
```

The formal argument of the function FuncMat can now be defined with a pointer to a float pointer:

```
int FuncMat(float **mm) // correct
    {....}
```

with the advantage of being able to give precisely those dimensions which are required by the problem, releasing storage with delete when the matrix is no longer of any use.

Using this approach, storage can be managed dynamically. In FORTRAN, this is not possible.

There are some drawbacks. The matrix dimensions M and N have to be passed, using the list, so that the function FuncMat can manage the matrix mm. The user has to manage memory dynamically with the operators new and delete. The data are separated from the functions which manipulate them. In short, a procedural, rather than an object-oriented approach is used (see Chapter 12).

5.6   return Function

A function can *interact with variables*, which are *external to it*, in three ways, by using:

(1)   global variables;
(2)   pointers or references used in function's formal arguments;
(3)   function return.

> Using return can pass the value of a single variable, even a complex class object or a result produced by an expression.
> When there is more than one variable involved, exchange of information has to be carried out with the function argument, using pointers or references.

Example:

```
.....
return var;
....
return (expression);
```

The type of variable that a function passes with its return is established while defining the function.

Example:

```
int Func1(....) // type int return
float Func2(....) // type float return
Matrix Func3(....) // type Matrix return
int *Func4(....) // pointer to type int return
void Func5(....) // no variable is passed
float &Func6(....) // return type reference to float
```

As far as return is concerned the same principle as that adopted for variables in the argument is valid. return passes a *value* to the calling function, and not a variable.

> For the time being, we cannot discuss return in relation to:
>
> (1) class objects
> (2) pointers;
> (3) references.
>
> They will be explained in greater depth in Chapter 10.

It is not a problem if a function passes a basic type variable with its return. The function passes the *value* calculated which can be used by the calling function.
Example:

```
int i=Func1(..); // Func1 with return to int
float x=Func2(..); // Func2 with return to float
```

> The key word void is used in C++, when a function does not return any value.

Example:

```
void Func(int i);
```

5.7 Recursive Functions

Recursive functions can be used in C++, a feature it inherited from C.

Definition: *Recursive function*
A function is said to be recursive if it calls itself from the block containing its definition.

Example:

```
float Func(void)
    {
    statements;
    float x = Func(); // calls itself
    statements;
    };
```

A function can also be indirectly recursive – when it calls another function and it, in turn, calls the first function.

> Recursive functions have to contain within them a mechanism for bringing the sequence of calls to an end, to avoid creating infinite loops.

For example, say you wanted to implement a function to calculate the factorial of a number: n!. As we know n! is equal to 1, if n = 0. And it equals n(n-1)(n-2)...1, if n is different to 0. The function can be implemented as follows:

```
int Factorial(int n)
    {
    if(n == 0)
    return 1; // avoids circular loop
    else
    return n*Factorial(n-1); // recursive
    }
```

> Recursive functions can very simply solve some problems that would otherwise be difficult to tackle. So the code is often more compact and easier to read.

> You should bear in mind two possible problems.
>
> (1)   With numerical algorithms, the non-recursive alternative almost always leads to codes which are faster in terms of calculation time.
> (2)   When a function is called recursively, the compiler has to store in the stack (see Chapter 6) the values of the items present when the function is called, to permit recovery of such values later when control returns inside the block which is calling the function. If the number of calls is very high, it can use up all the available memory.

One situation where use of recursive functions is essential is in implementing the *quicksort* algorithm for ordering a vector's elements.

> One drawback of the *quicksort* algorithm, when implemented without necessary precautions, is that it may fully use up memory when a large vector has to be ordered.

Function recursivity can help you solve the following problem easily and effectively: the user calls the function in a syntactically correct, but semantically inappropriate way.

The function highlights the syntactic error, corrects it and calls itself again – this time correctly.

For example, the function needs two different objects of the same type. The user calls the function with the same object, which is repeated twice. Syntax is respected and the compiler cannot pick up the error which can, instead, be picked up inside the function. The function creates a new object which is different from the one it receives and uses the one it receives to initialize it. Now, if the function calls itself again, semantics are also respected; the two objects are different (see Chapter 12).

5.8 Questions

Have a look at the following fragment:

```
void Func(float v)
    {
    v=5.;
    }
.....
float w=0.;
Func(w);
```

What is w's value after the Func call?
If the definition of Func is swapped with:

```
void Func(float &v)
```

what is w's value now?

In the first case, its value is 0, as the value is passed. In the second case, its value is 5, as a reference is passed.

If in the first case:

```
Func(&w);
```

had been used, what would w's value have been?

The compiler would flag an error: The actual and formal arguments do not agree.

Look at the following:

```
int v[10];
Func(v);
....
void Func(int *w)
    {
    for(int i=0;i<10;*w++=i;++)*w++=i;
    }
```

What does `*w++=i;` mean? Can the pointer w be varied even though we know that v is constant (you cannot have v++)? What is v's value after Func has been called?

The meaning of `*w++=i;` is as follows; the value of i is assigned to the content of w; w is incremented by 1. As w is initialized with v, this means that it is now pointing to v[1]. Thus, vector v is modified and its final value is v[0]=,..v[9]=9.

Notice that w is a variable pointer, even though v is a constant pointer.

Given the matrix:

```
float a[10][20];
```

say what Func's formal argument should be:
if a call is made with Func(a);
if a call is made with Func(&a[0]);
if a call is made with Func(&a[0][0]);

In the first two cases: (float (*m)[20]); and in the third: (float *m). In fact, &a[0][0] is the address of a float. In the last case, the function Func sees the matrix as a vector.

5.9   Examples

Calculation of the Median of a Vector

The median is a measure which is used to determine the central value of a distribution. It is defined as the value which divides into equal parts all the elements of the distribution, if they are odd in number. However, it is defined as the arithmetic mean between two central elements, if they are even.

To be able to calculate a median, the vector of the elements must therefore be ordered, using `Sort`, a function specially designed for that purpose. The function for calculating the median point is very simple:

```
float Median(int n,float *x)
  {
  Sort(n,x); // orders the elements of x
  int n2 = n/2;
  int n2m1 = n2   1;
  return ((n%2) ? x[n2] : .5*(x[n2m1] + x[n2]));
  }
....
// use of Median function
static float x[5]=
    {4.,5.,1.,3.,2.};
float median = Median(5,x);
```

The following points are to be noted in this short function:

(1)   As we are using a vector, x, which has already been defined (by C++ and C), it will have an index which varies between 0 and n-1.

(2)   `return` uses two operators: division of an integer by %, which provides the remainder of the operation; and the ternary operator ? : (see Chapter 2). If n is odd, the remainder of n%2 is 1, the test is true and the response is x[n2]. If n is even and the remainder 0, the test is false and the response is .5*(x[n2m1] + x[n2]).

(3)   As the function is written procedurally, the dimensions of the vector should be passed as well as the vector data.

Swapping Variables

A value swap is needed between two `float` variables. The following function `Swap` makes this possible:

```
void Swap(float *x,float *y)
  {
  float temp = *x; // initializes temp
              // with the content of x
  *x = *y; // assigns value *y to *x
  *y = temp; // completes the exchange
  }
....
```

```
// Example of how it is used
   float x = 3.,y = 5.;
   Swap(&x,&y); // address pass
```

It can be seen that two pointers to `float` type variables are passed into the argument. Access can be gained, inside the function `Swap`, to the address in which the two variables are stored. And the variables' content can thus be accessed and swapped using the auxiliary variable `temp`.

Sorting a Vector

Now let's have a look at how to construct an effective function for sorting a `float` vector. Many algorithms have been suggested to solve the problem and they all have their good and bad points. But the one that really seems to be the best, and the one that I prefer, is *heapsort*.

Anyone coming to C++ from FORTRAN rarely has cause to consider data structures that are different from ordinary vectors and matrices. Conversely, it is normal in C and C++ to exploit different types of structures to store data groups: trees, lists, queues, stacks etc. This greater flexibility stems from two basic features of the languages – pointers, and the ability to define new `struct` or `class` variables. We will see how to exploit one of these special structures for implementing sparse matrices in Chapter 13.

Recourse to special structures, or the recursive capacity of C and C++, is not needed to construct the `Sort` function based on the algorithm of heapsort.

A vector should be seen as a heap, so let's look at a its characteristics.

(1)   A *heap* is a special binary tree consisting of n nodes. (Binary trees are considered a hierarchy of nodes, in which two nodes can be added to any given node. The totality of the nodes, and the links between them, take on the form of a tree. Each node has two branches (or children). The starting point is a base node and the tree structure is built up from this.

(2)   Node 1 does not have parents and has (or can have) two children: nodes 2 and 3. Node 1 is on level 1, and nodes 2 and 3, should they exist, are on level 2.

(3)   Node 2 has (or can have) two children, nodes 4 and 5. Node 3 has (or can have) two children – 6 and 7. Nodes 4, 5, 6 and 7, if they exist, are on level 3.

(4)   To move to a higher level, the preceding level must have been filled starting from the node on the left.

(5)   For this generic binary tree to be a heap, *the value contained in a node must be inferior or equal to that contained in its parent node.*

> Try to visualize a vector, which not only consists of a sequence of elements, but also has a structure which enjoys the properties listed above – that is, a heap.

Example of a 6-node heap:

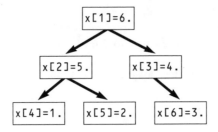

Because this is a heap, the values of the vector's coefficients have the following property:

```
x[2] <= x[1];        x[3] <= x[1];
x[4] <= x[2];        x[5] <= x[2];
x[6] <= x[3];
```

If a structure is a heap, element 1 contains the greatest value. The *heapsort* algorithm exploits this important characteristic.

Suppose we have a vector which has been converted into a heap. The first and last elements would now be swapped, and the last element would therefore contain the greatest value of the vector. Because of this exchange, the vector with n-1 elements (excluding the last one) would no longer be a heap. To convert this vector, which would have been reduced by one coefficient, into a heap, the elements would have to be swapped accordingly. If the procedure were repeated (swapping node 1 with the last but one node, and then with the last but two node, and so on, at each stage reconstructing a heap for a vector with one element fewer) by the end of the process, the vector would be ordered.

To sum up, three stages are required to construct the function:

1. The initial vector must be transformed, swapping variables, so as to form a heap.

2. Coefficient 1 is exchanged with coefficient i-th, so as to place the greatest value of the vector with i elements in i.

3. A heap is reconstructed for i-1 elements

Points 2 and 3 are repeated for i which varies by n from 2.

```
//    *******************< Sort >********************
//    *   Purpose: to sort an array of floats        *
//    *   Example:                                    *
//    *     float x[5]={3.,2.,5.,1.,4.};              *
//    *     Sort(5,x);                                *
//    *******************************************************
```

```
void Sort(int n,float *x)
    {
    if(n <= 1)return;
    int node,i,j,k,ik,jk;
    for(node = 1;node < n;node++)
        {
        i = node;
        j = ((i+1)/2)-1;
        while(i != 0 && x[j] <= x[i])
            {
            Swap(x+j,x+i);
            i=j;
            j=((i+1)/2)-1;
            }
        }
    for(i = n-1;i >= 1;iñ)
    {
    Swap(x+i,x);
    k = i-1;
    ik = 0;
    jk = 1;
    if(k >= 2 && x[2] > x[1])jk=2;
    while(jk <= k && x[jk] > x[ik])
        {
        Swap(x+jk,x+ik);
        ik = jk;
        jk = (2*(ik+1))-1;
        if(jk+1 <= k)
        if(x[jk+1] > x[jk])jk++;
        }
    }
}
```

This example is deliberately complicated. But its aim is to prevent the reader from confusing the complexity of an algorithm with the complexity of the language's syntax. Readers should not, in this example, concern themselves too much about understanding the algorithm and should, instead, analyse individual statements and understand them *individually*. If the above list is analysed again in this spirit, it will be seen that the individual statements are not all that complicated.

Program Structure in C++

Hic sunt leones.

There are lions here.

Indicated unexplored regions on maps of Africa.

6.1   Introduction

Generally a C++ program has a very articulated structure, for the following reasons.

(1)   It is very advisable, I would say indispensable, to break down a program into various files, as well as various functions, objects and modules. One or more functions (generally those which are linked to each other) are collected in each of these files.

(2)   Declarations of function prototypes and any other information common to the various files require one or more header files to guarantee a uniform declaration of common quantities.

(3)   Class (`class`, `struct`, `union`) and `enum` definitions are usually filed separately.

(4)   Class member functions are usually developed in other files.

(5)   Some functions, particularly those which are used to manage video efficiently, are hardware dependent. All non-portable functions should be collected into a single file, which is compiled separately.

A C++ program comprises a great number of files, for the reasons outlined above.

> There are two complications in choosing the identifiers of the files in which the various elements of a C++ program are held.
>
> (1)   The maximum length of the identifier depends on the working environment: DOS, UNIX and so on.
> (2)   There is no universally recognized convention covering file extensions.
>
> I will use the following convention.
>
> (1)   Maximum length 8 characters + 3 extension characters (as in DOS);
> (2)   The files which contain the `main` and functions will have the extension name `.CPP`; and those containing class definitions and function prototypes, the extension `.HPP`. Files with the extension `.CPP` have to be compiled. Files with extension `.HPP` are *header files*.

Valid examples (in the proposed style):

`MATRIX.CPP, UTILITY.CPP, VECTOR.HPP`

The purpose of subdividing the program into different modules is to enable small portions of the program to be compiled independently, so that they can be debugged efficiently. If a compilation error is found, only a small portion of the program needs to be recompiled, which has the advantage of both speed of compilation and detecting programming errors.

Pre-Compiler Directives

> Before compiling a module, C++ causes a *pre-compiler* to intervene, which, as its name suggests, executes some important operations before it compiles a file. The appropriate commands, containing the symbol # as the first character of a line have to be written in order to communicate to the pre-compiler which tasks it has to carry out.

A particularly important task carried out by the pre-compiler is the inclusion of header files, which is executed using the command `#include` and which can use three formats. The first is used to tell the pre-compiler that the task involves a library header file. The compiler automatically finds these files, as it knows in which directory they are located.

Example:

```
#include <stdio.h> // library file
```

The other two formats are used to include header files which are implemented by the user. If the header file is in the same directory as the file which includes it, explicitly writing the directory itself can be avoided. But this is not possible when the header file is in a different directory.

There are also minor differences in the inclusion of files according to the working environment, because of the different criteria which are used to define the directories in which the files are contained. I will use the DOS symbol \ to separate sub-directories.

Example:

```
#include "MATRIX.HPP" // same directory
#include "C:\BUMATH\UTILITY.HPP" // different directory
```

The definition of constants, executed using the #define directive, is another important task.
Example of definitions of constants:

```
#define PI 3.14
#define TRUE 1
```

Defining a constant by using the #define directive is characteristic of C style. C++ does it in a much more efficient way: it uses the modifier const. There is, therefore, the additional advantage of being able to check the *type* of constant, when it is used in a function.

Examples of recommended style for defining constants (see Chapter 2):

```
const float PI = 3.14;
const char TRUE = 1;
```

Defining a new type of enum variable is another very useful option in situations where constants are linked.

Example of recommended style for defining constants which are linked:

```
enum Arrow
   {
   UP, DOWN, RIGHT, LEFT
   };
```

> We will not consider all the possibilities offered by the pre-compiler.

Program Structure in C++

A C++ program therefore consists of several files divided into two categories – those which have to be compiled (with extension .CPP) and header files (with extension .HPP). One compiled file – and one alone – must contain a function called main.

Example of a program module (with extension .CPP):

```
#include <stdio.h>  // library header
#include "MYHEADER.HPP" // my header

const float PI=3.14; // global constant
float xglob; // definition of a global variable

void main(void)
    {
    statements; // body of the main
    }
float Func(int i)
    {
    statements; // body of Func
    }
```

For example, the following would occur in the file MYHEADER.HPP:

```
extern const float PI;// declaration of PI
extern float xglob; // declaration of xglobal
float Func(int i); // prototype of Func
```

The meaning of the keyword extern will be explained later on.

6.2   Declaring and Defining

C++ is a strongly typed language and so the compiler must be able to check the coherence in the use of a variable or a function in different parts of the program. The ability to declare a variable which has been defined elsewhere was introduced for this purpose. And here it is necessary to understand the difference between *defining* and *declaring*.

> Beware: Many books fail to make the distinction between defining and declaring, or even worse, they alternate them, as if the two meant the same.
>
> *cont.*

> *cont.*
> The problem is exacerbated by the factors outlined below:
>
> (1) It is impossible to give one single definition for the two terms, which is valid for each variable type and which is universally accepted.
> (2) Many compilers have different conventions of relaxation of the rules for converting a declaration into a definition, when they deem it necessary.

I believe it is right to attempt to uphold a precise distinction between defining and declaring, to avoid confusion and to attempt to come up with rules which can be followed.

> An identifier is *defined*, if the compiler can establish the *variable type* with which it is associated and the *amount of storage required to allocate* any such variable. An identifier is *declared* if the compiler can establish the variable type with which it is associated.

Basic Type Variables

The above rules must be made more precise when dealing with basic type variables since the compiler knows exactly the storage necessary for each type of variable.

Definition: *Variable declaration*
A variable *declaration* announces that a variable with a certain type of identifier exists.

Definition: *Variable definition*
A variable is *defined* when it is *declared* (that is, a name is assigned to it and its type is selected) *and it is assigned an amount of storage to allocate it.*

Example:

```
int i;        // i is defined
int j=0;      // j is defined and initialized
```

There are two *definitions* in this example: indeed the compiler has enough information to assign the right amount of storage to the variable.

> The keyword `extern` is used to tell the compiler (and whoever that reads the code) that a *declaration* and not a *definition* is needed.

Example:

```
extern int k; // declares that k has been defined
              // elsewhere of type int
```

If the keyword **extern** is used in declaring a variable, but the variable is initialized at the same time, this is a *definition* and not a *declaration*.

Example:

```
extern int k=1; // variable k is defined
```

 Many compilers take a declaration to mean a definition, if they only find declarations of the same identifier in the various files into which the program has been subdivided.

Example:

```
extern int k; // declaration of k in a file
....
extern int k; // declaration of k in another file
```

One of the two declarations is promoted to a definition in the example above.

 The following rules should be followed to avoid confusion:

(1) Always execute one *definition* of an identifier – and one alone – without the keyword **extern**.
(2) *Never* initialize a variable when the keyword **extern** is being used.

Example:

```
extern int k=1; // NO!!!! Danger of confusion
```

Derived Type Variables

Defining and declaring derived variables or new types of object follow the same rules as for basic type variables. (See Chapter 10 for *initializing* and *assigning* objects.)

   Example of a defining a **float** pointer and a **Matrix** type object:

```
float *ptr = new float; // defined and initialized
Matrix A; // variable A is defined
        // as type Matrix
Matrix B(3,4)j // B is defined as type Matrix and
        // initialized with a constructor
```

Example of declaring a `float` pointer and a `Matrix` type object:

```
extern float *ptr;
extern Matrix A; // variable A is declared
                 // as type Matrix
extern Matrix B; // variable B is declared
                 // as type Matrix
```

Functions

A distinction between defining and declaring must also be made for functions.

Definition: *Function definition*
A function definition consists of four parts (see Chapter 5).

(1)   Identifier.

(2)   Body of function within { and }.

(3)   List of argument variables.

(4)   `Return` type.

Example of a function definition:

```
int Func(float x)
    {
    statements;
    }
```

Definition: *Function declaration*
The declaration of a function acts as the *prototype* of that function; it consists of three parts: the function identifier, the list of arguments in the function and the `return` type. An identifier does not need to be given to the list of variables in the argument – saying what type they are is enough. The declaration *must* end with `;`.

Example:

```
int Func(float);
Matrix Func1(const Vector &v);
```

It is a good idea *always* to put an *identifier which recalls the meaning* of the variable in the list of argument variables, to make the code more comprehensible.

Example:

```
int Func(float *,int); // NO: unclear
                       // even if it is allowed
int Func(float *array,int dimensions); // OK
```

C++ inherited from C a form of relaxation in function declarations and a function can be declared – that is, what kind of prototype it has can be announced without using the keyword extern.
If, when declaring the function, the keyword extern is used, but the function's body is given (contained within { and }) at the same time, this is a *definition* and *not* a declaration.

Example of declaring a function:

```
int Func(float x);                // remember the ;
extern float Func1(int j); // extern is optional
```

The following is a definition, not a declaration:

```
extern int Func(int i){return 3*i;} // definition
```

Some authors suggest the use of the keyword extern in *declaring* a function. It seems to me that the difference between *defining* and *declaring* a function is obvious.
The characteristics of a declaration are as follows:

(1)   ; is present.
(2)   The body of the function {...} is not present.

I will *not*, therefore, use the keyword extern in function declarations.

Defining a New Type of Variable

One of the foundation stones of C++ is the ability to create *new types of variables*, or even better, *new types of objects*.

Do not confuse the definition of new type of object with the definition of an *object of that type.*
The former is an abstract description of a new type of entity, whereas the latter is the realization of an instance of that entity – a real object is created.

Definition: *Defining a new variable type*
A new variable type is *defined* using the declaration of the members of which it consists.

Example of defining a new variable type:

```
class Matrix // Matrix is declared from here
   {
   int numRows,numColumns;
   float **matrix;
public:
   .....
   }; // Matrix is defined from here
```

Definition: *Declaring a new variable type*
A new variable type is *declared* using its identifier, preceded by the keyword of the class to which it belongs (`class`, `struct`, `union`) and followed by a semi-colon `;`. The keyword `extern` is optional as in declaring function prototypes.

Example of declaring a Matrix type variable:

```
class Matrix; // Matrix is declared from here
class Matrix; // the declaration can be repeated
```

Notice that the compiler does not assign any storage space to the identifier, which denotes a new variable type. The variables, which are its members, are *only declared and do not take up any storage space* until a new object of that type is created. On the other hand, the compiler has enough information, after the identifier has been *defined*, to know how much storage is needed by an object of that type.
This *does not* happen after a simple *declaration*.

The following can be members of a new variable type (see Chapter 9):

(A)   Variables

   (1)   Basic and derived variables intrinsic to C++.

   (2)   Variables of a *different type* to the one which is being defined, provided that the variable type is defined.

   (3)   Pointers or references to variables of the type which is being defined and to other types of variables, provided that they have been declared.

(B)   Functions

   (1)   Member functions.

   (2)   Operators.

   (3)   Constructors.

   (4)   Destructor.

The following considerations are important.

(1) A class (`class`, `struct`, `union`) is *defined* only when it is enclosed by a curly bracket,`}`, which indicates the end of a definition block. The compiler can only know the size of the new object at this point.

(2) The identifier of the new variable type, preceded by the keyword `class`, `struct`, or `union` is sufficient to *declare* a new type of variable.

(3) An object of the variable type which is being defined cannot be a member of that variable (as the variable has yet to be *defined* inside the block).

(4) A *pointer* or a *reference* to a variable type which is being defined can be a member of that variable (as the variable is *declared* in the block).

(5) An *object* belonging to a different class can be a member of a class only if its *definition* precedes that of the class.

(6) A *preliminary declaration* is needed in order to use *pointers* or *references* to objects of a different class which has not yet been defined.

Example:

```
class Sample; // preliminary declaration of Sample
class Demo
    {
    Demo *ppp; // OK pointer to Demo
              // Demo is declared
    Demo pv;   // NO error
              // Demo is not defined
    Sample *pin; // OK pointer to Sample type
            // Sample has been preliminarily declared
    Sample sin; // NO error Sample type variable
          // has not yet been defined
    void Func(const Sample &xx); // OK reference
    ......
    };
class Sample
    {
    Demo *pal; // OK Demo is declared here
    Demo plpl; // OK Demo is defined
    ..........
    };
```

> Notice that *member variables cannot be initialized while a new type of variable is being defined*, since storage cannot be assigned to them during the definition of a new type of variable.
>
> They are only allocated the necessary storage when an object of that type is being defined and so only then can they be initialized.

enum type variables are *defined* by using a list of enumerators.
Example of defining `Direction`:

```
enum Direction
    {
    NORTH,EAST,SOUTH,WEST; // enumerators
    };
```

I have already stressed (see Chapter 4) that enumerators – unlike class members – are defined, automatically initialized or can be initialized while the type enum is being defined and they do not require the type specification.

An enum variable is *declared* by using its identifier, preceded by the keyword enum, and followed by `;`.
Example of declaring `Direction`:

```
enum Direction;
```

Declaring with `typedef`

> An identifier which is synonymous with an existing type (whether basic or derived) can be declared with the keyword `typedef`. But an identifier which has been declared synonymous with an existing type *must not* be the same as another type which already exists, even if it is defined by the programmer.

Example:

```
typedef int Integer;
typedef int float; //          NO error
```

Integer can be used instead of `int` to define an `int` type variable.
Example:

```
Integer i=5;
```

When `typedef` is used, *a declaration and not a definition* of a new variable type is executed and it can be repeated without creating errors.

Example:

```
typedef int Integer;
typedef int Integer // OK is a declaration
```

> A declaration carried out with `typedef` can improve a program's legibility and portability.

We shall see further on how a program's legibility can be improved. As for portability, consider the following problem. We saw in Chapter 2 how C++ does not guarantee the exact size of a basic type variable, only its minimum size. For example, an `int` can be 2 bytes long for a 2-byte compiler but for another 4-byte compiler it will be 4 bytes long and equivalent to a `long int` on the first compiler. Type Integer can be used in a program, if a guarantee of working with integers of 4 bytes is wanted.

`Integer` will be declared as follows, depending on the circumstances:

```
typedef long int Integer;
```

for the first compiler. Or:

```
typedef int Integer;
```

for the second. Modification of a single statement in this way is sufficient to move from one compiler to another.

How to Interpret Complex Definitions and Declarations

As we saw earlier on, C++ requires a variable type to be associated with each identifier.

In order to be able to understand what variable type an identifier is associated with in a complex definition or declaration, it should be borne in mind that there are four unary operators, which can be used to modify an object's definition. They are: the *indirect value* operator, `*`, the *address* operator, `&`, the *function* operator, `( )`, and the *array* operator, []. (A fifth operator, `::`, the *scope* operator, will be discussed later on).

While operators `*` and `&` go on the left of the identifier, because they associate to the right, the other two, `( )` and `[ ]`, go on the right, because they associate to the left.

The operators `( )` and `[ ]` have equal precedence, which is superior to that of the operators `*` and `&`, which also have equal precedence.

Of two operators with equal precedence, the one which is nearest to the name dominates.

Round brackets are used to change the order of precedence.

Definitions and declarations are sometimes very complex, in which case expressions are read in three stages:

(a)   start with the *identifier* of the item which is being defined;
(b)   move to the *right*, to the end of the expression (taking into account the brackets, which highlight variations on precedence);
(c)   Carry on to the *left*, to the beginning of the definition.

Here there are two important considerations.

(1)   Wherever the function operator, ( ), occurs, the definition refers to the variable type that is passed back by `return` from that point onwards.
(2)   If one or more operators, `[ ]`, occur, the definition up to that point constitutes *the name of an array*.

Let's consider a few typical definitions:

```
char *vect[NCHAR];
```

In this definition the following occurs, (`[ ]` has precedence over `*`):

(a) `vect`	`vect`
(b) is a vector with the dimension `NCHAR`	`vect[NCHAR]`
(c) of pointers	`*vect[NCHAR]`
which are variable, of type `char`	`char *vect[NCHAR]`

```
float matr[M][N];
```

(a) `matr`	`matr`
(b) is a vector, with dimensions `M`	`matr[M]`
of vectors with dimensions `N`	`matr[M][N]`
(c) of `float` type variables	`float matr[M][N]`

or, alternatively:

(a) `matr[0],..,matr[M-1]` are `M` identifiers	`matr[M]`
(b) of vectors with dimensions `N`	`matr[M][N]`
(c) of `float` type variables	`float matr[M][N]`

or, alternatively:

(a) `matr[0][0],..,matr[M-1][N-1]`
    are MxN identifiers   `matr[M][N]`
(c) of `float` type variables   `float matr[M][N]`

`float Fw(int n);`

(a) `Fw`   `Fw`
(b) is a function   `Fw(int n)`
(c) with a `float` type `return`   `float Fw(int n)`

The above is not a definition, but a function *declaration*.

`float *Fw(int n);`

Here, the following occurs (the function operator ( ) has precedence over *****):

(a) `Fw`   `Fw`
(b) is a function   `Fw(int n)`
(c) the `return` of which is a pointer `*Fw(int n)`
    to a `float` type variable   `float *Fw(int n)`

Neither is this a definition. It is a function *declaration*.

`float (*Fw)(int n);`

(a) `Fw`   `Fw`
    is a variable pointer   `(*Fw)`
(b) to a function   `(*Fw)(int n)`
(c) with a `float` type `return`   `float (*Fw)(int n)`

Conversely, this is a variable pointer *definition* and not a function *declaration* (see Chapter 7).

Note the difference between the last two examples – it is due to the swapping of precedence between the function operator and the operator *****. The introduction of the brackets in the second example, `(*Fw)`, constrains the normal priority of *****.

`int *&pti;`

(a) `pti`   `pti`
(c) is a reference   `&pti`
    to a pointer   `*&pti`
    to an `int` type object   `int *&pti;`

`float (*(*(*w)[N])(int n))[M];`

This complicated definition is read as follows:

(a) w	w
(b) is a variable pointer	(*w)
to a vector with dimensions N	(*w)[N]
of pointers	(*(*w)[N])
to function	(*(*w)[N])(int n)
which return pointers	(*(*(*w)[N])(int n))
to a vector with dimensions M	(*(*(*w)[N])(int n))[M]
(c) of float type variables	float (*(*(*w)[N])(int n))[M]

Do not use definitions which are too complicated, as not all combinations are acceptable.

For example, the definition below is unacceptable because a function cannot have a vector as a return.

```
float Fw(int n)[M];  // NO ILLEGAL
```

Remember that the names of a vector and a function are the names of their respective initial *addresses*.
So both names are *constant pointers*.

```
float fl[N];  // fl name of a constant pointer
int matr[M][N]; // matr name of a constant pointer
 // matr[0], matr[M-1] names of constant pointers
float Fw(int n); // Fw name of a constant pointer
```

Notice how the example above differs from the example below (see Chapter 7).

```
float (*pfw)(int n); // pfw Variable function
      // pointer
```

The typedef construct is useful for simplifying complex definitions.
Remember that the identifier is declared synonymous with everything else that appears in *declarations* which are executed with typedef.

For example, the declaration:

```
typedef int (*CompareType)
         (void *element1,void * element2);
```

declares `CompareType` as synonymous with:

```
int (*)(void *element1,void * element2)
```

So here I can write:

```
CompareType CompareFunc;
```

instead of:

```
int (*CompareFunc)(void *element1,void * element2);
```

6.3 Accessibility, Duration and Scope of an Identifier

A variable in a SUBROUTINE (or in a FUNCTION) in FORTRAN has a length of existence which lasts throughout the program and cannot be accessed outside of the SUBROUTINE, unless it is put in an argument or in a COMMON.

C++ offers a far greater range of possible alternatives, whether in terms of the duration of variables or in terms of their accessibility. Variables can: last for the whole program; exist only inside a function, or inside a block nested inside another block; and they can begin and end their existence at points which have been pre-selected by the programmer. Variables can be accessed: in all files; in a single file; in a single block, and only by using objects.

Codes which are more compact, more secure and less prone to errors caused by data corruption can be written thanks to C++'s greater flexibility.

For example, in FORTRAN, if a matrix is used in a SUBROUTINE, you are forced to put it in the argument list or in a COMMON, otherwise that storage space could not be used outside of the function. But the space could be inadvertently violated, because it is shared with the rest of the program.

The way the problem is overcome, which stems from C, is to hide variables in functions (and inside classes, in C++) as much as possible, without them taking up storage when a function is not being used. This involves a substantial change in writing styles in large programs.

It would be too costly in FORTRAN to create a large number of SUBROUTINES because each would have variables which would take up space throughout the program. Instead, it is advisable in C and C++ to write small functions, which offer the advantages of greater control over the correctness of codes and less likelihood of creating errors.

Here, let's analyse two problems: the duration and accessibility of an identifier; and the possibility of having the same identifier for different items at different points in the program.

Categories of Identifiers

As we have seen, identifiers can refer to different types of items: to basic and derived variable types; to a new type of variable object; to a function; or they can be one of the enumerators, etc.

C++ subdivides items, which have an identifier, into four categories.

(1)   Label identifiers, to which gotos transfer control.

```
goto out_of_bounds;
..........
out_of_bounds: // example of label
```

(2)   Identifiers of new variable types, which are defined using class, struct, union and enum constructs.

```
class Matrix // Matrix: new type, defined using class
   {
   ......
   };
enum Color // Color: new type defined using enum
   {
   .....
   };
```

(3)   Class (class, struct and union) member identifiers.

```
class Matrix
   {
   int numRows; // numRows: variable member
   Vector Solve(Vector b); // Solve: function member
   };
```

(4)   Identifiers of any type of variables, functions, typedefs and enumerators.

```
int x; // x type int variable
Matrix A; // A type Matrix variable
int Func(float x); // Func function name
typedef int Integer; // Integer declared
      // equivalent to int
```

```
enum Color
   {
   BLUE,RED; // BLUE, RED enumerator names
   };
```

It is important to know to which categories an item which is characterized by a given identifier belongs, in order to know what the consequences of using the same identifier in other parts of the program are. *Two items belonging to two different categories can have the same identifier without giving rise to problems.*

Example:

```
class demo // demo new variable type
   {
   int demo; // demo class member
   ....
   };
float demo(int xa) // demo name of function
       // xa name of variable
   {
   if(xa>10.) goto xa;
   else goto demo;
   xa:    // xa name of label
   ....
   demo: // demo name of label
   ....
   }
```

The identifiers demo and xa are used in different contexts without any problem, as they belong to different categories.

Avoid giving the same identifier to items which belong to different categories.

Where Items are Stored

An item can be stored in four different memory locations in C++. They are:

(1)   Compiled module.

(2)   Registers.

(3)   Stack.

(4)   Free store (or heap).

The modifier `register` has to be used in a variable definition in order to use register storage, which is the most efficient.

There are limitations to using this storage.

(1) Only local variables, that is, variables which are defined within a function block without the `static` modifier (see below), can be defined with the `register` modifier.

(2) The number of variables which can be defined with the `register` modifier depends on the working environment and is, in any case, very limited (only a pair of variables can be defined within each function).

(3) There is *no* guarantee that a variable, which is defined with the `register` modifier, is located in the registers.
The compiler uses stack storage, if it does not have sufficient available `registers`. Thus, `registers` can be thought of as a more efficient type of stack.

It should be noted that C has one further limitation, which C++ does not share; the addresses of variables stored in registers cannot be used.

The compiler attempts automatically to execute a rational selection, if the programmer does not define any variables with the `register` modifier.

I will not use the `register` modifier. I will leave the honour of choosing to the compiler, because the option is linked to the working environment.

It is essential to understand the difference between *stack* and module memory, as opposed to free store, which is linked to the duration of a variable.

Duration of an Item

Definition: *Duration of an item*
The duration of an item is the period of time during which the item takes up storage available to it.

An item has three types of length of existence, which correspond to where the item is stored.

(1) Global or static duration.

(2) Local or automatic duration.

(3) Dynamic duration.

An item has *global* or *static* duration if it occupies storage from the beginning to the end of the program. The item is stored in the module of the compiled file.

Identifiers have a global or static length of existence in each of the two cases below:

(1)   Its definition is outside of any block {}; and therefore outside of all functions and class definitions.

(2)   The modifier `static` is used, if it is inside a block.

Example:

```
int x,*pt; // static duration variable
void main(void)
    {
        // static duration variable
    static float a[10]={1.,2.,3.,4.,5.,6.,7.,8.,9.10.};
    static int count;
    .....
    }
```

Local or *automatic* duration is the period in which a variable enters into stack storage (or into registers), when the execution of the program passes over the variable definition, and exits from memory as soon as that variable is no longer needed – i.e., at the end of the block,}, in which it was defined. The compiler takes care to use the stack storage when necessary and to release it when it is no longer needed.

Example:

```
void Func(void)
    {
    ......
    float a[10]; // local duration variable; memory
                 // needed is created in the stack
                 // by the compiler from here
    .....
    }  // memory is automatically released
       // on exit from the block in which the
       // variable was defined
```

By contrast, dynamic duration is actively managed by the user, using the operators `new` and `delete`. The amount of memory needed is sought in free store.

Example:

```
void Func(void)
    {
    . . . . . . .
            // memory needed is requested in free store
    float *pta=new float[10]; // 10 float vector
            // with dynamic length of existence
    . . . . .
    delete pta;   // storage of 10 float is released from
                  // free store when no longer needed
    . . . . . . . .
    }             // pta storage released from stack
```

It is important to understand the difference between local (automatic) and dynamic duration. Let's consider the last example.

(1) The pointer `pta` has local length of existence, and its address is placed automatically by the compiler in the stack and it has an identifier.

(2) The operator `new` creates dynamically space in *free store* for 10 `float` type elements, which do not have an identifier.

(3) The pointer `pta` is initialized with the initial address of the vector created with `new`.

(4) The content of the vector's elements: `pta[0],..,pta[9]` are not automatically initialized. It is the programmer who is responsible for giving these elements a reasonable value.

(5) If the operator `delete` (with `delete pta`) is used, storage taken up by the vector in free store is dynamically released. Stack memory which was taken up by the pointer `pta` is, instead, released automatically when `pta` leaves scope, that is, when the block in which it had been defined is closed (see below).

(6) If the `delete` operator *is not* used and the `pta` pointer leaves scope, it is no longer possible to recover storage taken up in free store by the vector created with `new`.

Example:

```
void Func(void)
    {
```

```
. . . . . . .
float *pta=new float[10];
}    // pta leaves scope, can no longer be used
    // the 10 element vector
    // takes up unrecoverable storage
```

> All variables are static type in FORTRAN – they take up memory throughout the program, even when the function is not used and even when the function is *no longer being used.*
>
> The problem is particularly serious when large matrices are defined in a function. All FORTRAN programmers are familiar with the acrobatics they have to perform with work vectors, in order to limit damage.

Scope of an Identifier

Definition: *Scope of an identifier*
The scope of an identifier is that part of the program in which the identifier *can potentially* be used.

Definition: *Accessibility of an identifier*
It may be that an identifier, which can potentially be used, cannot be accessed. Inaccessibility can be *total*, in the sense that it is not possible to access the identifier, or *partial*, in the sense that it can be accessed, but not directly.

> *Beware*: Current terminology can be very confusing. Indeed, *accessibility* is often considered the same as *visibility* and the practice of calling an *inaccessible* identifier *hidden* stems from this.
>
> We will not be able fully to clear up this confusion until Chapter 14. But it is just as well to bear this in mind from here onwards: *hidden* is not an equivalent of *invisible,* but of *inaccessible,* and, as stated above, inaccessibility can be *total* or *partial.*

C++ has five different scopes.

(1)   FILE scope.

(2)   Block scope.

(3)   Class scope.

(4)   Function prototype scope.

(5)   Function scope.

> An identifier cannot be defined several times inside the same scope, *unless* it belongs to different categories. *Overloaded* functions (which we will discuss in Chapter 7, are (apparently) the exception.

Example:

```
float Func(void)
    {
    int i;
    int i=10; // error same scope same category
    .....
    }
```

FILE Scope

Identifiers which are defined externally to any block (because they are external to any function or class) have a FILE scope.

Their scope *begins at the point of definition* and extends to the end of the file in which they are defined. In other words, they can potentially be used from the point of their definition to the end of the file, *even inside functions*, provided that the functions were defined between these two points.

Example:

```
int jj;         // FILE scope
void main(void)
    {
    statements; // jj can potentially be used
    }
float tt;       // FILE scope beginning here
void Func(float x)
    {
    statements; // jj and tt can potentially
                // be used
    }
```

> Functions which are not class members have a FILE scope, as they are defined outside blocks. They can, therefore, be potentially used from the point at which they are defined up to the end of the file in which they have been defined. They must be declared (usually in a header file), in order for them to be used in the same file before they are defined or in other files.

Example:

```
.....
void Func(float x) // Func has a FILE scope which
                   // can be accessed
    {              // by other files with the declaration
```

```
statements;        // void Func(float x);
}                  // can be accessed in this file from
                   // here unless not already declared
                   // at some previous point in the file
```

> If an identifier, which has been *defined* outside all the blocks in a file, is *declared* outside all the blocks in another file (usually by means of a header file), it has a FILE scope and can be accessed from the declaration up to the end of the *file*. If the same identifier is *declared only* inside the block of a function, defined in another file, only that function can access the variable in that file.
>
> But, if, while an identifier is being *defined* (outside blocks), the *keyword* static is used, the identifier's scope remains limited to the file in which it was defined. It cannot be used outside of that file. This applies *both to variables and to functions*. Inaccessibility in the other files is total.

Example:

```
void Func(float x); // Func declared
                    // defined in another file
                    // Func can be used from here
extern float xx; // as for Func
static int FuThaFu(void) // FuThaFu has a FILE
            // scope but limited to this file even
            // if it is declared in another file
    {
    extern int iglo; // iglo declared
                    //defined as global in another
                    // file in this file can be
                    // accessed only by FuThaFu
    statements;
    }
static float va; // as for FuThaFu
```

If the declarations are made in another file:

```
int FuThaFu(void);
extern float va;
```

neither the function FuThaFu nor the variable va can be accessed in that file. It would cause an error in linking the program.

Many authors maintain that the `static` modifier is not easy to understand. It is used in three situations in which its effects are not completely consistent. We have already met two of them and shall see the third in Chapter 9.

The confusion arises from the fact that the term *static* is used both for the *duration* of a local variable and the *scope* of a global variable.

Let's have another look at the two situations in which we have already come across the keyword `static`.

(1)   Variable which is defined outside all blocks with a `static` modifier.

(2)   Variable which is defined inside a block with `static` modifier.

Both have a global, *static* duration. But in the first case there would be a static duration even without a modifier. Conversely, the `static` modifier does not change the *scope* in the second case, but it does in the first. Indeed, in the first case, the scope is now limited to the file where the variable was defined.

To sum up: *accessibility* in the first case is now limited to the file where the variable or function is defined. In the second case, the *length of existence*, which is now static and global, is modified.

Example:

```
static float xglob; // scope, accessibility is modified,
                    // not the length of existence
void Func(void)
    {
    static int i; // duration is modified,
                  // not the scope
    statements;
    }
```

The identifier of a new type of variable has a FILE scope, if it is defined outside of blocks.

Example:

```
class Matrix // Matrix has a FILE scope
    {
    statements;
    };
```

Care should be paid to the definitions with a FILE scope in the following two cases:

(1)   new type of variable;

(2)   variable defined with the modifier `const`.

> Inside the file in which definition takes place, the definition of a new type of variable occurs from the point at which the definition block is closed.
> The definition *cannot* be repeated inside the file and must be repeated in files which use that type of variable. A *declaration* of a new type of variable in the files which use it is *not* sufficient.

Example: the variable type `Demo` is defined in a file:

```
class Demo; // a preliminary declaration can be made
.......
class Demo
    {
    members;
    }; // Demo is defined
.....
class Demo; // can be declared even if not needed
....
class Demo // cannot be redefined
    {
    members;
    };
```

In another file, where the `class Demo` is required:

```
class Demo; // declaration is not enough
class Demo // class needs to be redefined
    {
    members;
    };
```

> The definition of variables of a new type, which have a FILE scope (in practice they are the most commonly used), should always be put into a header file (normally one for every new type, unless the definitions are particularly short and linked to each other).
> The name of the header file should be as similar as possible to that of the new type of variable, with the extension `.HPP`. If the name of the new type is too long, you will not be able to use all of it.
> Example: `MATRIX.HPP`, `VECTOR.HPP`.
>
> *cont.*

---

cont.

The following trick, which exploits the *pre-compiler*, is useful in avoiding several executions of a definition in the same file:

```
#ifndef MATRIX_HPP
#define MATRIX_HPP
class Matrix
{
members;
};
#endif MATRIX_HPP
```

It means: if `MATRIX_HPP` does not exist, it is defined, as is the `class Matrix`. If `MATRIX_HPP` is already defined, the definition of `Matrix` is ignored. I will use the new type's name, written in capitals and followed by `_HPP` as the identifier to put into the pre-compiler test.

Even variables with the modifier `const` are irregular.

Their *default* scope is limited to the file in which they are defined. It is as if the `static` modifier were always present.

Further on, we will lay down rules for defining and declaring variables with the modifier `const`.

Block Scope

Identifiers which are defined inside a function block have block scope. Scope *begins at the point of the definition* and finishes where *the block concerned* closes with `}`.
A definition *cannot* be repeated inside the same block.

Example:

```
float Func(void)
    {
    ....
    int i;      // i enters scope
        {
        ...
        float x; // x enters scope
        ...
        }          // float x exits from scope
```

```
....
float i;    // error definition repeated
int x;      // OK different block
}           // int x and int i exit from scope
```

> The variables in a function's argument are considered to be *inside* the function block itself and consequently *cannot* be redefined.

Example:
```
float Func(int i,float x)
    {
    int i;// error i defined in the same block
        {
        double x; // OK other block
        }
    }
```

> Potentially, the identifier can be used in blocks which have blocks nested inside them.
> If the same identifier with block scope is redefined inside nested blocks, only the internal identifier is accessible, while the others are hidden. The external identifiers are totally inaccessible.
> If an identifier with a FILE scope is redefined inside a function, the identifier with block scope hides the identifier with a FILE scope. Inaccessibility is in this case only partial. The identifier with a FILE scope can be accessed by using the unary scope operator ::.

Example of variables with blocks and FILE scopes:

```
int i=5,j=5;     // FILE scope
float Func(int i) // i block scope,
                 // hides i of FILE
    {
    i=10;            // block superior to FILE
                 // block i hides FILE i
                 // but FILE i can be accessed
                 // with FILE scope ::
    ::i = 3;     // global i is modified to 3
    j=10;        // modify j with FILE scope
                 // j can be directly accessed
        {
        float i=3.14; // the internal block i hides both
```

```
        ::i=15;          // modification i with FILE
                         // scope using ::
                         // here FILE i equals 15;
                         // external block i equals 10;
                         // internal block i equals 3.14
                         // external block i cannot be
                         // accessed here
        }
    // external block i equals 10 here
    // internal block i is no longer defined
    }
// i with scope FILE equals 5
// the other i's are not defined
// j equals 10 here
```

An initialized variable in the expression in which the initial conditions for a
for loop are given has a scope which is external to the for and it cannot
therefore be redefined in the block which encloses the for.

Example:

```
for(int i=0;i<10;i++) // equivalent to
                      // int i;
                      // for(i=0;i<10;i++)
    {
    statements;
    }
int i; // error
```

The compiler will flag an error in the situation below:

```
for(i=0;i<10;i++)
    for(int j=0;j<20; j++)// NO error
                         // j cannot be initialized
        {
        statements;
        }
```

Were the compiler not to flag an error, the external for would only act on the
initialization of j. Indeed, the preceding code is equivalent to:

```
for(i=0;i<10;i++)
    int j = 0;
for(j=0;j<20; j++)
```

```
{
statements;
}
```

An identifier with a new variable type has a block scope if it is defined inside a function. But its definition is subject to several limitations. For example, functions must all be of inline type (see Chapter 7).

Example:

```
float Func(void)
    {
    struct Sample // block scope
        {
        ......
        };
    Sample plpl;  // Sample can only be used
                  // inside Func
    ....
    }
```

I will avoid defining new variable types by using `struct`, `class` and `union` constructs with a local block scope.
Furthermore, it should be noted that the construct `typedef` cannot be used inside a function.

Class Scope

Identifiers which are declared inside a class definition block have the scope of that class. Class member identifiers are hidden from the rest of the program. If variables, or functions, with a FILE scope are reused as class members, they are hidden by those with a class scope – but they can still be accessed by using the unary scope operator `::`.
A variable with block scope hides a class member identifier if it is defined with the same identifier inside a member function. The class identifier can still be accessed by using the binary operator `::`, preceded by the class name.

Example:

```
float xyz=10.;
class Demo
```

```
    {
    float xyz; // hides xyz with FILE scope
    void Func(void)
        {
        xyz = ::xyz; // member variable uses
                     // the one with FILE scope
        float xyz;   // variable with block scope
                     // which hides both
        xyz = ::xyz; // use the one with FILE scope
        xyz = Demo::xyz; // use the Demo class one
        }
    };
```

Example:

```
int Func(int i) // Func with FILE scope
    {
    statements;
    }
class Demo
    {
    int Func(int i,float x) // hides FILE Func
        {
        int j=::Func(i); // FILE Func can be accessed
        ...
        }
    ...
    };
```

If possible, it is better to avoid these acrobatics by using different identifiers for variables with the three different scopes: FILE, class and block.

Notice that there is an important difference between block and class scope. With block scope, an identifier begins its scope at the point where the block is defined and is not defined from the beginning of the definition block, whereas the scope of class members extends to the whole class.

Example:

```
class Demo
    {
    void Func(float x)
    {xPin = x;} // xPin can be used
    float xPin; // even if declared after
    }
```

```
float FuFu(int i)
    {
    float x;
    x=y; // error y not defined
    float y=10.;
    }
```

> Defining one class inside another is equivalent to what would be obtained by putting it immediately outside. Nested class identifiers *do not* have a class scope.

Example:

```
class Demo
    {
    struct Sample
        {
        ......
        };
    };
```

is equivalent to:

```
struct Sample
    {
    ....
    };
class Demo
    {
    ......
    };
```

> I will avoid defining new variable types by using the constructs `struct`, `class` and `union` which are nested within the definition of another class.

The `typedef` construct behaves in a similar way, so it is *not* a good idea to use it within class definitions.

> Defining a new `enum` type within a class definition has unusual characteristics.
>
> (1)   The *identifier* of `enum` type has a scope which is *outside* the class in which it is defined.
> (2)   The *enumerators* have a scope which is *inside* the class in which `enum` type is defined.
>
> *cont.*

> *cont.*
> Identifiers of enum type can thus be accessed from outside the class.
> Enumerator identifiers can be accessed inside the class in the usual way but externally only by means of the class scope (class name followed by : :).
> This has the advantage of isolating enumerators inside the class, minimizing possible clashes with the names of other identifiers.

Example:

```
struct Demo
    {
    enum DemoEnum
        {
        ONE, TWO
        };
    DemoEnum xDemoEnum; // OK: DemoEnum can be accessed
    void Func(void)
        {
        xDemoEnum = ONE; // OK: ONE can be accessed
        )
    };
......
DemoEnum yDemoEnum; // OK: DemoEnum can be accessed

yDemoEnum = Demo::ONE; //OK: with class scope
yDemoEnum = ONE; // error: cannot be directly accessed
const float ONE=1.; // OK no clash
```

Function Prototype Scope and Function Scope

The arguments inside a function prototype are *dummy* variables. The identifiers can even be left out. Their scope is restricted to the inside of the prototype and does not cause interference of any kind with identifiers which have other scopes.

The only identifiers which have a function scope are labels. They are used by a goto. Labels have one limitation – they must be different within the same function.

Example:

```
void Func(void)
    {
    ......
    xy_unknown:
        {
        ......
```

```
        xy_unknown: // error: the same label cannot be
                    // used even in different blocks
          }         // within the same function
      }
void Func2(void)
      {
      ......
      xy_unknown:// OK in different functions
      }
```

Initializing Variables

We have already seen that a distinction must be drawn between *initializing* and *assigning* in C++ – initializing only occurs when a variable is assigned a value at the moment when it is defined.

```
float x=10.; // x defined and initialized
float y; // y defined
y=15.; // assigned
```

We shall return later to the problem of initializing user-defined objects.

It is important here to stress the difference in initializing variables between those which have static duration (variables with FILE scopes and `static` variables with block scope) and those with local duration.

> Variables of static or global length of existence are automatically *initialized at zero*, if they are not explicitly initialized.
> Those which have a local duration have an *indefinite* value, if they are not explicitly initialized. So it is always risky to use a variable or, even worse, a pointer with a local length of existence, if they have not been initialized or if no value has been assigned to them.

Example:

```
float xglo,yglo=15.; // xglo initialized at 0.
void main(void)
      {
      float z; // z of indefinite value
      static float r; // r equal to 0.
      static int i[10]; // i[0]=..i[9]=0
      int j[3]; // j[0]..j[2] of indefinite value
      ...
      }
```

A variable with static duration is initialized *before* the execution of main. The value assigned to that variable remains unchanged, until it is explicitly modified. If during the execution of the program control returns to the statement in which the variable is defined, the variable is not re-initialized, but maintains the value it has at that moment.

Conversely, a variable with a block length of existence which has been explicitly initialized is re-initialized *every time* the execution of the program passes over its definition.

Example:

```
void main(void)
    {
    for(int k=1;k<=10;k++)
        {
        static int m=1;
        int n=1;
        m=m+1;
        n=n+1;
                // k = 10 m = 11 n = 2
        }
    }
```

Initializing a variable or an object with a static duration occurs *before the* main *is called*. This can be used to execute particular operations, with which working environments can be prepared – for example, in opening particular files, video set-up, calculating useful variables (see Chapter 10).

Furthermore, the same variables and objects *leave scope after* main *has finished*. We shall see that an object is de-initialized when it leaves scope and this makes the execution of other operations possible after main has finished – for example, closing files which were opened during initialization.

Example:

```
const float MACH_EPS = MachEps();
void main(void)
    {
    ....
    if(x < MACH_EPS)
    ....
    }
```

The constant `MACH_EPS` can be preliminarily initialized and used anywhere in the program.

> If several variables or objects are initialized with a global scope, and if the initializations are in a different file, it is risky to rely on the order in which they are initialized.
> There can be no guarantee that they will be initialized in the same order, unless they are all in one file.

We will pick up the threads of this discussion again in Chapter 10.

> An array type variable (a vector or matrix) *must* be a variable with a global duration for it to be initialized (when defined). Many compilers automatically make a vector with a local scope `static`, when it is being initialized, even if the modifier `static` is not explicitly being used.

Example:

```
float vc[3]={1.,2.,3.}; // OK
void main(void)
    {
    float va[3]={1.,2.,3.}; // error or it is being
        // transformed in static
    static float vb[3]={1.,2.,3.}; // OK
    }
```

> It is preferable *always* to use the keyword `static` when a vector with a *local scope* is being initialized.

6.4   When Should Declarations and Definitions be Used?

Of course, declarations are important only in those cases where identifiers have a FILE scope. So how do you know when you should *define* and when you should *declare* a variable or a function?

> Let's look at a variety of situations:
>
> (1)   Basic, or derived type, *variables, objects* belonging to types defined by the user, *functions*. This is the norm.
> (2)   *Constants with an identifier.*
>
> *cont.*

cont.

(3) Inline *functions* (see Chapter 7).

(4) Definition of a *new variable type* with the `class`, `struct`, `union` and `enum` constructs.

(5) `static` class members (see Chapter 9).

(6) `typedef` construct.

Example:

```
class Matrix // new variable type
    {
    static int ERROR; // static member (see Chapter 9)
    ...
    };
int Func(void) // function definition
    {
    float x; // variable definition
    int *ip; // pointer definition
    Matrix A; // object definition
    ...
    }
const float PI = 3.14; // constant
                       // with identifier
inline float Max(float x,float y) // inline
                                  // function
    {
    return x > y ? x : y; // See Chapter 7
    }
```

Normal Variables, Objects and Functions

A *variable*, an *object*, or a *function* can be *defined* only once in the whole of a program. This stems from the fact that an adequate amount of storage is set aside when these items are defined and the storage space must be unique, if the variable, object or function is to be accessed in a single way.

Variables (or *objects)* defined with the same identifier, but with different scopes, are different. In the same way, a *function* with the same identifier, but with different *scope*, is a different function.

Variables or objects with a FILE scope are *defined* in one file and *declared* in other files where they are required.

> Variable and object declarations with FILE scope are grouped together in header files and included where necessary. I would advise against declaring a global variable inside a function, defined in another file, with the `extern` modifier in such a way as to make it accessible only to that function. In my opinion it is better to use this option exceptionally, otherwise it may confuse you.

Example of definitions using a FILE scope, which cannot be repeated in other files:

```
float xglob=10.;
float a[2][3]=
    {
    {1.,2.,3.},
    {4.,5.,6.}
    };
char *menu[3]=
{
"1 First",
"2 Second",
"9 End"
};
```

and of how they are declared respectively in a header file:

```
extern float xglob; // remember not to initialize
extern float a[2][3]; // careful **a is wrong
extern char *menu[3]; // careful **menu wrong
                      // would be permitted in C
```

> It is good practice to keep global type variables to a minimum to avoid unintended side-effects.
> Instead, bear in mind the following alternatives which are less risky.
>
> (1) Variables or functions defined outside blocks using the `static` modifier are in the scope of the file in which they are defined, so other modules cannot access them. Inside that module, they behave like globals.
> (2) Defined variables inside a function with the `static` modifier have a duration which lasts for the whole of the program and are initialized only at compilation level (and so, in this respect, they behave like a global variable). But they are accessible only inside the block.
> (3) Later, we will see that a class member can be made `static` (see Chapter 9).

A function's prototype has to be declared for the function to be used before it is defined, or used in different files from the one in which its definition occurs. There are two ways in which this can be done.

(1)   List the prototypes of all the functions used inside every function and at the beginning of the function block.

(2)   Put the prototypes in a few header files, grouping them appropriately, and include these header files wherever one of those functions is needed.

The first method has the advantage of immediately providing the user with a list of functions used inside a function. But it becomes wordier and more difficult to implement in that, each time the prototype of a particular function needs to be changed, you have to find and modify the prototypes in all the functions that use it.

> I will use the second method.
> Declarations of function prototypes which have FILE scope and which are not `static` are grouped in appropriate header files with the extension `.HPP`.

Constants with an Identifier

> Constants with an identifier, that is, variables defined with the `const` modifier – even if they are defined outside blocks and without the `static` modifier – have a scope which is limited to the files in which they appear. So they can be redefined in other files, without creating errors during program linking.

One way of dealing with this is to insert *definitions* of constants with an identifier in header files – each file, including the header file, makes a copy of the constant. This is not a problem when dealing with basic type variables, but it can become storage critical with large objects.

> I will adopt the following strategy for dividing up constants with an identifier into several files – the identifier is defined `const` in a single file, with the extension `.CPP`, where it is also initialized. It is declared with `extern const` in a header file bearing the extension `.HPP`. This is included in every file with the extension `.CPP`, in which it is used. This can be done because a `const` variable is not a true `static` variable, even though it has as default a scope which is restricted to the definition file. A simple declaration is all that is needed for it to be accessible in other files in which it is used, and it does not create errors during linking.

Example of definitions of constants with identifiers (executed in a single file):

```
const int M=2,N=3;
const float MACH_EPS = MachEps(); //can initialize it
        // with the function call which must
        // be declared here. Initialjzed
        // before the beginning of the main
const int NITEMS=3;
const Matrix A("MATR.DAT"); // const object
                            // Matrix type
```

and their respective declarations in a header file to be included in every file uses them:

```
extern const int M,N;
extern const float MACH_EPS;
extern const int NITEMS;
extern const Matrix A;
```

New Variable Type

> The definition of a new variable type is unusual, in that storage is not allocated to any item in the definition. As has already been stressed, we are dealing with an abstract description of a new type of entity and not the definition of a real object.
>
> The definition of a new variable type *cannot* be repeated in the same file, whereas it *must* be repeated in every file in which an object of that type needs to be defined. This enables the compiler to be aware of the amount of storage necessary for the object.

We have already seen the strategy I intend to follow.

Construct `typedef`

The construct `typedef` is always used to *declare* and never to *define*.

> The construct `typedef` cannot be inserted into a function block and it is not a good idea to insert it into the definition block of a class.
>
> It should go at the beginning of the file (with the extension `.CPP`) in which it is being used, if it relates only to that file, or in a header file, if several files are involved.

6.5 Questions

> Given:
>
> ```
> extern int i =0;
> ```
>
> is this a declaration or a definition?

It is a definition because the variable is initialized, even though the modifier extern is used.

> What errors have been committed in the following definition of Demo?
>
> ```
> class Demo
>     {
>     Demo dd;
>     Sample *ss;
>     void Func(const Demo &d);
>     int iDemo=0;
>     }
> ```

Objects of Demo cannot be allowed in its definition.

A preliminary declaration of Sample is needed, so that a pointer to one of its objects can be used.

iDemo cannot be initialized. The ; which is needed to complete the definition of Demo is missing.

> Interpret the following definition:
>
> ```
> float (*(*x)[M]))(void);
> ```

x is a pointer to a function pointers vector sized M with a return of type float.

> What will the following program print?
>
> ```
> #include <iostream.h>
> int i=1;
> main()
>     {
>     cout << i << ',';
>         {
>         int i=2;
>         cout << i << ',';
> ```
> *cont.*

cont.

```
      ::i=3;
      cout << i << ',';
      i=::i;
      cout << i << ',';
      ::i=4;
      }
    cout << i ;
  }
```

It will print: 1,2,2,3,4.

Consider the following program:

```
#include <iostream.h>
void main(void)
    {
    Func();
    }
void Func(void)
    {
    int i=5;
    cout << i+1;
    }
```

What is being printed?

Nothing. The compiler flags an error because the function `Func` is not defined in the `main` – the declaration of the prototype is missing.

What effect does the modifier `static` have on a variable with a FILE scope and on one with a local scope?

A variable with a global scope, defined with the modifier `static`, can only be accessed inside the file. It is the *accessibility* which is changed.

A variable with a local scope, defined with the modifier `static`, has global duration. In this case, it is the *length of existence* which is modified.

What is the scope of the following identifiers: `Matrix`, `numRows`, `main`, `x`, `j`, `A` and `x_different_from_5`?

```
    class Matrix
```

cont.

```
cont.
        {
        int numRows;
        ...
        }
    void main(void)
        {
        float x=5.;
        Matrix A;
        for(int j=0;j<10;j++)
        if(x !=5.)goto x_different_from_5
        ....
        x_different_from_5:
        ...
        }
```

`Matrix` and `main` have a global scope. `numRows` has a class scope. `x, j, A` have a block scope. `x_different_from_5` has a function scope.

✓ Is the following declaration with `typedef` correct?

```
class Matrix
    {
    int numRows;
    ...
    };
typedef float Matrix;
```

It is an impossible declaration: two pre-defined types of variable cannot be made synonymously.

7 Functions

To choose time is to save time.

Francis Bacon, *Essays*

7.1 Introduction

In Chapters 5 and 6 we saw how functions are *defined* and *declared* in C++.

 All functions have to be given a *prototype* before they can be used and this means that the compiler can check whether the function's actual and formal arguments agree. This has three merits.

(1) The compiler selects the function which is most suitable for the actual argument in use, if several functions bear the same identifier. This means that function identifiers can be overloaded, as we shall see later on.

(2) A compilation error will result if the actual and formal arguments are different in type or in the number of variables. A compilation error will also occur if the compiler cannot convert the values of the variables in the actual argument in such a way as to change them unambiguously into the types required by the formal argument. This process highlights *compilation* errors which would otherwise have been very difficult to detect while *running* a program.

cont.

cont.

(3)   If the actual argument contains variables which are of a different type from those in the formal argument, but the compiler can convert the data, conversion is carried out automatically. Whoever has programmed such a conversion is responsible for its reliability.

Example:

```
#include <iostream.h>
#include "matrix.hpp"
int Func(int i); // Func declared
void main(void)
    {
    Matrix A; // defines a type Matrix object
    cout << Func(5.3); // pass Func a double value
    Func(6,8); // compilation error
    Func(A); // compilation error
    }
int Func(int i)  // Func defined
{
return i+5;
    }
```

The compiler automatically converts the value 5.3 into an integer, 5. The result is 10. A Func call with more than one variable, or with a variable that the compiler cannot transform into an int, results in a compilation error.

The compiler would not generate an error in FORTRAN in the following program:

```
PROGRAM PRO
PRINT *, FUNC(5.3)
STOP
END
FUNCTION FUNC(L)
FUNC=L+5
RETURN
END
```

but the result would be meaningless.

 As stated earlier, I will follow the practice of always giving an identifier to the variables of a function's formal argument while it is being declared, even though this not strictly necessary. But it does highlight the meaning of the variables in the argument and makes reading a program easier.

7.2 Function Arguments

I will use the style below to pass variables into a function argument.

(1) If the variable does *not* have to be modified by the function:
    (a) The value is passed, in the case of variables.
    (b) A `const` *reference* is passed in the case of `struct` or `class` type objects.
(2) A *pointer* is always used, if the object must or can be modified by the function.

This option avoids the need to initialize objects of the formal argument every time a function is called, because only the object's address is passed.

Because data structures, or rather, pointers or references to structures, can be passed using a function argument, the number of elements to be put in the argument can be dramatically cut. The code becomes much easier to understand.

In FORTRAN, for example, the number of rows and columns must be provided, as well as the matrix identifier, to pass a matrix using a function argument:

```
CALL SAMPLE(A,M,N)
```

In a language which accepts structures, it would look like this:

```
Sample(A);
```

Now let's analyse some of the characteristics of a function argument which were not looked at in Chapter 5.

Default Argument

The possibility of giving one or several argument variables a default value has been introduced into C++.

Variables automatically assume the default value, if they are not given any value in actual arguments, when functions are called.

The value that can be assigned as default must be such that it can be determined at compile time – so it must be a constant or an expression consisting of constants.

Example:

```
int Func(int i,float x=5.,int k=6); // default values in the
                                    // prototype formal argument
......

int s = Func(3); // x=5.k=6 default
int j = Func(4,7.); // k=6 default
int h = Func(5,8.,1); // all three are
                      // given values
```

> Giving variables in a function argument a default value is subject to certain constraints.
>
> (1) Variables with a default argument must be grouped last, so variables with and without a default value cannot be alternated.
> (2) Default values can be assigned either in the function definition or its declaration, *but not both*.

Example:

```
int Func(float x=0.,int i,int j);// NO: default must
                                 // be at the end!
float FuFu(int i=1,float x,int j=3); // NO: default must
                                     // be at the end!
float FiFi(int i=1,float x=2); // NO:
.... //default in the declaration
float FiFi(int i=1,float x=2) // and in the definition
{
statements;
}
```

> Default values should be put in the *declaration* of a function rather than in the *definition*. Putting them in the declaration alone ensures that they can actually be used when the function is called.

Example:

```
int Func(int n); // declaration without default
int FuFu(void) // FuFu uses Func
  {
    return Func(); // error: different prototype
  }
```

```
int Func(int n=0) // default in the definition
   {
   return n;
   }
```

The compiler would generate an error in this example, because the prototype of Func has an int as its argument, whereas Func(void) is called in the function FuFu. The function FuFu cannot be aware that n is assigned a default value in the subsequent definition of Func.

> I believe the following rules should be adhered to:
>
> (1) Always put any default variables you may need to use in the *declaration* of the prototype and never in the definition.
> (2) Never misuse this facility.

Functions with a Variable Number of Arguments

Suppose you wanted to write a generic function for displaying on screen a menu which allows the user to choose from several possible options. The number of elements to be passed to the function cannot be fixed in advance, as the function must be such that it can be used in different situations.

C++ inherited this facility for writing functions with argument lists of variable length from C.

> It has two merits.
>
> (1) You can write generic functions which can be adapted to different requirements. The merit here is that *codes can be reused*, since a particular function, adapted to the specific requirements of a problem, does not need to be written for every new problem. For example, you could write a function, Menu, which accepts an indefinite number of options to choose from – and only that function would be used.
> (2) You can generate *codes which are more compact*, because one function carries out the task for which several functions would otherwise have been needed. For example, if you want to display different kinds of menus, you could use the same function, Menu, again and again, instead of writing one for each particular situation.

There are some constraints on solving this problem and you should follow a few rules.

There are three constraints both in C and in C++.

(1) Variables of an unknown number *must all be of the same type and the type must be known.*
(2) At least one variable must appear in the function argument, before the indeterminate number list.
(3) Information on how many variables there are must be passed.

Pre-defined macros in the header file `<stdarg.h>` have to be used to write functions with lists of variable length. They are: `va_list, va_start, va_arg`.

You should adhere to following rules:

(1) You must include the header file `stdarg.h`.
(2) The function is *defined* as if it were a normal function with two particular details in the formal argument – there must be at least one known type and the argument must end with three full-stops (`...`). The same prototype is used if the function has to be *declared*.
(3) A type `va_list` identifier has to be *defined* in the body of the function. The identifier to be defined is a pointer of type `va_list`.
(4) The correct initial value must be assigned to the pointer, using the other macro `va_start`. The syntax for this is as follows:

`va_start` (identifier pointing to `va_list`, identifier of the last fixed variable)

(5) Accessing the variable arguments is carried out using the third macro `va_arg` which takes two arguments:

variable identifier = `va_arg` (identifier pointing to `va_list`, variable type of the variable list).

(6) The end of the list is determined, assigning as the last element a value which can be recognized as such – for example, by using an empty string, `""`, when strings are passed. A better option is to put the number of terms in the list at its head. A third option, which is valid with formatted strings, will be considered when sending error messages is discussed (see Chapter 8).
(7) The pointer to `va_list` can be released using the macro `va_end` with the syntax:

`va_end` (pointer to `va_list`);

Let's take as an example writing a function for a menu of variable length which you want to display.

```cpp
#include <stdarg.h>
#include <iostream.h>
int Menu(char *optionFirst ...); // declares
                                 // the function
void main(void)
    {
                    // ends with 0
    int choice = Menu("Open","Close","Quit",0);
    cout<< "\n The option is:"<<choice;
    }
int Menu(char *optionFirst...)
    {
    va_list argumentList; // defines argumentList
    va_start(argumentList,optionFirst); // assigns
                    // value to argumentList
    char *option=optionFirst; // initializes option
    int count=0,choice;
    do  // executes loop until 0 is found
        {
        cout<<++count<<"."<<option<<"\n";
        }
    while((option = va_arg(argumentList,char *)) != 0);

    cout<<"\n";
    cin>>choice; // reads choice
    return(choice > 0 && choice <= count) ? choice : 0;
    }
```

Once the program has begun to run, and 2 has been keyed in, the output is:

```
1. Open
2. Close
3. Quit
2
The option is: 2
```

This plus feature of the C language is totally outclassed by the C++ ability to pass one object as an argument.

Variable List in Main

 C++ inherited from C a facility for adding information to the line where a program is called, so that the program itself can use the information.

Calling a program which automatically opens a specific application file is a typical example of this:

```
word myfile.doc
```

To understand how to construct a program which can exploit information added by the user when the program is called, you have to see which declaration of main is in one of its overloaded versions:

```
int main(int argc,char **argv);
```

The variables in the argument are initialized as below, when a program is called with the identifier constructed by the compiler with the extension .exe, followed by a list of information separated by a white-space character:

argc gives the number of pieces of information passed;
argv[0] contains the program's name;
argv[1] contains the first piece of information after the program's name;

The process is carried on up to argv[argc-1]. Remember that a vector sized n begins with [0] and ends with [n-1].

 Each element of the vector argv[i] contains a string of variable length, which depends on the information transmitted. Each string can then be manipulated as appropriate in the main.
It must be emphasized that the user must know in which order the various arguments to be used in the main are to be passed.

Suppose the program is progr.exe. The call could look like this:

```
progr filein.dat fileout.ris 77
```

Four strings are passed in this example. The main can manipulate them in order to use argv[1] to open an input file, argv[2] to open an output file, argv[3] to initialize an type int variable. C++'s library functions can be used to carry out these operations. For example, the function atoi is used to convert the string argv[3] = "77" into the number int 77:

```
int k = atoi(argv[3]);
```

A single piece of information in a program call consisting of two words is treated as if it were two separate pieces of information.
It should be remembered that every blank character separates one piece of information from another.

7.3   Inline Functions

Suppose that you wanted to search for the maximum value between x and y in a particular program. You can solve the problem by using the ternary operator ?:. The following would be obtained:

```
x > y ? x : y;
```

Alternatively, you can define a function which searches for the maximum value of two float type variables:

```
float Max(float x,float y)
    {
    return (x > y ? x : y);
    }
```

The alternatives would appear in the program as follows:

```
float max1 = x > y ? x : y;
float max2 = Max(x,y);
```

 Using a function instead of an explicitly written statement has a number of advantages in a situation like this.

(1)   It makes reading the program easier, in that the choice of function identifier highlights the purpose of the operation.

(2)   If you want to modify something to improve operational efficiency or for other reasons, the modification is situated in the function's body, and you do not need to search for all the possible applications.

(3)   Good programming requires functions which can be reused and which do not need to be rewritten when they are required again in other programs.

(4)   The type of variable involved can be checked. Errors of usage would be picked up by the compiler.

(5)   It is guaranteed that the function will be identical in all applications.

(6)   Expressions can also be used as the function's actual argument. There are no side-effects, as only the resulting numeric value is passed.

But using a normal function would have one disadvantage, when the number of statements involved is very small (just one statement in the example), and the operations are very simple. There is a penalty in terms of calculation speed, as function call and data transfer time have to be added on. Of course, the additional time is negligible, if the function is called only infrequently. But the increase in calculation time can be substantial, if the function is called a great number of times in an iterative cycle.

> In C++, you can enjoy all the advantages of a function and avoid the disadvantage outlined above, by introducing `inline` functions.
> A function is considered as `inline` if the keyword `inline` is used when it is defined.

Example of defining an `inline` function:

```
inline float Max(float x,float y)
    {
    return (x > y ? x : y);
    }
```

The compiler does not treat functions in the usual way, if it finds the keyword `inline` in the function definition: it substitutes the statements which go to make up a function for the function call. The code which results is similar to the result that would be obtained by directly writing the statements, instead of the function.

For example, the statement:

```
float max2 = Max(x,y);
```

is elaborated by the compiler as something like this:

```
float xx=x,yy=y;
float max2 = xx > yy ? xx : yy;
```

Working on auxiliary variables `xx` and `yy`, rather than directly on `x` and `y`, has the advantages outlined below, when `x`, or `y`, or both are expressions.

(1)   The expressions are calculated only once.

(2)   If in calculating an expression a variable is modified by a preceding calculation, the result is just as correct, because the expression is calculated only once, and its numeric equivalent is being worked on. Side-effects can thus be avoided.

> `inline` functions should not be abused. Indeed, if `inline` functions contain numerous statements, the size of the code increases, while a negligible amount of calculation time is saved.
>
> *cont.*

> *cont.*
>
> Do take account of the fact that there is no guarantee a function defined as `inline` will actually be developed as `inline`. The compiler decides whether or not to do this.

C and, consequently, C++ provide an alternative to `inline` functions – defining *macros*, which the pre-compiler then elaborates. C++'s `inline` functions provide a better solution, for two reasons:

(1)   Because they are functions, the type of variable involved can be controlled.

(2)   Macros can have side-effects which are well known to programmers working with C.

> So macros should never be used and functions should be substituted for them. Only functions with one or, at most, two statements should be defined `inline`.

> `inline` functions do not behave like other functions, as far as FILE scope and the distinction between definitions and declarations are concerned. An `inline` function is static by *default* and is thus only defined in the file in which it is defined. If you want to use an `inline` function, its definition must be repeated in all of those files.

> The most logical and simple solution is to define the function `inline` in a header file and include it wherever the function is needed.

7.4   Function Overloading

A drawback of procedural languages is that functions with the same identifier cannot be defined for the same type of operations, when different types of variable are involved.

> A new and fundamentally important idea has arisen in object-oriented languages – *polymorphism*. The term denotes that identical messages can be sent to different types of object which react characteristically and in conformity with their nature. The concept of polymorphism will be fully developed only in reference to real objects (see Chapter 14).

FORTRAN 77 was, perhaps, the first language, albeit a procedural one, to move in this direction. In comparison to FORTRAN IV, it was a step forward and it is underlined here, because it has not received due recognition. Indeed, many functions which are *intrinsic* to FORTRAN 77 – such as SIN-, COS-, TAN-, and so on – can use different types of data, while retaining the same name. The great limitation of FORTRAN 77 is that polymorphism stops there. And users cannot define their own overloaded functions.

In C++, you can overload function identifiers, so that one identifier is used for functions which operate with different types of variables. It is a crude but very useful form of polymorphism.

Suppose you want to find the maximum value between two numbers – of type float, double, int, char, long, or of a new, user-defined type. Each of these functions would need to be given a different identifier in a procedural language. For example: MaxFloat, MaxInt, MaxDouble.

It is much better to define a single identifier, Max, for example, and, depending on the variables in the argument, leave selection of the right function to the compiler.

Example:

```
float Max(float x,float y)
    {
    statements;
    }
double Max(double x,double y)
    {
    statements;
    }
int Max(int x,int y)
    {
    statements;
    }
void main(void)
    {
    double xd=10.,yd=7.;
    float xf=4.,yf=3.;
    int xi=9,yi=0;
    float f=Max(xf,yf); // use Max(float,float)
    int i=Max(xi,yi); // use Max(int,int)
    double d=Max(xd,yd); // use Max(double,double)
    }
```

Function overloading is a boon which stems from the strong type control of C++.

cont.

> *cont.*
> Exploiting the opportunities that it offers results in programs which are both easy to read and to write. And you do not need a host of identifiers which are both difficult to remember and – particularly in FORTRAN – to decode.

You should stick to a few rules, in order to be able to overload two or more functions.

> Overloading the identifiers of two or more functions requires each identifier to be *distinguishable* from the others, *either* because the *number* of variables in the argument is different, *or* because at least one of them is of a different *type*. The compiler flags an error if it finds any application which is not clear; if, that is, it does not manage clearly to select an alternative.
> So function overloading does not really break the rule which prohibits the same identifier in the same scope for an item of the same category (see Chapter 6). Functions with the same identifier, but with different arguments, are different functions as far as the compiler is concerned.

Example:

```
float Max(float x,float y); // arguments
double Max(double x,double y);// of different type

int Func(int i);// different number of variables
float Func(int i,float x);// in the argument
```

> Two functions with different `returns` are *not* overloaded and are *not* accepted by compilers.

Example:

```
int Func(int i,float x);
unsigned int Func(int j,float y); // error
```

> Two functions with different scopes (see Chapter 6) but the same identifier *are not overloaded; one hides the other*. It does not matter that the arguments are the same or not. It is possible to use a hidden function through the scope operator, if it can be accessed (see Chapter 14).

Example:

```
int Func(int i,float x);
class Demo
```

```
{
float Func(int i, float x); // not overloaded
...                          // but hides global
};
```

The `Func` class member is used inside `class` Demo. If the one with global scope is to be used, `::Func(i,x);` has to be written.

> Remember that an identifier declared with `typedef` *does not* create a new data type. It simply provides an *alternative name* for an already existing type. It follows that substituting an identifier, which is declared equivalent to that type by using a `typedef`, is *insufficient* to overload two functions' identifiers.

Example:

```
typedef int Integer; // Integer is equivalent to int
int Func(int i,float x);
void Func(Integer j,float y); // error
```

> If two functions have the same identifier and can be distinguished only by the different number of argument variables, but the values of the excess variables of the function which has most variables are default, the functions are not recognized as different in applications in which they are given only non-default values.

Example:

```
int Func(int i,float x);
int Func(int j,float x,int k=2);
....
int k=Func(3,1.,4); // OK use the second one
int w=Func(2,5.); // error: ambiguity
```

> I will not assign default values to variables, when one function is overloaded with another. This means that confusion over which function is actually being used and, consequently, a possible source of errors are avoided.

7.5 Function Pointers

Remember (see Chapter 5) that a function identifier is a constant pointer and, being constant, cannot be modified. However, it can be useful in some circumstances to have a *variable function pointer*. A definition like this:

```
float *Func(int i)
    {
    statements;
    }
```

is wrong. The meaning of this definition, as already shown in Chapter 6, is as follows:

(a)	identifier Func	Func
(b)	is a function	Func(int i)
(c)	the return of which is a pointer to a type float variable	*Func(int i) float *Func(int i)

Precedence between the function operator and the unary operator * must be switched using brackets to define a variable function pointer.

A correct definition is as follows:

```
float (*pointFunc)(int i);
```

Now pointFunc is a variable function pointer with a float type return.

> *Beware*: a variable function pointer is *not* a function. *You must not use the function's body when the variable function pointer is defined.* Once a variable function pointer has been defined, it can be assigned any function address *as long as they have the same argument and the same type of* return.
>
> A variable function pointer can also be initialized – it can be assigned a value as soon as it has been defined. The keyword extern must be used in the declaration of a variable function pointer.

Example:

```
float Func(int i)
    {
    statements;
    }
float (*pointFunc)(int i ) = Func; // define pointFunc
        // and initialize it with Func's address
```

or:

```
float (*pointFunc)(int i); // define pointFunc
pointFunc= Func; // assign it Func's address
```

Note that a function call through a pointer can be in an explicit form:

(*<pointer identifier>) (actual argument);

or in a contracted form:

<pointer identifier> (actual argument);

The contracted form of function invocation uses syntax which is the same as in normal function calls.

Example:

```
float Func(int i)
    {
    statements;
    }
....
float (*ptrFunc)(int i) = Func; // pointer to Func
float x;
x = (*ptrFunc)(3); // explicit form
x = ptrFunc(3);    // contracted form
x = Func(3);       // syntactically the same
```

Variable function pointers are useful for writing general programs which can be reused with different functions and so solve a variety of problems.

Variable function pointers are used mainly in two situations.

(1) *To pass a function name as the argument of other functions.*
It is possible to develop a general algorithm with this device, leaving indeterminate the name of the function to which the algorithm is to be applied. This situation occurs again and again in numerical problems – you only have to think of optimization programs and solving algebraic or differential equations. In all such cases, the algorithm used is always the same, but the function to which it is applied varies. Thus, all you have to do is define a variable function pointer in the argument of the function which implements the algorithm. If the algorithm is required for a specific function, the general function is called, using the identifier in the argument (that is, the address) of the specific function.
For example, in the function FindMax, which has the following prototype:

```
float FindMax(float (*pointFuncMax)(float x),
                  <list of other variables>);
```

an algorithm has been implemented for univariate maximization. Now, the maximum value of a particular function `MyFuncMax` needs to be found. The prototype of this function must coincide as arguments and returns with the definition of the pointer `pointFuncMax`:

```
float MyFuncMax(float x);
```

The following statement is all that is required to use the function FindMax:

```
float xmax;
xmax = FindMax(MyFuncMax,<list of other variables>);
```

(2) *To be able to assign different function names to a single variable pointer and then to use it for the rest of the program.*
Suppose you have a program that employs a library of similar (that is, with the same prototype) function, of which only one is needed at a time. And suppose that the user selects a particular function from the library and that it is used on different occasions during the program. A `switch` has to be inserted every time one of these functions is invoked.

> This approach has two drawbacks.
>
> (1) The code becomes difficult to read and considerably larger as the number of sparse `switch`es increases.
> (2) If you want to introduce a new function not included in the library, the whole program has to be revised and all the `switch`es found and modified. It is highly likely that you will make a mistake.

If a variable function pointer is used, you can write a more efficient code. The point in the program at which the function is to be selected can be determined. At that point, a function pointer is assigned a function identifier, which is selected with a `switch`, and from that point of the program onwards a variable function pointer. Using this approach, you only need one `switch`. And that part of the code which has to be changed, should the function library need to be modified, is confined to this `switch` point.

A vector of variable function pointers can be created as an alternative to a local `switch`, and the vector's index can be used to select the appropriate function. This means there will be no more `switch`es in the program.

> In fact, you can define a vector of variable function pointers.
> For example:
>
> ```
> void (*pointFuncVec[NMAX])(void);
> ```

The definition means: pointFuncVec is a vector of NMAX size of function pointers with a void type return.

As an application, let's exploit a vector of function pointers to select a function, with the selection occurring in the program call (see *variable argument* of main, discussed earlier).

```
// Prototypes
void Func1(void);
void Func2(void);
void Func3(void);

// include necessary for function library
#include <stdio.h>
#include <stdlib.h>
#include <conio.h>

int main(int argc,char **argv)
    {
    const int NUM_FUNC = 3;
    const int NMAX =NUM_FUNC + 1;// to leave from 1
     // vector of function pointers
    void (*pointFuncVec[NMAX])(void);
     // assignments
    pointFuncVec[1] = Func1;
    pointFuncVec[2] = Func2;
    pointFuncVec[3] = Func3;
    (*pointFuncVec[atoi(argv[1])])();// explicit form
    // or
    // pointFuncVec[atoi(argv[1])](); // contracted form
    return 0;
    }
// Func1, Func2, Func3 defined
.....
```

If the compiled program is called prog.exe, the following call is used to execute it with function 3.

```
prog 3
```

The meaning of the expression:

```
(*pointFunzVec[atoi(argv[1])])();
```

is as follows. The string argv[1] is transformed into an integer:

```
atoi(argv[1])
```

using the library function `atoi`. The number becomes the function pointer vector's argument, which was initialized with the various functions at an earlier point. The function `Func3` is executed.

 Using a variable function pointer to avoid `switches` in a program is a crude form of polymorphism. Only one identifier is used during the program to solve problems in a variety of situations.

C++ also uses a technique which is much more effective and which is made possible by two characteristics of object-oriented programming: *inheritance* and *virtual functions* (see Chapter 14).

7.6　Generic Functions

Many algorithms do not depend on the types being manipulated. For example, sorting and searching can be applied to all data types, such as `int`, `float`, `double`, strings and `struct` objects.

 Two of C++'s features allow you to write functions for handling data of any type.

(1)　The use of `void *` type pointers which can be converted into object pointers of the type required, whatever that type may be (see Chapter 3).
(2)　The use of variable function pointers which can receive the function address suitable for that type of object.

For the time being, we will not attempt to produce a general-purpose function. Instead, we will only look at how a function which has already been created by others can be used. (Remember that C++ is particularly suitable for using functions, or rather classes, which have already been implemented.)

For example, suppose an efficient function, `Sort`, has been created to order a vector of generic elements. How a particular type of object is used needs to be known before `Sort` can be used.

`Sort` is declared as follows:

```
typedef int (*CompareType)
            (void *element1,void *element2);
void Sort(void *data,int numElements,int elementSize,
          CompareType CompareFunc);
```

The items in the argument mean:

void *data is the address of the beginning of the vector that needs to be ordered. Because it is of void * type it can accept the address of any type of object;
int numElements is the number of elements in the vector;
int elementSize is the size of an element in the vector;
CompareType CompareFunc is the function with which you can ascertain which is the larger and which the smaller of two elements. Because a typedef has been used, the function is equivalent to:
int (*CompareFunc)(void *element1,void *element2);
CompareFunc is function pointer with a return of type int. The argument consists of two void * pointers on the elements which are to be compared.

The way Sort was implemented means that the return of CompareFunc must be equal to 1, if the content of element1 is less than that of element2. If the opposite is true, the return must be 0.
Which function should be used for comparison when a float vector is involved?

```
int CompareFloat(void *element1,void *element2)
   {
   return *((float *)element1) < *((float *)element2);
   }
```

Below is an analysis of the function's return statement.

((float *)element1) executes a conversion (*cast*) of the pointer and coerces it into becoming a float (see Chapter 2).
*((float *)element1) is the content of the storage to which element1 is pointing.
The return is 1, if *((float *)element1) < *((float *)element2) is true; if not, it is 0.
Suppose you want the vector to be ordered:

```
static float vect[]=
   {
   3.,6.,2.,6.,1.,11.,34.,2.,45.
   };
```

The function calling Sort is:

```
Sort((float *)vect,sizeof(vect)/sizeof(vect[0]),
     sizeof(vect[0]),CompareFloat);
```

Notice:

the *cast* `(float*)` to coerce the use of `float` pointers:
`sizeof(vect)/sizeof(vect[0])` in which the first `sizeof` gives the total amount of storage taken up by the vector, and the second the amount taken up by a `float` − a `sizeof(float)` could be used for a simple vector like this.
`sizeof(vect[0])` which is equivalent to `sizeof(float)` gives an element's size;
`CompareFloat` provides the function with which the two `floats` can be compared.

7.7   Library Functions

C++ has a host of pre-defined functions. They can be subdivided into two categories − portable functions, common to all C++ compilers, and particular functions for a compiler on a specific kind of computer.

It is essential to know the portability of each function, its syntax, the header file that must be included, and, of course, its intended purpose.

Such information can be found in manuals on compilers or in specific literature.

> Mathematical functions require the header file `<math.h>`, which must be included in every program based on numerical calculation.

Example:

```
#include <math.h>
#include <iostream.h>
main()
    {
    cout << exp(3.);
    return 0;
    }
```

Input/Output functions

One of the major obstacles to using a language efficiently is learning how to master the functions of data input/output.
You should bear in mind two basic aspects of the problem.

(1)   You need to exploit special functions available in the language to write efficient codes. For example, many C++ compilers have a wide selection of video functions, enabling you to create professional screens quickly. The

problem is the same for reading and writing certain kinds of data in files. Consequently the number of special functions is very large.

(2) Functions dedicated to managing interfaces are affected by the environment in which they are used – DOS, OS/2, UNIX, MACINTOSH and so on. For example, if data needs to be written in a *file*, the *file* must be assigned a name which follows the conventions of the system in which it is used. Even special and particularly efficient video functions are specific to the system in which they were created. That part of the code which interfaces with the outside world depends on the system and cannot be ported from one system to another.

> Since we are on the subject of data input/output, let's have a look at one or two special situations which are important when it comes to numerical problems. I will refer to DOS as the environment. But the differences between it and other environments, in terms of the problems which are analysed below, are minimal. The situations are:
>
> (1) Reading and writing numerical data (int and float), formatted to produce an ASCII file that can be read by a normal word processor.
> (2) Reading and writing blocks of numerical data to produce a binary file.

Formatted Data

We have already seen that you can read numerical data from the keyboard or write them on the screen using the operators cin >> and cout <<.

The procedure is very simple.

(1) Include the header file <iostream.h>.

(2) Use the following statement to read a number (int, float or double):

```
cin >> var;
```

(3) Use the following to write a numerical value to the screen:

```
cout << var;
```

The same result can be produced using the dedicated C functions scanf and printf. The procedure in this case is as follows:

(1) include the header file <stdio.h>.

(2) to read an integer, i:

```
scanf("%d",&i); // remember &
```

by contrast, to read a `float, var`:

```
scanf("%f",&var); // remember &
```

(3)   to write an `int, i` and a `float, var`:

```
printf("%d %f",i,var);
```

> Important points:
>
> (1)   Both `scanf` and `printf` accept a variable number of arguments.
> (2)   The functions are divided into two parts – in the first, the reading or printing statements are enclosed in `""`; in the second, the variable identifiers are listed.
> (3)   The variable identifiers in the function `scanf` must be preceded by `&` because it requires the addresses of those variables.

Comments can be inserted between the `""` in `printf`.
Example:

```
printf("Value of i=%d and of var= %f",i,var);
```

Depending on the type of variable you want to read or write, you have to use a special symbol, preceded by `%` – for example, `%d` for an `int` and `%f` for a `float`. Consult a C manual to find out more about the possible variants.

To write data which is formatted in a file, you can choose between functions available in C, or a C++ procedure, similar to the one above.

Here, we will only look at the C procedure.

The two functions under consideration are `fprintf` and `fscanf`. The new and important point here is having to open and close the *file* to which you want to read and write.

Let's look at a practical example – writing a vector:

```
#include <stdio.h>
void main(void)
   {
   const int n = 5;
   static vect[n]=
      {1.,2.,3.,4.,5.}
   FILE *fptr; // pointer to FILE
   fptr = fopen("TEXTFILE.TXT","w"); // w to write
   if(fptr == 0) // control
      {
```

```
            fprintf(stderr,"Can't open file TEXTFILE.TXT");
            exit(1);
            }
      fprintf(fptr," %d\n",n); // writes n
      for(i=0;i < n; i++) // writes coefficients
      fprintf(fptr," %f",vect[i]);
      fclose(fptr); // closes file
      }
```

Important points.

(1)   A pointer to FILE has to be created.
(2)   The pointer is assigned a value returned by the function fopen, which contains the file name associated with the pointer.
(3)   "w" is used, because data is to be written to the file.
(4)   It's a good idea to check whether the file can be opened without difficulty. If fopen returns 0 (NULL), problems arise and it is advisable to stop by sending a message to the *standard error file*, stderr.

The function fprintf is entirely the same as printf, except for the use of the FILE pointer.

When printing has finished, the file is closed with the library function fclose. To read the vector:

```
#include <stdio.h>
void main(void)
    {
    FILE *fptr; // FILE pointer
    fptr = fopen("TEXTFILE.TXT","r"); // r for read
    if(fptr == 0) // control
        {
        fprintf(stderr,"Can't open file TEXTFILE.TXT");
        exit(1);
        }
    fscanf(fptr," %d\n",&n); // remember &
    float *vect = new float[n]; // size vect
    for(i=0;i < n; i++)
    fscanf(fptr," %f",&vect[i]); // remember &
    ...
    delete vect;
    fclose(fptr);
    }
```

Important points.

(1)   "r" is put in the file opening function, because you want the *file* to be read.
(2)   The vector is sized dynamically to the exact size required.
(3)   The addresses of variables that are to be read must be used in fscanf.

C and C++ have some pre-defined FILE pointer identifiers which do not require the use of fopen.

They are:

stdin	*standard input device*	keyboard
stdout	*standard output device*	screen
stderr	*standard error device*	screen
stdprn	*standard printing device*	printer

Example:

```
fprintf(stdout,"This appears on screen");
```

It has already been mentioned that "w" must be used for writing a file and "r" for reading. The possible combinations are as follows:

"r"   Read only. The file must already exist.

"w"   Write only. If the file exists, its contents are deleted. If not, a file is created.

"a"   Write only. If the file exists, its contents are saved and the new data added at the end of the file If not, a file is created.

"r+"   Read and write. The file must already exist.

"w+"   Read and write. If the file exists, its contents are deleted. If not, a file is created.

"a+"   Read and write. If a file exists, its contents are saved and the new data added at the end of the file If not, a file is created.

Non-formatted, binary data

Numerical data can be read by any word processor, provided that it is written in a *formatted file,* using, for example, the function fprintf, as it is written as an ASCII file. So data can easily be ported from one environment to another, or from one compiler to another.

Reading and writing large blocks of data (vectors or matrices for example) to files will create difficulties if the blocks are treated as formatted data.

Reading and writing to formatted files has two big drawbacks.

(1) A number takes up much more space, because it has to be stored as a list of characters.
(2) The data are read and written one at a time rather than in one single block.

It is a good idea to treat large numbers of numerical data in the form in which the computer uses them.

C and C++ have some very efficient and, above all, extremely versatile functions for reading and writing blocks of data: vectors, matrices, structures, vectors of structures and matrices of structures.
And particular parts of blocks of data can be accessed to read or correct them.

Reading and writing non-formatted data means you have to:

(1) add b (for binary) to r, w, when the file is opened.
(2) use other types of functions: fread, and fwrite.

You want to write the same vector as before, but non-formatted:

```
#include <stdio.h>
void main(void)
    {
    const int n = 5;
    static vect[n]=
        {1.,2.,3.,4.,5.}
    FILE *fptr; // FILE pointer
    fptr = fopen("TEXTFILE.BIN","wb"); // b binary
    if(fptr == 0) // control
        {
        fprintf(stderr,"Can't open file TEXTFILE.BIN");
        exit(1);
        }
    if(fwrite(&n,sizeof(int),1,fptr) != 1)
        {
        fprintf(stderr,"Can't write in TEXTFILE.BIN");
        exit(1);
        }
```

```
if(fwrite(vect,sizeof(float)*n,1,fptr) != 1)
    {
    fprintf(stderr,"Can't write in TEXTFILE.BIN");
    exit(1);
    }
fclose(fptr);
}
```

Important points.

(1) The file is opened with `"wb"` and the data is written in binary and non-formatted form.
(2) The function `fwrite` is used instead of `fprintf`.
(3) `fwrite`'s syntax is: address of the start of the block, size of block, number of blocks of that size, FILE pointer.
(4) The block's size is calculated using the operator `sizeof`.
(5) The function passes back the number of blocks which it has successfully written. In the above example, a check is made on whether writing a data block was successfully executed.

To read the vector back in:

```
#include <stdio.h>
void main(void)
    {
    FILE *fptr; // FILE pointer
    fptr = fopen("TEXTFILE.BIN","rb"); // b binary
    if(fptr == 0) // check
        {
        fprintf(stderr, "Can't open file TEXTFILE.BIN");
        exit(1);
        }
    if(fread(&n,sizeof(int),1,fptr) != 1)
        {
        fprintf(stderr,"Can't read in TEXTFILE.BIN");
        exit(1);
        }
    float *vect = new float [n];
    if(fread(vect,sizeof(float)*n,1,fptr) != 1)
        {
        fprintf(stderr,"Can't read in TEXTFILE.BIN");
        exit(1);
        }
```

```
...
delete vect;
fclose(fptr);
}
```

7.8   Questions

Which of the following declarations is incorrect?

```
void Func(float x=3.,int i=2);        // a
float Func(float x);                  // b
float Func(int i=0,float x);          // c
float Func(float x,int i);            // d
void Func(float x,int i,float y=0.);  // e
```

a and d cannot be overloaded because they differ only by the return.

c because the default must be at the end.

b cannot be used because it is ambiguous in relation to a.

It is better not to define a function like e which could become ambiguous in relation to a.

Which of the following definitions is wrong?

```
void Func(int i){statements;}
void *Func(int i){statements;}
void (*Func)(int i){statements;}
```

The last one. A pointer, rather than a function is being defined, so it should not have the body of a function.

What is the output of the following program, compiled with the identifier lastname.exe and called with: lastname Buzzi Ferraris?

```
#include <iostream.h>
int main(int argc,char **argv)
    {
    cout << argv[1];
    return 0;
    }
```

Only Buzzi would be written, because Ferraris is separated by a blank character and stored in argv[2].

7.9   Examples

As the last example of functions with an unspecified number of arguments, a function will be written which searches for the highest number in a variable number of int.

```cpp
#include <stdarg.h>
#include <iostream.h>
int Max(int numVar,char *message,...); // declaration
void main(void)
    {
    int big=Max(3,"Highest number of 5,1,7 is",5,1,7);
    cout<< big;
     return 0;
    }
int Max(int numVar,char *message,...)
    {
    cout<<message;
    va_list pointList; // pointList pointer to va_list
    // assigns value to pointList
    va_start(pointList,message);
    int x,max;
    max = va_arg(pointList,int);
    for(int i = 2;i <= numVar;i++)
        {
                // va_arg needs to know that its actual
                // argument is int type
        x = va_arg(pointList,int)
        if(x > max)max = x;
        }
    va_end(pointList);
    return max;
    }
```

The execution of the program produces the following output:

```
The highest number of 5.,1.,7. is: 7.
```

Setting up a Program Library for Scientific Use

And here Alice began to get rather sleepy, and went on saying to herself, in a dreamy sort of way, 'Do cats eat bats? Do cats eat bats?' and sometimes 'Do bats eat cats?' for, you see, as she couldn't answer either question, it didn't much matter which way she put it.

Lewis Carroll, *Alice's Adventures in Wonderland.*

8.1   Introduction

It is not the aim of this book to explain numerical methods, but to demonstrate how object-oriented programming is able to solve classic numerical problems through a newer approach.

The purpose of this chapter is to lay the basis for building a numerical library in the object-oriented way. Chapters 12, 13 and 15 will develop the topic.

Developing a scientific math library, it is worthwhile to group together:

(1)   elementary but fundamental functions and objects;

(2)   variables which depend on the working environment.

We are not yet in a position to consider creating objects. So this chapter will describe that part of a basic library which requires no objects, just procedural programming.

Useful functions and constants, along with variables which depend on the working environment, have been grouped together in two files: a header file for declarations and a file for definitions. Their respective file names are: `UTILITY.HPP` and `UTILITY.CPP`.

In `UTILITY.HPP` and `UTILITY.CPP` you can find:

(1) Global type numerical constants, which depend on the working environment, and three general-purpose variables.

(2) An error messages function.

(3) A function for sending messages.

(4) A few, very short `inline` functions, which exploit identifier overloading.

(5) A few functions for controlling overflow, swapping variables and searching for the largest and smallest elements in vectors.

(6) A few functions for adding, subtracting and multiplying `float` vectors.

(7) A function for efficiently calculating the square root of the sum of the squares of a `float` vector, and a function for a `double` vector.

(8) A function for sorting `float` vectors.

(9) A class for creating distinct file identifiers. (See Chapter 10 for a description of this class.) The class is defined in these files, as some of its parts depend on the working environment.

Examples of applications of the functions described in this chapter can be found in the file `EXUTY.CPP`.

8.2   Constants and Global Variables

In the file `UTILITY.CPP`. are the following definitions:

(1)   Two identifiers for using files in I/O:

```
FILE *bzzFileOut = stdout;
FILE *bzzFileIn = stdin;
```

These identifiers are frequently used inside other functions and objects. For example, the function `Message` uses `bzzFileOut`. The two pointers are initialized with the *standard input* and *output devices*. Since the identifiers are defined with a global scope, they can be accessed by every file which includes

UTILITY.HPP. Users can, if they so desire, change the files they point to anywhere in the program – for example, to send messages to any particular files that are different from *standard* files.

(2)   The variable bzzYesNo:

```
char bzzYesNo = 'Y';
```

which is used to enable and disable print messages.

(3)   We have already discussed the computer precision, MACH_EPS, (see Chapter 2) and seen how it can be calculated. MACH_EPS is a constant and so it is defined with the const modifier. Furthermore, it can be used anywhere in the program, because it is global.

```
const float MACH_EPS = MachEps();
```

The function MachEps, which is necessary for the calculation, is defined in the same file.

(4)   The maximum and minimum values of each variable type in the DOS environment are defined in the same file:

```
const float BIG_FLOAT =                         3.4e+38;
const float TINY_FLOAT =                        3.4e-38;
const double BIG_DOUBLE =                       1.7e+308;
const double TINY_DOUBLE =                      8.e-307;
const long double BIG_LONG_DOUBLE =             3.4e+4932;
const long double TINY_LONG_DOUBLE =            3.4e-4932;
const char BIG_CHAR =                               127;
const char TINY_CHAR =                             -128;
const unsigned char BIG_UNSIGNED_CHAR =            255;
const unsigned char TINY_UNSIGNED_CHAR =             0;
const int BIG_INT =                              32767;
const int TINY_INT =                            -32768;
const unsigned int BIG_UNSIGNED_INT =            65535;
const unsigned int TINY_UNSIGNED_INT =               0;
const long int BIG_LONG =                   2147483647;
const long int TINY_LONG =                 -2147483648;
const unsigned long int BIG_UNSIGNED_LONG =  4294967295;
const unsigned long int TINY_UNSIGNED_LONG =          0;
```

All the constants are also declared (with the keyword extern and with no initializations) in UTILITY.HPP, so that any other file which includes it can use them.

8.3 Errors and Messages

Errors and messages can be managed in a variety of ways, one of which is to create an *object* dedicated to this purpose. The right approach, in my opinion, is a *procedural* one, defining the two functions Error and Message. Both functions exploit the opportunity offered in C++ of using a variable number of arguments. The function Error differs from the function Message in *three* respects:

(1)   the message is sent to the *standard* error file stderr;

(2)   the message is always sent;

(3)   the program is interrupted.

     Conversely, in the function Message:

(1)   users can choose the file to which they want to send the message, giving bzzFileOut a different name to the default (the default file is the standard file for message output: stdout);

(2)   users can disable the print message by having the global value of bzzYesNo equal to 'N' (its default value is equal to 'Y');

(3)   the program continues after the message has been sent.

The definitions of the two functions are:

```
//   ********************< Error >********************
//   * Purpose: Send error messages to file stderr      *
//   * Description: As for Message, but stop the program *
//   * Example: if(x < 1) Error("x = %f",x);             *
//   ****************************************************
void Error(char *myFormat,...)
   {
   va_list argPointer;
   va_start(argPointer,myFormat);
   vfprintf(stderr,myFormat,argPointer);
   va_end(argPointer);
   exit(1);
   }


//   ********************< Message >********************
//   * Purpose: Send messages to FILE bzzFileOut       *
//   * Description: To be used like printf             *
//   *              Do not stop the program            *
//   *              To disable it bzzYesNo = 'N'        *
//   *              To enable it bzzYesNO = 'Y' (default)*
//   * Example: Message("Longlive n. %d",3);           *
//   ****************************************************
```

```
void Message(char *myFormat,...)
   {
   if(bzzYesNo != 'Y')return;
   va_list argPointer;
   va_start(argPointer,myFormat);
   vfprintf(bzzFileOut,myFormat,argPointer);
   va_end(argPointer);
   }
```

Messages for the most common errors have been defined to make using the two functions easier.

All error message identifiers begin with ERR_. Both pointers and content have been made const in the definition of the messages, so that neither can be corrupted.

```
//========== Error Type ==============
const char *const ERR_RANGE=
     "\nIndex out of range\n";
const char *const ERR_SPACE=
     "\nNo room in heap\n";
const char *const ERR_OPEN_FILE=
     "\nImpossible to open FILE\n";
const char *const ERR_CLOSE_FILE=
     "\nImpossible to close FILE\n";
const char *const ERR_READING_FILE=
     "\nImpossible to read FILE\n";
const char *const ERR_WRITING_FILE=
     "\nImpossible to write FILE\n";
const char *const ERR_CHECK_DIMENSION=
     "\nDimension check failure\n";
const char *const ERR_OUT_OF_SCOPE=
     "\nOut of Scope\n";
const char *const ERR_FACTORIZED=
     "\nFactorized Matrix\n";
const char *const ERR_IMPLEMENTATION=
     "\nFunction not implemented\n";

//============ Function Type =============
const char *const ERR_FUNCTION="\nFunction: ";
const char *const ERR_CONSTRUCTOR="\nConstructor: ";
const char *const ERR_OPERATOR="\nOperator: ";
```

The same rules as for the library function printf should be followed to use the two functions.

Example:

```
// all you have to put not to print messages is
// bzzYesNo = 'N';
// at any point of the program
if(x > 10.)
    Message("The value of x is:  %f",x);
if(i < 1)
Error("\nIn %sFunSample%s",ERR_FUNCTION,ERR_RANGE);
```

8.4   Commonly Used Inline Functions

Absolute Value of a Variable: Abs

A function which computes the absolute value of a variable is commonly used. Unfortunately, C++ took from C functions with identifiers that are different, depending on the variable involved in the operation (in C, functions cannot be overloaded). If you do not use the right function, errors which are difficult to detect may occur.

For example, you want to check whether the absolute value of a variable, x, of type float, is larger than an assigned quantity. You carry out the test below:

```
if(abs(x) > .0001)
.......
else
......
```

Since the function abs, which is valid for int, is being used instead of fabs, which is valid for float, the compiler does *not* produce an error because it can change a float into an int. But in changing float into int, x is equal to 0 when it is less than 1. The test is executed incorrectly and the error cannot easily be detected.

Abs functions have been overloaded in UTILITY.HPP to obtain the absolute value of type int, float and double variables.

```
// **********************< Abs >**********************
// * Purpose: to have one single function for        *
// *             absolute value                       *
// * Description: overload float, int, double         *
// * Example: float x = Abs(y);                        *
// ****************************************************
inline float Abs(float a)
   {return fabs(a);}
inline double Abs(double a)
   {return fabs(a);}
```

```
inline int Abs(int i)
  {return abs(i);}
```

Using this function, the compiler automatically selects the appropriate function for the type which is being used.
Example:

```
int i = -3;
float x = -.007;
int j = Abs(i);
float y = Abs(x);
```

Maximum and Minimum Elements of Variables

The functions for finding the maximum and minimum elements (including absolute values – Max, Min, MaxAbs, MinAbs (see Chapter 7) – have been overloaded and defined inline. The same identifiers are overloaded in other files to search for the largest and smallest elements of vectors or matrices.

8.5   Other Commonly Used Functions

Some of the functions below are very short and could be defined inline.

Overflow Control

I will frequently use the device outlined below to ensure that calculation results do not overflow. Calculations are executed in double and results are limited within float's range of validity. A similar procedure can be adopted by executing calculations in long double, if you want the results in double.

```
// ********************< Control ********************
// * Purpose: To control overflow                   *
// * Description: Can be used for both float and double *
// * Example: float x = Control(y);                  *
// ****************************************************
float Control(double value)
   {
   if(value > BIG_FLOAT)return BIG_FLOAT;
   else if(value < -BIG_FLOAT)return -BIG_FLOAT;
   return value;
   }
double Control(long double value)
```

```
{
if(value > BIG_DOUBLE)return BIG_DOUBLE;
else if(value < -BIG_DOUBLE)return -BIG_DOUBLE;
return value;
}
```

Example:

```
float x[5] = {1.,2.,3.,4.,5.};
float y[5] = {5.,4.,3.,2.,1.};
double s = 0.;
float dot;
for(int i = 0;i < 5;i++)
    s += x[i]*y[i];
dot = Control(s);
```

Swapping Positions: Swap

If you want to swap two variables, for example, two variables x and y of type float, the function you need is (see Chapter 5):

```
Swap(float *x,float *y)
{float temp = *x; *x = *y; *y = temp;}
```

The function Swap is used in the following way:

```
float x = 3.,y = 6.;
Swap(&x,&y);
```

> You can swap two vectors and two matrices simply by exchanging their pointers at the head of the vector or the matrix.
> The same identifier, Swap, will be used to exchange objects, which I will define later – two Vector type or Matrix type objects will be swapped, even though they are different sizes.

For example, to swap one variable pointer for another, the function looks like this:

```
Swap(float **x,float **y)
{float *temp = *x; *x = *y; *y = temp;}
```

The swap functions could even have been written by putting *references* in the arguments instead of *pointers*, in which case the example would have looked like this:

```
Swap(x,y); // instead of Swap(&x,&y);
```

> I chose to swap variable pointers and not references, to stress that variables are modified in value.

Maximum and Minimum Elements of a Vector

The following are functions for finding the maximum and minimum elements of a vector, with the same identifier as the one already used, for the same purpose, where just two variables are involved: `Max`, `Min`, `MaxAbs`, `MinAbs`.

Example:

```
//   ********************< Max >********************
//   * Purpose: Max of array                      *
//   * Description: gives the Max of an array      *
//   *              If the index im is used        *
//   *              it also gives its position     *
//   * Example: y = Max(10,x,im);                  *
//   **********************************************
float Max(int n,float *x,int &im)
   {
   if(n < 0) return x[0];
   float temp = x[0];
   im = 0;
   for(int i = 1;i < n;i++)
     if(temp < x[i])
        { temp = x[i]; im = i; }
   return temp;
   }
```

An index, to which is assigned the default value 0, is used in the argument when the function is declared, since you sometimes want to know the position of the maximum or minimum element. If you are not interested in the position of the maximum element, you call the function omitting that term from the argument. Conversely, if you are interested in it, you call the function with one additional term.

Example:

```
int sizes = 3;
static float vector[3]={2.,5.,1.};
float  x = Max(sizes,vector);
int i;
     // in y the maximum and in i the position
float  y = Max(sizes,vector,i);
```

8.6 Sum, Subtraction and Products of Vectors

These operations are of the utmost importance, because they form the foundation of all numerical calculations. Calculations are carried out in double in all implementations and results are checked before they are changed into float.

There are three functions for vector sum and they share the same identifier, Sum, depending on whether or not the result is overloaded with one of the two vectors. The functions are:

```
//   ************************< Sum >************************
//   * Purpose: Sum of two vectors                        *
//   * Description: Addition of two arrays with check      *
//   * Example: Sum(n,x,y,z); z = x + y;                   *
//   ******************************************************
void Sum(int n,float *lval,float *rval,float *result)
    {
    double sum;
    for(int i=0;i < n;i++)
        {
        sum = (*lval++) + (*rval++);
        *result++ = Control(sum);
        }
    }

//   ************************< Sum >************************
//   * Purpose: Sum of two vectors                        *
//   * Description: Sum is substituted for first vector    *
//   * Example: Sum(n,x,y) x = x + y                       *
//   ******************************************************
void Sum(int n,float *lvalAndResult,float *rval)
    {
    double sum;
    for(int i=0;i < n;i++)
        {
        sum = (*lvalAndResult) + (*rval++);
        *lvalAndResult++ = Control(sum);
        }
    }

//   ************************< Sum >************************
//   * Purpose: Sum of two equal vectors
//                                                         *
//   * Description: Sum is substituted for vector          *
//   * Example: Sum(n,x) x = x + x                         *
//   ******************************************************
```

```
void Sum(int n,float *lvalRvalAndResult)
   {
   double sum;
   for(int i=0;i < n;i++)
      {
      sum = (*lvalRvalAndResult) + (*lvalRvalAndResult);
      *lvalRvalAndResult++ = Control(sum);
      }
   }
```

Similar functions, Difference, are valid for the difference between vectors. The function for calculating the product of two vectors is:

```
// ***********************< Dot >***********************
// * Purpose: Dot product of two vectors              *
// * Example: float c = Dot(n,x,y);                   *
// ****************************************************
float Dot(int n,float *lval,float *rval)
   {
   double result = 0.;
   for(int i=0;i < n;i++)
      result += (*lval++) * (*rval++);
   return Control(result);
   }
```

Apart from the functions mentioned above, there are others for scaling a vector (that is, for multiplying or dividing it by a float) – Product and Division.

```
// ********************< Product >********************
// * Purpose: Product of a float multiplied by a vector *
// * Description: Multiplies n terms of vector          *
// *                 v by c the result in r             *
// * Example: Product(n,c,v,r)                          *
// ****************************************************
void Product(int n,float lval,float *rval,float *result)
   {
   for(int i=0;i < n;i++)
      *result++ = Control(lval * (*rval++));
   }
```

```
// ********************< Product>********************
// * Purpose: Product of a float multiplied by a vector *
// * Description: multiplies n terms of vector          *
// *                 v by c is substituted in  v        *
// * Example: Product(n,c,v)                            *
// ****************************************************
```

```
void Product(int n,float lval,float *rvalAndResult)
   {
   for(int i=0;i < n;i++)
      *rvalAndResult++ =
         Control(lval * (*rvalAndResult));
   }

// *******************< Division >*******************
// * Purpose: Divide a vector by a float            *
// * Description: Divide n terms of vector v by c    *
// *                 the result in r                  *
// * Example: Division(n,v,c,r)                       *
// ***************************************************
void Division(int n,float *lval,float rval,float *result)
   {
   if(rval == 0.)rval = TINY_FLOAT;
   for(int i=0;i < n;i++)
      *result++ = Control((*lval++)/rval);
   }

// *******************< Division >*******************
// * Purpose: Divide a vector by a float            *
// * Description: divide n terms of vector v by c    *
// *                 is substituted in v             *
// * Example: Division(n,c,v)                         *
// ***************************************************
void Division(int n,float *lval,float rval)
   {
   if(rval == 0.)rval = TINY_FLOAT;
   for(int i=0;i < n;i++)
      *lval++ = Control((*lval)/rval);
   }
```

The same identifiers will be used in Chapter 12 for operations involving matrices and vectors considered as objects.

8.7   Euclidean Norm of a Vector

The Euclidean norm of a vector, defined as below, is a commonly used function.

$$\| \mathbf{x} \|_2 = \sqrt{\sum_{k=1}^{n} x_k^2}$$

Calculating this value seems very simple and could be reached as follows:

```
float Norm2(int n,float *x)
  {
  float norm = 0.;
  for(int i=0;i < n;i++)
        norm += x[i]*x[i];
  return sqrt(norm);
  }
```

This implementation presents a number of problems

(1)   If any one of the vector's coefficients is too large, its square may overflow with unpredictable effects or program crash.

(2)   If any of the coefficients is too small, an underflow may occur, raising it to the square. If this happens, the compiler normally gives the result as equal to zero. If other coefficients are large enough, the result is correct within the limits set by the precision. But, if all the coefficients are very small, and trigger an underflow if raised to the square, the result is zero, and thus incorrect.

(3)   If the vector consists of a large number of small coefficients and of one or two which are very large, you run a risk in summing their squares. Take, for example, a vector comprising a thousand coefficients with a value of 1, and one coefficient with the value $1.e+4$; if the sum begins with the square of $1.e+4$, all the other terms are disregarded.

In FORTRAN, (for example in the SUBROUTINE SNRM2 which is held in the BLASs of the LINPACK library) you would adopt the following ways round the problem:

(1)   You look for the maximum element in terms of absolute value in the coefficients of **x**.

(2)   If this is neither too large nor too small, you carry on as normal, because no overflow or underflow problems arise. If they do, you create a vector **y**, obtained by dividing all the x_i, in absolute value, by the largest element found.

(3)   You carry out the sum of **y**'s squares.

(4)   You multiply the square root of the sum of the squares by the largest element obtained.

By transforming vector **x** into vector **y**, you avoid overflow and underflow problems.

When you create **y**, the calculation time is doubled, since n divisions are necessary.

Moreover, if the sum begins with the largest terms, you do not remove the danger of the smallest coefficients, relative to the others, being disregarded. To lessen the chance of this snag occurring, you have to order the vector **y** with a `Sort` function, so that the sum begins with the smallest coefficients in absolute value. Even this device is costly in terms of calculation time, where large size vectors are involved.

The algorithm (apart from `switches` where the largest coefficient is neither too large nor too small) is:

C++ offers a much more efficient way of solving the problem than the above algorithm.

The solution is very simple, where floats are involved. All you have to do is ensure that operations are carried out in double. Remember that double operations are default and also that the library function `sqrt` (taken from C) works in double.

The function is:

```
// *******************< SqrtSumSqr>*********************
// * Purpose: Calculation of Euclidean norm for float    *
// * Description: Executes calculations in double, to     *
// *              remove risk of overflow, to give the    *
// *              correct result when all elements are    *
// *              small or when some are large and        *
// *              some small                              *
// * Example: float x[100]; x[0]=.....                    *
// *          float norm = SqrtSumSqr(n,x);               *
// ****************************************************
float SqrtSumSqr(int n,float *x)
   {
   if(n <= 0)
      Error("%s%sSqrtSumSqr",ERR_RANGE,ERR_FUNCTION);
   double norm = 0.,aux;
   for(int i = 0;i < n;i++)
      {
      aux = x[i];
      norm += aux*aux;
      }
   norm=sqrt(norm);
   if(norm > BIG_FLOAT)norm = BIG_FLOAT;
   return norm;
   }
```

Two options are available when the vector is of type `double`. You can either:

(1) Use the technique, set out above, which is normally used in programs written in FORTRAN. But it is laborious, if you also want to solve the problem of the vector containing one or two large, and many relatively small, elements. Here, you would have to order the vector with a `Sort` program; or

(2) Work with a higher precision (`long double`), as you do for `float` type vectors. I think the second option is the best, even though things are a little more complicated in this kind of situation. There are two reasons for this:

    (a) calculations in `long double`, unlike those in `double`, are not the C and C++ default calculations. So they require long calculation times and are only used when strictly necessary.

    (b) Coercing the execution of `long double` calculations would not, in itself, provide a solution, because the function `sqrt` (taken from C) works with double precision (`double`).

> The following is used to overcome the two problems.
> You work in `double`, if you see that the largest element is neither too large nor too small, and if the relationship between the largest and the smallest element is not large, in relation to the precision `double`.
> If not, a `long double` calculation is carried out, and, before the function `sqrt` is called, the sum of the squares is divided by the square of the product of n and the largest element (to prevent overflow). Once the root has been executed, the result is multiplied by the square root of the previous factor, to remove the preceding correction. A check is carried out to prevent overflow. This strategy avoids all the possible pitfalls, without forcing you to build up a new auxiliary vector y and, consequently, without calculation time being doubled.

The function for vectors in double is:

```
// *******************< SqrtSumSqr >*******************
// * Purpose: Euclidean norm for double              *
// * Description: Work in long double, if necessary   *
// * Example: double x[100]; x[0]=.....                *
// *          norm = SqrtSumSqr(n,x);            OK *
// *******************************************************

double SqrtSumSqr(int n,double *x)
   {
   if(n <= 0)
      Error("%s%sSqrtSumSqr",ERR_RANGE,ERR_FUNCTION);
   double aux, xmax = 0.,xmin = BIG_DOUBLE;
   for(int j = 0;j < n;j++)
```

```
      {
      aux = Abs(x[j]);
      if(xmax < aux)xmax = aux;
      if(xmin > aux)xmin = aux;
      }
   if(xmax == 0.)return xmax;
   if (xmin == 0.)xmin = TINY_DOUBLE;
   long double longaux =
      (long double)xmax/(long double)xmin;
   aux = sqrt(BIG_DOUBLE/((double)n));
   // to avoid problems of
   if(xmax < aux &&                       // overflow
      xmax > TINY_DOUBLE/MACH_EPS && // small numbers
      longaux < 1./MACH_EPS)         // sort
      {
      double norm = 0.;   // no problems: double
      for(int i = 0;i < n;i++)
         {
         aux = x[i];
         norm += aux*aux;
         }
      return sqrt(norm);
      }
   else  // if there are problems, work in long double
      {
      long double norm = 0.;
      for(int i = 0;i < n;i++)
         {
         longaux = x[i];
         norm += longaux*longaux;
         }
      if(norm < BIG_DOUBLE && norm > TINY_DOUBLE)
         return sqrt(norm);
      longaux = (long double)xmax*(long double)n;
      norm /= longaux; // prevents overflow
      norm /= longaux;
      norm = longaux*sqrt(norm); // renormalizes
            // prevents overflow
      if(norm > BIG_DOUBLE) norm = BIG_DOUBLE;
      return norm;
      }
}
```

Object-Oriented Programming: the Class Type

Festina lente.

More haste, less speed.

Attributed to Emperor Augustus by Suetonius.

9.1   Encapsulating and Hiding

From now on I will start abandoning ever more decisively the terminology appropriate to procedural programming and I will try to use one which is appropriate to object oriented programming.

The first step to make, when confronted with a specimen of a new type of variable, is to try to think of an *object* and *not* of a variable. Another necessary change is to use the term *class* instead of new type of variable or new type of object.

An object, therefore, is a specimen of a class.

Definition: *Encapsulating*
An object is composed of variables, objects and functions encapsulated together in a single construct.

Definition: *Hiding*
Not all components (data and/or functions), describing an object, can be *accessed* by the user.

You should bear in mind that in C++ the `struct` type is practically equivalent to the `class` type. I also remind you that I shall use the `struct` construct in those instances where *encapsulating and hiding* do not both operate, and the `class` construct where *either encapsulating or hiding or both* do occur.

Therefore, in the style used by me, objects will always be `class` type specimens.

Let's see now how C++ manages to encapsulate data and functions and to hide data and functions by way of the `class` construct.

In defining a class, encapsulating is obtained through the possibility of declaring the `class` members in terms of variables, objects and functions. The class members may be:

(A)   *Variables*

(1)   Variables of the basic and derived type.
(2)   Pointers or references for objects of the class which is being defined and for objects of other classes, as long as their class is defined or declared.

(B)   *Objects*

(1)   Objects belonging to classes *different* from the class which is being defined, as long as the class has been *defined*.

(C)   *Functions*

(1)   Member functions.
(2)   Operators.
(3)   Constructors.
(4)   Destructor.

Example:

```
class Sample
   {
   //  Sample definition: it must be defined
   //  because Demo uses one of its objects
   .....
   };
class Demo
   {
   int dim;   // variable of the basic type
   float *puntf;   // pointer to basic type
   float vet[10]; // array
   Demo *ptrDemo; // pointer to Demo (self-reference)
   Sample *ptrSample; // pointer to Sample
   Sample objSample; // object of Sample type
   float Func(int i,float x); // function member
   void Gga(int dd){dim = dd;} // function inline
                               // (see later)

   void operator =
          (const Demo &pin); //(see Chapter 11)
   Demo(void); // constructor (see Chapter 10)
   ~Demo(void); // destructor (see Chapter 10)
   };   // remember the ;
```

> In the definition of a class the *hiding* is obtained through three degrees of access to `class` members, be they variables, objects or functions: `private`, `protected`, `public`.

The rules governing the hiding levels are as follows.

(1)   The default level in a `class` is `private`. The default is assumed when the class definition block begins without signalling the level.

(2)   The various hiding levels can be alternated and repeated without limits.

(3)   The following can have access to members declared after the keyword `private`:

  (a)   the class members;

  (b)   the class objects which are defined within functions or classes which are `friend` of the class (the meaning of `friend` of a class will be explained later);

cont.

cont.

    (c)   the objects of classes which are derived from the class (see Chapter 14 for the derivation of a class from another) if defined within functions or classes which are f r i e n d of the class.

          The class objects and those of the derived classes, which are *not* defined in functions f r i e n d of the class, and the members of the derived classes do *not* have access to the private members of the class.

(4)   The members defined after the keyword p r o t e c t e d are different from those defined as p r i v a t e by the simple fact of being accessible for the members of the classes which are *derived* from the class itself. They are *not* accessible for the objects of the class and for the objects of the derived classes which have not been defined in functions or classes f r i e n d of the class.

(5)   The members defined after the keyword p u b l i c are accessible for the members and the objects of the class, for the functions and for the classes f r i e n d and for the members and objects of the *derived* classes.

Example:

```
class Demo
    {
private: // can be omitted (default in class)
    int dim; // access for member functions only
protected:
    float ProtectedFunc(int aa);// accessible also
                    // by members of derived classes
public:
    int PublicFunc(void); // accessible by Demo
            // objects and by derived classes
private:
    float var; // accessible by member functions only
    int PrivateFunc(void); // idem
    }; // remember the ;
....
Demo objDemo; // Demo object
objDemo.dim = 1; // NO dim private
objDemo.ProtectedFunc(3); // NO protected
objDemo.PublicFunc(); // OK
objDemo.var = 2.; // NO var private
objDemo.PrivateFunc(); // NO private
```

In C++ the only difference between c l a s s and s t r u c t is given by the fact that in s t r u c t the default is p u b l i c, while in c l a s s it is p r i v a t e.

Example:

```
struct Demo
    {
    int dim; // default public
    .....
    };
class Sample
    {
    int dam;  // default private
    .....
    };
```

> I will follow this style.
>
> (1) The levels are never repeated.
> (2) First comes the private level (because the most characteristic members of the class are declared in this level), followed by the protected, followed by the public.
> (3) The private level is always declared when defining a class.
> (4) The keywords private, protected and public are aligned on the first column while all the members are moved to the right by three characters. Thus the level to which the members belong is highlighted.

Example:

```
class Demo
    {
private: // can be omitted, but I use it nevertheless
    int dim; // accessible by members only
    float var; // idem
    int PriFunc(void); // idem
protected:
    float ProFunc(int aa); // accessible also
                // by members of derived classes
public:
    int PubFunc(void); // accessible also by Demo
                // and derived classes objects
    };  // remember the ;
```

> An important detail should be noted (even if it is not possible at the moment to understand why it is important): hiding in C++ is obtained through *access limitation* for data and functions, and *not* by making them *invisible* to the objects from whom they should be hidden.
> We'll come back to this in Chapter 14.

9.2   **Functions Which are Members of a class**

Definition: *Methods*
In the terminology of object-oriented programming, a function which is a member of a class is also called a method.

A function, which is a normal member of a class, is *declared* within the definition of the new object type and then *defined* elsewhere (usually in another file).

> When a function is *defined within the definition of the class*, it is deemed inline, with no need of the inline modifier.

Example:

```
class Demo
    {
private:
    int dim;
public:
    .....
    void Func(int i){dim=i;}  // function inline
    };
```

> As for all inline functions, it would be right to define as such only those made up of one, or two at the most, very simple statements. An inline function could also be *declared* within the definition of the class and then defined elsewhere with the inline modifier. I will *never* use this alternative: if we want a member function to be inline, the definition will *always* be carried out during the definition of the class.

> The definition of a function which is a member of a class is quite similar to the definition of a normal function, except for one detail: here the function identifier is preceded by the identifier of the class to which the function belongs, and the scope binary operator :: is located between the two identifiers. This syntax is indispensable in order to tell the compiler to which class the function belongs. As a matter of fact its name may be also used in other classes or have a FILE scope (see Chapter 6).

Example:

```
class Demo
```

```
    {
public:
    .....
    float Func(int i); //  Func declaration
    };
......
float Demo::Func(int i) // Func definition
          // of Demo class. Note Demo::
    {
    statements;
    }
```

A possible error, in defining a function member of a class, is to forget the class scope.

Example:

```
class Demo
    {
public:
    float Func(int i); //  Func declaration
    ...
    };
...
float Func(int i) // NO: float Demo::Func(int i) !!
    {
    statements;
    }
```

The definition of a class member functions is put in a separate file, where the header file with the class definition must be included. The file where functions have been located will have a similar name (the same, if possible) to the `class` name and the `.CPP` extension.

A function which is a class member has direct access to all class members, whether `public`, `protected` or `private`.
In other words, a member function does *not* need an object, or specimen of the class, in order to access the other class members.

Example:

```
Class Demo
```

```
    {
private:
    int i;
    void PrivateFunc(void);
public:
    void Func(int j);
    };
...
void Demo::Func(int j)
    {
    i = j; // direct access to i and j
    PrivateFunc(); // direct access to PrivateFunc
    }
```

9.3   The Hidden Pointer `this`

In order to access a class member (accessible) from a function which is not a class member, we need to use an object or a reference to the class object and the operator . or a pointer to a class object and the operator ->.

The class member functions follow a different procedure. Apparently, they do not need an object in order to access a class member (variable or function). In reality, as we'll see shortly, they use a hidden pointer, whose address is automatically assigned by the compiler, having the keyword `this` as identifier.

The address of the hidden pointer `this` is that of the object calling the class member function (which in turn may call other class functions or may use class variables).

Example:

```
class Demo
    {
public:
    int iii;
    void Func(int j)
        {iii = j}; // Func accesses iii directly
    ...
    };
.....
Demo xDemo;
xDemo.iii = 5.; // access with an object
xDemo.Func(3); // access to a member function
Demo *ptrDemo = &xDemo;
ptrDemo->iii = 45.; // access with pointer
                    // to object
ptrDemo->Func(6); // access to a member function
```

Another situation may arise which may seem unclear. When defining a certain type of object, this object possesses its own copy of class members' data (not declared as static).

Example:

```
class Demo
   {
   int pin;
public:
   void FunPin(int j){pin = j;}
   };
....

Demo o1,o2;
o1.FunPin(2);
o2.FunPin(7);
```

Both o1 and o2 have their *own value* of the member variable pin. For object o1 it is 2, for object o2 it is 7.

Vice versa, the member functions are *not* duplicated for every defined object: *they are shared by all the objects.*

One may ask: how can a function know to which object the member being manipulated belongs?

And in the previous example, how can FunPin know that the first time pin belongs to object o1 and the second time to object o2?

> Here again, the trick is in the hidden pointer with the this identifier which contains the address of the object which is calling that function.
> The hidden pointer this is automatically added by the compiler to the front of the argument list of a class member function.
> The pointer is used automatically to access the members of the object which is calling the function.

Still in same example, it is as though the FunPin(int j) function were as follows:

```
void FunPin(class Demo *this,int j){this->pin = j;}
```

Since this contains the address of the object calling the function, the first time pin belonging to o1 is modified, and the second time the one belonging to o2.

> An important consequence of the automatic introduction of a term hidden in an argument of a class member function is that the real function prototype is different from the one shown.

Let's suppose we want to use the `FindMax` function (see Chapter 7) having the prototype:

```
float FindMax(float (*puntaFunc)(float x),...);
```

and having a class:

```
class Demo
    {
public:
    float MyFuncDemo(float x);
    ...
    };
```

Although the `MyFuncDemo` function prototype seems to coincide with the one required in the `FindMax` function, this is not true.

In fact, the `MyFuncDemo` argument is interpreted by the compiler as:

```
(Demo *this,float x)
```

not as:

```
(float x)
```

Some programmers use the pointer explicitly in functions when using a class member.
For example:

```
 void FunPin(int j){this->pin = j;}
```

This kind of use, though legitimate, is redundant and useless. It is better to avoid it.
Later we'll see those instances where it is necessary to use the `this` pointer explicitly.

Care must be taken when using an identifier in a formal argument of a member function, which is identical to that of a class member. Bear in mind that an identifier with local scope hides one with class scope.

If, for instance, we write:

```
class Demo
    {
    int pin;
```

```
public:
   void FunPin(int pin){pin = pin;}
   };
```

we do not obtain the desired result because the pin with *blocking scope* hides the pin with *class scope* (see Chapter 6).

In order to obtain the desired result the this pointer may be used:

```
void FunPin(int pin){this->pin = pin;}
```

A better technique would be using the *class scope*:

```
void FunPin(int pin){Demo::pin = pin;}
```

Better still would be avoiding repeating the identifiers unnecessarily:

```
void FunPin(int j){pin = j;}
```

9.4   static Type Members

Objects of a certain class have their own copy of all the class members.

Sometimes it is useful to have all objects of a class sharing one or more data items.
For example:

(1)   a common variable for a test;
(2)   a counter indicating the number of active objects of that class;
(3)   a pointer to the free memory shared by the class;
(4)   an error message which locates the class objects.

In these cases C++ gives a better alternative to using a global type variable: using static type class members.

A variable which is a class member and declared as of the static type has the following advantages over the global type variable.

(1)   It can be made accessible only to the class members by making it private: in this way the possible dangers of tampering will be limited.
(2)   The scope of the variable stays within the class and it will not create conflicts with other variables with the same identifier.

In order to make a class member `static` it is sufficient to name it as such when defining a class.

Example:

```
class Demo
     {
private:
     static int sta1;
public:
     static float sta2;
     static float Func(int i);
     .....
     };
```

> A class member declared as `static` enjoys some features which make it different from other members.
> Both class member variables and functions can be declared as `static`.

`static` variables

How can a class member variable be initialized and declared as `static`?

> (1) It is not possible to initialize it during the definition of the class.
> (2) Initialization must be outside the class definition block and it is carried out by the compiler before any class object is defined.
> (3) The type of variable must be specified and the identifier must be preceded by the class identifier, putting the scope binary operator `::` between the two identifiers.
> (4) The keyword `static` must *not* be inserted during initialization.
> (5) The variable can be initialized even when defined as `private` in the class.
> (6) Only one initialization can be made throughout the program.
> (7) If the variable is not explicitly initialized, it will be set equal to zero by the compiler.

Example:

```
class Demo
     {
private:
     static float sta1;  // can be private
                         // cannot be initialized here
     ....
     };
```

```
.....
float Demo::sta1=45.;   // OK even though private
Demo::sta1=45.; // NO  float needed
static float Demo::sta1=45.; // NO static not needed
float sta1=45.; // NO  class name needed
float Demo::sta1=45.;  // NO already defined
```

> It is preferable not to place the initialization of a class member variable, declared as static, in a header file, because it would risk being initialized several times and cause errors when linking the program. Initialization must be placed in the file where the class functions are implemented!

How can a member class variable, declared with static, be *accessed*?
How can it be *assigned* a new value?
How can its value be *known and used*?

> In order to *access* a member variable declared by the static modifier, the following rules must be followed.
>
> (1) The class member functions have access to a static member variable in the same way as normal members.
> (2) The objects of that class have access to that member variable as if it were a normal member and therefore only if it were declared as public. This way of accessing a static member *must be avoided*. In fact, it is better not to use a particular object, since that member variable is in common with all objects of the class.
> (3) The member variable can also be accessed *directly* by using the class scope. This alternative is preferable. Access, though, is limited to public data.

Example:

```
class Demo
    {
private:
    static int ii;
public:
    static float xx;

    // Func1 can assign a value to ii
    // even if private
    // and as if it were a normal variable
    void Func1(int i){ii = i;}
```

```
// Func2 can use ii
int Func2(void){return ii;}
....
};
......

int Demo::ii=10; //I initialize ii even if private
float Demo::xx=3.; // I initialize xx
int i = Demo::ii; // access forbidden: error!
Demo::ii = 123; // assignment forbidden: error!
float x = Demo::xx; // use allowed
Demo::xx = 33.; // assignment allowed
Demo pp;  // pp Demo type object
int j= pp.ii; // use forbidden: error!
pp.ii = 7; // assignment forbidden: error!
float y = pp.xx; // use lawful, but not advisable
pp.xx = 55.; //assignment lawful, but not advisable
```

(1) To assign an initial value to a static variable, I will always use initialization.

(2) The initialization will be placed in the file where the class functions are implemented.

(3) To modify the value, through an assignment, I will never use an object, but I will always resort instead to direct access through the class scope.

(4) To use the value I will never use an object, but I will always resort instead to direct access through the class scope.

static Functions

Let's assume we have a class member function which uses *only* static *declared members*. If this member function were of the normal type, it would need an object of the class in order to be called up.

Example:

```
class Demo
    {
private:
    static int numDemo;
public:
    int GetNumDemo(void){return numDemo;}
    ....
    };
```

```
.....
Demo o1;
int num = o1.GetNumDemo(); //  object needed
```

This procedure is not very coherent because we are forced to link a datum, shared by all objects, to a particular object. Moreover, we are obliged to create at least one class object even in those cases where it would not be necessary.

The possibility of defining a member function as `static` has been introduced in order to solve these problems.

A class member function declared as `static` follows these rules.

(1) It is *defined* as a normal member function: that is, it requires class scope.

(2) It can access *directly only those members* which have been *declared* as `static`. Therefore, it *cannot* access normal members directly.

(3) It does not have the `this` hidden pointer added as an argument and, therefore, it *cannot* use it either implicitly nor explicitly.

(4) To access *non-`static`* class members, it *must use a class object* given possibly as an argument.

(5) It could be called up by a class object as a normal function (only if declared `public`), but it is better to avoid this possibility.

(6) It is better to call it up through the class scope without using any object. Here again, in order to be accessible the function must have been declared as `public`.

Example:

```
class Demo
    {
private:
    float flDemo;  // normal member
    static int numDemo; // static members
    static void SetNumDemo(int i,float x);
public:
    static int GetNumDemo(void)
       {return numDemo;} // inline
    static char CompareDemo
       (const Demo &lvalue,const Demo &rvalue);
    ....
    };
.....
// definition as normal  member function
void Demo::SetNumDemo(int i,float x)
```

```
      {
      numDemo = i; // OK: static member
      flDemo = x;  // NO: error, non static member
                   // uses this implicitly
      }
char Demo::CompareDemo
        (const Demo &lvalue,const Demo &rvalue)
      { // can access non static members
        // through objects
        if(lval.flDemo == rval.flDemo) return 1;
        else return 0;
      }
....
Demo::SetNumDemo(5,2.); // error in compilation
                // not accessible because private
int num = Demo::GetNumDemo(); //  object not needed
Demo o1;
num = o1.GetNumDemo(); // better avoided
```

> It is important to underline a consequence of the fact that in a static
> function, which is member of a class, the this hidden pointer is not
> introduced as an argument: in the case of static functions, unlike normal
> member functions, the prototype coincides with the one which appears in
> the declaration.

Therefore, given the FindMax function having the prototype:

```
float FindMax(float (*puntaFunc)(float x),...);
```

and the class :

```
class Demo
   {
public:
   static float MyFuncDemo(float x); // now it is static
   ...
   };
```

it is possible to call the FindMax function by:

```
float xm = FindMax(Demo::MyFuncDemo(x),...);
```

Note that to use the function, the class scope Demo:: must be used.

9.5   `const` Type Members

A class may be involved in items defined as `const` in two situations.

(1)   When a *variable*, which is its member, is declared by the `const` modifier during the definition of the class.

(2)   When a class object is defined by the `const` modifier.

In Chapter 10 we'll see how to solve the problem of initializing both the variable and the object: being constant, they cannot be given a value except through initialization.

Now let's see how C++ solves another problem: once a `const` object of a certain class has been defined and initialized, how can it be prevented from modifying, either directly or through a member function of that class, its own member data?

Example:

```
class Demo
    {
private:
    const float xxx; // how to initialize it? Chapter 10
    int jjj;
public:
    int iii;
    void Func(int j){jjj = j;}
    };
......
const Demo pro; // how to initialize it? Chapter 10
pro.iii = 5;  // how to prevent it?
pro.Func(5); // how to prevent it?
```

> If an object defined by the `const` modifier tries to modify any member of its own class, either directly or through a function, the compiler will give an error message or a danger warning.

A `const` object, though, can access the class members without the compiler giving danger signals, by means of *member functions* which have been declared as `const`.

> The member functions which have been declared as `const` follow these rules.
>
> *cont.*

cont.

(1)   A const defined object may only use member functions themselves declared as const. Otherwise, the compiler will give a danger warning.

(2)   The class programmer determines which functions are safe (they do not modify data) and which are not. The safe ones will be declared as const. However, if a function which modifies a class member variable is declared as const, a warning will appear during compilation.

(3)   The keyword const must be present *both in the declaration and in the definition* of functions which are not inline.

(4)   The keyword const must be placed between the function argument and the *;* in the *declaration*, while in the *definition* it is placed between the argument and the opening of the function block, {.

(5)   A const declared function can overload other functions having the same identifier. It is also possible to overload a function which only differs by the keyword const. In this case, one or the other function is called, depending from whether the calling object is const or not.

Example:

```
class Demo
    {
private:
    int iii;
    float *ptff;
public:
    int GetValue(void) const;  // declarations
    void Set1(float xxx) const;
    void Set1(float xxx); // overloaded without const
    void Set2(float *yyy) const;
    };
.....
int Demo::GetValue(void) const    // definition
    {
    return iii;  // OK does not modify
    }
void Demo::Set1(float xxx) const    // definition
    {
    *ptff = xxx;  // OK can modify
                  // the *ptff content
    }
void Demo::Set1(float xxx) // overloaded function
    {
    *ptff = xxx;  // OK
```

```
            iii = 0; // OK the function is not const
            }
     void Demo::Set2(float *yyy) const    // definition
            {
            ptff = yyy;  // error: it cannot modify
                         // the pointer
            }
     ......
     const Demo co; // co can only use
                        // Demo const functions
     Demo va;
     co.Set1(3.); // uses Set1 const
     va.Set1(5.); // uses Set1 NOT const
```

> The functions should be given names which indicate, as clearly as possible, whether they are meant to change some data or simply use data without any modification. For example, SetValue would be inappropriate for a const function.

9.6 friend

There are situations where *hiding*, which can be obtained by the keyword private, can be too restrictive. For instance, if we want a given function to have simultaneous access to the private data of two separate classes, it will not be possible to make the function a member of one of the two classes without blocking the access to the data of the other.

C++ allows for a more flexible access to *non*-public data of a class by using the keyword friend.

> The following can be declared as friend of a class:
>
> (1)   a single function;
> (2)   a function which is a member of another class;
> (3)   a whole class.
>
> This purpose is achieved by simply putting the keyword friend before the declaration. The declaration must be present within the definition of the class whose *non*-public data and functions are to be accessed. This way, the functions or classes which can access the *non*-public data of a class will be decided by the class programmer. The *non*-public data class accessibility is therefore preserved.
> *cont.*

cont.

The declarations of a `class friend` or of a function `friend` can be placed in the `private, protected` or `public` areas of the class definitions.

If the `class` intended to be made `friend` is not *defined* as the class which is being defined, a *forward declaration* is needed and sufficient.

Example:

```
class Sample; // forward declaration
class Zaza; // forward declaration
class Demo
    {
    friend class Sample; // class friend
private:
    friend void Func1(float x); // function friend
public:
    friend int ZaZa::Func2(int i); // function
                                 // member of Zaza
    };
```

A function which is declared `friend` in a class is *not* a member of that class, even if it has been declared within the `class` definition. In other words, it *is not within the scope* of the `class`. Therefore:

(1)   within the function there is no direct access to the class members;
(2)   it is the objects of the class which has declared the function as `friend` which, when defined within the function, have access to all the members of their class, even those not `public`;
(3)   the class scope must not be used in defining the function;
(4)   the function has FILE scope;
(5)   even though the declaration has been placed in the `private` area, the function is accessible and does not need objects to be used. It is used and defined as a normal function and not as a class member.

Example:

```
class Demo
    {
    friend void Func(void); // private area by default
private:
    int demoPrivate;
protected:
    int demoProtected;
```

```
public:
    int demoPublic;
    };
.....
void Func(void)   // NON Demo::Func
    {
    demoPublic = 1; // error: it does not have direct access
    Demo dd; // dd Demo object
    dd.demoPrivate = 1; // OK it has access
    dd.demoProtected = 1; // OK it has access
    dd.demoPublic = 1; // OK it has access
    }
....
Demo demo; // demo Demo object
demo.demoPrivate = 1; // error: it has NO access
demo.demoProtected = 1; // error: it has NO access
demo.demoPublic = 1; // OK
Func(); // OK even though in the private area!
demo.Func(); // error: it is NOT a Demo member!
```

A function f r i e n d can overload another function. If several overloaded functions are intended to be f r i e n d of a class, *each* one of them must be explicitly declared as f r i e n d.

Example:

```
class Demo
    {
    friend int Func(int i);
    friend float Func(float x);
    double Func(double d); // overloaded, but NOT friend
    ....
    };
```

All the function members of a class which has been declared f r i e n d of another class become f r i e n d of that class: they can access *non*-p u b l i c members of the class which has declared them f r i e n d through the objects of that class. Note that the f r i e n d feature is *not transitive*.

Example:

```
class Demo; // forward declaration
class Sample
```

```
    {
    friend class Demo;
private:
    int privateSample;
    ....
    };
class Demo
    {
    void FuncDemo(void)
        {
        Sample objSample;
        objSample.privateSample = 1; // OK
        }
    };
```

The functions of the Demo class are friend of the Sample class, while the functions of the Sample class *are not* friend of the Demo class.

Finally, note that:

(1) a function or a class can be friend to more than one class;
(2) the functions friend play an important role in the operators overloading (see Chapter 11);
(3) a derived class must explicitly declare as friend a function which has been declared friend in the base class, if it is to remain friend (see Chapter 14).

The *classes* which have been declared friend of a class are placed at the beginning of the class definition, immediately after the opening of the class definition block and before the keyword private.
The *functions* which have been declared friend are placed where it is more appropriate (for instance, among the operators if the function is an operator).

friend Functions or Member functions

It could be asked when it is convenient to declare a function as a friend and when it is preferable to declare it as a member of a given class.

> The following situations should be noted.
>
> 1. The use of a `friend` function is compulsory.
> 2. The use of a `friend` function is preferred but not compulsory.
> 3. The use of a class member function is preferred but not compulsory.
> 4. The use of a class member function is compulsory.

The use of a `friend` function is *compulsory* when the function has to access simultaneously *non*-`public` members of many classes. In this case, there are two alternatives.

(1)   To make the function a `friend` of all the classes involved.

(2)   To make the function a member of one class and a `friend` of the others.

For symmetry's sake, often the first alternative is preferable.

For instance, in order to overload the operator, `*`, so as to multiply a vector and a matrix, it is necessary to access simultaneously the `private` data of both classes. The most reasonable choice here is to make the `operator` a `friend` of both classes.

Another case where a `friend` function is *compulsory* (see Chapter 11) is when overloading a binary `operator` where the first object involved in the operation is not a class object but a basic variable.

A situation where the use of a `friend` function instead of a class member function is *preferable*, though not compulsory, is when the function acts *symmetrically* on two object belonging to the *same* class.

This is a frequent case when overloading `operators` such as `*`, `+` and so on. (see Chapter 11).

Example:

```
class Point
   {
private:
   float x,y;
      // The Distance function is accessible
      // even though it is in the private zone
   friend float Distance(const Point &p,const Point &q);
   .....
   };
......
      // NON Point::Distance !!!!
float Distance(const Point &p,const Point &q)
   { // access to x and y through objects p and q
   return sqrt((p.x-q.x)*(p.x-q.x)+(p.y-q.y)*(p.y-q.y));
   }
   .....
```

```
void main(void)
   {
   // definition and initialization p and q
   Point p(1.,5.),q(5.,6.);
   // for initialization see Chapter 10
   // I can use Distance even though declared as private
   cout << "Distance between p and q: "<< Distance(p,q);
   }
```

The same function can be implemented as a member of the class, but the resulting code becomes less elegant and more difficult to use.

```
class Point
   {
private:
   float x,y;
public:
      // The member function  Distance is
      // accessible only if public
   float Distance(const Point &q); // note the different
                   // argument (this hidden)
.....
};
......
            // necessary Point::
float Point::Distance(const Point &q)
   { // note asymmetry in the access to data
   return sqrt((x-q.x)*(x-q.x)+(y-q.y)*(y-q.y));
   }
.....
void main(void)
   {
   Point p(1.,5.),q(5.,6.); // I define
                   // and initialize p and q
      // note asymmetry in using Distance
   cout << "Distance between p and q: "<< p.Distance(q);
   }
```

A situation which must be analysed case by case is when the function is used to initialize a function pointer. In order to solve this problem, the two alternatives to consider are the following.

(1)   static member function.
(2)   Function not member and friend.

> A normal member function is not correct because of the hidden pointer, `this`, introduced by the compiler.

Consider again the problem of using the function:

```
float FindMax(float (*puntaFunc)(float x),...);
```

Consider the class:

```
class Demo
    {
public:
    float Func1(float x); // normal
    static float Func2(float x); // static
    friend float Func3(float x); // friend
    ...
    };
```

As previously observed, `Func1` cannot be used because its prototype is different from the one required.

Instead, it is possible to use both the `static` and `friend` functions:

```
float x2 = FindMax(Demo::Func2(x),...);
float x3 = FindMax(Func3(x),...);
```

Note that in the case of the `static` function (which is a member of the class) the class scope *must* be used; in the case of the `friend` function (which is not a member of the class) the class scope *must not* be used.

> By using a `static` member function, there is the possibility of making the function inaccessible by placing it in the `private` zone.

> If, instead, the function is to be also accessible by a user, the `static` alternative becomes a disadvantage because it requires the class scope and a possible source of error is therefore introduced.

When a class function uses objects of two different classes, but conceptually is associated with the first, it is better to make the function a member of the first class and to declare it as `friend` of the second. This kind of situation appears when overloading the assign `operator` = (in this case C++ compulsorily requires that such an `operator` should be a member of the class and not a `friend`). The overloading of this `operator` allows us, for example, to write:

```
A = v;
```

where `A` is a matrix and `v` is a vector (see Chapters 11 and 12).

9.7 Pointer to a Class Member

A variable pointer can receive the address of a class member. This possibility becomes important above all for the member functions.

Pointer to a Class Member Variable

> In order to define a pointer, it is necessary to say which type it is.
> In the case of a pointer to a class member, it is necessary to insert the class scope through the following syntax:
>
> <type> <class name>:: *<identifier>;
>
> Once defined, that pointer can receive the address value of *any member of that class having the same type, provided it is accessible* (for example, it is `public`).
> The pointer can also be initialized (it can receive a value at the time of definition).

The definition:

```
float Demo::*punMember1; //note the position of *
```

should read:

The identifier	`punMember1`
is a pointer	`*punMember1`
to a `Demo` member	`Demo::*punMember1`
type `float`	`float Demo::*punMember1`

Example:

```
class Demo
    {
private:
    float www;
public:
    float xxx,yyy,zzz;
    ....
    };
.......
float Demo::*punMember1; // definition of punMember1
```

```
punMember1 = &Demo::xxx; // I assign to it
                         // the address of xxx
                         // belonging to the Demo
                         // class
punMember1 = &Demo::yyy; // I change assignment
                         // I initialize punMember2
float Demo:: *punMember2 = &Demo::zzz;
punMember2 = &Demo::yyy; // I change assignment
punMember2 = &Demo::www; // error: private
```

A pointer to a class member *does not* represent the address of a physical element: it is only so for any particular object of that class.

Therefore it can be used *only when associated to a particular object* through the operators .* for an object and ->* for a pointer to an object.

Example:

```
class Demo
    {
public:
    float xxx;
    ....
    };
.......
     // I initialize punMember1
float Demo:: *punMember1 = &Demo::xxx;
Demo o1; //  Demo type object
Demo *punDem = new Demo; // pointer to Demo
o1.*punMember1=12.5; // equal to o1.xxx = 12.5;
punDem->*punMember1=33.; // equal to punDem->xxx = 33.;
```

If the class member has been declared by the static modifier, things are different. In this case, in fact, the pointer behaves as a normal pointer *both* in the definition (it does not require the class scope) *and* in the use (it does not require a class object).

Example:

```
class Demo
    {
public:
    static float xxx; // now is static
    ....
    };
```

```
. . . . . . .
float *punMember1; // I define punMember1
                   // Demo :: must NOT be inserted
punMember1 = &Demo::xxx; // I assign to it an address
*punMember1=12.; // an object is NOT needed
                 // to access  xxx
```

Pointer to a Member Function

The pointers to a class member are particularly useful in the case when the member is a function. The use of a pointer to a function which is a member of a class has the same advantages previously observed in the case of pointers to normal functions (see Chapter 7).

When defining and using a pointer to a class member function, it is necessary to follow the same rules as for definition and use of pointers to class member variables.

> Bear in mind that in order to define a pointer to a function which has FILE scope, its `return` must be specified, the identifier preceded by `*` must be enclosed in brackets (to modify precedence) and the list of the variables in the argument must be provided.
>
> In the case of a pointer to a class member function, it is necessary to add the class scope by the following syntax:
>
> <type of return> (<class name>:: *<identifier>) <argument>;
>
> Once defined, that pointer can receive the address value of any member function of that class having the same type of `return` and the same argument, provided it is accessible (for example, it is `public`).
>
> Also, the pointer can be initialized (at the time of definition) either by a known address or by 0.

The definition:

```
float (Demo::*punFun1)(int i);
```

should read:

The identifier	`punFun1`
is a pointer	`*punFun1`
to a `Demo` member	`Demo::*punFun1`
of the function type	`(Demo::*punFun1)(int i)`
with a `float` type `return`	`float (Demo::*punFun1)(int i)`

Example:

```
class Demo
   {
public:
   float Func(int iii);
   ....
   };
.......
float (Demo::*punFun1)(int i); // definition
punFun1 = Demo::Func; // assignment ( & not needed)
           //initialization
float (Demo::*punFun2)(int i) = Demo::Func;
//initialization to 0
float (Demo::*punFun3)(int i) = 0;
punFun3 = punFun1; //I can assign another
```

> To use a pointer to a function it is necessary to *associate it to a particular object* through the operators .* for an object and ->* for a pointer to an object.

Example:

```
class Demo
   {
public:
   float Func(float xxx){return 2.*xxx;}
   ....
   };
.......
     //  initialization
float (Demo::*punFun1)(float x) = Demo::Func;
Demo o1; // Demo type object
Demo *punDem = new Demo; // pointer to Demo

          // equal to o1.Func(12.);
          // note brackets
float result = (o1.*punFun1)(12.);

          // equal to punDem->Func(3.);
          // note brackets
result = (punDem->*punFun1)(3.);
```

Even class member functions which have been declared with the `static` modifier behave in a peculiar way. In this case, a pointer to a function behaves as a pointer to a normal function *both* in the definition (does not require the class scope) *and* in the use (does not require a class object).

Example:

```
class Demo
    {
public:
    static float Func(float xxx); // now it is static
    ....
    };
.......
float (*punFun)(float x); // I define punFun
                    //  Demo :: must NOT be inserted
punFun = Demo::Func; // I assign an address to it
                    // ( & not needed)
float res;
res = (*punFun)(3.);// object not needed
res = punFun(3.); // shorthand notation
```

Note that the pointer can be used without the need to define an object of that class and that both the explicit form:

```
res = (*punFun)(3.);// explicit form
```

and the shorthand notation can be used (see Chapter 7):

```
res = punFun(3.); // shorthand notation
```

9.8 Questions

What is the conceptual difference between the definition of a class and that of an object?

The definition of a class is an abstract description of a new type of entity.
The definition of an object is the realization of a specimen of such entity.

Is the following definition of the function `Func` as an `inline` member of `Demo` correct?

```
class Demo
   {
private:
    int i;
public:
    inline void Func(int j)
       {this->i = j;}
   };
```

Yes, even though it is not necessary to write explicitly `this` and `inline`.

 Consider the following initializations of the `st` variable:

```
class Sample
   {
public:
 static float st = 3.;
 };
...
static float Sample::st = 3.;
float Sample::st = 3.;
```

Which are the correct ones?

The last only.

 Why is it better to access a class member which has been declared `static` through the scope `operator` rather than through an object of the class?

Because to use a particular object to access a shared datum would be confusing.

 In order to make a class as `friend` of another, should it be defined or would a preventive declaration be sufficient?

A declaration would be sufficient. This is important because in this way it is possible to make both classes reciprocally `friend` of one another.

Is a function declared as friend of a class within the scope of the class?

No. It has a FILE scope. Consequently, it must not be called up by a class object and the class scope must not be used in its definition.

 How can class members be accessed from a function declared as friend of that class?

Not being within the class scope, the function does not have direct access to the class members. The class objects defined within the function can access all members of the class, even the private ones.

 Given the following definition of the Sample class, define and initialize variable pointers to the members x1, x2, f1 and f2.

```
class Sample
    {
public:
    float x1;
    static float x2;
    void f1(float xx1){x1=xx1;}
    static void f2(float xx2){x2=xx2;}
    };
```

```
float Sample::*punx1 = &Sample::x1;
float *punx2 = &Sample::x2;
void(Sample::*punf1)(float xx) = Sample::f1;
void (*punf2)(float xx) = Sample::f2;
```

10 Using Objects

E questo ti sia sempre piombo a' piedi,
per farti mover lento com'uomo lasso
e al sì e al no che tu non vedi.

And let this always be lead on thy feet,
like a weary man, moving either
to the yea or the nay where thou dost not see clearly.

Dante, *Paradiso*, XIII.

10.1 Introduction

In C++ you can construct new classes, new types of objects and you can define objects belonging to these classes. Here, we will look at how class objects can be initialized and used.

 You should remember that you have to make the distinction in C++ between *initializing* and *assigning*.
Initializing takes place in the statement which defines a variable or object, whereas assigning applies to objects which have already been defined elsewhere and takes place in the assignment statement.

10.2 Initializing Simple Classes

You can define and initialize objects belonging to simple `structs` and `classes` in a way similar to that which is employed for vectors and matrices.

> In what sense a class is described as *simple* will be seen later on.
> An object must have *static duration*, for it to be initialized. That is, it must have global scope or local scope and the `static` modifier. Many compilers automatically convert an object into `static` if a local object is initialized.

Example:

```
struct Point
    {
    float x,y,z
    };
    ....
Point xyz=    // define and initialize xyz
    {
    5.,3.,1.
    };
```

Example:

```
struct Demo
    {
    int i;
    char *name;
    float x;
    };
....
Demo demo[4] =    // initialize 4 Demo type objects
    {
    {1,"Titian",3.2},         // demo[0]
    {2,"Leonardo",123.1},     // demo[1]
    {3,"Michelangelo",3.14}   // demo[2]
    {4,"Raphael",7.127}       // demo[3]
    };
```

> An object can be initialized as above only if it belongs to a very simple class. In fact, simple classes, of which the above is a sample, are subject to the following constraints.
>
> *cont.*

cont.
(1)   They cannot have constructors.
(2)   All of their members must be `public`.
(3)   They cannot be derived from other classes (see Chapter 14).
(4)   There cannot be any virtual functions in their definitions (see Chapter 14).

I will avoid using this method of initializing `class` type objects. *At least one constructor will be defined* in a `class`, so this type of initializing *cannot* be used.

But it is sometimes convenient for initializing `struct` type variables, which should contain neither functions nor constructors, and which should not have private members in the style that I have adopted.

10.3 Constructors and Destructor

When a *basic* type variable is defined, the compiler reserves for it the required amount of storage, which is automatically freed when the variable leaves scope.

In C++, objects, that is `class` specimens, can behave in the same way.

Example:

```
void Func(void)
    {
    ....
    Demo objDemo;  // enters scope
    ....
    } // objDemo leaves scope
```

When an object is defined, the compiler automatically calls a special function of the class, called a *constructor*. Constructors are used to *initialize* objects in a way which is established by whoever designs the class. For example, it can open files and allocate storage to a vector or matrix, and so on. When the object leaves scope, the compiler automatically calls another function of the class, called a *destructor*. A destructor is used to de-initialize the object and to execute other operations which are deemed to be important when the object leaves scope. The destructor restores the conditions prevailing before the object was defined – it closes files, de-allocates storage and executes any other operations which may be needed.

Because initializing and de-initializing are carried out automatically and remain hidden from the user, the codes become much simpler.

Example:

```
void Func(void)
    {
    Matrix A(3,5);
    ....
    } // A leaves scope
```

When object A of type Matrix is defined:

```
Matrix A(3,5);
```

a constructor is called automatically; it creates storage for a 3-row, 5-column matrix and initializes the coefficients with 0 (see Chapter 12). When A leaves scope, the destructor automatically frees the previously occupied storage.

Constructors

Definition: *Constructor*
A constructor is a special dedicated class member function which automatically initializes an object.

A constructor differs from a normal class member function for the following reasons:

(1) A constructor's identifier *must* be identical to the class identifier. And a constructor:
(2) does *not* have a return (not even of type void);
(3) is automatically called, when an object of that class is defined, or when a pointer to an object of that class is defined using the new operator, or when a function returns an object, or when a function is passed an object by the argument;
(4) can be used, without having been declared const, by objects which have been defined as const;
(5) *cannot* be declared as virtual (see Chapter 14);
(6) is *not* inherited by derived classes and consequently the appropriate constructors have to be redefined for each derived class (see Chapter 14).

Example:

```
class Demo
    {
private:
    int iii;
```

```
public:
    Demo(int i)    // same identifier
      {iii = i}; // no return
    };
......
Demo dd(5);  //initialize dd.iii with 5
Demo *pun = new Demo(7); //initialize pun->iii with 7
const Demo dc(8); // uses the constructor even if const
```

> A constructor behaves like a class member function in almost all other respects.
>
> (1) It is inline, if defined inside a class definition.
> (2) It can be *overloaded* with other constructors.
> (3) Constructor arguments can be *default*.
> (4) It can initialize object members and also execute any other action.
> (5) It can be public, protected or private.

A constructor which is not inline can be defined in a very similar way to class member functions, apart from the fact that it does *not* return values.

Example:

```
class Demo
   {
public:
    Demo(int i,float x); // same identifier
                         // no return
    .....
    };
......
// definition
Demo::Demo(int i,float x) // no return type
   {
   statements; // no return
   }
```

A constructor, when defined as private, can only be accessed by class member functions or by functions which have been defined as a friend of the class.

Definition: *Private Class*
A class in which constructors are all of type private is said to be private. Where this is the case, only class member and friend functions can define objects of that class.

Destructor

Definition: *Destructor*

A destructor is a special member function of a class the main purpose of which is to de-initialize objects. A destructor is called when an object leaves scope.

It has the following characteristics.

(1)   Its identifier *must* be identical to the class identifier and *must* be preceded by the symbol ˜.

(2)   It *cannot* have variables in its argument, which must consequently be of type `void`.

(3)   It *cannot* be overloaded, and so there is only one destructor for every class.

(4)   It *must not* have a `return` (not even of type `void`).

(5)   It is automatically called when an object leaves scope or when a pointer to an object which has been created with `new` is de-allocated by using `delete`. A reference to an object does *not* call a destructor when it leaves scope.

(6)   If it is placed in a `private` area, the `class` becomes `private` – only `class` member or `friend` functions can use objects of that `class`.

(7)   It can be declared as `virtual` (see Chapter 14).

(8)   It is normally used to free storage which has been requested by a constructor. However, it can carry out other operations, as it should be considered in every respect as identical to a function.

Example:

```
class Vector
{
private:
    int dimensions;
    float *vector;
public:
    Vector(int n); // constructor
    ˜Vector(void){delete vector;} // destructor inline
    ....
    };
....
Vector::Vector(int n)
    {
    dimensions = n;   // n elements
    vector = new float[n];
```

```
for(int i = 0;i < dimensions;i++)
    vector[i] = 0.;
}
```

It is important to grasp the difference between *de-allocating* and *de-initializing* an object.

A constructor does *not allocate memory* for the object – it *initializes* it. Storage may be allocated using the `new` operator as initializing is being carried out, but the compiler automatically allocates the storage the object requires.

In the example above, the constructor does *not* have to be involved in allocating storage for `dimensions` and for the `vector` pointer. Instead, its task is to allocate the storage to which `vector` is pointing. The destructor does not have to and cannot de-allocate the object's memory, which is the compiler's task. In the example, the destructor does not have to be involved in freeing the storage of `dimensions` and of the pointer `vector`. The destructor has to *de-initialize* the object – essentially it must retrace the constructor's steps, backwards. It has only to free the storage *to which* `vector` *is pointing*.

10.4 Defining Objects

A constructor is called automatically when a class object is defined. Let's have a look, here, at the rules for passing arguments to a constructor.

Passing arguments to a constructor, while an object is being defined, can be done explicitly and in a simplified form, and these options are *always* available.

If the constructor has *only one* argument variable, or if all the others have a *default* value, a second simplified form can be used.

An object which *explicitly* uses a constructor is defined as follows:

<class name> <object name> = <class name>(value of the variables);

The simplified form, always available, is:

<class name> <object name>(value of the variables);

Where there is *only one* argument variable, an object can be defined as:

<class name> <object name> = value of the variable;

cont.

cont.

When several constructors are overloaded, the constructor with the same number of data items and with variable types which correspond to those passed as arguments is chosen.

Example:

```
class Demo
    {
public:   // three overloaded constructors declared
    Demo(int i,float x); // two variables in argument
    Demo(float y); // only one variable
    Demo(int i); // only one variable of a different type
    ....
    };
......
// uses Demo(int i,float x);
Demo d1 = Demo(2,3.44); // explicitly defined

// uses Demo(int i,float x);
Demo d2(24,515.1); // general simplified form

// uses Demo(float x);
Demo d3 = 1.8; // special simplified form
              // with one variable

// uses Demo(int i);
Demo d4 = 5; // as above, using another constructor

// uses Demo(int i);
Demo d5(15); //general simplified definition
```

Warning!

(1)   A simplified definition with only one variable should be considered as *an initialization* rather than an assignment. We will look at the difference later on.

(2)   Where a constructor *has no variables* in the argument, the simplified definition is:

<class name> <object name>;

and *not*:

<class name> <object name>( );

Example:

```
class Demo
    {
public:
    Demo(int i); // constructor with only one variable
    Demo(void);  // constructor with no variables in
                 // argument
    ....
    };
......
Demo pp = 5; // initialized not assigned
Demo d1 = Demo(); // explicit definition OK
Demo d2; // simplified definition OK
Demo d3(); // error
```

10.5 Special Constructors

It is desirable to subdivide constructors according to their purpose.

> Constructors can be subdivided into four categories, depending on how they are used and what type of variables they have in their arguments.
>
> (1) *Default constructor.*
> (2) *Copy-initializer constructors* – for copying one object and initializing another object of the same type.
> (3) *Type conversion constructors* – for converting objects of different types into objects belonging to the defining class.
> (4) *Generic constructors.*

Default Constructor

A default constructor is defined with a `void` argument.
Example:

```
class Demo
    {
private:
    int iDemo;
    float xDemo;
public:
    Demo(void){iDemo=0;xDemo=0.;} // default constructor
    };
```

Warning – if all the variables in the constructor's argument are assigned by default, *it is not a default constructor*.

If only one object is defined and no value is assigned in the argument, there is no difference between a constructor with a `void` argument and one which is assigned by default. The difference stems from the fact that the former is used to initialize the *arrays* of objects, as we shall see later, but the latter is not.

Example:

```
class Demo
{
public:
    // is not a default constructor
    Demo(int i=0,float x=0.){iDemo=i;xDemo=x;}
    };
....
Demo objDemo; // is the same as default
             // for a single object
```

I believe that , it is useful *always* to introduce a default constructor into a `class` definition. In this way you can define arrays of objects without problems.

Conversely, I will *not, in any circumstances*, use a constructor in which all variables have been assigned by default.

Constructors for Copying and Initializing Objects

This type of constructor is fundamentally important and is used automatically in three situations.

(1)   When one object is *initialized* by another of the same type.
(2)   When a function is *passed* an object.
(3)   When an object is *returned* by a function.

Constructors for copying and initializing can assume one of the forms below, where `Demo` denotes the class name and `dd` its object.

```
Demo(const Demo &dd);
Demo(Demo &dd);
Demo(const Demo &dd,int i=0,float x=0.);
Demo(Demo &dd,int i=0,float x=0.);
```

cont.

> *cont.*
> As can be seen from the last two examples, if the first variable is a reference
> to the class object and all the others have a default value, the constructor is a
> copy-initializer constructor.

If the c l a s s does *not* have an *explicit* definition of a constructor of this type,
the compiler automatically defines one which makes a simple copy of the object's
data.

Example:

```
class Vector
    {
private:
    int dimensions; // vector   dimensions
    float *vector;
public:
    Vector(void); // default constructor
    Vector(int size); // another constructor
    };
......
Vector dd(10); // Vector(int size) constructor
Vector pp = dd; //constructor generated by the compiler
              // pp.dimensions = dd.dimensions;
              // pp.vector = dd.vector;
```

> Simple copying is acceptable, if the data in a c l a s s are all of basic type,
> but, if they are not, copying can be *extremely dangerous*.
> There are two drawbacks in the example above.
>
> (1)   Only the value of the pointer v e c t o r, and not its content, is copied.
>   The two objects pp and dd share v e c t o r's data. By modifying the
>   data of one, the other's data is also changed.
> (2)   If the object dd has initialized the pointer with n e w and then uses
>   d e l e t e to release storage, the object pp is left with a pointer which
>   *no longer has storage available* – and this is a serious error.

These problems could be overcome if the following constructor for copying
and initializing were defined instead.

```
Vector::Vector(const Vector &dd)
    {
    dimensions = dd.dimensions;
    vector = new float [dimensions]; // gives vector dimensions
            // vector pp is now different from dd
```

```
for(int i = 0;i < dimensions;i++)
    vector[i] = dd.vector[i]; //copies values
}
```

Two possible errors in defining a copy-initializer constructor should be
avoided.

(1)   Defining it with a class object, rather than a *reference* to a class
       object. Here, the constructor should recall itself to initialize the object,
       but this is precluded by the compiler, which would flag an error.

(2)   Defining it with a *pointer* to the object. *This would not be a copy-
       initializer constructor*, it would be a generic constructor, a category of
       constructor which is *not* called to copy or initialize an object.

Example

```
class Demo
    {
public:
    Demo(Demo dd); //compiler flags error
    Demo(Demo *dd); // this is NOT a copy-initializer
                    // constructor
    };
```

It is preferable *always* to define a constructor for copying and initializing in
order to avoid problems.
The following form will be used *in all circumstances*:

```
Demo(const Demo &dd);
```

and shows that the object used is *not* modified by the constructor.
Consequently, I will avoid those constructors that modify objects which are
used to initialize others. I will also ignore the option of supplying variables
with default values.

All three forms for defining a new object can be used, as the constructor has
only one variable in its argument:

```
Demo p1 = Demo(dd); // explicitly defined
Demo p2(dd); // defined in general simplified form
Demo p3 = dd; // defined in special form with a variable
```

cont.

> *cont.*
> The special form below will always be used:
>
> ```
> Demo p3 = dd; // defined in special form with a variable
> ```
>
> as it is similar to the form used for basic type variables.
> And remember – this is an *initialization* and not an *assignment*.

Example:

```
class Demo
    {
public:
    Demo(void); // default constructor
    Demo(const Demo &demo); // copy-initializer
                                // constructor
    ....
    };
........
Demo d1; // default constructor
Demo d2 = d1; // copy-initializer constructor
Demo d3; // default constructor
d3 = d1; // assignment operator
```

> Notice, in the example above, the difference between *initializing* the object
> d2, in which the copy-initializer constructor is used, and *assigning*, which is
> carried out for d3. The assignment operator, =, is called, rather than the
> copy-initializer constructor, so it must be defined in the Demo class to act
> on the objects of the class (Chapter 11 will deal with the problem of over-
> loading operators).

Copy-initializer constructors are also brought into play as objects are passed to
and from a function, as well as when one object is initialized with another of the same
type.

> Remember that only the value of a variable is passed to a function in C++,
> and *not* the variable itself. The same thing happens with objects: the
> corresponding object in the function's formal argument is initialized with
> the object of the calling function.
> And so a copy-initializer constructor is called automatically. If a constructor
> of this type has not been explicitly defined, the compiler defines one which
> makes a simple copy of the data. This can be dangerous, as we have already
> seen.

Example:

```
class Demo
    {
public:
    float Fun(Demo dd);
    ...
    };
....
Demo d;
float x = Fun(d); //  a copy of d is created
                  // and passed to Fun
```

An object will not be passed to a function, as pointed out in Chapter 7. Instead, one of the following is passed.

(1) a const *reference*, in situations where the object *does not* have to be modified by the function.
(2) a *pointer* to the object, where the object *does* have to be modified.

The copy-initializer constructor is *not* called if a reference or a pointer is passed, with a concomitant bonus in terms of memory and efficiency.

Example:

```
class Demo
    {
public:
    float Fun1(const Demo &dd); // dd does not have to be
                                // modified
    float Fun2(Demo *pp); // *pp can be modified
    ...
    };
....
Demo d;
float x1 = Fun1(d);//d is not modified
float x2 = Fun2(&d);//d is modified
```

Remember that even when a function returns a variable in C++, the *value* rather than the variable itself is passed. So here again, the copy-initializer constructor is called automatically and, if it has not been explicitly defined, a simple copy of the data is made. And this can be dangerous as we have already seen.

cont.

> *cont.*
> Often you cannot use a reference or a pointer, unlike those situations where a variable is passed to a function, for reasons which will be explained later. This is another reason why, if you want to prevent problems arising, it is essential explicitly to define the copy-initializer constructor.

How the copy-initializer constructor is used to `return` objects will be looked at later. first, you have to grasp how C++ creates hidden objects with no specific identifiers.

Constructors for Converting Objects

> This type of constructor is brought into play when you want to transform an object of a type which is different from but similar to the target object, into an object belonging to the class.
> Below, `Demo` denotes the class name, `dd` one of its objects which you want to define, `Sample` the name of another class and `pp` the name of one of its objects. The constructor for converting `pp` into `dd` can assume one of the following forms:
>
> ```
> Demo(const Sample &pp);
> Demo(Sample &pp);
> Demo(const Sample pp);
> Demo(Sample pp);
> Demo(const Sample &pp,int i=0,float x=0.);
> Demo(Sample &pp,int i=0,float x=0.);
> Demo(const Sample pp,int i=0,float x=0.);
> Demo(Sample pp,int i=0,float x=0.);
> ```

Example:

```
class Matrix
    {
public:
    Matrix(const Vector &vet);
    ....
    };
.....
Vector v(100);
Matrix A = v; // A is initialized with Vector v
```

The same conditions laid down for the copy-initializer constructor also apply to this constructor. The only important difference is that the compiler does not attempt to create this type of constructor and, consequently, the compiler flags an error if a constructor for converting one type of object into another is not created.

> The following form will *always* be used:
>
> ```
> Demo(const Sample &pp);
> ```
>
> when the object used is a class specimen; and the form:
>
> ```
> Demo(<type> identifier);
> // Example: Demo(int iii);
> ```
>
> when the conversion of a basic variable is required. This will also show that the object used is *not* modified by the constructor.
>
> Constructors which modify an object which is used for initializing another will be avoided, and the option of giving variables default values will be ignored. *All three* forms of defining a new object based on an object of a different type can be used, since the constructor's argument has only one variable.
>
> ```
> Demo p1 = Demo(pp); // explicitly defined
> Demo p2(pp); // defined in general, simplified form
> Demo p3 = pp; // defined with special form
>                // with a variable
> ```
>
> The following special form will be used:
>
> ```
> Demo p3 = pp; // special form with a variable
> ```
>
> as it is similar to the form of definition adopted for basic type variables. Here, too, *this is not an assignment* – a conversion operator, rather than the assignment operator =, is involved.

Generic Constructors

If a constructor does not fall into one of the three special categories described above, it is a generic constructor.

Example:

```
class Demo
    {
private:
    Demo(int i,double z); // private constructor
```

```
public:
    Demo(float x,int i);
    Demo(const Vector &v,Matrix *A,int i);
    .....
    };
```

10.6 Defining Pointers to Objects

The `new` operator can be used to define a pointer to an object.

> A constructor is automatically called when a pointer to an object is defined using the `new` operator, and a destructor is automatically called when the same pointer is de-allocated with `delete`. This could *not* be done with C's dedicated allocation functions `malloc`, `calloc`, `realloc` and `free`.

Below are the rules for passing the constructor the values in its argument.

> A constructor can only be called in the explicit form, when the `new` operator is being used.
>
> <class name>*<pointer name> =
>   new <class name>(value of variables);

Example:

```
class Demo
    {
public:
    Demo(int i,float x); //argument with two variables
    Demo(float y); // only one variable
     Demo(void); // default
    ....
    };
......
// uses Demo(int i,float x);
Demo *ptr1 = new Demo(2,3.44); // explicit form

// uses Demo(float x);
Demo *ptr2 = new Demo(1.8); // explicit form

// uses default
Demo *ptr3 = new Demo(); // explicit form
```

Defining the pointer can be separated from the call to the constructor, if so desired.

Example:

```
......
Demo *ptr1; //defines ptr1 without calling constructors
ptr1 = new Demo(2,3.44); // Demo(int i,float x)
```

> You should remember that a pointer does not automatically call a constructor or a destructor when it is defined or leaves scope. This happens *only* if the operators new and delete are used.

Example:

```
Demo *ptrDemo = new Demo(1,3.); // call a constructor
....
delete ptrDemo; // call the destructor
```

> It is a serious mistake to use the delete operator with a pointer that has not been initialized with the new operator.
> A second mistake is that of failing to use the delete operator with a pointer that has been initialized with the new operator, as the destructor is *not* called and the object is *not* de-initialized.

Example:

```
{
Demo objDemo,ptrDemo=&objDemo;
Demo *pt = new Demo(1,3.);
....
delete ptrDemo; // serious error
}    // *pt is not de-initialized
```

10.7 Defining Arrays of Objects

An array of objects is defined in the same way as an array of variables. So there are two possible ways in which an array can be defined, which make use of different storage locations; the first uses the operator [], while the second uses the new operator. In the former, the array has global *or* local duration, depending on where the definition is placed (see Chapter 6) and the compiler takes care of managing storage. In the latter, storage is used dynamically and the user must release it when it is no longer needed.

Example:

```
Demo vectDemo[10];
Demo *ptrDemo = new Demo [10];

delete [10] ptrDemo; // frees storage
                     // remember dimensions [10]
```

Warning – Do not confuse:

```
Demo *ptrDemo = new Demo(10);
```

with:

```
Demo *ptrDemo = new Demo [10];
```

In the former, I explicitly use a constructor to initialize the object to which ptrDemo is pointing with the value of 10, whereas I create storage for a 10-element array of type Demo in the latter.

Different rules for initializing data apply, depending on whether the array has been defined with the [] or new operator.

We saw at the beginning of this chapter how data can be initialized in situations where the [] operator has been used to define an array and the class is very simple (struct).

The procedure is different, but rather simple for initializing objects of a more complex class – what I would describe as a class. All that has to be done is to call the appropriate constructor in a list enclosed in a block {} for every object in the array.

The constructor has to be defined explicitly if it has more than one variable in its argument, while the special simplified form of definition can be used if it only has one.

Fewer terms in the list than have been declared can be used only if a constructor with a void argument (default constructor) has been defined, in which case the constructor is used to fill up the list.

The compiler automatically calls the destructor for each object when the array leaves scope.

Example:

```
class Demo
    {
public:
    Demo(int i,float x);
```

```
   Demo(float x);
   Demo(void);
   ~Demo(void);
   };
....
Demo vectDemo1[4] = // dimensions do not have to
                    // be supplied
   {
   Demo(3,1.56),  // first constructor
   Demo(7.18),    // second constructor
   5.3,   // second in simplified form
    Demo()   // default constructor
   };
Demo vectDem2[10] =
   {
   Demo(2,3.14),
   6.12,  // Demo(void) is used for the others
   };
Demo matDem2[2][2] =
   {
   {Demo(2,3.14),Demo(2,5.)},
   {5.1,Demo(1,2.)}
   };
```

Where the array has been defined with the new operator, objects cannot be initialized *explicitly*.

A default constructor (with a void argument), if it exists, is used.

If there is no default constructor, no other constructor of any other type should be present. Here, the compiler uses a default constructor which has been generated automatically. But it is a good idea to avoid this, because it can give rise to errors.

Example:

```
class Demo
   {
public:
   Demo(int i,float x);
   Demo(float x);
   Demo(void);
   };
   ....
   Demo *ptrDemo = new Demo [10];// Demo(void) is used
                                 // 10 times
```

```
. . . . .
delete [10] ptrDemo; // free storage
                     // uses the destructor 10 times
```

> If you have to de-allocate an array of objects initialized with new, *you have to place the dimensions* after the delete operator. If you do not, the destructor is called for only one object.

Example:

```
Demo *ptrDemo = new Demo [10];// Demo(void) is used
                             // 10 times

. . . . .
delete ptrDemo; // the destructor is called
               // only once
               // only one object is de-initialized
```

10.8 Initialization List

So far, we have considered only classes that consist of simple type members. If, however, a class member were to be an object of another class or a const type variable, the problem of how they are to be initialized would arise, as we know that this cannot be done in the class definition.

> There is another characteristic that distinguishes constructors from ordinary functions – variables and class member objects can be initialized with an initialization list.
> An *initialization list* has the following syntax.
>
> (1)   It is placed in a constructor's *definition*, and *not* in its *declaration*.
> (2)   It is inserted after the round brackets of the constructor's arguments and before the constructor's definition block is opened.
> (3)   The operator : (semi colon) is placed before it.
> (4)   The identifier, followed by a calculable expression or a numeric value in round brackets, is used to initialize a basic type variable.
> (5)   A copy-initializer constructor in a simplified but general form is used to initialize an object. If the class the object belongs to does not have its own copy-initializer constructor, one is created by the compiler and it copies all the data. A copy-initializer constructor for all classes should always be defined to prevent this from happening.
> (6)   A comma (the operator *comma*) separates variables and objects, if several of them are used.

Below is the first example of a class where you have to attempt to understand the difference between initializing and assigning variables:

```
class Demo
    {
private:
    int iDemo;
    float xDemo;
    public:
    Demo(int i,float x);
    };
```

The constructor `Demo` can be written so that the variables `iDemo` and `xDemo` are assigned values.

```
Demo::Demo(int i,float x) // no initialization
    {
    iDemo = i;    // assignment
    xDemo = x;    // assignment
    }
```

It can also be written with an initialization for both variables and no assignment.

```
Demo::Demo(int i,float x)
            : iDemo(i), xDemo(x) // initialization.
    { // no assignment
    }
```

A complex expression can also be placed in the variables' argument.

> There is no practical difference between initializing and assigning where normal variables are involved. But you have to initialize, where objects or `const` variables are involved.
> An object cannot be used by a `class` unless its type is *defined* for that `class`, as a *preventive declaration is not sufficient for this.*

Example:

```
class Sample; // Sample declaration
class Demo
    {
private:
    Sample objSample; // error: Sample must
                      // be defined
    };
```

Example:

```
class Sample // Sample declared from here
    {
    ......
public:
    Sample(const Sample &ss); // copy-initializer
                              // constructor
    }; // Sample is defined from here
     // a preventive declaration is not sufficient
class Demo
    {
private:
    Sample objSample;
    const float constDemo;
    int iDemo;
public:
    Demo(int i,float x,const Sample &oo);
     ...
    };
......
Demo::Demo(int i,float x,const Sample &oo)
      : constDemo(x),objSample(oo) //initialization
    {
    iDemo = i; // assignment(for this only)
    }
```

Notice that basic variables can use this syntax – a similar syntax to that of an object which is using a copy-initializer constructor – to be initialized only in a constructor's initialization list.

Example:

```
class Demo
    {
private:
    int iDemo;
    float xDemo;
public:
    Demo(int i,float x)
            : iDemo(i)  // OK pseudo copy-initializer
                        // constructor
```

```
    {
    xDemo(x);        // NO a copy-initializer
                     // constructor does not exist
    }
    };
```

Variables and objects initialized using an initialization list receive values *before* the constructor's body is executed.

```
class Demo
    {
private:
    int iDemo;
    int jDemo;
public:
    Demo(int i,int j) : iDemo(i) //iDemo initialized
        {jDemo = j + iDemo;} // iDemo is initialized
                             // before jDemo
    };
```

The initialization order in an initialization list is *the order in which the members appear in the* class *definition, not the order in which they are placed in the initialization list.*

```
class Demo
    {
private:
    int iDemo;
    int jDemo;
public:
    Demo(int i,int j);
    };
....
    Demo(int i,int j); : jDemo(j),iDemo(i)
            // Beware. iDemo is initialized first
        {} // no statement
```

Exploiting priorities, whether of initializing over assigning or inside initialization lists, will be avoided.
Once again, the importance of explicitly defining a copy-initializer constructor can be stated.

10.9 Defining Objects with Global Scope

Often a program requires some operations – opening files, preparing the screen for executing graphics and so on – before the program itself is run. Other operations which complement those preceding the program – closing files, restoring conditions in the screen and so on – are necessary at the end of the program.

In a procedural language, a commonly used technique is to call a dedicated initializing function as the first statement of `main`. Another function for de-initializing is called as the last statement in `main`.

> But this technique suffers from a serious drawback. If there is a break in program running due to a numerical error for example, de-initializing is not carried out. Detecting all the possible points where the program may be interrupted is a difficult and often impossible task.

C++'s solution to this problem is much safer and more elegant.

Chapter 6 set out how a variable with a global scope is initialized before `main` is executed and leaves scope after the program has been executed.

> This important characteristic can be exploited to respectively initialize and de-initialize *objects with a global scope* before the beginning of `main` and after the program has stopped running.

Example:

```
ManageFiles objManageFiles;
main()
    {
    statements;
    }
```

The object `objManageFiles` can open the files that are needed before the beginning of `main` and close them when the program is finished

> *Warning*: You are faced with a different kind of programming, which is made possible by an object-oriented approach.
>
> An object can also be seen as a kind of mini-program in itself. When the object is defined, it can carry out a series of quite complex operations; in other words, a program.
>
> In the case currently under consideration, the program can be thought of as being divided into three parts: initialization, generated in the definition of a global object, the program itself, managed by `main`, and de-initialization, generated when the object leaves scope.

10.10 Temporary, Hidden Objects with No Explicit Identifier

All languages, FORTRAN, C, C++, and so on, have a mechanism which is hidden from the user, but which is of fundamental importance. Suppose, for example, that you wanted to execute a series of operations in one statement:

```
a = b + 2.*c
```

The compiler has to store the result of each single operation, so that it can be used in subsequent calculations. The result of the multiplication 2.*c in the example above must be stored for it to be added to the variable b. The result of the addition is, in turn stored and finally assigned to variable a. These partial results are stored by hidden variables, which have no explicit identifier, but which have an identifier that only the compiler recognizes.

This mechanism, by which a hidden object is automatically created, should be fully grasped, because, in C++, objects that are different from basic variables can be created. In fact, if you restricted yourself to operating with basic type variables, there would be no need to worry about how and when the compiler creates and eliminates hidden variables. Everything runs automatically and smoothly. But where objects of a new type are concerned, programmers who created the new type of object are responsible for initializing and de-initializing the object. They must therefore know under what circumstances an object is created and when that object is eliminated.

Direct Call to a Constructor

When a constructor is called directly, the compiler automatically defines a hidden object.

Example:

```
class Demo
    {
public:
    Demo (int i,float x);
    void Func(int j);
    };
......
Demo(3,55.67).Func(4);
```

In this example, `Demo(3,55.67)` defines an object with an identifier which is unknown to the user, but known to the compiler, which calls the function `Func`. When the statement has finished, the object can no longer be accessed, and is still in scope (that is, it still takes up storage) until a block is closed, `}`.

> You should be very aware that a hidden object is created when a constructor is called explicitly and that prevents an error from creeping in.
>
> Suppose you have several overloaded constructors of the same `class`, and they share many operations. It would be a good idea to place all the shared operations into one function. *But you should take care*, because a shared function *should not be a constructor* – a constructor called by another constructor would work on a hidden and independent object, and never on the same object.

Example:

```
class Demo
    {
private:
    int iii,jjj;
public:
    Demo(int i,int j){iii=i;jjj=j;}
    Demo(int i){Demo(i,i);} // uses a constructor
    ....
    };
....
Demo dd(3,4);
Demo yy(7); // iii and jjj of yy are NOT initialized
```

In this example, the object `yy` calls the constructor `Demo(i)`, which, in turn, directly calls the constructor `Demo(i,i)`. This creates a hidden object, which is independent of the object `yy`. The hidden object initializes its own member variables `iii` and `jjj` and then leaves scope. So the object `yy` is not initialized.

Hidden Object Generated in Function Returns

C++ uses the mechanism outlined below when an object, which has been defined in a function, is `returned` by a function.

(1) A hidden object is created. It is initialized with the object which has been passed by an automatic call to the copy-initializer constructor.

(2) The object which has been passed leaves the function's scope and is automatically de-initialized by the destructor.

cont.

cont.

(3)   The hidden object is *defined,* with a scope which is local to the calling function, from the point at which the statement in which the function `returns` the object is made.

(4)   Users can *access* the hidden object *only in that statement* because they do not know the object's identifier.

(5)   The hidden object *leaves scope* only *when the block containing the statement in which the function is called is closed.*

Take the following definition of the `class Demo` and of a function, `Func`, which `returns` a type `Demo` object.

```
class Demo
    {
public:
    Demo (void);
    Demo (const Demo &dd); // copy-initializer
                           // constructor
    void Print(void);
    ~Demo(void);
    };
......
Demo Func(void) // returns type Demo object
    {
    Demo dLocFunc; // the object dLocFunc is created
    statements;
    return dLocFunc; // dLocFunc is passed
    }
......
```

Let's look at three different situations.

(1)   Initializing an object, with the object returned by a function:

```
Demo d1 = Func(); // initialize d1
```

The default constructor is called in `Func` to create `dLocFunc` and the statement sequence of the function is executed. Before the object `dLocFunc` leaves scope, it initializes a hidden object using the copy-initializer constructor. The object `dLocFunc` leaves scope and calls the destructor. The hidden object initializes the object `d1` by calling the copy-initializer constructor again.

 The hidden object stays in scope along with `d1` because it is defined in the same statement.

(2)   The object returned by the function is assigned to another object:

```
Demo d2;
d2 = Func(); // assign d2 with the object passed by Func
```

The process is very similar to the preceding example, until the hidden object is assigned to d2. The main difference consists in the fact that the assignment operator = is called, rather than the copy-initializer constructor, to copy the hidden object to the object d2. However, the assignment operator must be defined in class Demo for this operation between objects of type Demo to go ahead (see Chapter 11).

> The hidden object can be made to leave scope independently of the object d2. The statement in which the function Func is called needs only to be enclosed in a block that does not contain d2's definition.

Example:

```
Demo d2;
{d2 = Func();} // hidden object
               // immediately leaves scope
```

(3)   The returned object is used only in the statement in which the call to Func appears:

```
......
  {
   Func().Print(); // hidden object is created and used

   statements; // it cannot be used any longer
   } //hidden object leaves scope
......
```

Here, the hidden object is used to call the function Print(). This object cannot be used in subsequent statements and leaves scope only at the end of the block, }.

> It is advisable to enclose the statement, in which a function passing an object and thus creating a hidden object is called, in a block,{}, so that the hidden object can be immediately destroyed by making it leave scope.

10.11 Function returns

We can now go into the options presented by functions returning variables, objects, pointers or references in greater depth.

> Remember that however large the object returned, a copy of that object is used to initialize a hidden object of the same type. If the object is a basic type variable or a normal type of derived variable – pointers or references to basic variables – the compiler supplies the most suitable copy-initializer constructor. If the object was user-defined, it should be ensured that a suitable copy-initializer constructor is explicitly defined. Whatever the case, the hidden object passes the value rather than the variable (it could equally be an expression) that appears in the return.

We have seen that to pass a variable to a function by using its argument, it is advisable to use a pointer or a reference when the object to be passed is large – an operation to copy just the address, rather than the whole object, is executed. The procedure is completely safe because the object's address is copied and it remains safely in scope throughout the function call.

> Is it possible not to return an object and so avoid creating a hidden object? Can a pointer or reference be used in a return, so that only an address is passed, storage saved and efficiency boosted (because they do not have to initialize the hidden object), as was done for objects passed into a function argument?
> *Answer*: it depends on the duration and scope of the object which is being returned.

Now let's look in detail at the various options presented by returning a pointer or a reference to an object. A float type variable will be examined to keep presentation of the example as simple as possible, although the considerations below are just as valid for objects, however complicated they may be. The important thing here is to establish when passing an address is safe.

Objects with FILE Scope

Example:

```
float glob;// global variable

// float type return
float Fun1(float y){glob = y;return glob;}
```

```
// returns pointer to float
float *Fun2(float y){glob = y;return &glob;}

// returns reference to float
float &Fun3(float y);{glob = y;return glob;}
main()
    {
    float x1 = Fun1(3.);
    float *x2 = Fun2(3.);
    float x3 = Fun3(3.);
    }
```

The variable glob is defined of type float and is global. Its lifetime lasts throughout the program and it can be accessed by the three functions as well as by main.

> What follows below is intended only to demonstrate how an object behaves when it is returned. The object is global and is visible to all functions and, therefore, returning it with a function is not advisable for reasons of program clarity.

The value 3. is passed in the three calls to the variable with local scope y. The variable of global scope glob is then assigned the value y. Up to here, behaviour in all three cases is identical.

When Fun1 executes return, a hidden variable with a value equal to a glob is created and the hidden variable's value is assigned to x1.

When Fun2 executes return, a hidden pointer with the same address as glob's is created, which is valid. The address is assigned to the pointer x2. Since the variable glob only leaves storage at the end of the program, its address remains valid and there are no problems.

The same happens with the reference and the function Fun3.

Unlike the first case, a hidden pointer and *not* a hidden object is created in these two cases.

> I will not use returns for global type variables or objects, nor for a reference or a pointer to a global type reference, even though this does not give rise to safety problems.

Objects with the Scope of Called Functions

It is here that the greatest care possible should be taken.
Example:

```
// returns type float
float Fun1(float y){return y;}
```

```
    // returns pointer to float
float *Fun2(float y){return &y;}

    // returns reference to float
float &Fun1(float y){return y;}
main()
    {
    float x1 = Fun1(3.); //OK
    float *x2 = Fun2(3.); //help help help
    float x3 = Fun3(3.);  //help help help
    }
```

Once again, the value 3. is passed to the variable with local scope y which is thus initialized. y is a local variable, which is stored on the stack. Its lifetime lasts until the end of the function and it then leaves scope.

When Fun1 executes return, a hidden variable is created which is initialized by y, which can thus leave scope. The value of the hidden variable is then assigned to x1.

When Fun2 executes return, a hidden pointer is created and it is assigned the value of y's address, that is, one of stack's memory addresses, where y is temporarily located. The address is passed to the pointer x2, which can now access the address of stack, in which y is no longer located, but which the compiler may have used for other reasons. Whatever use is made of x2 can thus lead to unpredictable and disastrous results. The same goes for using the reference to a variable with local scope inside the called function.

> One of the most dangerous and insidious errors consists in returning a pointer or a reference to an object which has been *defined locally in a function.*

Suppose you have defined a class of type Matrix. The first definition of the function Add is correct, but the other two should be avoided.

```
    // returns type Matrix: OK
Matrix Add(const Matrix &left,const Matrix &right)
    {
    Matrix result;
    statement;
    returns result;    // OK
    }
    // returns pointer to Matrix: NO
Matrix *Add(const Matrix &left,const Matrix &right)
    {
    Matrix result;
    statements;
```

```
    return &result; // NO
    }

    // return reference to Matrix: NO
Matrix &Add(const Matrix &left,const Matrix &right)
    {
    Matrix result;
    statements;
    return result; // NO
    }
```

 You should never use functions to return pointers or references to objects which have been defined in the function, as the object has the function's local scope.

Chapter 12 looks at the device used by some authors to avoid copying the whole of a large object.

Dynamically Created Objects.

The difficulty you encounter in returning a pointer or a reference to a local variable is linked to the fact that its memory address can be used again during the program, because it is on the stack. You may think you are getting round this obstacle by dynamically defining the object in the called function, which means that the *storage* used is *free store* and the stack's memory is no longer used.

Example:

```
Matrix *Add(const Matrix &left,const Matrix &right)
    {
    Matrix *result = new Matrix;;
    statements;
    return result;
    }
....
Matrix *mat = Add(A,B); // A and B are two Matrices
....
delete mat; // frees memory
```

Let's look at what happens next. The pointer result is defined in the function Add. The appropriate memory for the Matrix type object to which result is pointing is found with the new operator in free store. But the identifier result is local and is stored on the stack.

When Add calls the return, the pointer result, before leaving scope, is copied to a hidden pointer, which is passed to mat. The hidden pointer, like result before it, points to an address of free store. So in this case the address remains valid and the storage needed for the object remains reserved for it. And you may think you have got round the obstacle.

Unfortunately, there are two rather serious drawbacks.

(1) The procedure flies in the face of correct usage in object-oriented programming. Indeed, one of its greatest advantages consists in making the object manage all those operations involving the creation and release of storage necessary to the object itself. But, in the above example, users have to wipe out explicitly the storage associated with the object to which `mat` points, without it having been specifically requested by the users, and they must therefore know what happens inside the function `Add`.

(2) The second drawback is even more serious. If the hidden object, a pointer to a `Matrix`, for example, is only used in the statement calling the function without being assigned to a variable, (to `mat` in this case), it can *no longer be retrieved*. Thus the storage occupied by the object cannot be released, even though a usable object no longer exists.

Example:

```
Add(A,B)->Print();
```

In this example, the pointer to the object created by the function `Add` is used to print the result. When the statement is finished, the pointer cannot be retrieved, and so the object created inside the function `Add` cannot be de-initialized with `delete`.

Because of these drawbacks, *I will not use a function to* `return` *a pointer or a reference to an object which has been dynamically created inside a function.*

Objects with the Scope of Calling Functions

Here, a distinction should be made between whether the *called* function is or is not a member of the `class` of which the object is a member.

The Called Function is not a Class Member

When a called function is *not* a member of the class of which the object, defined in the calling function, is a specimen, the object *cannot* be returned by the called function, because it is not in its scope and thus cannot be accessed by the function unless a pointer or a reference to the object itself is passed by the called function's argument.

In which case, you may wonder what the point of returning objects is.

> When a pointer or reference to an object is passed with an argument, you may wish to return a specific part of the object rather than the whole object.

Example:

```
//returns type float
float Fun1(float *v,int n){return v[n];}

    //returns pointer to float
float *Fun2(float *v,int n){return &v[n];}

    // returns reference to float
float &Fun3(float *v,int n){return v[n];}
.......
void Func(void)
    {
    static float vv[5]={1.,2.,3.,4.,5.};
    float x1 = Fun1(vv,2);   // x1 = vv[2]
    float *x2 = Fun2(vv,2); // *x2 = vv[2]
    float x3 = Fun3(vv,2);   // x3 = vv[2]
    }
```

A variable pointer, v, is initialized in the various functions with the address of the beginning of the vector vv. Suppose the integer n is such that v[n] is inside the definition of vv, so that the vector v[n] can be used without giving rise to problems.

Let's see what happens in the three cases.

The variable v[2] is returned in the first case; but a hidden variable which is assigned the value of v[2] is created. The hidden variable is used to initialize x1.

In the second case, a hidden pointer which is initialized with v[2]'s address is created. The hidden pointer, that is, the *address* of v[2], is used to initialize x2. So the content of this address is the same as the content of vv[2]'s address.

The same thing happens with the reference but it does not necessitate use of the operator *.

> Three points are important here.
>
> (1)   The example demonstrates one of the defects in procedural programming. To know whether n is within the validity range of the vector, the two validity bounds inside the function have to be known.
> (2)   If n does fall within the vector's validity range, v[n]'s address is also valid and has the same scope as the object passed in the argument
>
> *cont.*

cont.

which, having been defined by the calling function, has the local scope of that function. So this address can be used inside the calling function without giving rise to difficulties.

(3)   The procedure can be used not only to *obtain* the values of a vector's coefficients, but also to assign them a value.

Let's use the functions Fun1, Fun2, Fun3 to write the following statements:

```
Fun1(vv,2) = 5.;      // error
*Fun2(vv,2) = 5.;     // content of the address = 5
Fun3(vv,2) = 5.;      // idem
```

The first statement cannot be executed and the compiler would flag an error because Fun1 is not an lvalue (see Chapter 12).

By contrast, the other two statements are accepted. What exactly do they do? In both cases, the numeric value to the right of the assignment is assigned to the variable whose address is that of the expression on the left of the assignment symbol (it becomes the content of that address). In other words, it is as if the following had been written:

```
vv[2] = 5.;
```

Class Member Called Functions

Where the called function is a member of the class to which the object belongs, it is accessed by the object itself.

Example:

```
class VectorDemo
    {
private:
    float v[10];
public:
    float &Value(int i)// returns reference to float
        {
        if(i < 0 || i >= 10) Error();
        return v[i];  // & should not be used
        }
    };
......
```

```
VectorDemo vv; // type VectorDemo object
vv.Value(2) = 12.; // assign a value
float x = vv.Value(2); // use a value
```

Information on the object to be manipulated is not passed to the function Value using the function argument. It is the object itself which sends the message to the function and receives it from the function. The function can manipulate the object's data and return a reference or a pointer to a member of the object. All this happens safely, because the object itself has a global scope or the scope of the calling function. finally, the object is aware of the vector's validity *range* and can control it.

> When a function returns a variable's address, the user can access the variable and change it. So great care must be taken to return pointers or references only when there are firm guarantees that errors will not be created.

For example, given the program fragment above, a variable pointer can be initialized with the vector's initial address and can then be used to violate v's data or to leave the definition range:

```
float *x; // define a pointer to float
x = &vv.Value(0); // assign v[0]'s address to x
*x = 5.; // assign value 5 to v[0]'s content
x[20] = 7.; // help help. May leave range
```

You run a similar risk when a pointer is returned.

> Where I believe it is right use a function to return a class member's address, I will choose a reference rather than a pointer, because using the function is simpler and more immediate since it does not require use of the * operator.

> There is another situation in which it is important to return a reference – when returning the reference to the object that has called the function. Here, we encounter a new kind of problem which is typical of objects and which may well appear just as baffling.

Suppose that a number of functions, Func1, Func2, Func3, etc. have been defined in a Demo class, with a void return. And suppose that an object has to call the functions in sequence but not in any predefined order. You would have to write the following:

```
Demo objDemo; // object defined
objDemo.Func1();
```

```
objDemo.Func3();
objDemo.Func2();
```

Instead, you can transform the function definitions so that they return a reference to class's object and write return *this in the definition.

For example, instead of defining:

```
void Demo::Func1(void)
    {
    statements;
    return;
    }
```

you can define it as follows:

```
Demo &Demo::Func1(void)
    {
    statements;
    return *this;
    }
```

> What does defining a function which returns a *reference to the* class *object* and writing *this in the return statement mean?
> Remember that this is the identifier of the pointer that the compiler creates automatically. It points to the object calling the function. Therefore, *this is the object which is calling the function. A reference returns the object and avoids calling the copy-initializer constructor.
> From the user's point of view the entity constituted by the object and the functions, united by the . operator, is still the object, even if it may be modified inside the function.

You can write the following, if the functions have been redefined to return a reference to the calling object:

```
Demo objDemo;
objDemo.Func1().Func3().Func2();
```

Since the . operator associates to the right, the function Func1 is called first, the object (which may have been modified) is returned by function Func1 and can, in turn, call the function Func3, and so on.

This technique is very important for two reasons.

(1) Once you have learned it, writing programs will come more easily to you and they will be easier to read.
(2) Mathematical objects such as Vectors or Matrices can be made to be very similar to basic variables. In particular, multiple assignments can be performed (see Chapter 11).

Example:

```
Matrix A = B = C + D;  // B = C + D; A = B;
A = B += C;  // B = B + C; A = B;
```

10.12 Questions

Can obj be initialized as below?

```
struct Sample
    {
private:
    int i;
public:
    float x;
    };
.....
Sample obj = {1,5.};
```

No, because i is private.

What errors have been made in the following program fragment?

```
class Sample
    {
private:
    int i;
    Sample(int ii){i = ii;}
public:
    void Sample(void){i=0;} // default constructor
    int GetValue(void){return i;}
    };
```

cont.

> *cont.*
> ```
> ....
> Sample obj(3);
> ```

The constructors should have neither the `return` type, nor `void`.

The constructor `Sample(int ii)` is private and cannot be used by an object, if it is neither defined in a member nor in a `friend` function of `Sample`.

 Which is the constructor that is convenient to define if you want to define an array of objects?

The default constructor, that is, the constructor with a `void` argument. This is always advisable, but you are obliged to define it, if other constructors exist.

 Why is the copy-initializer constructor fundamentally important?

Because it is brought into play in three situations – initializing an object, when the object is passed into a function argument and when an object is `returned` by a function.

 What type of constructor is the following?

```
class Demo
    {
private:
    float xDemo;
public:
    Demo(float x){xDemo = x;}
    };
```

A constructor for converting a type `float` variable into a type `Demo` object.

 What do the following definitions mean?

```
Sample *ptr1 = new Sample(5);
Sample *ptr2 = new Sample[5];
```

In the first case, the object which `ptr1` points to is initialized by a constructor of type `Sample(int i)`.

In the second, an array of 5 objects is defined of type `Sample`.

Which calls the destructor when it leaves scope – a pointer or a reference?

A reference never calls it. A pointer must have been initialized with the operator `new` and must call the destructor with the `delete` operator.

 How is a value assigned to a variable which has been declared a class member and which has the modifier `const`?

It cannot be initialized while the class is defined, because a class is not a real object. Neither can it be assigned a value in a function's or a constructor's body, because it is a constant. It can only receive a value if a constructor's initialization list is used.

 Why is a class with a destructor in its `private` area a `private` class?

Because only class member or `friend` functions can define class objects.
A normal function cannot define an object of the class since when the object leaves scope, the destructor cannot be called.

 Why does only one destructor exist for every class?

Destructors cannot be overloaded because they must always have `void` arguments.

 What is the `return` of a destructor?

A destructor, like constructors, does not have a `return`.

 Given the class:

```
class Sample
    {
private:
    int ii;
public:
    Sample(void){ii=0;}
    };
```

which of the following objects is defined correctly?

cont.

```
cont.
  Sample o1;
  Sample o2();
  Sample o3 = Sample;
  Sample o4 = Sample();
```

Objects o1 and o4.

Why is the following copy-initializer constructor wrong?

```
class Sample
    {
private:
    int ii;
public:
    Sample(Sample ss){ii = ss.ii;}
    };
```

Because it is defined with a Sample object and not with a reference. The compiler would flag an error. If it failed to do so, an infinite loop would be created.

Say whether the following fragment is acceptable.

```
class Demo
    {
    ... // Demo defined
    };
    ....
    Demo obj,*ptr=&obj;
    ....
    delete ptr;
```

The delete operator must never be used if the address has not been dynamically created with the new operator.

Why, when the storage of an array object is freed, do you have to write the array's dimensions?

Example:

```
Sample *ptr = new Sample [100];
...
delete [100] ptr;
```

Because only if this is done do all the array's elements call the destructor.

Should a constructor's initialization list be written in the definition or the declaration or both?

Only in the definition.

What is wrong with the `Vector` constructors below and what can be done to put it right?

```
class Vector
    {
private:
    int dimensions;
    float *vector;
public:
    Vector(int n);
    Vector(int n,float c);
    };
Vector::Vector(int n)
    {
    dimensions = n;
    vector = new float[n];
    }
Vector::Vector(int n,float c)
    {
    Vector(n);
    for(int i = 0;i < n;i++)
            vector[i] = c;
    }
```

The second constructor directly calls the first, thus creating a hidden object which is initialized instead of the right one.

Since both constructors have one part in common, it is useful to construct a function which is used by both.

10.13 Examples

Temporary File Management Class

You want to write a matrix or a vector or some other sort of data item in a temporary file which can be retrieved at a later date. The problem you face is to give every temporary file a unique name which can be retrieved when necessary. One possible solution consists in creating a class which associates with one of its objects the name of a file created automatically when that object is defined.

The class was implemented in the two files UTILITY.HPP and UTILITY.CPP, which are described in Chapter 8. The former is a header file, whereas the other is compiled.

The part of the file that goes in UTILITY.HPP is as follows:

```cpp
#ifndef TEMPFILE_HPP
#define TEMPFILE_HPP

// ===========================================================
// ==================  TempFile class   ================
// ===========================================================

class TempFile
   {
private:
   static int countTempFile;
   char *nameTempFile;
public:
   // default constructor TempFile ff[10];
   TempFile(void){nameTempFile = 0;}

   // constructor TempFile f1("D:"),f2("C:\\TEMP\\");
   TempFile(char *directoryTemp)
      {NewFileName(directoryTemp);}

   // destructor
   ~TempFile(void){delete nameTempFile;}

   // supplies unique name f1.FileName
   char *FileName(void){return nameTempFile;}

   // to be used after default ff[0].NewFileName("D:");
   void NewFileName(char *directoryTemp);
   };

#endif TEMPFILE_HPP
```

The part of the class that goes in UTILITY.CPP is as follows:

```cpp
// ********************< TempFile >********************
// *    Class for creating temporary files            *
// ***************************************************

int TempFile::countTempFile = 0;
```

```
// ********************< NewFileName >********************
// *   Purpose: Initializes when default constructor  *
// *            is used                               *
// *   Example: TempFile ff[10];                      *
// *            ff[0].NewFileName("D:");              *
// ********************************************************
void TempFile::NewFileName(char *directoryTemp)
    {
    nameTempFile = new char [strlen(directoryTemp)+10];
    strcpy(nameTempFile,directoryTemp);
    countTempFile++;
    strcat(nameTempFile,"T");
    char buff[5];
    itoa(countTempFile,buff,10);   // NOT ANSI
     strcat(nameTempFile,buff);
    strcat(nameTempFile,".TMP");
    }
```

The class consists of two items of data:

```
static int countTempFile;
char *nameTempFile;
```

The former is used to characterize all objects with a unique number. The variable `countTempFile` was defined `static` and initialized with zero. The name of the file which is being constructed in the class member function `NewFileName` is stored in `nameTempFile`. The name consists of the directory, supplied by the user in the definition of a class object, and of a unique name obtained by inserting the characteristic number of the object expressed as a string after the letter `T`. The file name ends with the extension `.TMP`. The library function `strcat` is used to link the strings. The library function `itoa` (complementary to `atoi` described in Chapter 7) is used to pass from the numeric value to a string. The function `itoa` is quite widespread, but is not officially included in the ANSI standard. I put the class in `UTILITY.HPP` for this reason.

Let's have a look at an application (in `EXUTY.CPP`):

```
void Ex_TempFile(void)
    {
    TempFile f1("C:\\TEMP\\");
    TempFile f2("C:\\TEMP\\");
    TempFile f3("C:\\TEMP\\");
    TempFile f4("D:");
    TempFile ff[10]; // uses default constructor
```

```
Message("\nFile %s",f1.FileName());
Message("\nFile %s",f2.FileName());
Message("\nFile %s",f3.FileName());
Message("\nFile %s",f4.FileName());
for(int k = 0; k < 10; k++)
    {
    ff[k].NewFileName("D:");
    Message("\nFile %s",ff[k].FileName());
    }
}
```

The file name associated with each object is obtained by calling the function FileName() with the object.

Notice that when a vector of objects is created:

```
TempFile ff[10]; // uses default constructor
```

the default constructor is called and objects cannot receive data. They must explicitly call the function NewFileName placing the name of the directory desired into its argument.

Operator Overloading

Cum grano salis

With a grain of salt

Pliny the Elder, *Natural History*.

11.1 Introduction

We saw in Chapter 7 that functions can be overloaded in C++ – the same identifier can be used for functions with different implementations, if their formal arguments are different. We also saw that it was a first step towards laying the foundation stone of object-oriented programming – polymorphism.

 Operator overloading takes us another large step towards genuine polymorphism.

All modern procedural languages employ a crude version of it. For example, when you execute the sum of two variables, you use the same symbol, +, independently of the fact that the variables are of type integer or floating point. The compiler automatically adapts itself to circumstances.

C extended the facility of using some operators to pointers. As we saw earlier, sum and subtraction operations on pointers automatically take account of the sizes of the variables to which the pointers point. Operators in languages of that kind are intrinsic to the language and may not be modified.

Other languages, which are specific to object-oriented programming, do *not* have intrinsic operators, and the user must define an operator for *every one* of its objects.

C++ stands mid-point between these two extremes, and I believe that this is the best solution. Operators are defined for basic type variables and for those which are intrinsic to the language by the language itself and *cannot* be modified. And so they can be written in the most efficient way possible. At the same time, the same operators in C++ can be redefined, and adapted to the particular demands of every object a user creates.

Thus, having defined `Matrix` type variables, you can, for example, add two matrices A and B to obtain a matrix C, as if they were two basic type variables, using the simple statement:

```
C = A + B;
```

A few constraints apply to overloading operators in C++.

(1) Intrinsic operators (those used by basic variables) cannot be over-loaded – at least one operand must be the object of a class.

(2) *Not all* operators can be overloaded. Table 2.4 of Chapter 2 shows which operators can and which cannot be overloaded.

(3) New symbols *cannot* be created for new operators. Symbols which already exist can be *combined only in ways laid down* by the language. Only combinations of symbols listed in Table 2.4 can be overloaded.

(4) Operator precedence cannot be modified. For example, the binary operator * always has precedence over the binary operator + (see Table 2.4).

(5) Operators' *arity* cannot be modified. A binary operator cannot be transformed into a unary operator and vice versa (see Table 2.4).

(6) The unary increment operator ++, and the decrement operator --, cannot be distinguished when they are applied to the right or left of an object, unlike intrinsic operators.

(7) The four operators [], (), = and -> must be `class` members and cannot be of type `static`.

For example, given two objects A and B:

```
A->.B; // ->. cannot be overloaded
A**3; // ** impossible combination
A + B * A // * is executed first then +
```

11.2 Syntax for Overloading Operators

The syntax for defining an operator changes according to whether the operator is unary or binary (the only ternary operator, ?:, *cannot* be overloaded) and according to whether the operator is declared as a class member or not.

There are three options for defining an operator. By:

(1)   Declaring it as a member of class.
(2)   Declaring it as a non-member of class.
(3)   Declaring it as a friend of class, rather than as a member.

The type of operator and access to class members determines which of the three options is to be preferred.

Before studying where and when to use one or another type of declaration let's have a look at the syntax which should be used in the definition.

The syntax used in the definition depends on whether the operator is declared a class *member* or *non-member*.

(1)   If it is a class *member*, the following syntax applies:

<return type><class name>:: operator <operator symbol> (argument) {statements;}

In the case above, the argument *must* be of type void, if the operator is unary; if the operator is binary, *one and only one* of the appropriate type of variable *must* be present.

(2)   If it is a *non-member* of class, this syntax is used:

<return type>   operator   <operator symbol>   (argument) {statements;}

In this case, the argument *must* be an object of the class, (or better, a reference) if the operator is unary. But if the operator is binary, *two and only two* variables must be present, of which *at least one must* be an *object* of the class or better, a reference.

The syntax you use is similar to that used for functions, whether operators are class members or not. You put the keyword operator, followed by the operator's symbol, instead of the function identifier.

For example, the unary ++ and the binary + operators are declared as members of Point class, while unary −, and binary * are declared as non-member and friend of Point class in the following fragment:

```
class Point
   {
// - unary
friend Point operator - (const Point &obj);

// * binary
friend Point operator * (float z,const Point &obj.);

// another binary * overloaded
friend Point operator * (const Point &obj,float z);
private:
   float x,y;
public:
   Point(void) // default constructor
      {x = 0.;y = 0.;}
   Point(const Point &obj) // copy-initializer
      {x = obj.x; y = obj.y;} // constructor
   Point(float xx,float yy) //generic constructor
      {x=xx;y=yy}

   // unary ++ with return reference to Point
   Point &operator ++ (void);

   // binary + with return object Point
   Point operator + (const Point &obj);
   ....
   };
......
// Definitions Point class members:
Point &Point::operator ++ (void)
   {
   x += 1.;
   y += 1.;
   return *this; // object which called ++
   }
Point Point::operator + (const Point &obj)
   {
   return Point(x+obj.x,y + obj.y);// hidden object
       // with direct call to constructor
   }
```

```
// Definitions for non-members
Point operator - (const Point &obj)
   {
   return Point(-obj.x,-obj.y); // hidden object
      // with direct call to constructor
   }
Point operator * (float z,const Point &obj)
   {
   return Point(z*obj.x,z*obj.y);
   }

// * overloaded

Point operator * (const Point &obj,float z)
   {
   return Point(z*obj.x,z*obj.y);
   }
```

Example of usage:

```
Point p1(3.,4.),p2(1.,6.); // generic constructor
p1++; // x=4., y=5.
Point p3 = -p1 + p2;// unary - and binary +
Point p4 = 2.*p1;  // binary *
```

Note the following points.

(1)   When an operator has to pass an object, using its argument, it is better to pass a *reference* to the object instead – you keep the same syntax, and the copy-initializer constructor is not called.

> References to objects were brought into C++ for the precise purpose of making operator overloading similar to intrinsic operations, while maintaining maximum efficiency.
>
> In fact, the two alternatives are as follows:
>
> (1)   Passing the object. Here, the copy-initializer constructor creates a hidden object and copies all the object's data; but this has obvious disadvantages (see Chapter 10).
> (2)   Using a pointer to the object. This would make the program read poorly.

If you use pointers instead of references when + is defined, the result is as follows:

```
Point p5 = &p1 + &p2 // instead of p5 = p1 + p2;
```

As was the case with normal functions, I will *always* use a `const` type *reference,* when an operator requires an object in its argument which must *not* be modified.

If an object can be modified during an operation, I will do the following.

(1) An operator will be used only if the intrinsic operator modifies the variable to which it is applied. The operators `++`, `--`, `=`, `+=`, `*=`, `-=` and `%=` fall into this category. They will always be implemented as class members, so that the modified object does not have to be transferred.

(2) In other cases, the user is obliged to use a function in which a pointer to the object is placed in the argument. For example, if you want to find the product of two matrices, `A` and `B`, and to put the result in matrix `B`, you have to use the function `Product(A,&B)`.

The unary `-` operator is a special case. The object to which the operator is applied remains unchanged, and another modified object is returned by the operator. If you want the object to be modified instead, you have to use a special function, `Minus`, not the operator.

(2) A hidden object is created if a direct call to a constructor is used to carry out a `return`. Before the object leaves its scope, it initializes another hidden object, which can be used in the calling function (see Chapter 10).

```
return Point(x+obj.x,y + obj.y);
```

(3) In the operator `++`, `return` was defined as a *reference* to an object of type `Point`.

```
Point &operator ++ (void); // return to Point &
```

Since the `return` is:

```
return *this;
```

the returned object is the one which called the operator.

The copy-initializer constructor is *not* called, because a reference is being returned and, at the same time, the object which called the operator can be accessed directly.

Example:

```
Point p4 = ++p1 + p2;
```

(4)   There is one element less in the argument of operators declared as class members, in comparison with what they would have, were they to be defined as non-members.

> Let me remind you that, where member functions (and consequently also operators) are concerned, the compiler adds as a first hidden argument a pointer to the object which calls the function. This explains why a member operator apparently has one element less in its argument.

For example, the operator:

```
Point Point::operator + (const Point &obj)
  {
  return Point(x+obj.x,y + obj.y);
  }
```

is treated as if it were:

```
Point Point::operator + (Point *this,const Point &obj)
  {
  return Point(this->x+obj.x,this->y + obj.y);
  }
```

(5)   In turn, operators can be overloaded. You have to follow the same rules as for functions.

> Variables in the argument must be of a different type to overload an operator.

In the example above, two * operators were overloaded:

```
Point operator * (float z,const Point &obj);
Point operator * (const Point &obj,float z);
```

11.3 Assignment Operator =

The assignment operator is used to assign one object to another of the same or a different class.

Example:

```
Matrix A = ....; // A is defined and initialized
Vector v = ....; // v is defined and initialized
Matrix B; // B is defined
```

```
B = A;  // object of the same class is assigned
B = v;  // object of another class is assigned
```

Example:

```
class Point
   {
private:
   float x,y;
public:
   Point &operator = (const Point &rval)
      {x = rval.x;y = rval.y;return *this;}
   };
```

> If an assignment operator is not explicitly defined in a class, and if an object of the *same* class is assigned to another, the compiler copies all the data in the first object to the second. This can be very dangerous, as was the case with copy-initializer constructors, for the same reasons (see Chapter 10). This danger should be avoided by defining an assignment operator in every class.

Example:

```
class VectorDemo
   {
private:
   int dimensions;
   float *vector;
public:
   VectorDemo(void)
      {dimensions=0;vector=0;}
   VectorDemo(int n,float x);
   };
....
VectorDemo::VectorDemo(int n,float x)
   {
   dimensions = n;
   for(int i=0;i < n;i++)
      {vector[i] = x;
   }
....
VectorDemo v(3,5.),w;
w = v;  // w.dimensions = v.dimensions;
        // w.vector = v.vector; // help help
```

The object w shares the vector with the object v, with disastrous consequences.

You must bear the following points in mind when planning to overload assignment operators.

(1) The operator (or operators, if you want to define more than one) must be a class member. It *cannot* be a non-member or friend function.

(2) The object must already have been defined for it to be able to receive the value of another object. *The copy-initializer constructor* is called and *not* the assignment operator, if the symbol = is used when an object is defined.

```
Matrix A = B; //initialized not assigned
```

(3) The object must be de-initialized before being overwritten by the new object.

(4) You have to go on to initialize the object so that it can receive a copy of the other object.

Thus, the assignment operator essentially consists in a merging of the operations executed by the destructor and the copy-initializer constructor.
In fact, two auxiliary functions are often created, one for de-initializing the object and the other for initializing it. The destructor and the assignment operator call the first function and the copy-initializer constructor and the assignment operator the second.

For example, consider this example;

```
B = A;  // assignment
```

If matrix B is not the same size as A, storage taken up by B has to be freed and the requisite space to store the coefficients of A has to be created.

I will follow the rules outlined below to make the assignment operator efficient and consistent with the intrinsic assignment operator.

(1) The return type is a reference to the object which calls the operator and so the return itself is;

```
return *this;
```

which makes a multiple assignment possible:

```
A = B = C;
```

cont.

> *cont.*
> (2)   The object used to assign values will not be modified, on any
>   occasion, during the assignment operation, and, for this reason, the
>   operator's argument will always be a `const` reference to an object.
> (3)   Library functions will be used wherever possible to copy data blocks,
>   when large size objects are being dealt with.

Chapter 12 will go into assignment operators for object classes such as
matrices and vectors.

11.4   Combined Assignment Operators

Operators of this type are very important, because their use obviates the need to use
`return`, with all the associated advantages that this brings (a hidden object is not
created and you do not have to copy the object using the copy-initializer constructor).

> Essentially, these operators consist of an assignment and a specific
> operation taken as one entity. Since assignments, in turn, are made up of de-
> initializations and initializations, these operators generally consist of three
> components (all three are not always present).

Example:

```
class Point
   {
private:
   float x,y;
public:
   Point(const Point &obj) // copy-initializer
      {x = obj.x; y = obj.y;} // constructor
   Point(float xx,float yy) //generic constructor
      {x=xx;y=yy;}
   Point &operator += (const Point &rval);
   ....
   };
......
Point &Point::operator +=
      (const Point &rval)
   {
   x += rval.x;
   y += rval.y;
   return *this; // object which called +=
   }
```

Example of how they are used:

```
Point p1(3.,4.),p2(1.,6.); // generic constructor
Point p3 = p1 += p2; // x = 4., y = 10.
```

Note that it is also convenient with these operators to carry out a return to a reference to the object which calls the operator, so that the operations can be linked to other assignments or initializations. In this example, the operator returns the object *this, which the operation produced. The object is used for initializing another object, p3, using the copy-initializer constructor.

11.5 Operator [ ]

Chapter 10 described how a function, Value, which has a reference to the element returned, can be used to access the elements of a class, VectorDemo.
Example:

```
class VectorDemo
   {
private:
   int v[10];
public:
   float &Value(int i)// return reference to float
      {
      if(i < 0 || i >= 10) Error(...);
      return v[i];  // do not put &
      }
   };
......
```

```
VectorDemo vv; // object of type VectorDemo
vv.Value(2) = 12.; // assign a value
float x = vv.Value(2); // use a value
```

 A code which mimics the behaviour of the vectors intrinsic to C and C++ and using the same technique can be obtained by overloading the operator [ ].

Example:

```
class VectorSample
   {
private:
   int v[10];
```

```
public:
   float &operator []
      (int i) // return reference to float
      {
      if(i < 0 || i >= 10) Error();
      return v[i];  // do not use &
      }
   };
......
```

```
VectorSample vv; // object of type VectorSample
vv[2] = 12.; // assign a value
float x = vv[2]; // use a value
```

Access to data in the vector vv is now entirely similar to what would have been used, had it been defined:

```
float vv[10]; // normal array
```

Chapter 12 will look at how this technique can be broadened to apply to matrices.

11.6 Operator ( )

The fact that you can also overload the function operator, (), considerably increases the flexibility of the language. This operator can solve specific problems, depending on the class involved.

> Note that any number of arguments can be used in the operator. It is brought into play by an object identifier, followed by the actual argument. The object directly calls a function, which has been defined by the operator ( ).

Example:

```
Demo objDemo; // object of the class Demo
int i = objDemo(3,5,19.); // uses the operator ()
```

As far as the classes that we will be looking at are concerned, overloading this operator can mean that the elements of a vector or a matrix are accessed in a similar fashion to the way they are accessed in FORTRAN.

```
class VectorSample
  {
private:
  int v[10];
public:
  float &operator ()
    (int i)// return reference to float
      {
      if(i < 0 || i >= 10) Error();
      return v[i];   // do not put &
      }
    };
......

VectorSample vv; // object of type VectorSample
vv(2) = 12.; // assign a value
float x = vv(2); // use a value
```

Here, the way data in the vector vv is accessed is entirely similar to the method used in FORTRAN, that is, by using round brackets.

Chapter 12 will show how this technique can be extended to matrices.

11.7 Differences between Member and Non-member Operators

As was the case with friend functions, you may wonder when an operator should be defined as a class member, a non-member and a class friend.

> The choice depends on how readily the class members involved can be accessed and on the type of overloaded operator.
> If the classes' source code is not available, a non-member operator and not a friend of the classes has to be selected. Overloading in this case can only be put into effect by operators which do not need to be class members and which can access the required data across the class interface.

For example, if the source code of the class Matrix cannot be accessed, but a function that enables access to the matrix's coefficients has been implemented, an operator can be defined to execute the sum of the two matrices.

Generally speaking, if the source code of the classes involved is available, it is better to implement an operator as a class member, or as a class friend. If it is implemented as a non-member and non-friend of the class, the result is a less efficient code, as the private members of the class cannot be directly accessed.

Now let's turn to when an operator should be chosen as a class member and when it should be declared as friend of the class.

You are occasionally compelled to opt for one of the two solutions and intermediate cases, as was the case in normal functions.

You are compelled to declare an operator as a class friend in two situations.

(1)   When you have to access private data in two different classes; when you want to implement an operator for finding the product of a Matrix and a Vector, for example, a situation which has already been analysed with regard to friend functions.

(2)   When a binary operator is involved and the first operand is a basic type variable.

For example, when you want to execute the following multiplication of a double type number 3.5 and a vector, v, of class Vector:

    x = 3.5 * v;

the operator * cannot be defined as a member of Vector class, because the first operand is not a member of the same class.

The operator cannot be defined as a class member when the first operand of a binary operation is a basic type variable.

The opposite is true for some operators.

The operators =, ( ), [ ] and -> must be defined as class members.

In situations which do not fall exactly into either category, you must do what you did with normal functions; if the operator affects two members of the same class, it is better to use a non-class member function, for reasons of symmetry. If the operator is unary, it is often better to convert it into a class member. For example, the binary operator +, if defined as a non-member of the classes involved in the operation, produces a neater and more symmetrical code. Conversely, the unary increment operator ++ is linked logically to the object which is using it and it is better to implement it as a class member.

11.8 Conversion Operators

You can convert one object into another in C++. For example, a `Vector` can be converted into a `Matrix`.

> An object can be converted into another in either of the *two* following ways.
>
> (1)   By using a constructor to carry out the conversion.
> (2)   By overloading the conversion operator (*cast*).

Chapter 10 dealt with using a constructor dedicated to this aim.

Here, we are looking at how it can be done by using a conversion operator.

Note that you *cannot use both alternatives* at the same time and you have to choose one of the two to implement the conversion. If you do not, the compiler will produce an error because it is faced with ambiguity.

Note, too, that when the term conversion is used, it does *not* refer to an assignment of an object of one type to an object of another type. Conversion takes place only when a conversion operator or constructor is implicitly or explicitly called, that is, only when a conversion operation on the object in question is carried out.

For example, consider the following situations – a constructor for converting a `Vector` into a `Matrix` (or a conversion operator, but *not* both) has been defined, but an assignment operator, with which a `Vector` can be assigned to a `Matrix`, has not. In the following operation:

```
A = v;  // A is a Matrix and v is a Vector
```

the `Vector` v is first converted into a `Matrix` and the hidden `Matrix`, which is thereby obtained, is assigned to `Matrix A`, because there is no assignment operator.

> The following rules should be followed when you want to overload a conversion operator with which an object of type `Atype` can be converted into one of type `Btype`.
>
> (1)   The operator must be a member of the `Atype` class.
> (2)   The syntax which should be used in the declaration is:
>
> ```
> operator Btype (void);
> ```
>
> (3)   The type of `return` must not be placed in the declaration or the definition, as the `return` is implicitly and automatically defined with the identifier `Btype`.
> (4)   But the type `Btype` `return` statement *must* be in the *definition*.
> (5)   The argument *must* be `void`.
>
> *cont.*

cont.

(6) Several conversion operators can be defined for the same class, but this must *not* be exploited for reasons which will be explained later.

(7) The Atype class must be a user-defined class. Conversion operators of basic type variables *cannot* be overloaded.

(8) But Btype can be *either* a user-defined class, *or* a basic variable type

(9) You cannot define a conversion operator and a constructor dedicated to the same purpose at the same time.

Example of a conversion operator of a Demo type object into an int type variable:

```
class Demo
   {
private:
   float xDemo;
public:
   Demo(float x)   // conversion constructor
      {xDemo = x;} // converts float into Demo

   // conversion operator: converts Demo into int
   operator int(void)  // type of return,
      {return (int)xDemo;} // not declared but
                           // return is an int

   int operator float(void); // error: return type
   operator double(int i); // error: non void argument
   ...
   };
...
Demo objDemo = 3.1; //calls the constructor: xDemo = 3.1
int n;
n = objDemo; // implicit call to int()
n = int(objDemo); //can be explicit (function type)
n = (int)objDemo; //another explicit form (cast type)
```

In the three statements above, the conversion operator is called, and it converts objDemo into a hidden int type object with a value of 3, which is then assigned to n.

Example of a conversion operator of a Sample type object into a Demo type object:

```
class Demo
   {
   ..... // Demo defined
   };
```

```
class Sample
  {
private:
  int iSample;
public:
  Sample(int i) // conversion constructor
    {iSample = i;} // converts an int into Sample

  // conversion operator
  operator Demo(void); // converts Sample into Demo
  ....
  };
...
// conversion operator defined
Sample::operator Demo(void)
  {
  statements;
  }
...
void Func(Demo objDemo); // use Demo object
...
Sample objSample(1);
Func(objSample); // objSample is converted into Demo
                 // with an implicit call of
                 // operator Demo()
```

Conversion Operator or Constructor?

We have seen that type conversion can be put into effect using the conversion operator or a conversion constructor (but never at the same time). You may wonder when should one or the other be used.

> You have to use the conversion operator to convert a user-defined class object into a basic type variable. In fact, you cannot build a constructor for a basic type variable.
>
> On the other hand, conversion operators must be implemented inside the class to which an object of another class is to be converted. To convert an Atype object into a Btype object, you must be able to access the Atype class. So you can define this conversion with a conversion operator, only by being able to access the code with which the Atype class is implemented.
>
> But the conversion constructor is implemented in the class Btype into which you want to convert the Atype object. In such cases you can carry out an implementation without having the source code of Atype's class.
>
> In all other respects, conversion constructors are equivalent to conversion operators.

Example:

```
class Sample
   {
public:
   // operator must be defined in Sample
   operator Demo(void); // convert Sample into Demo
   // constructor which converts Demo into Sample
   Sample(const Demo &objDemo);
   ....
   };
```

> Declaring several conversion constructors, or operators with which one type
> of object can be converted into several types of objects, produces an error,
> which is not directly recognized by the compiler and which should be
> avoided.

Example:

```
class Danger
   {
   ..... // Danger defined
   };
class Demo
   {
   ..... // Demo defined
   };
class Sample
   {
private:
   int iSample;
public:
   Sample(int i){iSample = i;} // constructor of Sample
   operator Demo(void); // converts Sample into Demo
   // it is possible, but dangerous to define another
   // conversion operator
   operator Danger(void); // converts Sample into Danger
   ....
   };
void Func(Demo objDemo); // use an object of \Demo
void Func(Danger objDanger); // Func overloaded
...
Sample objSample(1);
Func(objSample); //what is objSample converted into??
```

Unless you come across a situation such as the one created by `Func`, the compiler will not produce an error. But using `Func` creates ambiguity and the compiler produces an error. In fact, the function `Func` in one version accepts `Demo` type objects and in another, `Danger` type objects. When it is called with a `Sample` type object, the compiler does not know which conversion operator to use.

> To convert objects of a class into basic type variables, which is not really all that important in problems of numerical calculus, a conversion *operator* is used. In other cases, both options are valid. It is better not to overuse this facility and above all to remember *never* to define conversions of one object to more than one other object or variable.

For and Against Type Conversions

Assume you have N classes, `Dem1, Dem2, ..., DemN`, for which you want to overload the addition operator, +, the subtraction operator, –, etc. If conversions of the objects of the various classes were not defined, the respective operators for every pair of classes would have to be defined. As N grew, the size of the code would become unacceptably large.

> The advantage of using conversion operators and constructors is that you write more economic codes and you save time, because you avoid redefining large numbers of operators of similar functions.

But let's assume that the classes we are implementing describe different kinds of matrices; for example, normal, triangular, band matrices and so on. All these matrices can be converted to a single class – an unstructured class of matrices – and only the operations which are necessary for this class can be defined. Yet the calculation times and numerical precision of the results can change drastically, whether you do or you do not exploit the particular structure of a matrix.

To give an extreme example: working out a linear system with triangular or tridiagonal matrices is a very different thing from working out a system of the same size but with unstructured matrices.

> In many situations in numerical calculus, type conversions are best avoided, because they lead to a fall in the efficiency of calculations.

It is obvious that you have to weigh up the pros and cons of the alternatives carefully: writing all the functions for every combination; or doing it only for a class and converting objects of the other classes to those objects.

In creating complex classes, like different types of matrices, it is in any case useful to create conversion constructors with which you can define many different classes with special characteristics. Later, and one at a time, the most important classes and those which have been consigned to a more general fate can be defined.

11.9 Questions

Why is the following declaration of the operator [ ] wrong?

```
class VectorDemo
   {
friend float &operator [](int i);
private:
   int dimensions;
   ....
   };
```

The operators [ ], ( ), = and -> must be members of a class.

When are you forced to declare an operator a non-class member and not a friend of that class?

When you do not have the source code of that class.

What benefit is derived from defining the assignment operator with a *this return instead of a void return?

It makes multiple assignments possible.

What drawback ensues from the following definitions of the assignment operator?

```
class Point
   {
private:
   float x,y;
public:
   Point(float xx,float yy)
      {x=xx;y=yy;}
```

cont.

```
cont.
    Point &operator =
        (const Point &rval)
            {this=&rval;return *this;}
    ...
    };
...


Point p1(3.,4.),p2(4.,5.);
p2 = p1;
```

By having the this pointer equal to rval, the two objects p1 and p2 share the same data.

Given the following definition of the class VectorDemo:

```
class VectorDemo
    {
private:
    int dimensions;
    float *vector;
public:
    VectorDemo(int n)
        {
        dimensions=n;
        vector=new float[n];
        }
    float &operator()(int i)
        {return vector[i];}
    ...
    };
```

what happens when the following statements are used?

```
VectorDemo v(3);
v(5);
```

The constructor VectorDemo(int n) is called in the first statement. In the second, the operator () is called and it returns the value of vector[5], but it is not used.

12 Matrices and Vectors

Créer un poncif, c'est le génie. Je dois créer un poncif.

To write a potboiler, that is genius. I ought to write a potboiler.

Baudelaire, *Intimate Journals.*

12.1 Introduction

 Linear algebra has a basic and often undervalued importance for every field of numerical analysis. It plays a decisive role in the following situations.

(1) In solving systems of linear equations.
(2) In multivariate optimization.
(3) In the integration of partial and ordinary differential equations.
(4) In the construction of models (linear and non-linear regressions).

Operations between matrices and vectors are, in turn, the basis of linear algebra and are thus the basis of all numerical calculations.

We have already seen that problems arise in procedural languages, even sophisticated ones like C, when operations involving interactions between matrices and vectors have to be executed. The major drawbacks are listed below.

(1)   Operations between matrices and vectors are carried out via functions (or SUBROUTINES) which must have different identifiers, if the objects they operate on are different. Functions cannot be overloaded, that is, *polymorphism* is absent.

For example, if A, B and C are matrices, and x and y are vectors, it is not possible simply to write:

```
C = A*B; x = A*y;
x = 3.*y;
Product(A,B,&C);
Product(A,y,&x);
Product(3.,y,&x);
```

(2)   Vectors and matrices are unable to prevent themselves from being used incorrectly; in other words, they lack the ability to *hide* data. The user is thus responsible for subsequent use of a matrix, if one of its details is modified.

For example, users have uncontrolled access to the sizes of a vector or a matrix. If users modify them inadvertently, the results are disastrous.

(3)   Users are required to possess a much more detailed knowledge of function implementation than is necessary, that is, there is no *encapsulation of functions and data.*

For example, if users have to solve a linear system, they have to know that it is desirable to factorize the matrix with a function and then pass the factorized matrix to another function. If they have to solve a system in which only the right-hand side vector is changed, the procedure must be modified, since they have to access the second function without using the first. The 'matrix' object does not, by itself, dictate the right functions to be used at the right moment.

FORTRAN has added drawbacks, which are listed below.

(4)   You have to pass the sizes of the vector, or the matrix, on which you are working into the argument in every operation, because you cannot build structures. So the likelihood of making mistakes increases. And the number of terms in a function argument can grow considerably, making it difficult to use the function.

(5)   It is impossible to create vectors and matrices dynamically and so either storage space is wasted or there is not enough storage.

(6)   An auxiliary vector has to be passed by the argument to supply subroutines with the requisite dynamic storage. This working vector is extraneous to the function-user interface and often needs to be sized in a complicated and baffling way.

(7)   Calculations are inefficient because there are no pointers with which data could be accessed more efficiently.

Suppose you had this linear system:

$$\mathbf{Ax} = \mathbf{b}$$

in which matrix **A** is not squared and you want to find the vector x which minimizes the sum of the squares of the residuals. HFTI (notice how difficult it is in FORTRAN to understand a function's purpose from its identifier), an efficient and commonly used SUBROUTINE, requires the following list:

```
CALL HFTI(A,MDA,M,N,B,MDB,NB,TAU,KRANK,RNORM,H,G,IP)
```

It is essential to include the sizes of the various matrices involved (b and x can be either vectors or matrices) and three auxiliary vectors: H for floating point variables, G for integer type variables and IP to store the pivots, which are necessary for the calculation.

In C++, the equivalent could be this (see Chapter 15):

```
Solve(A,b,&x);
```

12.2 Class Plan for Vectors and Matrices

Some fundamental decisions have to be taken in order to make classes coherent and efficient.

> The main decisions are as follows.
>
> (1) What types of objects to consider using.
> (2) How to implement classes, so that calculations reflect algebraic laws and are, at the same time, efficient.
> (3) What type of `return` to use.
> (4) How to initialize class objects.
> (5) Which operations are essential, and which operators and functions can be used.
> (6) How to access vector or matrix elements.
> (7) How and where data should be stored and how to print a vector or matrix.

On Vectors and Matrices

It is not essential, as a general rule, to create an independent class for vectors, being, as they are, matrices with only one column. I decided to treat the vector class as autonomous from and independent of the matrix class for reasons of efficiency. For the same reason, I also rejected the option of deriving the vector class from the matrix class (see chapter 14). By keeping the two classes separate, you can store a vector column as if it were a vector row, with considerable benefits both in terms of calculation speed and storage used (a matrix with only one column and `M` rows requires `M` pointers).

The matrices that I will look at in this chapter are dense, store coefficients and have `float` type elements.

> I will restrict the analysis to:
>
> (1) unstructured matrices;
> (2) triangular matrices (Left or Lower, and Right or Upper);
> (3) symmetrical matrices.

The class names are, respectively: `Matrix`, `MatrixLeft`, `MatrixRight`, `MatrixSymm`. Vectors are treated like vector *columns* in the `Vector class`.

Matrices with other types of structure will not be studied. Chapter 13 examines sparse and unstructured matrices, and Chapter 15 some classes for solving linear systems. The classes considered in this chapter are implemented in the following files: `VECTOR.CPP, MATRIX.CPP, LEFT.CPP, RIGHT.CPP, SYMM.CPP` and use header files: `UTILITY.HPP, VECTOR.HPP, MATRIX.HPP, LEFT.HPP, RIGHT.HPP, SYMM.HPP`. Examples can be found in the files: `EXVECTOR.CPP, EXMATR1.CPP, EXMATR2.CPP, EXLEFT.CPP, EXRIGHT.CPP, EXSYMM.CPP`.

12.3 Implementation of Matrices and Vectors

Various data is required fully to define a vector or matrix. For the moment, we will only look at those that are strictly necessary – the dimensions and values of the coefficients for a vector, and the number of rows, columns and values of the coefficients for a matrix. A vector's dimensions have the following as an identifier.

```
int dimensions;
```

while the number of rows and columns of a matrix will be identified by:

```
int numRows,numColumns;
```

The choice of how to store the elements of vectors or matrices is practically made for you, if you want to use dynamic memory and maximize the efficiency of the implementation. The basic element of vectors is a floating pointer.

```
float *vector
```

while matrices have a pointer to a float pointer.

```
float **matrix
```

Here, the following decisions have to be taken.

(1)   Between which values to vary the indices of vectors and matrices.
(2)   How, physically, to store elements.

The simplest thing to do would be to follow C's standard method – indices that vary between 0 and the number of elements -1. But this choice would be damaging in terms of problems of numerical analysis, because all numerical algorithms deal with matrices with indices which start with 1.

> Vectors and matrices are implemented so that their indices (including extremes) can vary, for reasons of efficiency and convenience of use, in the following way.
> Vector indices vary between 1 and dimensions. Matrix indices vary between 1 and numRows for rows, and between 1 and numColumns for columns.

But now the following problem arises – how can you ensure in C and C++ that a vector with n dimensions is able to vary between the two indices n1 and n2, which are different from 0 and n-1?

The most commonly used solution is to add a constant – an offset – to the index or subtract one from it. Chapter 2 touched on this method.

Example:

```
float x[41] // between -20 and 20 there are 41 elements
for(int i = -20;i <= 20;i++)
    {
    x[i+20]=.....
    }
```

This operation can be made much safer and more automatic in C++ by inserting the offset between the vector's class members and by hiding the operations from the user.

> This kind of implementation can work well in other areas, but when it comes to intensive numerical calculations, it has a drawback – you have to carry out an unnecessary sum to access a vector's element. The efficiency of the algorithms suffers accordingly.

One alternative, which is used by some authors and which seems to work, is to solve the problem as follows:

```
const int n = 41;
float *x = new float [n];
x = x + 20; // use pointers algebra
for(int i= -20;i <= 20; i++)
    {
    x[i] =...
    }
```

The trick is to use a variable pointer and to add the offset directly to the pointer, rather than to the index. Remember that an integer can be added to or subtracted from the pointers and the compiler automatically takes into consideration the dimensions of the variable to which the pointer points.

In the example above, the variable pointer is moved by twenty float type elements by adding 20 to the pointer. Thus, the element x[-20] ends up where x[0] stood before.

> But there is a danger in this course of action – there is no absolute guarantee that the repositioning operation has been correctly executed, unless the storage to which the pointer with the added offset is pointing is a valid address. C and C++ guarantee that the pointer can be incremented or decremented *for as long as the vector stays within the bounds of its definition and not outside.*

Example:

```
float *x = new float[5]
// x += -1 or -10 or -100 are not guaranteed
// x += +5 or +200 are not guaranteed
x = x + 2; // the operation is safe
for(int i = -2; i <= 2;i++)
   {
   x[i] = i;
   ....
   }
```

NO	OK	OK	OK	OK	OK	NO
x-1	x	x+1	x+2	x+3	x+4	x+5

In this example, C++ guarantees that there will be no surprises if the pointer is re-positioned between x+0 and x+4, as these addresses can be safely accessed and are valid.

If you want to vary a vector between the indices 1 and dimensions (included) you have to subtract an offset of 1 from the pointer.

```
float *x = new float[dimensions]
x = x - 1;
for(int i = 1; i<= dimensions;i++)
   {
   x[i] = ...
}
```

I believe that this operation – subtracting 1 from the pointer which has been initialized with a valid address – can be considered safe in practice, even though the language does not guarantee it. Because of this doubt, and because I wanted as much as possible to avoid portability problems with programs, I decided not to use this approach.

> The alternative I chose in the case of vectors with an index that must vary between 1 and dimensions was to give the vector's dimensions an extra element (dimensions + 1), so that the element whose index is dimensions could also be accessed.
> This device remains hidden from the user, as it takes effect inside the object Vector.
> The price you pay is the waste of one float storage for each vector you use. The benefit consists in being sure of never having problems with using vectors, while maintaining maximum efficiency.

Example:

```
int dimensions = 10;
float *x = new float[dimensions + 1]

// including dimensions
for(int i = 1; i <= dimensions;i++)
   {
   x[i] = i;
   ....
   }
```

Before seeing how this technique can be extended to matrices, we have to look at the criterion normally used in creating a matrix A[M][N], using pointers (see Chapter 3).

First, a pointer to a float pointer is defined.

```
float **A;
```

Then, the operator new is used to create storage for the array of M pointers:

```
A = new float *[M];
if(!A)Error(...); // insufficient storage
```

Having placed the unary * operator in front of the required sizes, the operator new creates storage for an array of float pointers.

The last step is to create storage for the matrix's rows. The identifiers of this array are A[i], thus:

```
for(i=0;i<M;i++)
   {
   A[i]= new float [N];
   if(!A[i])Error(...); // insufficient memory
   }
```

The elements of every row of the matrix are allocated in different arrays in this type of implementation, each array with the same sizes as the number of the columns.

There are two flaws in this kind of implementation.

(1)   An array of pointers and M arrays of float have to be allocated and de-allocated, when a matrix is created and subsequently removed.

(2)   Individual rows have to be copied one at a time, if a matrix is to be copied.

The efficiency of the matrix can be improved if a single array is created and all the elements of the matrix are placed in it.

 It is possible to implement a class which deals with matrices with indices including 1 and the maximum number of rows and columns, with maximum safety and efficiency, and this is how it is doné:

(1) You create an array of pointers with sizes `numRows + 1`, which makes the array valid from 1 to `numRows`.
(2) You size a single array of `float` containing all the elements of the whole matrix + 1, using the element 0 from the previously mentioned arrays.
(3) The other pointers are positioned on this single array in the positions suitable for them.

Two additional items (one pointer and one `float`) are necessary for each matrix in this kind of implementation.

A general unstructured `Matrix` would look like this:

```
size = numRows * numColumns + 1;
matrix = new float *[numRows + 1];
if(!matrix)
    Error("...");
matrix[0] = new float[size];// single array
if(!matrix[0])
    Error("...")          ;
matrix[1] = matrix[0]; // position the pointers
for(int i = 2;i <= numRows;i++)
    matrix[i] = matrix[i-1] + numColumns;
```

Notice that every pointer points to a position preceding the physical beginning of the row to ensure that the index of every column can be made to vary between 1 and `numColumns`.

For example, consider the following 3 x 3 matrix:

```
1.    2.    3.
4.    5.    6.
7.    8.    9.
```

It is stored as follows:

Coefficients		1.	2.	3.	4.	5.	6.	7.	8.	9.
Position	0	1	2	3	4	5	6	7	8	9
Pointer	0,1			2			3			

A generic element, for example, the element **3,2** is found as follows – the pointer **3** is positioned on element **6**; from here you move 2 elements and you find the coefficient **8**. which is, in fact, coefficient **3,2** of the matrix.

Placing all the elements in a single array has the following advantages.

(1) Indices i and j of `matrix[i][j]` can be used between the extremes 1 and `numRows` and between 1 and `numColumns` *inclusive*. You forfeit only two items. `M + 1` pointers would be necessary if you were using matrices stored by rows.

(2) Only two vectors are allocated and de-allocated instead of `M + 1` vectors.

(3) Copying operations and those for executing addition, subtraction and multiplication of matrices prove to be more efficient as will be seen later.

It is very easy to handle triangular matrices (`MatrixLeft` and `MatrixRight`) and symmetrical matrices (`MatrixSymm`) using the same technique by cunningly giving the single array the same sizes as the elements of the matrix, as required (only half a matrix) and the row pointers the correct positions on the array.

The same symbols used for a normal matrix can be used for gaining automatic access to the correct element, without having to carry out multiplications and additions to transform the array's row index into the matrix's two indices, row and column.

`MatrixLeft` would look like this:

```
size = numRows*(numRows+1)/2+1;
matrix = new float *[numRows+1];
if(!matrix)
    Error("...");
matrix[0] = new float[size];
if(!matrix[0])
    Error("...");
matrix[1] = matrix[0];
for(int i = 2;i <= numRows;i++)
    matrix[i] = &matrix[i-1][i-1];
```

For example, look at this left-triangular matrix:

1.	0.	0.	0.
2.	3.	0.	0.
4.	5.	6.	0.
7.	8.	9.	10.

It is stored as follows:

Coefficients		1.	2.	3.	4.	5.	6.	7.	8.	9.	10.
Position	0	1	2	3	4	5	6	7	8	9	10
Pointer	0,1	2		3			4				

A general element $3,2$, for example, is found by positioning pointer 3 on element 3 and moving 2 elements from here to the coefficient 5. which is in fact the coefficient $3,2$ of the matrix.

But for right-triangular MatrixRight:

```
size = numRows*(numRows+1)/2+1;
matrix = new float *[numRows+1];
 if(!matrix)
    Error("...");
matrix[0] = new float[size];
if(!matrix[0])
    Error("...");
matrix[1] = matrix    [0];
for(int i = 2;i <= numRows;i++)
    matrix[i] = &matrix[i-1][numRows-i+1];
```

Look at the following right-triangular matrix:

```
1.    2.    3.    4.
0.    5.    6.    7.
0.    0.    8.    9.
0.    0.    0.    10.
```

It is stored as below:

Coefficients		1.	2.	3.	4.	5.	6.	7.	8.	9.	10.
Position	0	1	2	3	4	5	6	7	8	9	10
Pointer	0,1			2		3	4				

A general element, for example $3,4$, is found by positioning pointer 3 on element 5 and moving 4 elements to the coefficient 9. which is the coefficient $3,4$ of the matrix.

Symmetrical matrices are stored like left-triangular matrices, with the difference that in MatrixLeft the upper bound is zero, while MatrixSymm reflects the stored lower bound and you must bear this in mind during operations.

12.4 Operator and Function Returns

Chapter 10 went into the problems associated with returns of objects. In particular, we saw that pointers or references to objects with the scope of the called function cannot be passed, because their addresses are stored on the stack and cannot be safely returned.

For example, you should avoid the following implementation:

```
float *Func(void)
    {
    float *x;
    ....
    return x;
    }
```

Here the following problem arises. If, inside a function, I build a matrix and I cannot pass a pointer or a reference to the matrix itself, I must pass the whole matrix. Before the returned matrix leaves scope, it calls the copy-initializer constructor, which copies the matrix and creates a hidden object.

> There are two drawbacks.
>
> (1) A copy of the returned matrix is made, which wastes storage space.
> (2) All of a matrix's coefficients have to be physically copied, whereas it would be better to copy only one pointer.

Some authors get round the problem in the following way.

A pointer which points to a struct, containing all the data necessary to the matrix, is defined in the class. The pointer, rather than the whole matrix, is returned. And an index initialized to 1 is introduced, when the matrix is created. The index is incremented by 1 every time the copy-initializer constructor is used or a matrix is assigned to another, and decremented by 1 when the destructor is called. The destructor does not de-initialize the matrix unless the index is equal to 1. This trick is essential to enable the matrix, created inside a function, to be returned unharmed by the function.

Example:

```
Matrix A = B + C;
```

Operator + creates a matrix resulting from the addition and returns the pointer to the matrix. Before it leaves scope, the pointer is copied into a hidden pointer and the index is incremented. When the returned pointer leaves scope, it calls the destructor which decrements the index, bringing it back down to 1, but does not free storage used by the matrix, because, when the call was made, the value of the index was 2. The hidden pointer is then used to initialize the pointer which matrix A needs, by calling the copy-initializer constructor. The index is incremented and becomes again equal to 2. Matrix A shares the data with the hidden object, since both have a pointer which is pointing to the same address. The storage holding the data is de-allocated when both matrices – A and the hidden matrix – leave scope. It seems that everything is working well.

> This device removes the problem of having to pass a whole matrix and of having a copy of a matrix, because only a pointer is being passed and copied.
> But there's a snag. If a matrix is explicitly initialized with another, or if a matrix is set equal to another by an assignment, the two matrices share the same data, even though they are mathematically distinct from each other.

Example:

```
Matrix A = B; // A shares B's data
C = B; // now A, B and C share the data
C(1,3) = 5.; //modify C and also modify B and A
```

> It seemed to me that the possibility of several matrices manipulating the same data undermined one of the essential preconditions for avoiding calculation problems, as far as matrices which are to be used in numerical calculations are concerned. And that's why I discarded this option.

> There remain two other options, which have both good and bad points. You can either:
>
> (1)   Return the full object using `return`. Or
> (2)   Fail to carry out the `return` and use the function argument to pass a pointer to the object, which is then modified inside the function itself, with the object safely in the scope of the calling function.

return of an Object

If you want to overload operators (=, *, +, etc.) you have to use `return` to return the object resulting from the operation.

> The benefit obtained is that you can write simpler codes which are easier to read. For example, you can write an expression like this:
>
> ```
> A = B*C + D - 3.*E;
> ```

But using operators does have its disadvantages.

(1) Not all operations can be carried out using operator overloading, (remember that new symbols cannot be defined).
(2) Because the copy-initializer constructor has to be used, it creates a hidden object which in practice halves the computer's maximum capacity.
(3) Efficiency of calculation suffers, as a large object has to be copied.

The `return`, in cases of operators in which a matrix is created, is as follows:

```
Matrix operator *
        (const Matrix &value,const Matrix &rvalue)
    {
    Matrix result;
    ...
    return result;
    };
```

C and C++ have some very efficient functions for copying blocks of data from one storage position to another. Data transfer times are drastically cut, if these functions are used instead of copying coefficients one at a time.

For example, to copy one vector to another:

```
const int n = 5000;
float *x = new float[n];
float *y = new float[n];
for(int i = 0;i < n;i++) x[i] = i;
for(i=0;i < n;i++) y[i] = x[i]; // do not use this
memcpy(y,x,n*sizeof(float));   // use this function
```

On a 386 PC, the ratio between calculation times of the alternatives for large vectors turned out at around 7.2 (a 5000 `float` vector required 0.033 and 0.0044 seconds respectively). The difference between the alternatives considerably increases if you have to copy a matrix one coefficient at a time, or a matrix considered as one block.

It is important to bear in mind the suggestions below to limit the disadvantages of having hidden matrices and vectors at the same time.

(1) Whenever possible, preference should always be given to operators which do not `return` matrices.
(2) Isolate operations in blocks, {}, to make hidden objects generated by the compiler leave scope as quickly as possible.

Example:

```
A = A + B;  // NOT like this
A += B; // but like this
```

Example:
```
{A = 2.*B + C/3. + D*E;}  // use the curly brackets {}
```

Passing an Argument Pointer

It is possible to get round returning an object, if you pass in the function argument a pointer to the object which is being manipulated inside the function.

> You could even pass a reference to the object which is to be manipulated inside the function. Following the practice which I have stressed on several occasions, I will always use a pointer to an object, if the object is modified inside the function.

Using this technique, you can define overloaded functions which allow you to perform all the operations you consider useful.
Example:

```
void Product(const Matrix &A,const Matrix &B,Matrix *C)
    {
    statements;
    }
```

Even using overloaded functions and objects passed as argument pointers, it is still necessary in some situations to create matrices or auxiliary vectors inside a function.

For example, supposing you wanted to multiply two matrices and to substitute the matrix produced into the first of the two matrices, the function below would be used:

```
Product(A,B,&A);
```

If matrix A does not have the dimensions of the matrix produced, an auxiliary matrix, C, has to be created inside the function and copied into matrix A, because matrix A is being restored by the argument.

> Since the pointer to matrix A in this case has the scope of the calling function, it is possible to use a trick which gets round physically copying all the coefficients. All you have to do is swap the pointers in which the matrices are stored – a pointer is swapped instead of MxN coefficients. When
>
> *cont.*

cont.

matrix C leaves scope at the end of the function Product, it frees the old matrix A's storage. When the new matrix A subsequently leaves scope it frees storage created by matrix C inside the function Product, which treats the storage as if it were its own. Everything is executed with complete safety.

The advantages of overloaded functions are as follows.

(1) All possible operations can be implemented with a limited number of identifiers.
(2) Hidden matrices or unnecessary vectors are not created.
(3) Efficiency is boosted.

The main disadvantage is that the resulting code is less neat.

Example

```
C = A*B;
Product(A,B,&C);
```

Here the reader may wonder whether the second alternative is not the same as the solution that FORTRAN adopts. SUBROUTINES are also used in FORTRAN to find the product of two matrices, so what's the difference?

There is a fundamental difference – in FORTRAN data is passed to the function, while in C++, objects are passed.

12.5 Initializing

Different types of constructors were implemented for the various types of matrices, to make it easier to initialize objects in different circumstances.

Below, I will take only the class Matrix into account. Other classes have similar constructors.

The data needed to define a matrix are:

```
static const char *const ERROR;
static int count; // for whoAmI

float **matrix;
int numRows,numColumns;
int size;
int whoAmI;
```

The first item of data, ERROR, is used to make error messages inside the class uniform, as ERROR is called when an error occurs in all the functions of the class. Because it is common to all objects, it has been declared static. And it is const, because it does not have to be modified.

A second identifier, count, was defined static and initialized at 0. Its purpose is to count Matrix type objects as they are defined so that each object has a distinct value assigned to the variable whoAmI.

The two static items of data are defined in the MATRIX.CPP file, as follows:

```
const char *const Matrix::ERROR=
                "\n=========>>> Matrix error!!!!!!\n";
int Matrix::count = 0;
```

We have already discussed the other variables.

numRows and numColumns are respectively, the number of rows and columns.

size is the size of the array in which the matrix is stored and is equal to numRows*numColumns +1.

**matrix is the pointer to a float pointer where the coefficients are to be placed.

The constructors' task is to initialize the object Matrix: to allocate the storage necessary for the coefficients and to give the correct numerical value to all the variables.

Since the constructors have a first part in common, the function Initialize was introduced, with the task of creating the necessary storage for the elements of the matrix. The coefficients of the matrix are not initialized in this function, but they will be in different constructors.

```
// ******************< Initialize >*******************
// *    Purpose: Common functions for initializing    *
// *    Description: Chapter 12                        *
// *    Example: Initialize(rows,columns)              *
// ***************************************************
void Matrix::Initialize(int rows,int columns)
   {
   count++;
   whoAmI = count;
   if(rows < 1 || columns < 1)
      {
      numRows = numColumns = size = 0;
      matrix = 0;
      return;
      }
   numRows = rows;
   numColumns = columns;
```

```
size = numRows * numColumns + 1;
matrix = new float *[numRows + 1];
if(!matrix)
    Error("%s%s%sInitialize",
    Matrix::ERROR,ERR_SPACE,ERR_FUNCTION);
matrix[0]=new float[size];
if(!matrix[0])
    Error("%s%s%sInitialize",
    Matrix::ERROR,ERR_SPACE,ERR_FUNCTION);
matrix[1] = matrix[0];
for(int i = 2;i <= numRows;i++)
    matrix[i] = matrix[i-1]+numColumns;
}
```

The object Matrix is *de-initialized* in the destructor and other functions – in assignments, for example. It is useful to introduce a common function Deinitialize, to manage this task.

```
// *****************< Deinitialize >*****************
// *   Purpose: Shared functions for de-initializing   *
// *   Description: Chapter 12                          *
// *   Example: Deinitialize();                         *
// ****************************************************
void Matrix::Deinitialize(void)
    {
    if(matrix == 0) return;
    delete matrix[0];
    delete matrix;
    }
```

Private Constructor

In some cases it is important to give a matrix sizes without supplying a numeric value to the coefficients. This saves the time needed to supply all coefficients with a value which you know beforehand will have to be changed subsequently. As this can be risky, if a value is not supplied to the coefficients, I have rendered the constructor inaccessible to the user by putting it in the private area of the class.

Default Constructor

This serves to define a matrix of unknown sizes when it is defined.
    Example:

```
Matrix A;
```

Its implementation is very simple:

```
// ********************< default >********************
// *   Purpose: To define a Matrix that can receive    *
// *            an assignment                          *
// *   Example: Matrix A;                              *
// *            A = B;                                 *
// ****************************************************
Matrix::Matrix(void)
   {
   Initialize(0,0);
   }
```

> This constructor is extremely useful because it defines a matrix without allocating storage and the object thus becomes available to be automatically given sizes. It is worth using when a pointer is passed in the argument of a function which manipulates the object to which the pointer is pointing. It means you do not have to worry about the sizes the object assumes, because of what is happening inside the function.

Example:

```
// A and B defined and initialized
...
Matrix C;
Product(A,B,&C);
```

In the example above, it is not necessary to supply the sizes of matrix C: they are automatically defined inside the function.

> As already stated on several occasions the default constructor is essential if you want to initialize an array of matrices.

Example:

```
Matrix *V = new Matrix [10];
```

In the definition above, the *default* constructor is called ten times.

Copy-Initializer Constructor

This constructor is fundamentally important as it is called implicitly when a Matrix is passed by a function or operator return. It is also used for initializing a matrix with another matrix or with a result obtained by operations performed on other matrices.

For example, if A and B are matrices which already exist:

```
Matrix C = B;
Matrix D = A + 2.*B;
```

Its implementation is:

```
// ***************< Copy-Initializer >******************
// *   Purpose: used by Matrix in returns and in        *
// *                  initializations                   *
// *   Example:Matrix A=B;                               *
// *           Matrix A=B+2.*C;                          *
// *           return A; (used implicitly)               *
// *****************************************************
Matrix::Matrix(const Matrix &rval)
    {
    Initialize(rval.numRows,rval.numColumns);
    if(numRows != 0)
        memcpy(matrix[0],rval.matrix[0],size*sizeof(float));
    }
```

As you can see, the library functions memcpy is used. As the matrix is stored in only one array, the whole of the matrix can be copied in a block, and this brings about a significant improvement in efficiency.

Conversion Constructors

It is often useful to convert a special type of matrix or a vector into a general matrix, and so conversions of MatrixLeft, MatrixRight, MatrixSymm and of Vector in Matrix were implemented. For example, given the matrices L (MatrixLeft), R (MatrixRight), S (MatrixSymm) and the vector v (Vector), a generic matrix Matrix can be initialized:

```
Matrix A = L, B = R, C = S, D = v;
```

Generic Constructors

The other implemented constructors are as follows.

(1)   A constructor for giving sizes to a matrix. Coefficients are automatically initialized with the value 0 using the library function memset.

```
Matrix A(3,4);
```

The constructor is used to enable non-zero coefficients of the matrix to be assigned subsequently, using one of various modes of accessing coefficients which are described further on.

For example, to build the matrix I:

```
Matrix I(10,10);
   for(int i = 1;i <= 10;i++)
   I(i,i) = 1.;
```

(2)   A constructor for giving sizes to a matrix and assigning a value to all the coefficients:

```
Matrix A(2,4,
       1.,2.,3.,4.,
       5.,6.,7.,8.);
```

The coefficients must be arranged by row.

(3)   A constructor for giving sizes to a matrix and assigning to it an array's values. The coefficients must be arranged by row, following C's convention.

```
float w[] = {1.,2.,3.,4.,
            5.,6.,7.,8.,
            9.,10.,11.,12.};
Matrix A(3,4,w);
```

(4)   A constructor for initializing a matrix using a file written in ASCII. The data must be arranged as follows: number of rows, number of columns, coefficients arranged by rows. Each item of data must be separated from the others by one or more spaces. The file can be created by the user with a normal editor or result from it having been saved by the function Save, which I shall discuss later.

For example, the following is in the MATR.DAT file:

```
3 4
1. 2. 3. 4.
5. 6. 7. 8.
9. 10. 11. 12.
```

The constructor is used to initialize Matrix A, as follows:

```
Matrix A("MATR.DAT");
```

The pointer to FILE bzzFileIn, defined with a global scope in the UTILITY.CPP file, is used in this and other functions of the various classes.

It is implemented as follows:

```
// ******************< ASCII FILE >*********************
// *  Purpose: to initialize an ASCII file matrix      *
// *  Example: Matrix A("MAT.DAT");                     *
// ****************************************************
Matrix::Matrix(char *filematrix)
    {
    if((bzzFileIn=fopen(filematrix,"r"))==NULL)
        Error("%s%s%sFILE",
        Matrix::ERROR,ERR_OPEN_FILE,ERR_CONSTRUCTOR);
    int rows,columns;
    fscanf(bzzFileIn,"%d %d",&rows,&columns);
    if(rows < 1 || columns < 1)
        Error("%s%s%sFILE",
        Matrix::ERROR,ERR_CHECK_DIMENSION,ERR_CONSTRUCTOR);
    Initialize(rows,columns);
    float *w = matrix[0];
    for(int i = 1;i < size;i++)fscanf(bzzFileIn,"%f",++w);
    fclose(bzzFileIn);
    }
```

(5) A constructor for calling up a matrix saved on a file and written in binary, using another version of the function `Save`.
You have to use a character as the first argument, to let the compiler know that the file is written in binary and not in ASCII.

```
Matrix A('*',"MATR.BIN");
```

It is implemented as follows:

```
// ****************< from binary FILE >***************
// *  Purpose: to initialize a Matrix from binary FILE *
// *             using Save('*',namefile)              *
// *  Example: Matrix A('*',"MAT.BIN");                *
// ****************************************************
Matrix::Matrix(char,char *filematrix)
    {
    if((bzzFileIn=fopen(filematrix,"rb"))==NULL)
        Error("%s%s%sFILE",
        Matrix::ERROR,ERR_OPEN_FILE,ERR_CONSTRUCTOR);
    int rows,columns;
    if(fread(&rows,sizeof(int),1,bzzFileIn) != 1)
        Error("%s%s%sFILE",
        Matrix::ERROR,ERR_READING_FILE,ERR_CONSTRUCTOR);
```

```
    if(fread(&columns,sizeof(int),1,bzzFileIn) != 1)
        Error("%s%s%sFILE",
        Matrix::ERROR,ERR_READING_FILE,ERR_CONSTRUCTOR);
    if(rows < 1 || columns < 1)
        Error("%s%s%sFILE",
        Matrix::ERROR,ERR_CHECK_DIMENSION,ERR_CONSTRUCTOR);
    Initialize(rows,columns);
    if(fread(matrix[1],sizeof(float)*size,1,bzzFileIn) != 1)
        Error("%s%s%sFILE",
        Matrix::ERROR,ERR_READING_FILE,ERR_CONSTRUCTOR);
    fclose(bzzFileIn);
    }
```

(6) A constructor for generating a submatrix from a matrix. The submatrix has the same coefficient 1,1 as the base matrix and less than or the same number of rows and columns.

Example:

```
Matrix B(5,2,A);
```

where A is a matrix which has already been defined, with numRows >= 5 and numColumns >=2.
It is implemented as follows:

```
// ******************< from submatrix >*****************
// *   Purpose: from a submatrix with same beginning     *
// *   Example: Matrix B(4,5,A);                          *
// ******************************************************
Matrix::Matrix(int rows,int columns,const Matrix &rval)
    {
    if(rows < 1 || rows > rval.numRows)
        Error("%s%s%sSubMatrix",
        Matrix::ERROR,ERR_CHECK_DIMENSION,ERR_CONSTRUCTOR);
    if(columns < 1 || columns > rval.numColumns)
        Error("%s%s%sSubMatrix",
         Matrix::ERROR,ERR_CHECK_DIMENSION,ERR_CONSTRUCTOR);
    Initialize(rows,columns);
    for(int row=1;row<=numRows;row++)
        memcpy(matrix[row]+1,rval.matrix[row]+1,
            numColumns*sizeof(float));
    }
```

Notice how memcpy is used to copy the coefficients.

(7)   Another constructor for generating a submatrix. Here, the submatrix is inside the base matrix. The two indices that mark the beginning of the submatrix in the base matrix have to be supplied.

Example: given the matrix A(10,20):

```
Matrix B(2,3,4,5,A);
```

B is a 2x3 matrix, starting from coefficient 4,5 of matrix A.
It is implemented as follows:

```
// ***************< from internal submatrix ************
// *   Purpose: From internal submatrix                 *
// *   Example: Matrix B(m,n,i,j,A);       B(m,n) da i,j *
// ***************************************************
Matrix::Matrix(int rows,int columns,int irow,int jcol,
               const Matrix &rval)
    {
    if(rows < 1 || irow < 1
            ||
      irow>rval.numRows
            ||
      rows>(rval.numRows-irow+1))
        Error("%s%s%sSubMatrix",
        Matrix::ERROR,ERR_RANGE,ERR_CONSTRUCTOR);
    if(columns < 1 || jcol < 1 ||
      jcol>rval.numColumns ||
      columns>(rval.numColumns-jcol+1))
        Error("%s%s%sSubMatrix",
        Matrix::ERROR,ERR_RANGE,ERR_CONSTRUCTOR);
    Initialize(rows,columns);
    for(int row=1;row<=numRows;row++)
        memcpy(matrix[row]+1,rval.matrix[row+irow-1]+jcol,
            numColumns*sizeof(float));
    }
```

12.6 Operations

As has been underlined before, you can follow two different but parallel routes to implement satisfactorily operations between matrices and vectors – and it is desirable to do so. In fact, overloaded operators could bring benefits when executing some operations, while overloaded functions could be advantageous when executing others.

Operations involving inverse matrices are not implemented in these classes. For example:

$$x = A^{-1} b$$

Modern linear algebra avoids using matrix inversions and uses matrix factorization instead.
Classes for this purpose will be implemented in Chapter 15.

Operator Overloading

You have to be very careful when choosing symbols for overloading operators, to ensure that they follow the syntax for matrix calculation.

Your choice must take account of two very important factors.

(1)   Symbols must be as similar as possible to those used in matrix algebra.
(2)   Usual operator precedence must be respected, bearing in mind that operator precedence as defined by the compiler is maintained.

The choice of symbols for sums, subtraction and unary minus is pre-determined.

The most sensible symbol for the product of two matrices, of a constant and a matrix, or of a matrix and a vector is `*`.

For reasons of precedence, the operator `%`, which has the same precedence as `*` and a higher precedence than `+` and `-`, should be chosen for multiplication of a transposed vector, or of a transposed matrix and a vector or a matrix.

The operator `->*` is used for the same reason and because – with a little imagination – it re-invokes the operation for multiplying a vector or a matrix and a transposed vector or matrix.

The symbol `/` is used for dividing a matrix or vector by a scalar.

The C symbols `==` and `!=` are used to check whether two matrices are equal or different.

The symbol `||` is used to construct one matrix from two others positioned next to each other.

The symbol `&&` is used to append one matrix below another.

When the matrix or the vector appears on the right and left of an assignment, the composite assignment symbols `+=`, `-=`, `*=`, `%=` are used.

Function Overloading

The following functions are overloaded.

Sum	Operations involving the sum of two objects
Difference	Operations involving the difference of two objects
Minus	Unary minus
Product	Product of two objects.
Division	Division of an object by a float.

If the object on the left of a binary operation is a transposed matrix or vector the identifier is preceded by T. For example:

```
TProduct(A,B,&C);
```

executes the product between $\mathbf{A}^T$ and matrix $\mathbf{B}$.

Similarly, if the second matrix is transposed, a T is placed at the end of the function, while if both are transposed, one T is put at the start and one at the end:

```
ProductT(A,B,&C);
TProductT(A,B,&C);
```

The first example executes the following operation:

$$C = AB^T$$

while the second executes the following:

$$C = A^T B^T$$

The following four things can happen when binary operators are involved.

(1)   The result of the operation is placed in a distinct object.
(2)   The resulting object substitutes the left object.
(3)   The resulting object substitutes the right object.
(4)   If the two left and right objects coincide, there is a fourth possibility – the resulting object substitutes the only object present.

Example:

```
Product(A,B,&C);
Product(&A,B);        or      Product(A,B,&A )
Product(A,&B);        or      Product(A,B,&B);
Product(&A);          or      Product(A,A,&A);
```

The operations listed above correspond to the following operations:

$$C = AB$$
$$A = AB$$

B = AB
A = AA

The two rules can be combined. For example:

```
TProduct(A,&B);          or          TProduct(A,B,&B);
TProduct(&A);            or          TProduct(A,A,&A);
```

correspond to the operations:

B = A^{T}B
A = A^{T}A

12.7 Access to Elements

To gain access to the elements of a matrix, two operators are overloaded, producing a means of access which is similar to those employed by FORTRAN and C. It makes using matrices easier.

Here's an example of FORTRAN- and C-style access to a `Matrix A`:

```
A(3,4) = 5.; // the element 3,4 becomes same as 5.
x = A(3,4);  // x receives the value of A(3,4)
A[3][4] = 7.; // C style
x = A[3][4];
```

The same procedure is valid for other matrices: `MatrixRight`, `MatrixLeft`, `MatrixSymm` and for `Vector`.

> The operator function `()` is overloaded and a reference to a `float` is used as `return`, in order to access a matrix in way similar to that adopted by FORTRAN.
> The operator `[]` is overloaded and a `float` pointer `return` is used to gain access in C style.

The two functions are implemented as follows:

```
float &Matrix::operator () (int row,int col)
    {
    if(row < 1 || row > numRows
                || 
       col < 1 || col > numColumns) Error(...);
    return matrix[row][col];
    }
```

```
float *operator [] (int r)  // placed in the definition
   {return matrix[r];}      // of Matrix (inline)
```

In the first case, things are very simple if you remember what was said in Chapter 10 about returning a reference. A check on the validity of the indices is made. A reference to the element matrix[row][col] is returned. A reference is an *lvalue* and this can be placed on the left of the assignment operator.

To understand how the second case works have a look at how A[i][j] is used – the first index is called by object A and is thus overloaded to the pre-defined operator []. A floating pointer is returned and is the address of the i-th row. The operator [] is used again, but this time the operator which was pre-defined by the compiler is used because the call to the floating pointer was made. This pointer selects the element on column j of row i. As a pointer is returned, the final expression is also in this case an lvalue and can thus be placed on the left of an assignment in order to receive an element of the matrix.

This implementation is not without its risks.

(1) Chapter 10 went into the fact that there is a basic reason why functions must not be used with a reference or pointer type return; if they are, the facility to *hide* data goes by the board, in that the user can access data, in this case, matrix elements.

(2) A second problem arising from using FORTRAN-type symbols is that the operator () which is used to access data in the matrix may be confused with the initializing of a matrix. In both cases, you can write, for example, A(3,4). A user could mistakenly use such an expression with the intention of modifying the sizes of a Matrix. In reality, if the expression were used in isolation, it would not do anything useful, creating only a hidden float with the value of A(3,4).

However, I believe it is worth implementing these two possibilities because their advantages far outweigh their disadvantages.

Data hiding does not have to mean that the elements of a matrix must at all costs be kept secret from the user. In the case cited, modifying the selected element is explicitly allowed and is entirely appropriate. Of course, it is quite possible (have another look at the problem of returning pointers and references in Chapter 10) for users to create pointers themselves and change data illegally, but this only happens when this kind of access is deliberately willed, rather than accidental. As far as the second danger is concerned, you just have to remember never to use the operator () on its own.

Whatever the case, I also introduced two functions, SetValue and GetValue, to assign and receive function values, which do not return a pointer or a reference and thus guarantee that data will be hidden:

```
Matrix A(3,4);
A.SetValue(1,2,5.); // as A(1,2) = 5.;
float x = A.GetValue(1,4); // x = A(1,4);
```

> Note the following points.
>
> (1) C-type access, A[i][j], does *not* provide any checks on the validity
>   of the indices and the operator is defined *inline*. This method of access
>   is advisable – because a function is placed as inline, and because
>   there are no checks, it is faster – only if there is the certainty of
>   staying within the validity range of a matrix.
> (2) If A is a Matrix defined as const, the only way its coefficients can
>   be accessed is by using the GetValue function.

GetRow and GetColumn functions for accessing a Matrix row or column
were also implemented, along with SetRow and SetColumn for modifying a row or
a column.

For example, let two Vectors x and y be defined:

```
Matrix A(3,5);
A.SetRow(1,x);   // row 1 of Matrix A
                 // = x
Vector z = A.GetRow(3); // Vector z = row 3 of A

A.SetColumn(2,y); // column 2 of A = y
Vector s = A.GetColumn(2); //s = column 2 of A
```

With Get functions, the resulting vector is automatically given the correct
sizes. In Set functions, an error is flagged if the sizes are not congruent.

12.8 Assigning

One Matrix can be set equal to another using the assignment symbol, =, in which
case the new Matrix is completely independent and autonomous from the matrix that
generated it.

Example:

```
A = B;
```

You can also assign the result of a series of operations to a Matrix.
Example:

```
A = 2.*B +C%D*E;
```

It could be a multiple assignment.
Example:

```
A = B = C + 3.*D;
```

Since the matrix which receives the assignment must already have been defined, the new matrix completely destroys the old one (as is the case with any other type of variable).

If their sizes are the same, the new matrix uses the storage that has already been allocated. If their sizes are different, the requisite storage is created.

The assignment operator is implemented as follows :

```
// *********************< = >************************
// *   Purpose: Assigns a Matrix                     *
// *   Description: Uses memcpy                       *
// *   Example: A=B;       // simple                  *
// *            A=C+D;     // with multiple           *
// *            A=B=C+D;   // operations              *
// **************************************************
Matrix &Matrix::operator =(const Matrix &rval)
   {
   PrepCopy(rval.numRows,rval.numColumns);
   if(numRows != 0)
      memcpy(matrix[0],rval.matrix[0],size*sizeof(float)) ;
   return *this;
   }
```

The operator exploits `PrepCopy`, a private function, which is also used on other occasions when the same operator is overloaded.

```
// *****************< PrepCopy >******************
// *   Purpose: prepares an assignment               *
// **************************************************
void Matrix::PrepCopy(int rRows,int rColumns)
   {
   int who = whoAmI;
   if(numRows != rRows || numColumns != rColumns)
      {
      Deinitialize();
      Initialize(rRows,rColumns);
      count--;
      }
   whoAmI = who;
   }
```

Notice the following points.

(1)   The assignment operator `returns` a reference to the object to which `this` is pointing, that is to say to the matrix itself, which means that assignments can be linked. In fact, the reference can be used to assign the same `Matrix` to another and so on.

(2)   The variable `whoAmI`, which identifies the matrix, is left unaltered in the function `PrepCopy`.

(3)   The library function `memcpy`, which copies the array in which the matrix is allocated as a block, is used to make copying the coefficients efficient.

(4)   As was noted in Chapter 11 and as can be seen from the function `PrepCopy`, the assignment operator consists of a destructor and a copy-initializer constructor. If the object does not have the same sizes as the object which receives the values, it has to be de- and re-initialized.

The assignment operator was also overloaded so that either a `Vector` or one of the special matrices `MatrixLeft`, `MatrixRight` and `MatrixSymm` could be assigned to a `Matrix` object.

If `L`, `R`, `S` are matrices of type `Left`, `Right` and `Symm`, and `v` a `Vector`, the following are all assignments that are accepted:

```
Matrix A;
A = L;
A = R;
A = S;
A = v;
```

12.9 Constructing Matrices with **&&** and **||**

Matrices comprising several submatrices can be constructed with the **&&** and **||** operators.

The **&&** operator is used to append one matrix below another, with the same number of columns as the first. The **||** operator can be used to construct one matrix by placing two matrices with the same number of columns side by side.

The two operators can be used, at the same time, in a single statement.
Example:

```
A = ((B&&C)||(D&&E))&&F);
```

$$
A \;=\; \begin{matrix} \mathbf{B} & & \mathbf{D} \\ \mathbf{C} & & \mathbf{E} \\ & \mathbf{F} & \end{matrix}
$$

They are implemented as follows:

```
// ***********************< && >***********************
// * Purpose: constructs one matrix from two by         *
// *          placing the second under the first.       *
// *          They must have the same number of columns *
// * Description: Uses memcpy                            *
// * Example: A = B&&C;                                  *
// ****************************************************
Matrix operator && (const Matrix &lval,const Matrix &rval)
    {
    if(lval.numColumns != rval.numColumns)
        Error("%s%s%s&&",
        Matrix::ERROR,ERR_CHECK_DIMENSION,ERR_OPERATOR);
    Matrix result('*',lval.numRows+rval.numRows,
                  lval.numColumns);
    if(lval.numRows != 0)
        {
        memcpy(result.matrix[0],lval.matrix[0],
              lval.size*sizeof(float));
        float *r = &result[lval.numRows][lval.numColumns] + 1;
        memcpy(r,rval.matrix[0]+1,
              (rval.size-1)*sizeof(float));
        }
    return result;
    }

// ***********************< || >***********************
// *  Purpose: constructs one matrix from two           *
// *     by placing the second at the side of the first. *
// *     They must have the same number of rows          *
// *     Description: Uses memcpy                         *
// *     Example: A = B||C;                              *
// ****************************************************
Matrix operator || (const Matrix &lval,const Matrix &rval)
    {
    if(lval.numRows != rval.numRows)
        Error("%s%s%s||",
        Matrix::ERROR,ERR_CHECK_DIMENSION,ERR_OPERATOR);
    Matrix result('*',lval.numRows,
                  lval.numColumns+rval.numColumns);
    float **s=lval.matrix;
    float **d=rval.matrix;
    float **r=result.matrix;
    if(result.numRows != 0)
```

```
    {
    for(int i=1;i<=lval.numRows;i++)
        {
        memcpy(r[i]+1,s[i]+1,
               (lval.numColumns)*sizeof(float));
        memcpy(r[i]+lval.numColumns+1,d[i]+1,
               (rval.numColumns)*sizeof(float));
        }
    }
  return result;
  }
```

12.10 Logical Operators

Tests which mirror the symbols of tests carried out on basic variables can be carried out on class objects with the == and != operators.

For example, given two matrices A and B and two vectors x and y:

```
if(A == B)
    {
    statements; // if the matrices are the same
    }
if(x !=y)
    {
    statements; // if vector x is different from y
    }
```

Note that the variable whoAmI and the library function memcmp are used. All the individual coefficients need not be compared, and this is another advantage of having placed the matrix in one vector.

== and != are implemented as below:

```
// ********************< == >************************
// *   Purpose: if == return 1 otherwise 0          *
// * Example: if( A == B )                           *
// ***************************************************
char operator == (const Matrix &lval,const Matrix &rval)
    {
    if(lval.whoAmI == rval.whoAmI)return 1;
    char ch = 1;
    if(   lval.numRows != rval.numRows
```

||

```
                    lval.numColumns != rval.numColumns) ch = 0;
        else
        {
            if(memcmp(lval.matrix[0]+1,rval.matrix[0]+1,
                    (rval.size-1)*sizeof(float))==0)ch=1;
            else ch = 0;
            }
        return ch;
        }


// ************************< != >**************************
// *    Purpose: If   != return 1 otherwise 0            *
// *    Example: if( A != B)                             *
// ********************************************************
char operator != (const Matrix &lval,const Matrix &rval)
        {
        if(lval.whoAmI == rval.whoAmI) return 0;
        char ch=0;
        if(lval.numRows != rval.numRows
                ||
            lval.numColumns != rval.numColumns)ch = 1;
        else
        ch = memcmp(lval.matrix[0]+1,rval.matrix[0]+1,
                    (rval.size-1)*sizeof(float));
        return ch;
        }
```

12.11 Implemented Operations

Table 12.1 shows all the operations which were implemented for the two classes, Vector and Matrix, in two versions: with operator overloading and function overloading. By contrast, table 12.2 shows the those operations which involve special matrices.

The operations are shown in the left-hand column, using normal matrix symbols; a lower case letter represents a scalar, a lower case letter in bold a vector, and a capital letter a matrix.

Table 12.1 *Operations involving Vectors and Matrices.*

x = a + b	x = a + b;	Sum(a,b,&x);
x = x + a	x += a;	Sum(&x,a);
		Sum(x,a,&x);
x = a + x		Sum(a,&x);
		Sum(a,x,&x);

Table 12.1 *cont.*

x = x + x		`Sum(&x);`
		`Sum(x,x,&x);`
x = a - b	`x = a    b;`	`Difference(a,b,&x);`
x = x - a	`x -= a;`	`Difference(&x,a);`
		`Difference(x,a,&x);`
x = a - x		`Difference(a,&x);`
		`Difference(a,x,&x);`
x = x - x		`Difference(&x);`
		`Difference(x,x,&x);`
x = - a	`x = -a;`	`Minus(a,&x);`
x = - x		`Minus(&x);`
		`Minus(x,&x);`
y = Ax	`y = A*x;`	`Product(A,x,&y);`
x = Ax		`Product(A,&x);`
		`Product(A,x,&x);`
y = 3x	`y = 3.*x`	`Product(3.,x,&y);`
x = 3x	`x *= 3.;`	`Product(3.,&x);`
		`Product(3.,x,&x);`
c = a^{T}b	`c = a %b;`	`TProduct(a,b,&c);`
		`c = Dot(a,b);`
y = A^{T}x	`y = A%x;`	`TProduct(A,x,&y);`
x = A^{T}x		`TProduct(A,&x);`
		`TProduct(A,x,&x);`
A = ab^T	`A = a->*b;`	`ProductT(a,b,&A);`
y = x/2	`y = x/2.;`	`Division(x,2.,&y);`
x = x/2	`x /= 2.;`	`Division(&x,2.);`
		`Division(x,2.,&x);`
C = A + B	`C = A+B;`	`Sum(A,B,&C);`
A = A + B	`A += B;`	`Sum(&A,B,);`
		`Sum(A,B,&A);`
B = A + B		`Sum(A,&B);`
		`Sum(A,B,&B);`
A = A + A		`Sum(&A);`
		`Sum(A,A,&A);`
C = A - B	`C = A-B;`	`Difference(A,B,&C);`
A = A - B	`A -= B;`	`Difference(&A,B,);`
		`Difference(A,B,&A);`
B = A - B		`Difference(A,&B);`
		`Difference(A,B,&B);`
A = A - A		`Difference(&A);`
		`Difference(A,A,&A);`
C = AB	`C = A*B;`	`Product(A,B,&C);`
A = AB	`A *= B;`	`Product(&A,B,);`
		`Product(A,B,&A);`
B = AB		`Product(A,&B);`
		`Product(A,B,&B);`
A = AA		`Product(&A);`
		`Product(A,A,&A);`

Table 12.1 *cont.*

$\mathbf{B} = 3.\mathbf{A}$	B = 3.*A	Product(3.,A,&B);
$\mathbf{A} = 3\mathbf{A}$	A *= A;	Product(3.,&A);
		Product(3.,A,&A);
$\mathbf{C} = \mathbf{A^T B}$	C = A%B;	TProduct(A,B,&C);
$\mathbf{A} = \mathbf{A^T B}$	A %= B;	TProduct(&A,B,);
		TProduct(A,B,&A);
$\mathbf{B} = \mathbf{A^T B}$		TProduct(A,&B);
		TProduct(A,B,&B);
$\mathbf{A} = \mathbf{A^T A}$		TProduct(&A);
		TProduct(A,A,&A);
$\mathbf{A} = \mathbf{A A^T}$		ProductT(&A);
$\mathbf{B} = \mathbf{A}/2$	B = A/2.;	Division(A,2.,&B);
$\mathbf{A} = \mathbf{A}/2$	A /= 2.;	Division(&A,2.);
		Division(A,2.,&A);

Table 12.2 *Operations involving special matrices.*

$\mathbf{A} = \mathbf{L} + \mathbf{R}$		Sum(L,R,&A);
$\mathbf{A} = \mathbf{R} + \mathbf{L}$		Sum(R,L,&A);
$\mathbf{R} = \mathbf{R1} * \mathbf{R2}$	R = R1*R2;	
$\mathbf{L} = \mathbf{L1} * \mathbf{L2}$	L = L1*L2;	
$\mathbf{y} = \mathbf{Rx}$	y = R*x;	
$\mathbf{y} = \mathbf{Lx}$	y = L*x	
$\mathbf{R} = 3\mathbf{R1}$	R .= 3.*R1;	
$\mathbf{L} = 3\mathbf{L1}$	L = 3.*L1;	
$\mathbf{R} = 3\mathbf{R}$	R *= 3.;	
$\mathbf{R} = 3\mathbf{R1}$	R = 3.*L1;	
$\mathbf{L} = 3\mathbf{L1}$	L = 3.*L1;	
$\mathbf{R} = 3\mathbf{R}$	R *= 3.;	
$\mathbf{L} = 3\mathbf{L}$	L *= 3.;	
$\mathbf{S} = \mathbf{L L^T}$		ProductT(L,&S);
$\mathbf{S} = \mathbf{L^T L}$		TProduct(L,&S);
$\mathbf{S} = \mathbf{R R^T}$		ProductT(R,&S);
$\mathbf{S} = \mathbf{R^T R}$		TProduct(R,&S);
$\mathbf{R} = \mathbf{R1}/2$	R = R1/2.;	
$\mathbf{L} = \mathbf{L1}/2$	L = L1/2.;	
$\mathbf{R} = \mathbf{R}/2$	R /= 2.;	
$\mathbf{L} = \mathbf{L}/2$	L /= 2.;	

Here, before analysing some of the implementations in more detail (the others are shown in diskette files), a very important point should be made.

More efficient codes can be written by making the most of the fact that matrices are stored on only one line.

We have already seen three advantages in this.

(1)   Only one array has to be allocated and de-allocated instead of `numRows` arrays.

(2)   Storage is saved if you want to have indices which vary between 1 and `numRows` and from 1 to `numColumns`.

(3)   The library functions `memcpy`, `memcmp` and `memset` can be used just once for the whole block of a matrix in copying operations and comparative operations, and in those for initializing coefficients at zero.

Now let's look at some ways of implementing operations which can save computing time.

 It is important to grasp this point fully because it demonstrates how an implementation which uses object-oriented programming can be not only safer and more convenient, but also *more efficient in terms of computing time.*

Consider three matrices; `A`, `B`, and `C`. To calculate `C` as the sum of `A` and `B` you have to write the following statement using matrix terminology:

```
C[i][j] = A[i][j] + B[i][j];
```

Two indices are used to access the three matrices.

If, instead, the matrices are stored like vectors and *it is certain that the pointers which point to the beginning of the matrix rows have not been swapped*, the sum can be carried out as if the matrices were vectors, that is, by accessing the coefficients with just one index.

Languages which use object-oriented programming guarantee that pointers have not been swapped, because the object itself controls access to them. But there can be no such guarantee in procedural programming, because the user, convinced that the matrix was still being treated as such, may have swapped the pointers at another point in the program.

So a *generic* function which uses a matrix as if it were a single vector and which, for example, uses a single index to access its coefficients *cannot* be written in a language which uses procedural programming.

You may be wondering exactly how computing time is saved. As I stressed earlier on, it is impossible to quantify comparisons of computing times because they depend on so many different factors. But there are some occasions when it can be stated that one implementation is intrinsically better than another – and this is one of those occasions.

Consider the following three ways of accessing a matrix coefficient:

```
a[i][j]
b[i][j]
*c++
```

The first two are syntactically the same; the difference between them consists in defining the matrix a as:

```
float a[M][N];
```

while the second, b, is defined using pointers.

The time taken to access the coefficients in the first two is determined by the context in which the statement is made, particularly if the row index, i, or the column index, j, are varied.

As an example, I obtained the following results on a 386 PC. The times reported relate to the time taken to carry out a multiplication.

1.08	a_{ij}	varying j
0.96	a_{ij}	varying i
0.92	b_{ij}	varying j
0.88	b_{ij}	varying i
0.84	*(c+j)	
0.78	*c++	

These numerical values can vary from one environment to the other but their hierarchical order cannot.

Addition and Subtraction

Functions built in the UTILITY.CPP file are used for adding and subtracting float type arrays.

> By putting all of a matrix's elements in one array, two matrices can be added, or one subtracted from the other, using only one index to move from one element to the next.

Of the functions implemented, consider the following:

```
// ********************< Sum >***********************
// *   Purpose: Sum of two matrices                 *
// *   Description: Uses sum from utility.cpp        *
// *   Example: Sum(A,B,&C); C = A + B;             *
// ************************************************
void Sum(const Matrix &lval,const Matrix &rval,
        Matrix *result)
    {
    if(lval.numColumns != rval.numColumns
                ||
            lval.numRows != rval.numRows)
```

```
        Error("%s%s%sSum",
         Matrix::ERROR,ERR_CHECK_DIMENSION,ERR_FUNCTION);
      if(result->whoAmI == lval.whoAmI)
         (*result) += rval;
      else if(result->whoAmI == rval.whoAmI)
         Sum(lval,result);
      else
      {

ChangeDimensions(lval.numRows,lval.numColumns,result t);
         Sum(rval.size-1,lval.matrix[1]+1,rval.matrix[1]+1,
            result->matrix[1]+1);
      }
    }
```

Notice the following points.

(1)   A check is carried out on the congruency of the operands.

> This is another advantage of object-oriented programming. In procedural programming, there is no guarantee that the actual sizes of matrices correspond to the dimensions given by the user. The user is responsible for the *real* (and not only apparent) congruency of matrices.

(2)   The matrix which results is checked to see that it is not one of the two operands. If it is, the appropriate functions are called and the resulting matrix can be overloaded.

> This check can only carried out in object-oriented programming because only in this case is the variable `whoAmI` safely and unequivocally associated with an object.

(3)   If the resulting matrix does not have to be overloaded onto one of the operands, its sizes are checked and changed, if necessary, using the function `ChangeDimensions`, so that its dimensions are congruent.

> Similarly, this check can only be carried out because the matrix is an object which is aware of its dimensions.

(4)   The resulting matrix can only be defined in the calling matrix and it does not have to be given the correct dimensions.

For example, given two matrices A and B:

```
Matrix C;
Sum(A,B,&C);
```

(5)   The function, constructed in the UTILITY.CPP file, is used to carry out the addition and it can be used with arrays. As was stressed earlier on, only one index is used to access all three matrices.

```
Sum(rval.size-1,lval.matrix[1]+1,rval.matrix[1]+1,
    result->matrix[1]+1);
```

Unary Subtraction Operator

To change a matrix's sign, two Minus functions and the unary subtraction operator − are overloaded.
Example:

```
B = -A;
Minus(A,&B);    // B = -A
Minus(&A);      // A = -A;
```

Multiplication

As shown in Table 12.1, several functions were used to multiply vectors and matrices, also transposed vectors and matrices.
As an example, consider how the function Product is used in multiplying a Matrix and a Vector:

```
Product(A,x,&y); // y = Ax
```

It is implemented as follows:

```
// *******************< Product >*******************
// *   Purpose: Multiplication of matrix by Vector       *
// *   Example: Product(A,x,&y); y = A*x;                 *
// ****************************************************
void Product(const Matrix &lval,const Vector &rval,
             Vector *result)
    {
    if(lval.numColumns!=rval.dimensions)
        Error("%s%s%s*",
        Vector::ERROR,ERR_CHECK_DIMENSION,ERR_OPERATOR);
    if(rval.whoAmI == result->whoAmI)
```

```
      {
      Vector aux;
      Product(lval,rval,&aux); // recursive call
Swap(&aux,result); // avoids copying
      }
      else
      {
         ChangeDimensions(lval.numRows,result);
         float *r = result->vector;
         for(int i = 1;i <= lval.numRows;i++)
            r[i] = Dot(rval.dimensions,lval.matrix[i] +1,
                   rval.vector + 1);
      }
   }
```

Note the point below – if the vector resulting from the operation, y, coincides with x, the test:

```
if(rval.whoAmI == result->whoAmI)
```

is true and the statements below are executed:

```
Vector aux;
Product(lval,rval,&aux); // recursive call
Swap(&aux,result); // avoids copying
```

> The first statement defines an auxiliary vector `aux`. Then, the function `Product` can be called *recursively*, because `aux` is distinct from the vector `rval`. The last statement uses the function `Swap`, so that the need to copy all the coefficients of the vector by the pointer exchange is avoided.

As a second example, look at the how the function `TProduct` is implemented to multiply a transposed matrix by another matrix:

```
// *******************< TProduct >*******************
// *   Purpose: Multiplication of a transposed matrix by *
// *              a normal matrix                        *
// *   Example: TProduct(A,B,&C);  // C = ATB            *
// **************************************************
void TProduct(const Matrix &lval,const Matrix &rval,
              Matrix *result)
   {
   if(lval.numRows!=rval.numRows)
      Error("%s%s%s %",
      Matrix::ERROR,ERR_CHECK_DIMENSION,ERR_OPERATOR);
```

```
if(result->whoAmI == lval.whoAmI)
   (*result) %= rval;
else if(result->whoAmI == rval.whoAmI)
   TProduct(lval,result);
else
{
   ChangeDimensions(lval.numColumns,
                    rval.numColumns,result);
   if(lval.whoAmI != rval.whoAmI)
      {
      float *p,*b;
      int np = lval.numColumns;
      int nc = rval.numColumns;
      float *v = result->matrix[1];
      for(int cc = 1;cc <= lval.numColumns;cc++)
         {
         for(int column = 1;column <= rval.numColumns;
                            column++)
            {
            double sum=0.;
            p = lval.matrix[1] + cc;
            b = rval.matrix[1] + column;
            for(int i = 1;i <= lval.numRows;i++)
               {
               sum += (*p) * (*b);
               p += np;
               b += nc;
               }
            *++v = Control(sum);
            }
         }
      }
   else  // matrices same ATA
   {
      int n = lval.numColumns;

      int m = lval.numRows;
      int i,j,k;
      float **a = lval.matrix;
      float **aTa = result->matrix;
      for(i = 1;i <=n;i++)
         {
         for(j = i;j <= n;j++)
            {
            double sum = 0.;
```

```
        for(k = 1;k <= m;k++)
            sum += a[k][i]*a[k][j];
        aTa[i][j] = Control(sum);
            }
        }
    for(i = 1;i <= n;i++)
        for(j = 1;j < i;j++)
            aTa[i][j] = aTa[j][i];
        }
    }
}
```

There are four possible outcomes when this function is used.

(1) The resulting matrix is the same as the left matrix of the multiplication.
(2) The resulting matrix is the same as the right matrix of the multiplication.
(3) The resulting matrix is different from both matrices, which are different from one another.
(4) The resulting matrix is different from both matrices, which are the same as each other.

In these cases the appropriate function is always called.

For example, if the matrices in the product are the same, the resulting matrix is symmetrical and requires half the number of calculations.

> All these choices remain hidden to the user and can only be achieved in object-oriented programming. In procedural programming, the user is responsible for choosing the correct function.

Example:

```
TProduct(A,B,&A);
TProduct(A,B,&B);
TProduct(A,A,&A);
TProduct(A,B,&C);
TProduct(A,A,&C);
```

Divisions

A matrix or vector can be multiplied or divided by a float constant.
Example:

```
A = 3.*B;
A = B/3.;
Division(x,3.,y);   // y = x/3.
```

12.12 Other Functions

Print, Save and Recover

The `Print` function allows you to write a comment, the number that characterizes a matrix, the number of rows and columns and the coefficients of a matrix in the `bzzFileOut` file:

Example:

```
A.Print("Matrix A");
```

```
// ***********************< Print >***********************
// *   Purpose: Prints matrix data                        *
// *   Description: Uses bzzFileOut global file            *
// *                    in utility.hpp *                   *
// *   Example: A.Print("Matrix A");                       *
// *******************************************************
void Matrix::Print(char *msg)
    {
    fprintf(bzzFileOut,"\nMatrix No.%d",whoAmI);
    if(*msg)fprintf(bzzFileOut," %s",msg);
    fprintf(bzzFileOut,"\nrows %d columns %d\n",
            numRows,numColumns);
    for(int row = 1;row <= numRows;row++)
        {
        for(int column = 1;column <= numColumns;column++)
            fprintf(bzzFileOut," %12.4e",matrix[row][column]);
        fprintf(bzzFileOut,"\n");
        }
    }
```

In some circumstances, it is useful to save a matrix in a file, so that it can be recovered later. To this end, two functions were implemented for saving files, `Save`, and two for recovering, `Recover`. (Formatted or binary files can be written or read.)

The file constructor (whether formatted or not) can be used as an alternative to the `Recover` function, which requires a matrix which has already been defined.

To save a matrix or a vector so that you have a formatted file, all you have to do is to place the file name, and if required, its directory, in the `Save` function's argument. To get a binary file, you have to specify a character, `'*'`, for example, before the file name in the argument list. The process is similar for recovery.

Example:

```
A.Save("MAT.DAT");  // ASCII file
B.Save('*',MAT.BIN"); // binary
.....
```

```
Matrix C("MAT.DAT"); // with ASCII file constructor
Recover(&C,'*',"MAT.BIN"); // from binary file.
```

A class was created in the UTILITY.CPP file for the purpose of generating a single name for a file (see Chapter 10) and it is very useful in a program where some temporary files are needed for saving matrices and vectors.

Example:

```
TempFile f1("D:"),f2("C:\\TEMP\\");
Matrix A(2,2,1.,2.,3.,4.);
A.Save(f1.FileName());
....
Matrix B;
Recover(&B,f1.FileName());
B.Save('*',f2.FileName();
Matrix C('*',f2.FileName());
```

Norms

It is often useful to be able to calculate the norms of vectors or matrices which are involved in numerical calculations. The most important norms were implemented for each class and they are simple to use. For example:

```
float normR = A.NormR();
float norm2 = v.Norm2();
```

Delete

Occasionally a matrix or a vector are no longer needed, even though they are still in their scope. You can use the Delete function, which has the task of freeing an object's storage, as an alternative to constructing a block {}, dedicated to causing the object to leave scope.

Example:

```
A.Delete();
```

ChangeDimensions

This function is commonly used inside those functions which go to make up classes, because it can be used to apply new dimensions to a matrix or a vector at any point in the program. If the dimensions coincide with existing dimensions, there is no need to de- and re-initialize the object, and the function simply sets the coefficients to zero.

Example:

```
ChangeDimensions(m,n,&A);
```

Transpose

The Transpose function is used to substitute for matrix **A** its transpose, $\mathbf{A}^T$. If matrix **A** is squared, an auxiliary matrix is not required. If it is not, the transpose is stored in a new matrix, which, before leaving scope, is swapped with the original matrix, using the Swap function. For reasons which were discussed earlier on in this chapter, the pointer to a matrix is swapped, rather than all the coefficients. When the matrix is not squared, you could in any case avoid creating an auxiliary matrix, because the matrix is stored in a single array and does not change its dimensions. It is the number of the row pointers and the positions to which they point that change. The implementation is not commonplace and I leave it to the reader as an exercise.

Example:

```
Matrix A(2,3,
         1.,2.,3.,
         4.,5.,6.);
Transpose(&A);
A.Print("Transpose(&A)");
```

It is implemented as follows:

```
// ********************< Transpose >********************
// * Purpose: Changes a matrix into its transpose      *
// * Description: If matrix is square, it is overloaded *
// * Example: Transpose(&A);                            *
// ******************************************************
void Transpose(Matrix *A)
   {
   int i,j;
   float **a=A->matrix;
   if(A->numRows == A->numColumns)
      {
      for(i = 1;i <= A->numRows;i++)
      for(j = i+1;j <= A->numColumns;j++)
         Swap(&a[i][j],&a[j][i]); // in utility.cpp
   }
   else
   {
      Matrix B('*',A->numColumns,A->numRows);
      for(i = 1;i <= A->numRows;i++)
         for(j = 1;j <= A->numColumns;j++)
             B[j][i] = a[i][j];
      Swap(A,&B);
      }
   }
```

SumRankOne

A frequently occurring operation in numerical problems is adding a rank one matrix to a squared matrix, which is obtained by multiplying a vector by another transposed vector.

$$A = A + cuv^T$$

Three functions bearing the identifier `SumRankOne` were overloaded to execute this operation in three subcases: c general, c = 1, c = 1/d.
Example:

```
Matrix A(2,2,
         1.,2.,
         3.,4.);
Vector u(2,7.,8.),vT(2,5.,6.);
PlusRankOne(3.,u,vT,&A);
A.Print("PlusRankOne(3.,u,vT,&A)");
```

Implementation in the special case c = 1 is as follows:

```
// ******************< SumRankOne >*******************
// *   Purpose: Addition of matrix to a rank one matrix  *
// *   Example: SumRankOne(u,vt,&A); A = A + u*vT         *
// ***************************************************
void SumRankOne(const Vector &u,
        const Vector &vT,Matrix *result)
   {
   if(u.dimensions != vT.dimensions ||
      u.dimensions != result->numRows ||
      u.dimensions != result->numColumns)
        Error("%s%s%sSumRankOne",
        Matrix::ERROR,ERR_CHECK_DIMENSION,ERR_FUNCTION);
   float *r = result->matrix[1] + 1;
   float *left = u.vector + 1;
   float *right = vT.vector;
   for(int i = 1;i <= u.dimensions;i++)
      {
      for(int j = 1;j <= u.dimensions;j++)
        *r++ = Control(*r + (*left) * right[j]);
      left++;
      }
   }
```

As can be observed, the method used was such that the resulting matrix could be accessed with just one index.

```
*r++ = Control(*r + (*left) * right[j]);
```

Swap

This function is very useful for swapping the addresses and sizes of two matrices without moving their coefficients.

```
// *********************< Swap >*********************
// *   Purpose: Swaps data of any two matrices          *
// *   Description: used for efficient copying           *
// *                when a matrix remains in scope       *
// *                and another one leaves, they swap    *
// *   Example: Swap(&A,&B);                             *
// ****************************************************
void Swap(Matrix *lval,Matrix *rval)
   {
   float **temp = lval->matrix;
   lval->matrix = rval->matrix;
   rval->matrix = temp;
   Swap(&lval->numColumns,&rval->numColumns);
   Swap(&lval->numRows,&rval->numRows);
   Swap(&lval->size,&rval->size);
   }
```

Special Functions for Vectors

The functions Normalize, Reverse and Sort were implemented in the Vector class, besides functions which are more or less similar to the ones used above for the Matrix class. Their purpose is to normalize vectors, while calculating their Euclidean norm at the same time, to invert the order of vectors' coefficients and to put them into ascending order.

Example:

```
Vector v(5,1.2.,3.,4.5);
float norm = Normalize(&v);
v.Print("Normalized");
Reverse(&v);
v.Print("Inverted");
Sort(&v);
v.Print("Ordered");
```

```
// *******************< Normalize >*******************
// *   Purpose: normalizes a vector (xTx = 1)           *
// *            returns the value of norm               *
// *   Example: float norm = Normalize(&x);             *
//    ****************************************************
float Normalize(Vector *result)
   {
   float norm = result->Norm2();
   if(norm==0.)return norm;
   float *w = result->vector;
   for(int i = 1;i <= result->dimensions;i++)
      *++w/=norm;
   return norm;
   }


// *******************< Reverse >*******************
// *   Purpose: To invert the elements of a vector      *
// *   Description: Swaps extremes                      *
// *   Example: Reverse(&x);                            *
//    ****************************************************
void Reverse(Vector *result)
   {
   int m = (result->dimensions+1)/2;
   int n = result->dimensions;
   int i,j;
   if(n < 2)return;
   float *v = result->vector;
   if(n == 2) Swap(v+1,v+2);
   else
   for(i = 1,j = n;i <= m;i++,jñ)
         Swap(v+i,v+j); // in UTILITY.CPP
  }


// ********************< Sort >********************
// *   Purpose: To order a Vector                       *
// *   Description: Uses UTILITY.CPP's heap sort        *
// *   Example: Vector x(150,w); Sort(&x);              *
//    ****************************************************
void Sort(Vector *result)
   {
   Sort(result->dimensions,result->vector + 1); //UTILITY.cpp
   }
```

Special Functions for **MatrixRight** and **MatrixLeft**

Given the importance (see Chapter 15) of this type of matrix in modern linear algebra, here are a few functions dedicated to solving linear systems, which have as coefficient matrix a right-triangular matrix **R**, or left-triangular matrix **L**.

The symbols used are the same as those adopted in Chapter 15, which should be referred to for further clarification.

Example for solving a system with a right-triangular matrix:

```
MatrixRight R(3,3,
             1.,2.,3.,
               4.,5.,
                 6.);
Vector b(3,6.,9.,6.);
Vector x;
Solve(R,b,&x);
x.Print("Solution");
```

There are four versions of the Solve function for right-triangular matrices. Depending on which one is selected, the solution either covers or does not cover the right-hand side vector; there can be either just one right-hand side vector or a matrix. The versions for a single vector are as follows:

```
// *******************< Solve >*******************
// *  Purpose: solves a Right system R*bx = bx        *
// *  Description: Given a Vector bx restores          *
// *                   the solution in bx             *
// *  Example:  Solve(R,&bx);                          *
//  ********************************************************
void Solve(const MatrixRight &R,Vector *bx)
    {
    if(R.numRows != bx->Size())
      Error("%s%s%sSolve",
      MatrixRight::ERROR,ERR_CHECK_DIMENSION,ERR_FUNCTION );
    double sum;
     float *r,tmp,*x = &(*bx)[0];
    float **mat = R.matrix;
    for(int i = R.numRows;i >= 1;iñ)
      {
      r = mat[i] + i;
      tmp = *r;
      if(tmp == 0.)
         {
         Message("%sSingular Matrix",MatrixRight::ERROR);
         x[i]=0.;
         }
```

```
    else
    {
        sum = x[i];
        for(int j = i+1;j <= R.numColumns;j++)
            sum -= *++r * x[j];
        x[i]=Control(sum/tmp);
        }
    }
}


// *********************< Solve >***********************
// *   Purpose: solves a Right system R*x = b          *
// *   Description: Given the Vectors b and x restores  *
// *                   the solution in X                *
// *   Example:  Solve(R,b,&x);                         *
// *****************************************************
void Solve(const MatrixRight &R,const Vector &b,Vector *x)
    {
    if(b.WhoAmI() == x->WhoAmI())
        Solve(R,x);
    else
    {
        *x = b;
        Solve(R,x);
        }
    }
```

It is useful sometimes to solve the system in which the matrix is transposed.

$$R^T x = b$$

The function TransposeSolve is used for this purpose. For example,

```
MatrixRight R(3,3,
             1.,2.,3.,
                4.,5.,
                   6.);
Vector b(3,1.,6.,14.);
Vector x;
TransposeSolve(R,b,&x);
x.Print("Solution");
```

There are two overloaded versions of the TransposeSolve function for right-triangular matrices and depending on which one is being used it does or does not cover the right-hand side vector.

```
// ****************< TransposeSolve >*****************
// *  Purpose: Solves a right system RT*bx = bx        *
// *  Description: Given the vector bx restores         *
// *                the solution in bx                  *
// *  Example:  TransposeSolve(R,&bx);                  *
// *****************************************************
void TransposeSolve(const MatrixRight &R,Vector *bx)
   {
   if(R.numRows != bx->Size())
     Error("%s%s%sTransposeSolve",
       MatrixRight::ERROR,ERR_CHECK_DIMENSION,ERR_FUNCTION );
   double sum;
   float tmp,*x = &(*bx)[0];
   float **mat = R.matrix;
   int n = R.numRows;
   for(int i = 1;i <= n;i++)
     {
     tmp = mat[i][i];
     if(tmp == 0.)
       {
       Message("%sSingular Matrix",MatrixRight::ERROR);
       x[i]=0.;
       }
     else
     {
       sum = x[i];
       for(int j = 1;j < i;j++)
         sum -= mat[j][i] * x[j];
       x[i]=Control(sum/tmp);
       }
     }
  }


// ****************< TransposeSolve >*****************
// *  Purpose : Solves a Right system RT*b=x           *
// *  Description: Given the Vector  x restores         *
// *                the solution in x                   *
// *  Example:  TransposeSolve(R,b,&x);                 *
// *****************************************************
void TransposeSolve(const MatrixRight &R,
                    const Vector &b,Vector *x)
   {
   if(b.WhoAmI() == x->WhoAmI())
     TransposeSolve(R,x);
    else
```

```
    {
        *x = b;
        TransposeSolve(R,x);
        }
    }
```

Functions for calculating the determinant, `Determinant`, and the condition number, `ConditionNumber`, (which will be discussed in Chapter 15) were implemented for these matrices.

Example:

```
double det = R.Determinant();
float cond = R.ConditionNumber();
```


12.13 Examples of Applications

Numerous examples of applications of the classes described in this chapter are shown in files : `EXVECTOR.CPP, EXMATR1.CPP, EXMATR2.CPP, EXLEFT.CPP, EXRIGHT.CPP, EXSYMM.CPP`.

Updating a Matrix with Broyden's Formula

Broyden's formula is often used to bring up-to-date the Jacobian matrix in Newton's method for solving systems of non-linear equations.

$$\mathbf{B}^{i+1} \;=\; \mathbf{B}^{i} + \frac{(\mathbf{f}^{i+1} - \mathbf{f}^{i} - \mathbf{B}^{i}\,\mathbf{p}^{i})(\mathbf{p}^{i})^{T}}{(\mathbf{p}^{i})^{T}(\mathbf{p}^{i})}$$

The formula can be implemented very simply either by using operators or by using the `SumRankOne` function.

Using overloaded operators:

```
B += (f1-f-B*p)->*(p/(p%p));
```

Using the `SumRankOne` function the necessary statement is:

```
SumRankOne(f1-f-B*p,p,Dot(p,p),&B);
```

13 Sparse Matrices

Provando e riprovando.

By proof and refutation

Dante, *Paradiso*, III.

13.1 Introduction

A matrix with a large number of null coefficients is called a sparse matrix.

I thought it was a good idea to create a special class, `MatrixSparse`, dealing with this type of matrix, because suitable techniques are necessary both for storing non-null coefficients and for implementing various operations. The header file is `SPARSE.HPP`, while `SPARSE.CPP` is the file in which the class is implemented. Examples of how the class is used can be found in the file `EXSPARSE.CPP`.

 Only a few operations which are useful to the class will be outlined, although it deserves to be examined in much greater depth, given its importance in all fields of numerical calculation.

The purpose of this chapter is to demonstrate how a matrix of large sizes can be stored and used with techniques which are not available in FORTRAN.

When a matrix is defined in FORTRAN as follows:

```
REAL A(100,200)
```

it is stored as *static*. Consequently, anyone who writes programs in FORTRAN gets used to thinking of using the storage and matrix as if they were something static.

In the last chapter, we moved a step closer to changing this attitude. `Matrix` objects are given dimensions dynamically at the point of definition, they can change sizes during their existence and release storage when they leave scope, that is, when they are no longer needed.

> The step we are about to take is much more challenging. We must begin to think of a matrix as an entity containing only the coefficients which are assigned a value or used in some way. When a coefficient is no longer needed it ceases to exist and frees the storage it previously occupied.
> It is the coefficients of a matrix, rather than the matrix as a whole, that have a dynamic existence.

If, for example, the following sparse matrix is defined:

```
MatrixSparse A(1000,1000);
```

storage to contain 1000×1000 coefficients is not created – only the formal dimensions of the matrix are assigned. If you want a coefficient to be equal to a certain numerical value, you just have to write an assignment:

```
A(123,271) = 6.;
```

Object A knows from now on that a non-null coefficient with the value of 6 exists at row 123 and column 271. If a coefficient, that had not until that point been defined, is used, object A creates the requisite storage for it and initializes it to zero. If object A discovers that a coefficient is no longer needed it eliminates it and dynamically releases the storage it occupied.

13.2 Storing Coefficients

It is not sensible to store a sparse matrix, when its sizes are large, as if it were a normal matrix, because storage set aside for null coefficients would be wasted.

> FORTRAN lacks two essential tools for storing sparse matrices efficiently – *pointers* and data *structures*.
> Structures allow all the information needed to identify a particular coefficient to be lumped together in one individual variable.
> Pointers are used to move from one structure to another, that is, from one non-null coefficient to another.

Auxiliary vectors are used in FORTRAN to store the coefficients of a sparse matrix.

One widely used method is the Gustavson method, in which non-null coefficients are stored sequentially in a vector. The index column of each coefficient that is different from zero is stored on a second vector. The position of the first non-null coefficient for every line in the first vector is stored in a third.

For example, the matrix:

$$
\begin{vmatrix}
1 & 0 & 0 & 3 & 0 \\
0 & 0 & 2 & 0 & 4 \\
7 & 0 & 1 & 0 & 5
\end{vmatrix}
$$

would be stored in the three vectors below:

$$
\begin{vmatrix} 1. & 3. & 2. & 4. & 7. & 1. & 5. \end{vmatrix}
$$

$$
\begin{vmatrix} 1 & 4 & 3 & 5 & 1 & 3 & 5 \end{vmatrix}
$$

$$
\begin{vmatrix} 1 & 3 & 5 \end{vmatrix}
$$

Storing like this – if implemented in a language that permits the three vectors to be given dimensions dynamically – is only efficient, if the matrix is used without being modified. Problems arise if you want to insert or remove a coefficient, swap two rows and so on.

A large number of techniques for grouping and finding data with particular characteristics can be developed by exploiting pointers and structures in modern languages like C. These techniques are essential for DATABASE programs.

For our purposes, we only have to consider the most simple form of such techniques: linked lists.

A non-null coefficient of a matrix can be characterized by the numerical value of the coefficient and by its position (that is, by the row and column which identify it). Another item of data is added to this – a pointer which points to the following non-null coefficient. You need the pointer to be able to move along the list. The last non-null coefficient is not, by definition, followed by any other data. The pointer is set equal to zero for the last coefficient on the list. Because no valid pointer has this address, the end of the list can be found.

The matrix could thus be stored using the following data structure.

```
struct Element
    {
    int row,column;
    float value;
    Element *next;
    };
```

The procedure may seem rather baffling, as it does not figure among the techniques used in FORTRAN. But, with practice, you realize that it is not complicated. What is baffling is the presence in the structure of a pointer, `next`, which points to the next structure. Chapter 9 dealt with how a class identifier (`Element` in this case) is *declared* (but not defined) inside the definition block of a class.

Therefore, it can be used to define pointers to an object which is being defined but not to proper objects. It is by using this pointer that you can construct lists and move along them, passing from one element to the next. Suppose that `elem` is a variable pointer to `Element` and that it points to an `Element` on a list. The information below follows directly:

`elem->row` : row where element is located
`elem->column` : column where element is located
`elem->value` : coefficient's value
`elem->next` : address where next `Element` is stored

All you have to write to move to the next element and to be able to run through the whole list is:

`elem = elem->next;`

Several authors suggest this type of implementation to deal with sparse matrices. But, in my opinion, it is *not* a very efficient way of dealing with sparse matrices where solving numerical problems is involved.

The following characteristics should be borne in mind for this specific objective.

(1)   The means by which rows are swapped must be efficient.
(2)   Access to a matrix element is not always typically sequential and is often fortuitous.
(3)   There is always at least one element in a row.

I decided to change the approach which is normally used to accommodate these characteristics.

An array of pointers is created and given the same sizes as the number of rows in the matrix, the elements of which contain the address at the head of a list. Thus, each list contains the elements of a row. In other words, I construct one list for each row, instead of constructing a single list for the whole matrix.

> The advantages which accrue are as follows:
>
> (1) The exchange of rows is direct, because only the initial pointer of the list has to be swapped.
> (2) Any row can be accessed efficiently.
> (3) Any element can be accessed efficiently, without always having to run through a large list. Because the matrix is sparse, the number of elements on each list is certain to be very small. Conversely, the *total* number of elements could be very large, if the number of rows is large.
> (4) Storage is saved generally. In fact, the solution makes use of an array of pointers, the sizes of which accord with the number of rows. But the index of the row where an element resides does not have to be stored in each of the elements. Since there is at least one element for every row, less storage is required.

struct Element should be modified as follows:

```
struct Element
    {
    int column;
    float value;
    Element *next;
    };
```

The position of an element in a row, the value of a coefficient and the address of the next element on the same row are defined in struct Element. The last element in each row has 0 as the value of next.

class MatrixSparse uses the following data:

```
class MatrixSparse
    {
private:
    int numRows,numColumns;
    Element **elementRow;
    . . . . . . . . . . . . . . . . . .
    };
```

Their meaning is as follows.

numRows and numColumns are the dimensions of the whole matrix.

**elementRow is a pointer to a pointer to Element. An array of pointers with the dimensions numRows+1 is placed in it (so the vector can be used from 1 to numRows included). Each pointer in the array points to the head of a list containing the non-null elements of that particular row.

13.3 Constructors and Destructor

Defining a function, Initialize (for initializing), that is common to the various constructors is useful even for the class MatrixSparse.

```
// *********************< Initialize >*********************
// *   Purpose: Common function for initializing            *
// *   Description: Chapter 13                               *
// *   Example: Initialize(rows,columns)                     *
// ***********************************************************
void MatrixSparse::Initialize(int rows,int columns)
   {
   if(rows < 1 || columns < 1)
      {
      numRows = numColumns = 0;
      elementRow = 0;
      return;
      }
   numRows = rows;
   numColumns = columns;
   elementRow = new Element *[numRows + 1];
   if(!elementRow)
      Error("%s%s%sInitialize",
            MatrixSparse::ERROR,ERR_SPACE,ERR_FUNCTION);
   for(int row = 0;row <= numRows;row++)elementRow[row] = 0;
   return;
   }
```

Its purpose is to create storage space for the array of pointers to Element:

```
elementRow = new Element *[numRows + 1];
```

and to initialize the pointers with zero.

Default Constructor

This constructor is used to enable an identifier of type MatrixSparse to be defined. It is then assigned a value, using the = operator.

Example:

```
MatrixSparse A;
A = B; // B defined elsewhere
```

Its implementation is very simple:

```
// **********************< default >********************
// *  Purpose: to define a MatrixSparse                *
// *           which then receives an assignment       *
// *  Examples: MatrixSparse A;                         *
// *            A = B;                                  *
// ****************************************************
MatrixSparse::MatrixSparse(void)
    {
    Initialize(0,0);
    }
```

Copy-Initializer Constructor

This constructor, as has been stressed on several occasions, is fundamentally important.

```
MatrixSparse A = B; // B defined elsewhere
```

Its implementation is as follows:

```
// ****************< Copy-Initializer >******************
// *  Purpose: to define and initialize from MatrixSparse  *
// *  Example: MatrixSparse A=B;                          *
// ****************************************************
MatrixSparse::MatrixSparse(const MatrixSparse &rval)
    {
    Initialize(rval.numRows,rval.numColumns);
    Copy(rval);
    }
```

The constructor uses the function `Copy` which is also used by the = operator.

```
// **********************< Copy >********************
// *  Purpose: Copies a sparse matrix                  *
// *  Description: Used in copy-initializer            *
// *               and in assignment                   *
// ****************************************************
void MatrixSparse::Copy(const MatrixSparse &rval)
    {
    for(int row = 1;row <= numRows;row++)
        {
        Element *elem,*elemRval;
        int first = 1;
```

```
for(elemRval = rval.elementRow[row];
              elemRval != 0;elemRval = elemRval->next)
    {
    Element *newElement = new Element;
    if(!newElement)
    Error("%s%s%sCopy",
        MatrixSparse::ERROR,ERR_SPACE,ERR_FUNCTION);
    newElement->column = elemRval->column;
    newElement->value = elemRval->value;
    newElement->next = 0;
    if(first == 1)
        {
        elem = elementRow[row] = newElement;
        first = 0;
        }
    else
        {
        elem->next = newElement;
        elem = elem->next;
        }
    }
    }
}
```

Copying is cyclical and happens row by row:

```
for(int row = 1;row <= numRows;row++)
```

Two variable pointers to Element are defined inside this loop, and the variable first is equal to 1:

```
Element *elem,*elemRval;
int first = 1;
```

for, which is used to scan the elements in the various rows, is the function's linchpin.

```
for(elemRval = rval.elementRow[row];
    elemRval != 0;elemRval = elemRval->next)
```

The pointer elemRval is initialized with the address stored in the array of pointers rval.elementRow[row], which contains the address of the head of the list to be copied. Storage for a new element, newElement, is created inside for, and useful data is copied. elemRval = elemRval->next is used to move along to the next element. for finishes when the last null element in next is reached.

If an element is the first in a row, `elementRow[row]` and `elem` are initialized with `newElement`. This is the address at the head of the list of elements for that row in the new matrix.

```
elem = elementRow[row] = newElement;
```

When it comes to the subsequent elements, `elem->next` is defined first, so that it points to the new element that has just been created, and `elem` moves to the new element:

```
elem->next = newElement;
elem = elem->next;
```

> Drawing a diagram of the elements on the list to see what happens geometrically helps you understand this and other functions that use a list. Each element can be represented by a box which contains its own data and which is linked to the next box with an arrow, representing the pointer `next`.

Constructor for Giving Dimensions to a Matrix

This constructor is used to supply the dimensions of a matrix without assigning non-null coefficients:

```
MatrixSparse A(1000,1000);
```

13.4 Access to Elements

> Overloading the operator ( ), described below, suggests new ways in which coefficients in a sparse matrix can be managed and demonstrates C++'s far-ranging flexibility.

The same syntax as in FORTRAN is used to access matrix elements:

```
A(305,466) = 3.;
float x = A(215,766);
```

You can do this by overloading the operator ( ), as in normal matrices.

> Here, the operator ( ) must be implemented by means of a series of devices. When it is used as an lvalue, it must be used to assign the value to an element, if that element has already been defined. It must also be used to create a new element by inserting it in the right place, if the element no longer exists. When it is used as an rvalue, it must return the correct value, if the element exists. If not, it has to insert a new element and set a zero value to it.

Example:

```
MatrixSparse A(1000,1000); // no coefficient

A(123,456) = 15.; // insert a coefficient
A(123,456) = 1.; // change it
float x = A(123,456); // use it
x = A(5,6); // use an undefined coefficient
```

The operator uses the function InsertElement, the purpose of which is to insert a new element appropriately. The function is used internally and is therefore *private*. The user inserts or uses the elements with the operator ().

> An in-depth study of the following functions is recommended, because they are typical examples of functions that intervene when lists are used to store data.

```
// ******************< operator () >*******************
// *   Purpose: to receive and assign control values    *
// *   Example: x = A(1,5); A(3,7) = 5.;                 *
// ***********************************************************
float &MatrixSparse::operator () (int row,int column)
   {
   if(row < 1 || row > numRows ||
      column < 1 || column > numColumns)
         Error("%s%s%s()",
         MatrixSparse::ERROR,
         ERR_CHECK_DIMENSION,ERR_OPERATOR);
   Element *elem = elementRow[row];
   if(elem == 0 || column < elem->column)
      return InsertElement(elem,row,column,1);
   if(elem != 0 && column == elem->column)
      return elem->value;
   for(;elem->next != 0;elem = elem->next)
      {
      if(column == elem->next->column)
         return elem->next->value;
      else if(column < elem->next->column)break;
      }
   return InsertElement(elem,row,column,0);
   }
```

Notice that both functions return a *reference* to a float. In fact, both functions are to be used also as lvalues.

The operator ( ) starts with a test to make sure that row and column indices are inside the permitted range of the matrix.

A new variable pointer to Element is defined and initialized with the value stored in the vector of pointers for the row requested by the user.

```
Element *elem = elementRow[row];
```

At this point, there are three options.

(1)   If there are no more elements in a row, or the first existing element has a column index that is higher than the one you want to insert or use, the element must be inserted first.

```
if(elem == 0 || column < elem->column)
    return InsertElement(elem,row,column,1);
```

Notice that in this case, the function InsertElement is called with 1 in its argument.

(2)   If the first test is *not true*, the check moves to the second – if the first is true you leave the function, by using return.

The second test checks whether the column index of the first element is the same as the one requested; if so, you should return the stored value, rather than insert any new element.

```
if(column == elem->column)
    return elem->value;
```

> Because a *reference* to float is returned, the statement:
>
> ```
> return elem->value;
> ```
>
> ensures that the value stored on the list is modified and assumes the value of the expression on the right of the assignment, if the operator is being used as an lvalue.

This point is important and not easy to understand, so have a look at the following example:

```
A(123,456) = 15.; // insert a coefficient
A(123,456) = 1.; // modify it
float x = A(123,456); // use it
```

In the first call, no elements exist on the row, so the first test is true and the element *inserted*. In the second call, the element exists and so the second test is true and 1. is assigned to elem->value by exploiting the *reference* to float. In the last statement, the existing coefficient is used as an rvalue. The second test is again true, but this time return returns the value and does not modify it.

(3)   If the two tests above are *false*, the check proceeds as follows:

```
for(;elem->next != 0;elem = elem->next)
   {
   if(column == elem->next->column)
      return elem->next->value;
   else if(column < elem->next->column)break;
   }
return InsertElement(elem,row,column,0);
}
```

for allows you to go through the whole list. elem does not have to be re-initialized in for's argument, as it has already been initialized. Three things may happen:

(a) The loop is interrupted, if the right column is found and the stored value is returned. The value is also either returned or assigned in this situation, depending on whether the operator is being used as an rvalue or an lvalue:

```
return elem->next->value;
```

(b) The column index requested turns out to be greater than the index of an element on the list. Since the elements are stored in ascending column index order, this means that the element no longer exists in that row. The loop is interrupted.

(c) The loop reaches the bottom and has not found the column requested. The function InsertElement is called in the last two cases, but with a 0 value in its argument:

```
return InsertElement(elem,row,column,0);
```

Now, let's look at the function InsertElement.

```
// ***************< InsertElement >******************
// *   Purpose: Inserts an element                  *
// *   Description: Internal use                     *
// ***********************************************
float &MatrixSparse::InsertElement
            (Element *elem,int row,int column,int first)
   {
   Element *newElement = new Element;
```

```
if(!newElement)
    Error("%s%s%sInsertElement",
            MatrixSparse::ERROR,ERR_SPACE,ERR_FUNCTION);
newElement->column = column;
newElement->value = 0.;
if(first == 1)
    {
    newElement->next = elem;
    elementRow[row] = newElement;
    }
else
    {
    newElement->next = elem->next; // is inserted after
    elem->next = newElement;
    }
return newElement->value;
}
```

The function arguments are: a pointer to Element, elem, which points to the element you want to insert; the row and the column in which the element is located; an index, first, to show whether the element should or should not be inserted first.

The function starts by creating storage for a new element:

```
Element *newElement = new Element;
```

The value of the column index is assigned to the new element and the coefficient's value is set equal to zero.

```
newElement->column = column;
newElement->value = 0.;
```

The last statement may appear strange – why assign the value zero to newElement->value? Because the function can be called when an element is being used as an rvalue, before it is inserted. The element has to have a value for it to be usable, and if no value is assigned to it, it must be equal to zero. If the element has already been inserted and is used as an rvalue, the function is not called.

Example:

```
float x = A(123,456); // use it
x = A(5,6); // use an undefined coefficient
```

In the first case, I use a coefficient which has already been defined, and the function InsertElement is not called.

In the second case, a coefficient which has yet to be inserted is used. The function is used to insert and initialize it.

Here two things may happen, depending on the value of the index first, that is, depending on whether the element should or should not be inserted as first on the list.

If the element is to be inserted first, the following statement sequence is executed:

```
newElement->next = elem;
elementRow[row] = newElement;
```

Here, elem contains the address of the former first element. The first statement turns it into the second element. The other statement substitutes the new address for the old one.

If the element is not first on the list, it must be inserted by the following:

```
newElement->next = elem->next; // is inserted after
elem->next = newElement;
```

Here, newElement has to be inserted after elem, because of the way for is interrupted in the operator ().

Finally, the last statement:

```
return newElement->value;
```

serves to return the value (which as we have seen is equal to zero), if the operator () is used as an rvalue, or to assign the value, if it is used as an lvalue.

Example:

```
// rvalue for InsertValue
x = A(5,6); // use an undefined coefficient

// lvalue for InsertValue
A(2,4) = 2.; // assign an undefined coefficient
```

13.5 Delete and Clean

To use a sparse matrix efficiently, you have to be able to eliminate, in a simple fashion, those coefficients, which, for some reason or other, are no longer useful, and to free storage space.

The functions DeleteElement, DeleteRow, DeleteMatrix and two overloaded versions of the function CleanMatrix were implemented to this end. The purpose of the first three is obvious from the identifier.

The two overloaded functions CleanMatrix are used to eliminate from the matrix all coefficients or those coefficients that are lower in absolute value than an assigned value, but without de-initializing the matrix. It can still be used again.

Example:

```
MatrixSparse A(1000,1000);
......
A.DeleteElement(321,125);
A.CleanMatrix(1.e-20);
A.CleanMatrix();
A.DeleteRow(500);
A.DeleteMatrix();
```

Have a look at the function DeleteElement, which enables an element to be removed from a list.

```
// ****************< DeleteElement >********************
// *   Purpose: To remove an element from the matrix     *
// *   Example: A.DeleteElement(i,j);                    *
// ****************************************************
void MatrixSparse::DeleteElement(int row,int column)
    {
    if(elementRow == 0)return;
    if(row < 1 || row > numRows)return;
    if(column < 1 || column > numColumns)return;
    Element *elem,*temp;
    elem = elementRow[row];
    if(elem == 0)return;
    if(column == elem->column)
        {
        elementRow[row] = elem->next;
        delete elem;
        return;
        }
    for(;elem->next != 0; elem = elem->next)
        {
        if(column == elem->next->column)
            {
            temp = elem->next;
             elem->next = elem->next->next;
            delete temp;
            return;
            }
        }
    }
```

The element on the list is removed and eliminated with delete.

It is interesting to see how a row is removed:

```
// ******************< DeleteRow >**********************
// *  Purpose: To remove a row from a matrix            *
// *  Example: A.DeleteRow(i);                          *
// *****************************************************
void MatrixSparse:: (int row)
   {
   if(row < 1 || row > numRows)return;
   if(elementRow == 0)return;
   Element *elem,*temp;
   elem = elementRow[row];
   while(elem != 0)
      {
      temp = elem;
      elem = elem->next;
      delete temp;
      }
   elementRow[row] = 0;
   }
```

The pointer elem is initialized with the first element's address:

```
elem = elementRow[row];
```

You have to move to a subsequent element before removing an element and this is done by exploiting the auxiliary pointer, temp.

13.6 Operators

A few operators were overloaded and some operations were implemented. In particular it is instructive to analyse the multiplication of a sparse matrix and a vector.

```
// ********************< Product >**********************
// *  Purpose: To multiply sparse matrix and vector    *
// *  Example: Product(A,x,&y); y = A*x;               *
// *****************************************************
void Product(const MatrixSparse &lval,const Vector &rval,
             Vector *result)
   {
   if(lval.numColumns != rval.Size())
      Error("%s%s%s*",
```

```
               MatrixSparse::ERROR,
               ERR_CHECK_DIMENSION,ERR_OPERATOR);
        if(rval.WhoAmI() == result->WhoAmI())
           {
           Vector aux;
           Product(lval,rval,&aux); // recursive call
           Swap(&aux,result); // avoids copying
           }
        else
           {
           ChangeDimensions(lval.numRows,result);
           for(int i=1;i <= lval.numRows;i++)
              (*result)[i] = 0:; // initializes
           Element *elem;
           for(int row = 1;row <= lval.numRows;row++)
              {
              elem = lval.elementRow[row];
              for(int column = 1;
                      column <= lval.numColumns;column++)
                 {
                 if(elem == 0)break;
                 if(elem->column == column)
                    {
                    float *temp = &(*result)[row];
                    *temp = Control(*temp +
                          elem->value * rval.GetValue(column));
                    elem = elem->next;
                    }
                 }
              }
           }
        }


// ************************< * >************************
// * Purpose: Multiplication of sparse matrix          *
// *          and vector                               *
// * Example: y = A * x;                               *
// ****************************************************
Vector operator *
        (const MatrixSparse &lval,const Vector &rval)
   {
   if(lval.numColumns != rval.Size())
        Error("%s%s%s*",
        MatrixSparse::ERROR,
        ERR_CHECK_DIMENSION,ERR_OPERATOR);
```

```
Vector result;
Product(lval,rval,&result);
return result;
}
```

The procedure is similar to the one for multiplying a normal matrix and vector, as we saw earlier. The most substantial difference consists of the different order in which multiplication of the function `Product` is executed. The purpose of this is to accommodate greater difficulties which arise in accessing sparse matrices.

13.7 Solutions to Sparse Systems

How to solve large, *unstructured* sparse systems is a numeric problem which is of great practical interest, but it goes beyond the scope of this book.

> Here, only the problem of how to solve systems with triangular matrices will be analysed.

Where right-triangular matrices are involved, the function implemented is:

```
// ******************< SolveRight >********************
// * Purpose: Solve a system with MatrixSparse Right    *
// * Example: A.SolveRight(&bx);                        *
// ****************************************************
void MatrixSparse::SolveRight(Vector *bx)
   {
   Message("\nSolveRight\n");
   if(numRows != bx->dimensions)
      Error("%s%s%sSolve",
      MatrixSparse::ERROR,
      ERR_CHECK_DIMENSION,ERR_FUNCTION);
   Element *elem;
   double sum;
   float temp,*x = bx->vector;
   for(int row = numRows;row >= 1;rowñ)
      {
      elem = elementRow[row];
      if(elem != 0 && elem->column < row)
         {
         Error("%s Matrix non Right",
                  MatrixSparse::ERROR);
         }
```

```
if(elem == 0 || (temp = elem->value) == 0.
              || elem->column != row)
    {
    Message("%sSingular Matrix",
            MatrixSparse::ERROR);
    x[row]=0.;
    }
else
    {
    sum = x[row];
    elem = elem->next;
    for(int column = row+1;
            column <= numColumns;column++)
        {
        if(elem != 0 && elem->column == column)
            {
            sum -= elem->value * x[column];
            elem = elem->next;
            }
        }
    x[row] = Control(sum/temp);
    }
  }
}
```

There should not be any great problem in understanding the function's statements.

14 Derived Classes and Polymorphism

Non est ad astra mollis e terris via.

The ascent to heaven from earth is difficult.

Seneca, *Hercules furens.*

14.1 Introduction

 One of the great merits of object-oriented programming is that it is easier to exploit already existing codes, which can be *reused* to meet new demands.

Reusing existing functions or SUBROUTINES is also common practice in procedural languages. The model of procedural programming was created for this specific purpose.

 The concept of an existing code being reused in an object-oriented language requires users to see various aspects of programming in a new light so that they can take into account all the possibilities it offers.

383

A class which has already been defined elsewhere can be reused in three different ways.

(1) The first consists simply in using an object in a program. This entails only a slight shift in perspective in relation to the concept of reusing an existing code. Just as procedures (functions or SUBROUTINES) can be reused in a procedural language, so objects belonging to classes defined elsewhere can be reused in an object-oriented language.

(2) An object can be used inside the definition of another class. The process by which a class uses an object of another class in its own definition is known as *composition*.

(3) Finally, there is a third way of using extant classes. It is typical of object-oriented programming and is one of its strong points. Since it is, unlike the first two ways mentioned above, completely alien to procedural languages, it is more difficult to understand and to use appropriately. But it is also what makes object-oriented programming so much better than its procedural counterpart. Expressed briefly, all you have to know is that, instead of taking an extant object and incorporating it into a new class, the previous class is extended, so that it is possible to create a new class similar to its predecessor, but with an addition or change of some sort to the way it works. This is known as an *extension* of use rather than reuse, as a *derivation* of extant classes and not as a composition.

How Objects are Used

Suppose you have to use a type `Matrix` object in a function:

```
void Func(void)
    {
    Matrix result(10,10); // type Matrix object
                          // being used

    .....
    };
```

> The term *reusing* can be applied to this method of exploiting an object belonging to a class that has already been defined and the method is similar to, but more efficient than, that used in procedural programming. An object is reused instead of a procedure. The object supplies greater guarantees of data protection (*data hiding*) and of appropriate use of functions which act on data (*encapsulation*).

Composition

Suppose you have defined the class `Point` and want to use it in defining another class, `class Circle`:

```
class Point // Point must be defined
    {      // forward declaration is not sufficient
private:
float xi,yi;
public:
void SetPoint(float x,float y){xi = x; yi = y;}
};

class Circle
{
private:
float radius;
public:
Point center;  // uses Point
void SetRadius(float r){radius = r;}
};
```

> The term *composition* can be applied to this method of exploiting an extant code. The new class is composed of the previous object and of other members (data or functions.) The relationship between the two objects is that of one object contained within another.

Chapter 10 dealt with how an object included in another class is initialized (by using an initialization list) and how constructors of the two classes interact. Now let's look at how an object included in a class is *used*.

Example:

```
Circle cir; // object type Circle
cir.SetRadius(3.); // assigns the radius
cir.center.SetPoint(4.,5.); // uses center with cir
```

As can be seen, cir, the object of class Circle, is used to access Circle's public members. If you want to access the public members (data or functions) of the encapsulated object, you must also use the object's name, center.

> This procedure is entirely valid for swapping messages *inside* a class. But it is stylistically clumsy and *violates one of the principles of object-oriented programming*, if it is to be used *externally* by the user, who is required to be aware of internal details of the class.

In the example considered above, it is necessary to know that an object of type Point is in class Circle and bears the identifier center.

class `Circle` could be more coherently implemented like this:

```
class Circle
   {
private:
   float radius;
   Point center;   // Point is private
public:
   void SetRadius(float r){radius = r;}
   void SetCenter(float x,y){center.SetPoint(x,y);}
   };
```

Now the internal object is *hidden* from the user, who can only access it across the interface of the type `Circle` object.

```
cir.SetCenter(4.,5.); // uses cir to use center
             // hidden to the user
```

Inheritance, Derivation, Extension

Suppose you have an already defined class, and one of its details needs to be changed. In C++, you can leave the original class unchanged and *derive* from it a new class which has the same characteristics as its predecessor, except those you do not want. *And you do not have to rewrite a whole amount of code to meet already satisfied needs.*

For example, let's assume the `class Demo` has been defined. It is quite satisfactory, apart from three details. You want to add an item of data of type `int` and a function, `Funx`, and to change the function `FunFun`. You can create a new class, `Sample`, which very simply meets these requirements:

```
class Sample : public Demo
   {
private:
   int newInt;
public:
   void Funx(void);
   float FunFun(int i);
   };
```

For the time being, let's not worry about the syntax used to derive the class.

```
class Sample : public Demo
```

So far, the following points should be stressed:

(1) derived class objects and members can directly exploit base class members as if they were its *own* members (with a few exceptions);
(2) deriving can often be carried out *without possessing the base class's source code.*

Let's look at another situation. You want construct a class library which has a clear hierarchical order. Some objects are more abstract and general, while others are more specific and complex. Here too, it is useful to be able to link classes, with those which are most developed exploiting the code of the simplest.

For example, let's go back to class `Circle`. Instead of *including* the object `Point` in class `Circle`, we derive class `Circle` from class `Point`:

```
class Point
   {
private:
   float xi,yi;
public:
   void SetPoint(float x,float y){xi = x; yi = y;}
   };
class Circle : public Point
   {
private:
   float radius;
public:
   void SetRadius(float r){radius = r;}
   };
```

Notice that `Circle` no longer defines a type `Point` object and does not have to supply a function in order to access `SetPoint`. At the same time, `Circle` can use all `Point`'s functions and accessible data with its object:

```
Circle cir; // type Circle object
cir.SetRadius(3.); // assigns radius
cir.SetPoint(4.,5.); // uses Point directly
```

This method of exploiting an already existing code is completely alien to procedural programming. So a few metaphors would be useful, and are indeed used, to describe this new method of tackling the problem.

(1) *Inheritance* highlights the fact that when a class is obtained in this special way by another, it inherits all those characteristics of the parent class that are not explicitly declared as different from the child class.

cont.

cont.

(2) *Derivation* underlines the fact that one class is derived from another and is not defined by itself.

(3) *Extension* underlines an important facet of this approach, and that is, that a class is extended to meet new demands. This has much more profound implications than can be followed up here. But we will return to the subject later.

Several other metaphors, and consequently, different names, exist to describe classes that generate others, and the classes that are generated.

(1) *Parent* and *child* classes.
(2) *Base* and *derived* classes.
(3) *Super-* and *sub-*classes.

Like all metaphors, they are both accurate and misleading.

I will not use a specific name to denote this method of exploiting an existing code, even though I prefer to use the term *derivation*. I will also use the terms *inheritance* and *extension*, depending on the circumstances.

But, when referring to relations between classes I will use the adjectives *base* (class or classes) and *derived* (class or classes).

14.2 Class Derivation

One class can be derived from another, in ways that we shall look at shortly. A derived class can, in turn, be used as a base class. And so a chain of classes, each one derived from another, can be created.

An even more articulated model of relations between classes can be drawn up using recent versions of C++.

Definition: *Simple and multiple derivation*
If one class is derived from another *single* class, this is known as a *simple derivation*. If conversely, a class is derived from *several* classes, this is called *multiple derivation*.

I will only look at simple derivation.
And remember that I consider only `class` specimens as being *objects*. I use `struct` and `unions` within the constraints and purpose of C.

Now let's look at how a derived class is defined.

The syntax to be used with a derived class is as follows:

`class` <derived class name> : <modifier> <base class name>
{derived class body};

Modifiers can be `public`, `protected` or `private`. Their purpose is to manage how base class *members* are hidden from derived class *objects*. The default modifier is `private` and intervenes if *no* modifier is written.

For example, let's assume that a class with the identifier `Base` has been defined; the `class Derived` can be derived from it:

```
class Derived : public Base // notice the semi-colon:
    {
    statements;
    };
```

It must be stressed that the base class *has to be defined* when the derived class is defined. *A forward declaration is insufficient.*

For example:

```
class Base; // forward declaration insufficient
class Derived : public Base
    {
    statements;
    };
```

Data Hiding in Derived Classes

Access to data and functions in classes can be managed very smoothly in C++.

When one class is derived from another, you have to understand *to what extent base class and derived class members are accessible to*:

(1) *base* class *objects*
(2) *base* class *member* functions
(3) *derived* class *objects*
(4) *derived* class *member* functions
(5) *base* class `friend` functions
(6) *derived* class `friend` functions
(7) `friend` functions of *both* classes

Have a look at the following two classes:

```
class Base
    {
    friend void BaseFriend(void);
    friend void BaseAndDerivedFriend(void);
private:
    int basePrivate;
protected:
    int baseProtected;
public:
    int basePublic;
    void BaseFunc(void);
    };

class Derived : <MODIFIER> Base
    {
    friend void DerivedFriend(void);
    friend void BaseAndDerivedFriend(void);
private:
    int derivedPrivate;
protected:
    int derivedProtected;
public:
    int derivedPublic;
    void DerivedFunc(void);
    };
```

Base Class Objects

A base class object *can only access members of its own class which have been defined as* `public`. It *cannot* access `protected` and `private` members of its own class, nor members of a derived class (not even those that are `public`).

Example:

```
Base objBase;
objBase.basePrivate = 1; // NO
objBase.baseProtected = 1; // NO
objBase.basePublic = 1; // OK
objBase.BaseFunc(); // OK
```

```
objBase.derivedPrivate = 1; // NO
objBase.derivedProtected = 1; // NO
objBase.derivedPublic = 1; // NO
objBase.DerivedFunc(); // NO
```

A base class object can access `protected` and `private` members of its own class, if it is defined in a `friend` function of the same class. It *cannot* access derived class members.

Example:

```
void BaseAndDerivedFriend(void) // or BaseFriend
    {
    Base objBase;
    objBase.basePrivate = 1; // OK
    objBase.baseProtected = 1; // OK
    objBase.basePublic = 1; // OK
    objBase.BaseFunc(); // OK
    objBase.derivedPrivate = 1; // NO
    objBase.derivedProtected = 1; // NO
    objBase.derivedPublic = 1; // NO
    objBase.DerivedFunc(); // NO
    }
```

A base class object can only access `public` members of the base class, if it is defined in a `friend` function of a derived class. It *cannot* access derived class members.

Example:

```
void DerivedFriend(void)
    {
    Base objBase;
    objBase.basePrivate = 1; // NO
    objBase.baseProtected = 1; // NO
    objBase.basePublic = 1; // OK
    objBase.BaseFunc(); // OK
    objBase.derivedPrivate = 1; // NO
    objBase.derivedProtected = 1; // NO
    objBase.derivedPublic = 1; // NO
    objBase.DerivedFunc(); // NO
    }
```

Base Class Member Functions

Base class member functions can *only* access *base* class members and *cannot* access members of any *derived* classes. This is to be expected, because base classes do not hold any information on any classes which could be derived, but which have yet to be implemented.

Example:

```
void Base::BaseFunc(void)
   {
   basePrivate = 1; // OK
   baseProtected = 1; // OK
   basePublic = 1          ; // OK
   BaseFunc(); // OK
   derivedPrivate = 1; // NO
   derivedProtected = 1; // NO
   derivedPublic = 1; // NO
   DerivedFunc(); // NO
   }
```

Derived Class Objects

 A derived class object can access members of its own class, which may have been defined as public. It cannot access protected or private members of its own class, unless it has been defined inside a class friend function. This is the usual rule that applies to class objects.

Example:

```
Derived objDerived;
objDerived.derivedPrivate; // NO
objDerived.derivedProtected; // NO
objDerived.derivedPublic; // OK
```

Example:

```
void DerivedFriend(void)
   {
   Derived objDerived;
   objDerived.derivedPrivate = 1; // OK
   objDerived.derivedProtected = 1; // OK
   objDerived.derivedPublic = 1; // OK
   objDerived.DerivedFunc(); // OK
   }
```

The modifier used in defining a derived class is brought into play, where access by the derived class object to *members of a base class* is involved.

(1)   `public` modifier. Access remains unchanged. Public members remain `public`, `protected` members, `protected`, and `private` members, `private`. Thus derived class objects can access `public` base class members.

(2)   `protected` modifier. Public members become `protected`, `protected` members `private`, while `private` members stay `private`. *Not all compilers accept this modifier.* Using it should therefore be avoided.

(3)   `private` modifier. All base class members become `private`. Derived class objects cannot access them.

If you use:

```
class Derived : public Base
```

the following results:

```
Derived objDerived;
objDerived.basePrivate; // NO
objDerived.baseProtected; // NO
objDerived.basePublic; // OK
```

If you use:

```
class Derived : private Base
```

the result is:

```
Derived objDerived;
objDerived.basePrivate; // NO
objDerived.baseProtected; // NO
objDerived.basePublic; // NO
```

Take a function which has been defined a `friend` of the derived class and not of the base class.
An object of the derived class, defined inside this function, has access to `public` and `protected` members (notice that *even* `protected` *members* can be accessed) of the base class, if the modifier with which the class was defined is `public`. The object cannot access any base class members, if the modifier is `private`.

Example:

```
// if defined with public modifier
void DerivedFriend(void)
    {
    Derived objDerived;
    objDerived.basePrivate = 1; // NO
    objDerived.baseProtected = 1; // OK Notice this
    objDerived.basePublic = 1; // OK
    objDerived.BaseFunc(); // OK
    }
```

Example:

```
// if defined with private modifier
void DerivedFriend(void)
    {
    Derived objDerived;
    objDerived.basePrivate = 1; // NO
    objDerived.baseProtected = 1; // NO
    objDerived.basePublic = 1; // NO
    objDerived.BaseFunc(); // NO
    }
```

Take a function which has been defined as friend of the base class and not of the derived.
A derived class object, defined inside this function, can access all base class members, independently of the modifier that is used in deriving the derived class. This object *cannot* access protected and private members of its *own* class.

Example:

```
// with public or private modifier
void BaseFriend(void)
    {
    Derived objDerived;
    objDerived.basePrivate = 1; // OK
    objDerived.baseProtected = 1; // OK
    objDerived.basePublic = 1; // OK
    objDerived.BaseFunc(); // OK

    objDerived.derivedPrivate = 1; // NO
    objDerived.derivedProtected = 1; // NO
    objDerived.derivedPublic = 1; // OK
    objDerived.DerivedFunc(); // OK
    }
```

If you also want to extend the privilege of f r i e n d for a function, defined as
f r i e n d in the base class, to the members of a derived class, the function
has to be explicitly defined as f r i e n d of the derived class.
Assume you have a function which has been defined as f r i e n d, both in a
base class and in a *derived* class. An object of the derived class, defined
inside this function, can access *all* the *base* and *derived* class members,
independently of the modifier used in deriving the derived class.

Example:

```
// with public or private modifier
void BaseAndDerivedFriend(void)
    {
    Derived objDerived;
    objDerived.basePrivate = 1; // OK
    objDerived.baseProtected = 1; // OK
    objDerived.basePublic = 1; // OK
    objDerived.BaseFunc(); // OK

    objDerived.derivedPrivate = 1; // OK
    objDerived.derivedProtected = 1; // OK
    objDerived.derivedPublic = 1; // OK
    objDerived.DerivedFunc(); // OK
    }
```

Derived Class Function Members.

A derived class function member can access all members of its own class.

A derived class function member *cannot access private base class members.*
So a user cannot violate the inaccessibility of a class's data simply by
deriving another class from it.

Let's sum up accessibility of p r i v a t e class members.

The following can access class members defined as p r i v a t e:

(1) class member functions (using the hidden pointer t h i s);
(2) functions which have been defined as f r i e n d *inside a class* with a
     class or derived class object (independently of the modifier used in the
     derivation);
(3) class member functions of a class which has been defined f r i e n d
     inside the class itself. These functions also require a class object of
     which they are f r i e n d or an object of a class derived from that class.

> Whoever designs the class always decides whether or not to permit access to its private members.

But there are many situations, where, in one sense, you want to give preference to classes which have yet to be derived.

> The keyword protected was introduced to enable a class to have some way of permitting its own members to be accessible for classes which have yet to be derived and, at the same time, of prohibiting objects of all classes, including its own, from being able to access them.
> So a derived class member function *can access* all base class members that have been declared as public or protected. *It cannot access* data declared as private.
> The accessibility of base class members is not influenced by the modifier that is used when a class is derived.

Example:

```
// with public or private modifier
void Derived::DerivedFunc(void)
    {
    derivedPublic = 1; // OK
    derivedProtected = 1; // OK
    derivedPrivate = 1; // OK
    basePublic = 1; // OK
    baseProtected = 1; // OK
    basePrivate = 1; // NO
    }
```

> Notice that access to those base class members which can be accessed (public and protected members) occurs in the same way as for members of the class to which a function belongs. This is the reason for the term *inheritance* – a derived class inherits public and protected members from its base class and can treat them *as if they were its own*.

Inaccessibility and Invisibility

In Chapter 9, I stressed the importance of one of C++'s characteristics, but failed to explain why.

> Data hiding is achieved by restricting access to data and functions, and not by making them invisible.

Look at how the class below is derived:

```
class Base
    {  .
public:
    void FuncBase(int i);
    void FuncBase(double d);
    };

class Derived : public Base
    {
public:
    void FuncDerived(int i){FuncBase(i);}
    };
```

The derived class can access the overloaded functions defined in the base class and it uses one of them, `FuncBase(int i)`, in its function, `FuncDerived`. What would happen if you now decided, for whatever reason, to place `FuncBase(int i)` in the `private` area?

Example:

```
class Base
    {
private:
    void FuncBase(int i);
public:
    void FuncBase(double d);
    };
class Derived : public Base
    {
public:
    void FuncDerived(int i){FuncBase(i);}
    };
```

In the C++ approach, the function `FuncBase(int i)` is inaccessible, but still *visible* to the derived class, so a compile-time error would be flagged.

If, instead, C++ made a function *invisible* in order to make it inaccessible, disaster would strike – the function `FuncDerived` would call the overloaded function `FuncBase(double d)`, which would be the only one visible to `FuncDerived`. The latter would use `FuncBase(double d)` with unpredictable results.

Classes Derived from other Derived Classes

The rules which govern the relationship between the first base class in a chain and the class derived from it apply to the relationship between all subsequent derived classes.

> The modifier which was used to define a derived class is brought into play, when a member of its base class has to be accessed by members of its derived class.

For example, access to members of a base class remains unaltered, if the modifier public is used.

If the modifier private is used in defining a derived class, members of its derived classes cannot access members of its base class.

> In practice, it is best to use the modifier public, so that the same level of accessibility can be maintained in the various derived classes.
> Only in exceptional cases should accessibility be modified in subsequent classes and the modifier private used.

> As a matter of style, I shall explicitly write the modifier used in deriving classes.

14.3 Deriving and Overloading Functions

We have seen that a derived class inherits all of a base class's members.

But you may wonder what happens, if a function with the same identifier as the one used in a base class is used in one of its derived classes.

> It is easy to make the mistake of confusing *deriving* a function member with *overloading* functions. You must always remember that a function's *scope* is shared by the class in which it is defined. The scope of a derived class is thus different to that of a base class. So, when a derived class uses a function with which it shares a common identifier, hide the function and *do not overload it.*

To understand the difference, let's use the following example to have another look at what hiding an identifier entails;

```
void Func(void)
   {
   statements;
   }

class Demo
   {
   ...
```

```
float Func(int i){statements;}
};
```

The global function Func is *hidden, but not invisible,* inside the class Demo. It would be a compile-time error to call Func(void) (which is hidden from Func(int)) inside the class functions, unless the scope operator :: were used. In fact, ::Func() would be permitted, and the global function, rather than the class function, would be used. The same happens with derived classes.

Example:

```
class Base
    {
public:
    void Func(void){statements;}
    float Func(int i){statements;}
    ...
    };

class Derived : public Base
    {
public:
    float Func(int i){statements;}
    ...
    };
.......
Derived objDerived;
objDerived.Func(1); // OK uses Derived's
objDerived.Base::Func(); // OK uses Base's
objDerived.Base::Func(1); // OK uses Base's
objDerived.Func(); // error Func() is hidden
                   // not overloaded
```

This is a very important and useful point to grasp.

> Two functions with the *same identifier* are *overloaded* only if they:
>
> (1)   have the same scope;
> (2)   have arguments that distinguish them.

If the same two functions do *not* have the same scope, *one hides, but does not overload* the other. And the hidden function is *only hidden and not invisible.*

Note the following points on hidden functions.

(1) Whether their arguments are the same or different is unimportant.
(2) All functions with a different scope are hidden at the same time, not just those with the same arguments.
(3) Hidden functions can be used even at the point where they are hidden, if they can be accessed, and if the scope operator : : is used.

So the compiler treats two functions that share the same identifier, with one defined in class Base, and the other in class Derived, as two *distinct* functions – one with Base: : scope, and the other with Derived: : scope.

This is of considerable practical importance. If a function can be accessed by objects of both classes, both a base class object and a derived class object call their own specific functions.
The same thing happens when using pointers to objects or references.

Example:

```
class Base
    {
public:
    void Func(void);
    ....
    };

class Derived : public Base
    void Func(void);
    ....
    };
....
Base objBase;
Derived objDerived;
objBase.Func(); //calls Base's
objDerived.Func(); //calls Derived's
Base *ptrBase = &objBase;
Derived *ptrobjDerived = &objDerived;
ptrBase->Func(); //calls Base's
ptrDerived->Func(); //calls Derived's
```

Assume you have three classes; one base, a second derived from it and a third derived from the second.

```
class Base
   {
public:
   float Func(void);
   ...
   };

class Derived : public Base
   {
public:
   float Func(void);
   ...
   };

class DerivedDerived : public Derived
   {
public:
   float Func(void);
   ...
   };
```

The function `Func` of class `DerivedDerived` hides the function with the same identifier in the classes from which it is derived. Thus, in the example:

```
DerivedDerived obj;
obj.Func();
```

the object, `obj`, of `DerivedDerived` calls `Func` which was defined in its class.

Being able to derive several classes in sequence means you can reuse existing code in a new way. Hidden functions can be called directly, helping to construct the definition of the function itself, since they can still be accessed by derived class functions.

For example, the function `Func` of the class `DerivedDerived` can use the following function calls inside itself:

```
Derived::Func() // Derived's Func
Base::Func() //  Base's Func
```

It is a good idea, when writing derived classes one after the other, to try to create functions in the lowest level classes, which do as much work as possible. You can then use them in derived classes.

14.4 Pointers to Derived Class Objects

Pointers to derived class objects are defined and initialized in the same way as pointers to base class objects.

Example:

```
Base objBase;
Derived objDerived;
Base *ptrBase = &objBase;
Derived *ptrDerived = &objDerived;
Base *pppBase = new Base;
Derived *pppDerived = new Derived;
```

> You may wonder what happens if a derived class pointer is assigned the address of a base class object and vice versa.

You have to look at both situations – a pointer to a derived class object, and a base class object.

Pointer to a Derived Class Object

A pointer to a derived class object *cannot* receive the address of a base class object.

Example:

```
Base objBase; // base class object
Derived *ptrDerived; // pointer to derived object
ptrDerived = &objBase;  // Error
Derived *pppDerived = new Base; // Error
```

Some compilers allow address conversions to be coerced, by using an explicit cast. In some very special circumstances, this technique could prove useful, if you wanted to reuse the pointer. Example:

```
Base *ptrBase = new Base;
Derived *ptrDerived;
ptrDerived = (Base *)ptrBase; // often accepted
```

> I shall avoid using explicit cast as a matter of style.
> So, a pointer to a derived class object *will not receive the address of a base class object*:
>
> ```
> ptrDerived = ptrBase; // Error
> ptrDerived = (Base *)ptrBase; // avoid
> ```

Pointer to a Base Class Object

If a pointer is defined as a pointer to a base class object, it may be assigned the address either of a base class object or of a derived class object.

Example:

```
Base objBase;
Derived objDerived;
Base *ptrBase;
ptrBase = &objBase; // OK
ptrBase = &objDerived; // OK
```

The same is true if the operator new is used to initialize the pointer.
Example:

```
Base *ptrBase = new Base; //OK
```

Example:

```
Base *ptrBase = new Derived; //OK
```

An implicit cast is carried out in the two statements:

```
Base *ptrBase = new Derived; //OK
ptrBase = &objDerived; // OK
```

and the cast transforms the address of a derived object into the address of a base class object – and all this happens safely and unambiguously.

> This is the first important point to be remembered – *a pointer to a base class object can receive the address of a derived class object.*

Now, we need to see how a pointer to a base class object can access members of two classes.

Have a look at the following two classes.

```
class Base
    {
public:
    int basePublic;
    void Func(void);
    };
```

```
class Derived : public Base
   {
public:
   int derivedPublic;
   void DerivedFunc(void);
   void Func(void);
   };
```

Now take the following two objects and two pointers:

```
Base objBase;
Derived objDerived;
Base *ptrBase;
Derived *ptrDerived;
```

It is obvious that if the assignment looks like this:

```
ptrBase = &objBase;
ptrDerived = &objDerived;
```

the two pointers behave normally towards their class members.
Suppose, instead, the assignment is:

```
ptrBase = &objDerived; // OK it can be done
```

The following statement:

```
ptrBase->basePublic = 1;
```

modifies the member basePublic of the object objDerived.

> The second point to remember is that *a pointer to a base class object which has been assigned the address of a derived class object can access members – if they are accessible – of that object which are common to the base class.*

How can derived class members that are not in the base class be accessed? If they are assigned:

```
ptrBase = &objDerived;
ptrDerived = &objDerived;
```

the following statements are valid:

```
ptrDerived->derivedPublic = 1;
ptrDerived->DerivedFunc();
```

```
((Derived *)ptrBase)->derivedPublic = 1;
((Derived *)ptrBase)->DerivedFunc();
```

that is, you can access either by using a pointer to a derived class object (as is obvious) or by a explicit cast with a pointer to a base class object which has been assigned the address of a *derived* class object (notice the brackets – they are essential).

 As a matter of style, I shall avoid using an explicit cast to access derived members with a pointer to a base class object. The members will be accessed using a pointer to a derived class object.

```
ptrDerived->derivedPublic =1; // OK

// best avoided
((Derived *)ptrBase)->derivedPublic = 1;
```

What happens if the two classes have a function with the same identifier?

Which function is called, the base class function or the derived class function with the following statements, in the case under consideration here?

```
ptrBase = &objDerived;
ptrBase->Func();
```

The *base* function is called, as was stressed earlier on.

An explicit cast would be necessary, here, to be able to access class Derived's Func:

```
((Derived *)ptrBase)->Func(); // calls Derived's Func
```

This can be done because the function is hidden, rather than invisible.

An important variant in this analysis consists in using *references* instead of pointers. In particular, let's see what happens when an a function argument has a reference to a Base class object:

```
void FunSample(const Base &obj);
```

The object obj can access all the accessible members of the class Base, in particular Func(), in the definition of the function FunSample:

```
void FunSample(const Base &obj)
    {
    ....
    obj.Func();
    }
```

What happens if the function `FunSample` is used and a `Derived` class object is placed in its actual argument?

```
Derived objDerived;
FunSample(objDerived);
```

Which function `Func()` is used in `FunSample`?
Here again, the *base* class's `Func()` would be used.

> *Warning*: The second shift in perspective brought about by the introduction of class derivation begins here. (The first was occasioned by the different method of reusing existing codes.) In C++, you can define special functions, called virtual functions, for reasons and in a form that will be clarified later. In defining virtual functions, *a pointer (or a reference) to a base class object, which has been assigned the address of a derived class object, accesses the function member of the derived, rather than the base class.*

If `Func` had been one of these virtual functions in the example above, `FunSample` would have used the derived class's `Func`, rather than the base class's.

> This characteristic may seem wasteful and of little importance at this point. On the contrary, we shall see that it is the keystone of genuine object-oriented programming, that is, of genuine polymorphism and of extending existing codes. This goes far beyond the simple class derivation that we have seen so far.

A short recap would be useful here.

(1)   A pointer to a base class, `Base`, can receive the address of a derived class, `Derived`:

```
ptrBase = &objDerived;   // OK
```

(2)   The `public` members of the object `objDerived` defined in `Base class` can be accessed with this pointer. `ptrBase` has to be defined in a `friend` function of `Base` to access its `protected` or `private` members.

(3)   The `public` members of the `objDerived`, defined in the class `Derived`, can be accessed only by using an explicit cast. `ptrBase` has to be defined in a `friend` function of `Derived` (remember that a `friend` property cannot be inherited) to access the `protected` or `private` members of `Derived`.

(4)   The pointer *directly* accesses – without an explicit cast – *virtual* member functions of `objDerived`, which have been defined in the `Derived` class. Levels of accessibility to this kind of function will be discussed later.

The above also applies to references.

14.5 Virtual Functions

So far, you may have had the impression that derived classes form a kind of long chain, with one class being derived from another, from which is derived another and so on.

But, here, you must also consider the possibility of class derivation having a more *horizontal* dimension – a base class from which many other classes are derived on the same level. You could think of a base class as a common platform for a number of classes.

The same kind of horizontal dimension could apply in cases which are complementary to the one above, where the base class is a general form of many similar situations.

In the light of the above, we must now focus attention on the following simplified problem – derived classes differ only in the way they implement a given function.

And suppose that, having foreseen a number of possible situations, there is a fair probability that you will have to consider others.

How could an efficient code be implemented?

The first option is to construct a program in which alternative functions are selected with switches, which are managed by an index chosen by the user. But this method is not very efficient, because if a new option is introduced, the whole program has to be modified and recompiled.

A second, more acceptable option is to use function pointers, as demonstrated in Chapter 7. This is the method used in procedural languages like C.

A third option is to exploit the technique mentioned above, but within the context of objects, that is, by exploiting pointers to class member functions.

C++ offers a fourth option, which is much more efficient than those listed above and which, in practice, is an automatic version of the technique described in the third option. To this end, C++ introduces *virtual* functions.

The rules governing how functions are specified virtual are as follows:

(1) Functions *must* be class members. Functions which are not class members cannot be virtual.

(2) The keyword virtual has to be written in *declarations of function prototypes*, while *classes are being defined*.

(3) All class member functions of *derived classes with the same prototypes* (identifiers, return types, formal arguments) are automatically virtual.

cont.

cont.

(4) If functions are declared as virtual in a class, which is a base class for other classes, declaring prototypes is *not* by itself sufficient – they *must* also be *defined* in that class or *must* be declared as *pure virtual functions* (by setting them equal to zero – we shall see what this entails later).

(5) The definition of virtual functions is identical to definitions of normal class member functions. You do *not* have to write the keyword `virtual` in the functions' *definitions*.

(6) Virtual functions can be `inline`.

(7) They *cannot* be `static`.

(8) Overloaded operators *can* be declared as virtual.

Example:

```
class Base
   {
public:
   void Func1(int i);
   virtual int Func2(void);
   virtual float Func3(int i);
   ...
   };

class Derived : public Base
public:
   virtual void Func1(int i);
   virtual int Func2(void);
   virtual float Func3(void);
   ...
   };
```

In this example, only the function `Func2` is virtual for the class `Derived`. In fact, the function `Func1` was not declared with the keyword `virtual` in the base class; it does not matter whether `Func1` was then declared as `virtual` in the derived class.

`Derived class`'s `Func3` does not share a prototype with the base class's `Func3`, which behaves as if the keyword `virtual` did not exist.

Thus, a pointer to a base class object, which has been assigned a derived class object's address, calls `Func3`, which has been defined in the base class.

Warning: one error that may creep in here is to use different prototypes in derived functions when you think you have a virtual function.

Once again, I must stress that functions remain virtual in derived classes only if the same prototype is kept.

cont.

cont.

This does not mean that a virtual function cannot be declared with a different prototype in a derived class. You just have to be aware of the consequence, which is that the function is not virtual for that class.

By deriving a class from a derived class with a different function prototype, and by declaring the prototype correctly in the new class, a virtual function is obtained once again and you can skip a generation.

But it is best not to play around like this.

Example:

```
class Base
    {
public:
    virtual void Func1(int i);
    ...
    };

class Derived : public Base
public:
    void Func1(float x); // is not virtual for Derived
    ...
    };

class DerivedDerived : public Derived
public:
    void Func1(int i); // is virtual for DerivedDerived
    ...
    };
```

The keyword `virtual` can be omitted from derived classes and from those derived from them, since a function remains virtual for all classes derived from the class in which the function is so declared.

 Even if the keyword `virtual` does not have to be repeated in the declarations of derived class prototypes, I would nevertheless advise re-writing it as an *aide-mémoire*.

Example:

```
class Base
    {
public:
    virtual void Func1(int i);
```

```
   virtual int Func2(void);
    ...
   };

class Derived : public Base
public:
   void Func1(int i); // valid, but not advisable
   virtual int Func2(void); // better
   ...
   };
```

> If a function is not redeclared as a virtual function (and thus not re-defined) in a derived class, its class objects use the function of the base class from which the class is derived. Thus, a virtual function *does not have to* be redeclared and redefined in all derived classes.

Example:

```
class Base
   {
public:
   virtual int Func(void){return 0;}
   };

class Derived : public Base
public:
   ...// Base's Func is used
   };
```

> But the *definition* of a function, which was declared as virtual in the base class, has to be supplied, if this function is declared in the derived class.

Example:

```
class Base
   {
public:
   virtual int Func(void){return 0;}
   };

class Derived : public Base
public:
   virtual int Func(void); // assembly error
                        // if it is not also defined

   };
```

A derived class can, in turn, introduce new virtual functions for classes derived from it.

Example:

```
class Base
    {
public:
    virtual void Func1(int i);
    ...
    };

class Derived : public Base
public:
    virtual void Func1(int i);
    virtual int Func2(float x);
    };
```

DerivedDerived, (a class derived from Derived), has two virtual functions – the first, Func1, is inherited from Base, while the second Func2, is inherited from Derived.

A derived class, in which a virtual function has been redefined, can still access the virtual base class function with the scope operator. Data hiding does not mean invisibility – and that applies to virtual functions as well.

Example:

```
class Base
    {
public:
    virtual int Func(int i)
    {return i;}
    ...
    };

class Derived : public Base
public:
    virtual int Func(int i)
    {return 2*i + Base::Func(i);}
    };

class DerivedDerived : public Derived
public:
    virtual int Func(int i)
```

```
{return 3*i + Derived::Func(i) + Base::Func(i);}
};
```

Either `Derived`'s or `Base`'s `Func` can be accessed in the `DerivedDerived` function `Func`.

14.6 Advantages of Virtual Functions

Why are virtual functions important and in what way are they useful?

Let me remind you, for your convenience, of two points I stressed while discussing pointers to a base class object.

(1) A pointer to a base class object can receive the address of a *derived* class object.

(2) A pointer to a base class object, which has been assigned the address of a derived class object, can access those object members that are accessible and which are shared with the base class.

We have also seen that a pointer or a reference to a base class object, that has been assigned the address of a derived class object, calls the base class function, if the base and derived classes define a normal member function with the same identifier.

```
class Base
   {
public:
   void Func(void);
   };

   class Derived : public Base
{
public:
   void Func(void);
   };
.....
Derived objDerived;
Base *ptrBase;
ptrBase = &objDerived;
ptrBase->Func(); // calls Base's Func
```

A explicit cast is needed to access class `Derived`'s `Func` with the pointer `ptrBase`:

```
((Derived *)ptrBase)->Func(); // calls Derived's Func
```

If a function has been declared as *virtual* in a base class, a pointer to a base class object, which has been assigned the address of a *derived* class object, accesses the derived class function, rather than that of the base class.

Example:

```
class Base
    {
public:
    virtual void Func(void); // only virtual is changed
    };

class Derived : public Base
    {
public:
    virtual void Func(void);
    };
.....
Derived objDerived;
Base *ptrBase;
ptrBase = &objDerived;
ptrBase->Func(); // now calls Derived's Func
```

Essentially, what the compiler does is to produce an implicit, automatic cast, the purpose of which is something more than just making the process easier to manage, as we shall see.

We have also seen an important option, that is, a function which contains a reference to a Base object in its argument.

```
void FunSample(const Base &obj);
```

obj can access all the accessible class Base members, in particular Func() in the definition of FunSample.

```
void FunSample(const Base &obj)
    {
    ....
    obj.Func();
    };
```

What happens if FunSample is called by placing an object of Derived's in its actual argument?

```
Derived objDerived;
FunSample(objDerived);
```

If the function `Func()` has been declared as virtual, the `Func` of the derived class is called in `FunSample`.

FunSample can now act as an automatic `switch` *which chooses a function belonging to the derived class whose object it was passed.* This is a neat and fast method of implementation, and it solves the problem we faced.

> Use of an existing code can be extended without modification by using virtual functions.

Indeed, suppose you wanted to implement a new class with a `Func` that was different from those used before. All you have to do is derive the new class from the `Base` class. `FunSample`, *unmodified*, automatically calls the function, if an object of the new class is passed to it by its argument.

> You can also use this procedure by putting a *pointer* to a base class object in the function's formal argument, and an *address* of a *derived* class object in the actual argument, when the call to the function is made.

Using a pointer to a base class object instead of a reference to a `const` is to be preferred in two situations.

(1)   When the object is modified.

Example:

```
        // obj is NOT modified
void FunSample(const Base &obj)
    {
    ....
    obj.Func();
    }

    // *ptrBase can be modified
void FunDemo(Base *ptrBase)
    {
    ....
    ptrBase->Func();
    }
....
Derived objDerived;
FunSample(objDerived);
FunDemo(&objDerived);
```

(2)   When the pointer is an element in a vector of pointers.

Take three classes derived from `Base`: `DerivedOne`, `DerivedTwo`, `DerivedThree`:

```
void FunDemo(Base *ptrBase) // pointer to Base
    {
    ....
    ptrBase->Func();
    }
....
DerivedOne      objDerivedOne;
DerivedTwo      objDerivedTwo;
DerivedThree    objDerivedThree;

Base *base[3]; // vector of pointers to Base
base[0] = &objDerivedOne;
base[1] = &objDerivedTwo;
base[2] = &objDerivedThree;

for(int i=0;i < 3; i++)
    FunDemo(base[i]);
```

An element of the vector of pointers, `base[i]`, which was assigned the address of a derived class, is passed to `FunDemo`. The function `FunDemo` calls the appropriate `Func` for that class, if `Func` was declared *virtual* in `Base`.

> *Warning*: the procedure only works if the *address* of an object (a reference is an implicit address) is passed. It does *not* work if an object of the base class is placed in the argument.
> *A derived class object cannot be used instead of a base class object.*

Example:

```
void FunSample(Base obj)
    {
    ....
    obj.Func();
    };
....
Derived objDerived;
FunSample(objDerived);  // compile-time error
```

14.7 Example of How Virtual Functions are Used

Have a look at the following simple example. It may help to understand the advantages that can accrue from using virtual functions.

Take three classes: SolveOne, SolveTwo, SolveThree, derived from the class SolveBase. In it, a function, Solution, which is different in each class, is implemented.

Suppose you have the following main:

```
#include <iostream.h>
#include <stdlib.h>
#include <math.h>
main()
    {
    SolveOne    one;
    SolveTwo    two;
    SolveThree  three;

    // vector of pointers to SolveBase
    SolveBase *solveBase[3];

    // addresses of derived class objects
    solveBase[0] = &one;
    solveBase[1] = &two;
    solveBase[2] = &three;

    for(int i = 0;i<3;i++)
        {
        cout << "Solution Method";
        cout << Solve(solveBase[i]);
        }
    }
```

Three objects are created in main, one for each derived class. Their addresses are assigned to an array of pointers to base class objects with the identifier solveBase.

Solve, the function with FILE scope, is called, using one of the three pointers as its actual argument,

Let's see how the classes and the Solution functions are implemented, *without* using virtual functions.

One possible version (*which should be inserted before* main) is as follows:

```
enum SolutionMethod {ONE,TWO,THREE};

class SolveBase
    {
public:
    SolutionMethod method;
    int Solution(void)
```

```
   { cout << "Unusable"; return 0; }
   };

class SolveOne : public SolveBase
   {
public:
   SolveOne(void) // default constructor
      {method = ONE;}
   int Solution(void)
      {return 1;}
   };

class SolveTwo : public SolveBase
   {
public:
   SolveTwo(void) // default constructor
      {method = TWO;}
   int Solution(void)
      {return 2;}
   };

class SolveThree : public SolveBase
   {
public:
   SolveThree(void) // default constructor
      {method = THREE;}
   int Solution(void)
      {return 3;}
   };

// function with FILE scope
int Solve (SolveBase *ptrSolve)
   {
   switch(ptrSolve->method)
      {
      case ONE:
         return ((SolveOne *)ptrSolve)->Solution();
      case TWO:
         return ((SolveTwo *)ptrSolve)->Solution();
      case THREE:
         return ((SolveThree *)ptrSolve)->Solution();
      default:
         cout << "Unusable";
         exit(1);
      }
   }
```

Note the following points.

(1)   `method`, a variable, has to be introduced to characterize the various classes.

(2)   A constructor must initialize this variable for each class object.

(3)   The function with FILE scope, `Solve`, for selecting the appropriate member function of the classes `Solution`, must use a `switch`, based on the variable `method`.

(4)   An explicit `cast` is needed to access the class functions `Solution`:

```
((SolveOne *)ptrSolve)->Solution();
```

But, using *virtual functions*, the implementation, which once again is inserted before `main`, could look like this:

```
class SolveBase
    {
public:
    virtual int Solution(void) = 0; // pure virtual function
    };

class SolveOne : public SolveBase
    {
public:
    virtual int Solution(void)
        {return 1;}
    };

class SolveTwo : public SolveBase
    {
public:
    virtual int Solution(void)
        {return 2;}
    };

class SolveThree : public SolveBase
    {
public:
    virtual int Solution(void)
        {return 3;}
    };

// function with FILE scope
int Solve (SolveBase *ptrSolve)
    {
    return ptrSolve->Solution();
    }
```

Note the following points.

(1)   A special variable to identify class objects does not have to be introduced and so it does not have to be initialized by a constructor.

(2)   The function with FILE scope, `Solve`, does *not* have to choose the appropriate `Solution` class members with a `switch`.

(3)   An explicit `cast` is not needed to access `Solution` class member functions.

> Here, let's sum up the advantages gained by using virtual functions.
>
> (1)   Derived class objects do not have to be labelled with an identifier, `method`, for the choice of the appropriate function during run time to be made.
> (2)   The function `Solution` is much simpler and does *not* require a `switch` for a function to be chosen, or an explicit `cast` to coerce the pointer.

The advantages so far are important, but not essential.

> The following, however, are of *fundamental* importance.
>
> (1)   If a new class with different characteristics is to be introduced the code written previously does *not* have to be modified. You simply have to derive a new class from the class `SolveBase`.
> (2)   Even more important is the fact that a new class can be introduced *without the person who designed it possessing the source code of those classes that have already been defined.*

If you want to introduce a new class, `SolveFour`, all you have to do is compile the following code and assemble it with the code above.

```
class SolveFour : public SolveBase
    {
public:
    virtual int Solution(void)
       {return 4;}
    };
```

`main` is now as follows:

```
main()
    {
    SolveOne     one;
    SolveTwo     two;
```

```
SolveThree   three;
SolveFour    four;
SolveBase *solveBase[4];

solveBase[0] = &one;
solveBase[1] = &two;
solveBase[2] = &three;
solveBase[3] = &four;

for(int i = 0;i<4;i++)

   {
   cout << "Solution Method";
   cout << Solve(solveBase[i]);
   }
}
```

Functions – in this case the sole function `Solve` – that use virtual functions – in this case `Solution` – do *not* have to be modified and recompiled; and *nor* do previously defined classes – in this case `SolveBase`, `SolveOne`, `SolveTwo`, `SolveThree`.

 This simple example turns the spotlight on an entirely new meaning of the concept of reusing an existing code. In the case under consideration here, it is more appropriate to describe it as extending existing codes. We are dealing with something that is more significant than a simple derivation of one class from another, and it is enabled by the use of virtual functions.

 The disadvantage in using virtual functions is that you get an `.EXE` file which is slightly larger, but this is compensated for by the fact that the source code is generally more compact.

For instance, the `.EXE` files of the two codes above obtained with the compiler Turbo C++ are, respectively: 19072 and 21380 Kb, while their source codes are: 1285 and 821 Kb.

14.8 Early and Late Binding

Virtual functions demonstrate their power when they are used in the execution of *interactive* programs, that is, in programs where decisions that could not be foreseen at compile time have to be taken at run time.

It is important to make the distinction in object-oriented languages between *early* or *static binding* and *late* or *dynamic binding* of a function.

If an object is associated by the compiler to a function at compile time, this is called *early binding*. If, by contrast, the compiler cannot associate the object to a function at compile time, and the function to be associated with the object is chosen at run time, this is called *late binding*.

C++ offers both early and late binding.

Normal and class member functions are associated to objects at compile time. But virtual functions allow you to exploit late binding.

Consider the two implementations of the function with FILE scope `Solve` in the previous example.

The first implementation is valid when the `Solution` functions *are not virtual*:

```
int Solve (SolveBase *ptrSolve)
    {
    switch(ptrSolve->method)
        {
        case ONE:
            return ((SolveOne *)ptrSolve)->Solution();
        case TWO:
            return ((SolveTwo *)ptrSolve)->Solution();
        case THREE:
            return ((SolveThree *)ptrSolve)->Solution();
        default:
            cout << "Unusable";
            exit(1);
        }
    }
```

The second is valid when the `Solution` functions *are virtual*:

```
int Solve (SolveBase *ptrSolve)
    {
    return ptrSolve->Solution();
    }
```

In the first case, the compiler is able to associate the function `Solution` to the class that governs it at compile time: the explicit *cast* is needed for precisely this reason. In the second case, this is not possible. The user can choose the class to which the function refers at run time, for example, by selecting interactively.

Late binding is firmly linked to the concept of polymorphism: objects which are similar to, but nevertheless different from, each other are able to respond

cont.

> *cont.*
>
> to a common message *which may be sent at any moment and which cannot be foreseen during the program project.* Each object reacts in its own way to the message.

For some authors, polymorphism applies only when:

(1) An identical message is sent to different objects.

(2) The message is sent to an object which was not foreseen at compile time.

(3) The message is interpreted by the object which reacts according to its own characteristics.

> Polymorphism, in the strongest sense of the word, is linked to the concepts of encapsulation and data hiding. Different, but logically related, objects can be treated in exactly the same way, without the particular details which distinguish one object from another having to be dealt with. Objects thus remain *hidden to the user* and *encapsulated* in themselves.

In a procedural language, the code users have to know a great number of details about general-purpose functions which they have not implemented, in order to be able to use them coherently.

> In an object-oriented language, different objects can be dealt with in the same way, simply by a message being sent to an object which is then left to sort things out in the most appropriate way (*polymorphism*). The specific characteristics of that object do not need to be worried about. And they remain opaque to the user (*data-hiding*) and encapsulated in the object itself (*encapsulation*).

> There is another important aspect of the issue which should be underlined – since the definition of a class of which an object is a specimens and the hierarchical relations between various classes are *encapsulated in the object and opaque to the user*, they can be changed without the user code having to be changed, provided that the object's public interface is not modified.

This is an advantage when writing large codes in object-oriented programming.

Obviously attempts are made in procedural programming to reach this objective, but much more severe constraints apply. Users are always involved in data swapping between functions and their actions depend on the implementation being used. Modifying functions can involve users directly and so they are forced to modify their part of the program.

For example – the function `Solve` is among those that will be implemented to solve linear systems in the next chapter.

The interface with the user is as below:

```
Solve(A,b,&x);
```

where A is a matrix, either square or rectangular, it does not matter which, and b and x are two vectors or matrices. The user can quite happily ignore what is going on inside the function. If whoever implemented the classes involved in `Solve` subsequently decides to modify something, even the method of solving the system, the user would not need to be concerned. Users realize that the function has been modified only by a different efficiency and computation precision. Consider the function mentioned in Chapter 12.

```
CALL HFTI(A,MDA,M,N,B,MDB,NB,TAU,KRANK,RNORM,H,G,IP)
```

It is clear that there is a more wide-ranging and complex interaction between the user and the function, and changing the method of solution without having to change the user code is unthinkable.

14.9 Interactions between Virtual and Normal Functions

A virtual function should be considered to all intents and purposes as a non-`static`, class member function, apart from the one particular detail we have already encountered; the compiler *implicitly* applies a `cast` to the pointer or reference to a base object, which has been assigned the address of a derived class object.

A virtual function that can be accessed (see below) can be called by any function that is not a member of those classes for which it is virtual. It uses:

(1)   a base or derived class object;
(2)   a pointer or a reference to a base class object or to derived classes with an address of an object of their class;
(3)   a pointer or a reference to a base class object with the address of derived class objects. Here, the characteristics of virtual functions would come into play.

Example:

```
class Base; // forward declaration for FuDemo
void FuSample(void); // prototype
float FuDemo(const Base &obj); // prototype
```

```
class Base
    {
public:
    virtual float Func(void){return 2.;}
    };

class Derived : public Base
    {
public:
    virtual float Func(void){return 3.;}
    };

void FuSample(void)
    {
    Base objBase;
    Derived objDerived;
    Base *ptrBase = &objBase;
    Derived *ptrDerived = &objDerived;
    float y;

    y = objBase.Func();       // Base's Func; y = 2.
    y = objDerived.Func();    // Derived's Func; y =3.
    y = ptrBase->Func();      // Base's Func; y = 2.
    y = ptrDerived->Func();   // Derived's Func; y = 3.

    // these are the interesting cases
    ptrBase = &objDerived;
    y = ptrBase->Func();      // Derived's Func; y = 3.
    y = FuDemo(objBase);      // y = 2.
    y = FuDemo(objDerived);   // / y = 3.
    }

float FuDemo(const Base &obj)
    {
    return obj.Func();
    }
```

A virtual function can be called by a member function which is *not* virtual for those classes for which the first function is virtual.

Example:

```
class Base
    {
public:
    virtual float Func(void){return 2.;}
```

```
   float NonVirtualBase(void){return Func();}
   };

class Derived : public Base
   {
public:
   virtual float Func(void){return 3.;}
   float NonVirtualDerived(void){return Func();}
   };
```

A base class object that calls `NonVirtualBase` uses the base class's `Func`.

A base class object cannot by itself call `NonVirtualDerived`.

A derived class object that calls `NonVirtualBase` uses the derived class's `Func`.

A derived class object that calls `NonVirtualDerived` uses the derived class's `Func`.

A *pointer* to a base class object, which has been assigned the *address* of a *derived* class object, that calls `NonVirtualBase`, uses the derived class's `Func`.

The other possible combinations should be obvious.

> A virtual function can be called by a function which is also virtual and which is a member of the classes for which it is virtual. This situation is similar to the one above, apart from one particular detail. Since the calling function is now virtual, the object that called the first function selects which function is to be called. And there does not necessarily need to be a call to the other virtual function in all versions of the functions that are called first.

Example:
```
class Base
   {
public:
   virtual float Func(void){return 2.;}
   virtual float Virtual(void)
      {return Func();}// calls Func
   };

class Derived : public Base
   {
public:
   virtual float Func(void)
      {return 3.;}
   virtual float Virtual(void)
      {return 55.;} // does not call Func
   };
```

Base and derived class constructors *can* call a virtual function, without the compiler flagging an error, but the function does *not* behave like a virtual function. Calls to virtual functions by a constructor should therefore be avoided.

A virtual function can be declared as friend in a class that is not derived from the class in which the function is declared as virtual.
What was said about normal derived class functions applies equally to virtual functions – friend is not a property that functions in derived classes inherit from their base class. A function is friend only if it is declared as friend.

Example:

```
class Base
    {
public:
    virtual void Func(const Demo &objDemo);
    };

class Derived : public Base
    {
public:
    virtual void Func(const Demo &objDemo);
    };

class Demo
    {
private:
    iDemo;
public:
    Demo(void){iDemo = 0;} // default constructor
    // notice Base:: scope
    friend virtual void Base::Func
                      (const Demo &objDemo);
    // friend has to be declared
    // it is not automatically friend
    friend virtual void Derived::Func
                      (const Demo &objDemo);
    };

void Base::Func(const Demo &objDemo)
    {             // behaves like a normal friend
    objDemo.iDemo = 1; // it can access Demo's
                      // private data.
    }
```

```
void Derived::Func(const Demo &objDemo)
    {
    objDemo.iDemo = 2; // it can access Demo's
                       // private data
    }
.....
Base objBase;
Derived objDerived;
Demo objDemo;
Base *ptrBase;
ptrBase = &objBase;
ptrBase->Func(objDemo); // calls Base's Func
ptrBase = &objDerived;
ptrBase->Func(objDemo); // calls Derived's Func
```

14.10 Level of Protection for Virtual Functions

The level of protection afforded to a function called by a class object follows the usual rules.

> If a virtual function is called by a pointer or a reference, the protection level is linked *to the pointer or the reference of the object that invokes the function and not of the object whose address the pointer or the reference bears.*

Example:

```
class Base
    {
protected:
    virtual float ProtectedBasePublicDerived(void)
        {return 1.;}
public:
    virtual float PublicBaseProtectedDerived(void)
        {return 2.;}
    };

class Derived : public Base
    {
protected:
    virtual float PublicBaseProtectedDerived(void)
        {return 3.;}
```

```
public:
   virtual float ProtectedBasePublicDerived(void)
      {return 4.;}
   };

float Func(const Base &obj)
   {
   return obj.PublicBaseProtectedDerived();
   }
....
float x;
Base objBase,*ptrBase;
Derived objDerived,*ptrDerived;

x = objBase.ProtectedBasePublicDerived(); // NO
x = objBase.PublicBaseProtectedDerived(); // OK x = 2.

x = objDerived.ProtectedBasePublicDerived(); //OK x = 4.
x = objDerived.PublicBaseProtectedDerived(); //NO

ptrBase = &objBase;
x = ptrBase->PublicBaseProtectedDerived(); // OK; x = 2.

ptrDerived = &objDerived;
x = ptrDerived->PublicBaseProtectedDerived(); // NO

// these are important
ptrBase = &objDerived;
x = ptrBase->PublicBaseProtectedDerived(); // OK; x = 3.
x = ptrBase->ProtectedBasePublicDerived(); // NO

x = Func(objBase); // OK; x = 2.

// and this is important
x = Func(objDerived); // OK; x = 3.
```

In the statements:

```
ptrBase = &objDerived;
x = ptrBase->PublicBaseProtectedDerived(); // OK; x = 3.
x = ptrBase->ProtectedBasePublicDerived(); // NO
```

the pointer ptrBase has the address of an object of class Derived and calls
Derived's function, but the protection level is linked to the fact that ptrBase is
defined as a pointer to objects of the class Base.

Similarly:

```
x = Func(objDerived); // OK; x = 3.
```

Even if a reference to one of `Derived`'s objects is passed and `Derived`'s virtual function is called, the protection level is linked to the `Base` object that appears in the function `Func`'s formal argument.

14.11 Pure Virtual Functions and Abstract Classes

In constructing a class hierarchy, you can go from one extreme, where derived classes differ by minute details from the base class, which is thus able to implement the greater part of common functions, to the other extreme, where the base class is unable to implement any functions and is used only as a common foundation for derived classes.

Remember that a class that declares a virtual function must decide whether to:

(1)   Declare the function as a pure virtual function, by setting it equal to zero.
(2)   Supply a definition of the function.

In the first case, derived classes must, in turn, decide whether to declare the function as a pure virtual function or to supply a definition of the function.
In the second case, the function is used as default for all the subsequent classes that do not declare their own version of the function.
The syntax for declaring a pure virtual function looks like this:

virtual <return type> <identifier> (argument) = 0;

Example:

```
class Base
    {
public:
    virtual float Func1(int i) = 0; // pure virtual
    virtual int Func2(void)
        {Message("Func2 not implemented");}
    };
```

```
class Derived : public Base
   {
   public:
   virtual float Func1(int i);
   virtual int Func2(void);
   };

// Derived's definition of Func1
float Derived::Func1(int i)
   {
   statements;
   }

// Derived's definition of Func2
int Derived::Func2(void)
   {
   statements;
   }
```

Notice that the function Func1 has been defined as a pure virtual function in Base class; thus in the derived class Derived, a choice has to be made between re-defining it as a pure virtual function or supplying a definition of the function.

Func2 was also declared in Derived, but it must be redefined.

Definition: *Abstract class*
A class is called abstract, if a *function* is defined as *virtual and pure* in the class. Objects which belong to an abstract class cannot be defined.

Example:

```
class Base  // Base is an abstract class
   {
public:
   virtual float Func1(int i) = 0; // pure virtual
   };
...
//error: a Base object cannot be defined
Base objBase;
```

Notice that objects belonging to an abstract class cannot be defined, but *pointers* or *references* to objects of an abstract class *can* be defined (abstract classes are defined for this precise purpose). Naturally, only addresses of objects of derived classes can be assigned to these pointers or references.

Example:

```
class Base  // Base is an abstract class
   {
public:
   virtual float Func1(int i) = 0; // pure virtual
   };

class Derived : public Base
   {
   ...
   };
...
void FunSample(const Base &objBase); // OK
....
Base *ptrBase; // OK
Derived objDerived;
ptrBase = &objDerived; // OK
FunSample(objDerived); // OK
```

You have three options from which to choose, if you do not know how to implement a virtual function, particularly in a base class:

(1)   To declare it as *pure and virtual*. Objects of that class will consequently not be able to be defined.
(2)   To define it with an *error* function, which interrupts calculations.
(3)   To define it with a *message* that allows calculations to continue.

Example:

```
class Base  // Base is an abstract class
   {
public:
   virtual float Func1(int i) = 0; // pure virtual
   virtual void Func2(void)
      {Error("\nFunc2 not implemented");}
   virtual void Func3(float x)
      {Message("\nFunc3 not implemented");}
   };
```

14.12 Constructors and Destructors in Derived Classes

Base class constructors are very similar to those of classes which have not generated any derived classes.

A technique similar to the one employed to initialize objects of other classes, which have been defined inside a class, needs to be used for derived class constructors – in other words, the initialization list has to be used (see Chapter 10).

A derived class constructor initialization list has the following syntax:

(1)   The list should be placed in the constructor's *definition, not in its declaration.*

(2)   The list should be positioned between the round closing bracket of the constructor's argument and the opening curly bracket of the constructor's body.

(3)   The list is preceded by **:** (colon).

(4)   One of the constructors of the class from which the class is derived is placed on the list.

(5)   The comma operator is used, if there are several items to be initialized.

(6)   If the base class has a default constructor, it does not need to be placed explicitly in the initialization list, as the compiler does this.

Example:

```
class Base
    {
private:
    int privateBase;
public:
    Base(void){privateBase = 0;} // default
    Base(int i){privateBase = i;} // Base's constructor
    ....
    };

class Derived : public Base
    {
private:
    float x;
public:
    Derived(void) : Base() {}
    // or, also, Derived(void){}
```

```
    Derived(int i) : Base(i){}
    ....
    };
```

Notice that the bodies of the two derived class constructors do not have statements, {}. This practice is fairly widespread and is used when the base class constructor completes the task of initializing the object.

Often the definition of derived class constructors is coerced, so that their bodies are empty.

Example:

```
class Base
    {
private:
    int privateBase;
public:
    Base(int i){privateBase = i;} // Base's constructor
    ....
    };

class Derived : public Base
    {
private:
    float xDer;
public:
    Derived(int i,float x) : Base(i), xDer(x){}
    ....
    };
```

Notice that a dummy copy-initializer constructor (see Chapter 10) is used to initialize xDer.

> *Warning*: constructors are *not* inherited by derived classes; in this respect, they do not behave like normal class member functions. So every derived class *must* redefine its own constructors. Notice, as well, the benefits of being able to call the appropriate base class constructor in the initialization list.

Example:

```
class Base
    {
private:
    ....
public:
    Base(void); // default
```

```
Base(const Base &obj); // copy-initializer
Base(int i); // other constructor
....
};

class Derived : public Base
    {
public:
    void Func(void);
    };
.....
Derived objDerived(5); // error: does NOT have a constructor
```

 C++ permits one or two shortcuts in initialization lists. But I strongly urge you to avoid them by *always writing the explicit form of the constructor of the base class that you want to use at that point.*

You have to remember that the base class constructor's task in the initialization list is that of initializing that common part of the object that is considered important for that particular derived class constructor.

Example:

```
class Base
    {
private:
    int iB;
public:
    Base(void){iB = 0;} // default
    Base(int i){iB = i;} // other constructor
    ....
    };

class Derived : public Base
    {
private:
    float xD;
public:
    Derived(void) : Base(), xD(0){}
    Derived(int i) : Base(i),xD(0){}
    Derived(int i,float x) : Base(i),xD(x){}
    ....
    };
```

One example of a short cut – and it is particularly irritating for anyone reading the program – is that you can omit the class identifier with which the constructor in the initialization list is labelled (by writing only the actual argument of the base constructor):

```
class Base
    {
private:
    ib;
public:
    Base(int i); // constructor
    ....
    };

class Derived : public Base
    {
public:
    Derived(int i) : (i){} // better : Base(i)
    ....
    };
```

> Note that the order in which constructors are called is: first, the base constructor, followed by the successive hierarchies (if there is more than one of them). But the order for destructors is the opposite; first the destructor of the last derived class, and so on, up to the base class constructor.
>
> These rules are logical, as the base class supports the derived classes. To initialize an object the absolutely essential parts must first be supplied, then the detailed parts – and vice versa for de-initializing.

Four types of constructor can be distinguished, as is the case with all classes: the default constructor, the copy-initializer constructor, constructors for converting objects and general-purpose constructors.

The default constructor (for initializing vectors) and the copy-initializer constructor (for function `returns` and for initializing objects) are of fundamental importance to base and derived classes.

> I recommend always defining both the default and copy-initializer constructor for every base and derived class to avoid difficulties possible with the constructors automatically defined by the compiler.

> And I recommend trying to group together in one common function – not a constructor – for each class the part needed to initialize that part of the class which governs the formation of objects, so that it can be made available for all overloaded constructors and for the assignment operator. The same procedure is adopted for de-initializing.

This technique will be demonstrated in Chapter 15.

Constructors and Virtual Functions

> Constructors *cannot* be declared virtual. Remember that they are not inherited, and therefore it would be senseless to make them virtual.

Example:
```
class Demo
    {
private:
    int iDemo;
public:
    virtual Demo(void){iDemo = 0;} // error
    };
```

> One error that tends to creep in, undetected by the compiler, is when a virtual function is used inside a constructor. When a base class constructor calls a function, the version of the function defined in the base class is always called.

Example:

```
class Base
    {
private:
    int iDemo;
public:
    virtual void Func(void){iDemo = 0;}
    Base(void){Func();}
    };

class Derived : public Base
    {
public:
    Derived(void){Func();}
    virtual void Func{iDemo = 1;}
    };
...
// Base's Func is called with the constructor
Base *ptrBase = new Derived;
```

> You must avoid using a virtual function in a constructor, because this would only create confusion.

Virtual Destructors

> The destructor can be, and thankfully is, declared as virtual. It cannot however, be declared as *virtual and pure*.

Suppose there are some constructors that initialize some members in the base class `SolveBase` and in the classes derived from it, `SolveOne`, `SolveTwo`, `SolveThree`. If the following technique is used for de-initializing objects:

```
main()
    {
    SolveOne    one;
    SolveTwo    two;
    SolveThree  three;

    // notice use of new
    // so that delete can be used
    SolveBase *solveBase = new SolveBase [3];
    solveBase[0] = &one;
    solveBase[1] = &two;
    solveBase[2] = &three;
    .....
    delete [3] solveBase;
```

the class destructor must be declared `virtual`. If not, the class `SolveBase`'s destructor is called, rather than `solveBase[i]`'s, because `solveBase` has been defined as a pointer to that class. The alternative would be to carry out a `switch` and use explicit casts, but you would lose the advantage of polymorphism.

> Note this interesting fact: derived class destructors have a different name from base class destructors. Despite this, if the base class destructor is declared as `virtual`, derived class destructors are automatically virtual.

Example:

```
class Demo
    {
public:
    virtual ~Demo(void); // virtual destructor
    ...
    };
```

One error that tends to creep in is using a *virtual function* inside a base class destructor, thinking that it remains as such. The version of the function *which is defined in the base class* is always called, even if the base class destructor itself is virtual, when a virtual function is called by the base class destructor.

 Using a virtual function in the destructor should be avoided because it only leads to confusion.

14.13 Questions

 Are two functions that are members of two separate classes with the same identifier overloaded?

A class member function has the scope of its own class, so two functions which are members of two separate classes always have a different scope and cannot be overloaded.

 To what does a derived class object, defined in a base class `friend` function, have access?
(1)   Base class `public` members.
(2)   Base class `protected` members.
(3)   Base class `private` members.
(4)   `public` members of its own class.
(5)   `protected` members of its own class.
(6)   `private` members of its own class.

It can access the first four members.

 Can a derived class object access base class `protected` members?

No, if the function in which the object is defined is not a `friend` of the base class. `Derived` class member functions can access them.

 Which of the following statements is wrong?

```
Base objBase,*ptrBase;
Derived objDerived,*ptrDerived;
ptrBase = &objBase;
```

cont.

cont.
```
  ptrDerived = &objBase;
  ptrBase = &objDerived;
  ptrDerived = &objDerived;
```

A derived class pointer cannot be assigned the address of a base class object, so the statement below is wrong.

```
ptrDerived = &objBase;
```

Given the definition:

```
ptrBase = &objDerived;
```

in a non-friend function of a class, say which members of objDerived can be accessed with ptrBase.

Public members defined in the base class; public members of the class derived only by an explicit cast; derived class virtual functions that are public *for the base class* without an explicit cast.

What happens if a function defined as virtual in the base class has a different argument in a derived class?

The function is *not* treated as if it were virtual for that class.

If Solution is a virtual function of SolveBase and Solve is a function with FILE scope defined with:

```
void Solve(SolveBase objBase)
    {
    objBase.Solution();
    }
```

what happens if Solve is called with a class object derived from SolveBase?

There is a compile-time error.

Why did I advise against using virtual functions in constructors and destructors?

Because they are not recognized as virtual and would sow confusion.

15 Program Design for Linear Algebra

Memento audere semper.

Be daring.

Gabriele D'Annunzio.

15.1 Introduction

The subjects treated in this chapter are of fundamental importance to numerical calculation. Since the purpose of this book is not to explain numerical analysis, as I have emphasized on several occasions, I shall not dwell on the details of implemented algorithms.

I am much more concerned here to bring out the advantages of, and the opportunities provided by, constructing derived classes that use virtual functions and that enable polymorphism in the full sense of the word to be exploited.

I must, however, make a brief digression into the field of numerical analysis to explain the purpose of these classes.

It is very instructive to look at how methods of solving linear systems have developed, because it illustrates very clearly the difference between methods conceived for manual calculation, which use an extremely limited number of calculations, and methods of using modern computers. And it illustrates the more subtle, but more important difference between the concepts of *classical analysis* and those of *numerical analysis*, in which round-off errors play a fundamentally important role.

Some methods of solving linear systems have become obsolete, particularly the following.

(1) Cramer's rule, because of the length of calculation time it requires and its lack of precision.
(2) The use of inverse matrices:

$$x = A^{-1}b$$

for the same reasons.

Inverse matrices have also been banished from many formulae, because it is possible and advantageous to solve problems in which inverse matrices appear without physically inverting the matrices.

For example, it may be necessary in statistical analysis of a regression to calculate the variance of a forecast of a model, corresponding to a given point, using the equation:

$$V(y) = f^T(F^TF)^{-1}f\,\sigma^2$$

The formula seems to suggest that the matrix F^TF should be inverted. But $V(y)$ could equally be calculated without inverting the matrix, as will be demonstrated below.

Even Gauss-Jordan elimination has greatly declined in importance, but I have not included it in the category of obsolete methods for two reasons.

(1) It is still effective in one particular situation – when you want to invert a matrix (as stated above, this is only done if inverting the matrix itself is important) by overloading the inverse matrix on the original matrix. One or more linear systems can be solved during inversion using this method. All other methods of inverting matrices require *two* separate matrices, so storage space can be saved by using this method, known as Gauss-Jordan elimination.

(2) Because old hands at programming are particularly fond of the method. Personally, I was very proud of one of my programs (written in FORTRAN of course) in which a system was solved and the matrix inverted simultaneously and on the spot.

Gauss-Jordan elimination has two major disadvantages.

(1) It requires a threefold increase of computation time when you want to solve a linear system but are not interested in inverting a matrix.

(2) It can solve one or more systems in which right-hand side terms are known at the point of inversion of the matrix. But if you *subsequently* want to solve a new system an inverse matrix has to be used, entailing a serious loss of accuracy.

At one time, the calculation of the determinant of a matrix of coefficients was used, in order to judge the condition of a linear system. That judgement was based on Cramer's celebrated rule: if the determinant of a matrix of coefficients, in a linear system of N equations in N unknowns, is different from zero, there is a unique solution.

In solving a linear system numerically, you may think it sensible to ask whether the determinant you have found is sufficiently different from zero. If the determinant is large you have a good solution, because you have a system which is well-conditioned. If the determinant is on the limits of numerical zero, you have a poor solution because the system is ill-conditioned, there are an infinity of numerical equivalents or, worse, none at all exist.

But this is very dangerous.

Numerical analysis has shown that the condition of a system *cannot* be judged on the basis of the determinant's value, when this value is not exactly equal to zero. Systems with very large determinants can be ill-conditioned, and systems with very small determinants can be well-conditioned.

A change of approach is needed to gauge the condition of a linear system. Your viewpoint has to shift from classical to numerical analysis, that is, you must be aware of the fact that calculations are subject to numerical error and that *there is no sense in holding that a property, which is deduced with the procedures of classical analysis and which is valid when an exact value of a quantity holds, is almost valid, when the numeric value of the same quantity approximates its theoretical value.*

A new concept is now used instead of the determinant – the condition of a system, which is quantifiable with the *condition number*. Here, all we need to know is that a condition number indicates the degree to which errors are propagated in relation to the solution.

For example, if the seventh significant figure of the right-hand side is an error and the condition number is 1000, an error in the coefficients of the solution on the fourth significant figure is to be expected – three significant figures are lost. The larger the condition number, the less precise the solution. The nearer the condition number is to 1 (theoretical minimum), the more stable the system.

> Here, the different way of viewing Gauss elimination is the most important shift in perspective that needs to be underlined.

Gauss elimination consists in effecting linear combinations of the rows of a matrix, so as to eliminate those elements below the main diagonal. The resulting matrix is a right-triangular matrix **R**.

> If some coefficients that intervene in Gauss elimination are stored in a left-triangular matrix **L** it will be discovered that the product of the matrices **L** and **R**, **LR**, is equal to the initial matrix of the system **A** (the problem of the exchange of rows is ignored here for the sake of simplicity).

Why is this result important?

> Because it entails a new perspective on how the problem of solving linear equation systems is tackled.

Above all, it means that the matrices **L** and **R** have to be seen in a new light. In Gauss elimination, the matrix **L** does not have any particular significance during elimination. Certain coefficients are obtained that are useful for calculating the matrix **R**, with which a simplified linear system can be solved. The coefficients in themselves are not of any interest.

> In the new way of looking at the problem, **L** and **R** are two particular matrices which enjoy a special property – their product is equal to the original matrix, **A**.
> The new perspective transforms Gauss elimination into a way of *factorizing* the matrix, rather than a solution to a system.

> Three important consequences flow from this.
>
> (1) Problems can be solved in succession.
> (2) The matrices **L** and **R** can be directly deduced using special techniques.
> (3) You may wonder whether there are other ways of factorizing the matrix **A** that could be used to solve linear systems.

Suppose we have to solve in succession a number of problems with the same matrix **A**, and various values for the coefficients $b = b_1$, b_2 and so on.

Using the old approach to the problem, **L** was considered a sequence of coefficients used during the process of solving the problem, rather than a *matrix*. The procedure had to be repeated to solve a system with a different right-hand side vector. Even today, if you wanted to solve by hand a system with small dimensions, this is the way that Gauss elimination works and it was conceived for this purpose.

If, instead, Gauss elimination is thought of as a method of factorizing the matrix **A** in the two matrices **L** and **R**, the following procedure can be used:

$$\mathbf{Ax = LRx = L(Rx) = Lc = b}$$
$$\mathbf{Rx = c}$$

If the matrices **L** and **R** are known, the solution to the system is:

$$\mathbf{Lc = b}$$

obtaining vector **c**.

Since the matrix **L** is triangular, the solution is immediate. The vector **x** is deduced according to the following system:

$$\mathbf{Rx = c}$$

in which the matrix **R** is triangular.

The operations as a whole are identical in the two approaches when a single system has to be solved. But, using the first approach, the operations must be repeated for every new value of **b**, as the property of the matrices **L** and **R** are not exploited. Here, calculation times come into the picture.

It can be demonstrated that as the dimensions of systems increase, so the weight of the determination of coefficients of the matrices in relation to the subsequent solution of the two triangular systems becomes preponderant. If the two matrices are stored and not calculated again and again, calculation times are shorter.

The matrices **L** and **R** can also be directly deduced from the coefficients of the matrix **A**, in that each coefficient of the two matrices can be expressed explicitly with the coefficients a_{ij}.

And so there are two new methods for calculating the coefficients of the two matrices; they bear the names of their originators, Crout and Doolittle. In particular, Crout factorization has an advantage over the others: the coefficients of the two matrices can be calculated by carrying out operations (the sums of products) in double precision. In some situations the resulting algorithm is more precise (particularly if you are working in FORTRAN, where the default is simple precision).

Are there any options to factorizing **LR**?

> The basic characteristic of factorizing **LR** consists of the fact that the two new systems:
>
> *cont.*

> *cont.*
> **Lc = b**
> **Rx = c**
>
> are easy to solve and require short calculation times in comparison with solving the original system.
> Two new methods of factorizing, known as **QR** (or **LQ**) and *Singular Value Decomposition* respectively, are very important.
> The former is mainly used in solving systems with rectangular matrices.
> The second is an extremely versatile and powerful tool, which is used in a great number of situations, but which is too complicated to be dealt with here.

I shall only look at factorizing **QR** and **LQ** as an alternative to Gauss eliminations. **Q** is an orthogonal matrix, that is, a matrix with the following property:

$$Q^T Q = I$$

If a factorization of this type is known, the system can be solved as follows:

$$Ax = QRx = b$$
$$Q^T QRx = Q^T b$$
$$Rx = Q^T b$$

The procedure is similar for factorizing **LQ**.
There is a variant in both factorizations:

$$PA = R$$
$$AP = L$$

The matrices **P** are also orthogonal. Depending on the circumstances, it is preferable for the matrix **Q** or **P** to be known.

Factorizing **QR** is very important because, if the system is over-determined, the solution obtained using this method minimizes the sum of the squares of the residuals. Linear regression is one application of this that is of great practical importance.

The central problem of linear regression (and consequently also of non-linear regression, linked to the former by the Gauss-Newton method) consists in finding the parameters, **b**, of a model:

$$y_i = b_1 f_1(x_i) + b_2 f_2(x_i) + \ldots + b_p f_p(x_i)$$

in which the values of the dependent variable, y_i, are known, in correspondence with the experimental points x_i. The following system is obtained:

$$Fb = y$$

The system is over-determined (there are more equations than unknowns), as the number of experimental observations must be higher than the number of the model's parameters. Furthermore, because of the experimental errors in the dependent variable **y**, the equations are not compatible – a compromise value for the parameters **b** has to be chosen.

A sensible choice, proposed by Gauss, is to seek the parameters, **b**, which minimize the sum of the squares of the residuals.

$$(\mathbf{Fb} - \mathbf{y})^{\mathrm{T}}(\mathbf{Fb} - \mathbf{y})$$

It is easy to demonstrate the conditions under which the minimum leads to the solution of the system:

$$\mathbf{F}^{\mathrm{T}}\mathbf{Fb} = \mathbf{F}^{\mathrm{T}}\mathbf{y}$$

which is called a *normal system*. The system can be solved efficiently using a special method (Cholesky decomposition) that exploits the matrix $\mathbf{F}^{\mathrm{T}}\mathbf{F}$'s property of being symmetrical and positive definite. It looked as if the problem had been solved optimally, until the condition number of the system was considered.

In fact, by moving from the original system:

$$\mathbf{Fb} = \mathbf{y}$$

to the normal system, there was a deterioration in the system's condition number for the following two reasons:

(1)   The condition number of the matrix $\mathbf{F}^{\mathrm{T}}\mathbf{F}$ is the square of the condition number of the initial matrix **F**. If the residuals are small, this brings about a serious decline in the accuracy of the calculations.

(2)   Round-off errors in the calculations may lead to a normal system that has lost vital information present in **F**: that is, the matrix $\mathbf{F}^{\mathrm{T}}\mathbf{F}$ becomes ill-conditioned.

> The way the problem was tackled was reversed by factorizing **QR**. Using the old approach, the least value of the sum of the residuals was sought – the solution to *this* problem leads to the solution of the normal system.
> Using the new approach, a solution to the over-determined system is sought:
>
> $$\mathbf{Fb} = \mathbf{y}$$
>
> The solution to *this* problem leads to factorizing **QR**, which has the property of minimizing the sum of the squares of the residuals.

Thus, instead of solving the normal system to deduce the parameters that minimize the sum of the squares of the residuals, a direct solution to the system is currently preferred:

Fb = y

by factorizing **QR**.

Factorizing **QR** means that other problems linked to linear systems can be solved. If we return to the formula for calculating the variance of y:

$$V(y) = f^T(F^TF)^{-1}f \, \sigma^2$$

it can be seen that the value of $V(y)$ can be obtained without inverting the matrix, F^TF, if the matrix **F** has been factorized as:

F = QR

Then:

$$(F^TF)^{-1} = (R^TQ^TQR)^{-1} = (R^TR)^{-1} = R^{-1}R^{-T}$$

from which:

$$V(y) = f^T(F^TF)^{-1}f \, \sigma^2 = (R^{-T}f)^T(R^{-T}f)\sigma^2$$

If we know the matrix **R** we can solve the system:

R^T x = f

and thus $V(y)$ is deduced:

$$V(y) = x^Tx\sigma^2$$

As can be seen, the inversion of the matrix is avoided and the calculation is very efficient, since the system to be solved is elementary, with **R** being a triangular matrix.

In contrast, factorizing **LQ** is used in cases where the number of equations is less than the number of unknowns. In this case, by using this method, the minimum Euclidean norm for the vector **x** can be found among an infinity of solutions.

Now that this very quick and, unfortunately, limited digression into numerical analysis is over, let's see how systems can be solved by implementing classes.

The matrix factorizations below were considered.
(1)   Gauss.
(2)   Crout.
(3)   **A = QR.**
(4)   **PA = R.**
(5)   **A = LQ.**
(6)   **AP = L.**

15.2 **Implemented Classes**

The full listings of the classes described in this chapter can be found on the enclosed diskette. The header files are: FACTORED.HPP, FACTPLR.HPP, FACTQRLQ.HPP, and the files to be compiled: FACTORED.CPP, FACTPLR.CPP, FACTQRLQ.CPP.

Classes that are used to solve linear equation systems have many parts that can be commonly shared, and it is a good idea to create a base class from which others can be derived. The purpose of the base class is also to provide a framework for derived classes, so that they all have an identical interface.

The base class, Factored, is abstract; objects of it cannot be defined.

The derived classes under consideration can be divided into two strands: Gaussian derived classes, in which **LR** factorization is used (or put better, **PLR** in order to take account of the interchange of rows), and derived classes of the **QR** and **LQ** family.

The two classes derived from Factored, which are the founding family members of the two strands of classes, are called FactoredPLR and FactoredQRLQ. These two classes are also abstract. The two classes, FactoredGauss and FactoredCrout are derived from the first of these two classes, FactoredPLR.

The classes FactoredQR and FactoredLQ are derived from the second, FactoredQRLQ.

Objects can be defined with the four classes FactoredGauss, FactoredCrout, FactoredQR and FactoredLQ.

The matrices defined as objects of these classes differ from those which are definable as objects of the class Matrix in the following respects.

(1)   They can be factorized with their own class's method.

(2)   They can only be manipulated in certain ways.

(3)   Possible interactions with the factorization can be controlled internally.

A priori, Matrix could be used as the base of all these classes. But this was not done, in order to prevent the calculations of Matrix from being weighed down with all the controls used in this case. A special function, CommuteMatrixToFactored, was introduced so that type Matrix objects could be transformed into objects of classes with which factorization can be carried out. In this way it is possible to perform the required operation using the object of the class Matrix and then to transform it into an object of a factored class.

It is used as follows:

```
Matrix A;
FactoredGauss B;
. . . . .
CommuteMatrixToFactored(&A,&B);
```

As a result of this transformation, the matrix A is copied to B and destroyed (note the use of the pointer to matrix A – this means that the object is being manipulated, as stressed on several occasions). In reality, the coefficients are not physically copied, and there is a simple interchange of pointers. Matrix A becomes unusable for this reason. If you want to save matrix A, you can use an initialization or an assignment.

```
FactoredGauss B = A; // initialized

// or
FactoredGauss B;
B = A;  // assigned
```

Using one of these options, the matrix that is to be used to solve a system can use all the operations available for Matrix objects that are more efficient.

15.3 The Base Class Factored

The base class is called Factored and it is an *abstract class*. Essentially, it is a similar class to Matrix. Controls are placed in Factored on all possible operations, and interface prototypes for numerical methods of linear algebra are added to it.

Control over Acceptable Operations

Two variables of type enum are used to control the environment of the object matrix:

```
enum factorizationStatus
    {
    UNFACTORED,
    FACTORED
    }factorizationStatus;
enum matrixStatus
    {
    AVAILABLE,
    DESTROYED,
    MODIFIED
    }matrixStatus;
```

The first variable, factorizationStatus, initialized with UNFACTORED, is set equal to FACTORED, if the matrix has been factorized.

The second variable, matrixStatus, is initialized with AVAILABLE and is set equal to DESTROYED, if the matrix is filled with coefficients of the factorization. The matrix can then be made inaccessible and can no longer be modified.

Sometimes you want to save the original matrix, so an additional pointer to a floating point was defined to this end.

```
float **matrix;
float **factored;
```

The variable `matrixStatus` is set equal to `MODIFIED`, if the matrix has been factorized and stored independently of the original matrix, and if functions which modify its coefficients are used. If the matrix needs to be factorized subsequently, it is automatically refactorized.

Initialization and De-Initialization

The class `Factored` is dedicated to initializing the common part of all the derived classes. A function (*not a constructor*, see Chapter 10) that carries out this task was implemented, as many constructors share a common part.

```
// ******************< Initialize >*********************
// *   Purpose: Shared function for initializing          *
// *******************************************************
void Factored::Initialize(int rows,int columns)
    {
    count++;
    whoAmI = count;
    singular = 0;
    norm = 0.;
    factorizationStatus = UNFACTORED;
    matrixStatus = AVAILABLE;
    factored = 0;
    if(rows < 1 || columns < 1)
        {
        numRows = numColumns = size = 0;
        matrix = 0;
        return;
        }
    numRows = rows;
    numColumns = columns;
    size = numRows * numColumns + 1;
    matrix = new float *[numRows + 1];
    if(!matrix)
        Error("%s%s%sInitialize",
        Factored::ERROR,ERR_SPACE,ERR_FUNCTION);
    matrix[0]=new float[size];
    if(!matrix[0])
        Error("%s%s%sInitialize",
        Factored::ERROR,ERR_SPACE,ERR_FUNCTION);
```

```
    matrix[1] = matrix[0];
    for(int i = 2;i <= numRows;i++)
        matrix[i] = matrix[i-1]+numColumns;
    }
```

If a function requires the matrix to be factorized using a matrix which is independent of the initial matrix, storage has to be created for the second matrix, factored:

```
// **************< FactoredInitialize >****************
// *  Purpose:Initializing factored                  *
// ****************************************************
void Factored::FactoredInitialize(void)
    {
    factored = new float *[numRows + 1];
    if(!factored)
        Error("%s%s%sFactoredInizialization",
        Factored::ERROR,ERR_SPACE,ERR_FUNCTION);
    factored[0]=new float[size];
    if(!factored[0])
        Error("%s%s%sFactoredInizialization",
        Factored::ERROR,ERR_SPACE,ERR_FUNCTION);
    factored[1] = factored[0];
    for(int i = 2;i <= numRows;i++)
        factored[i] = factored[i-1] + numColumns;
    memcpy(factored[0],matrix[0],size*sizeof(float));
    }
```

It is also a good idea to use a common function to de-initializing either matrix or factored:

```
// ******************< Deinitialize >******************
// *  Purpose: Common function for de-initializing    *
// ****************************************************
void Factored::Deinitialize(void)
    {
    FactoredDeinitialize();
    if(matrix != 0)
        {
        delete matrix[0];
        delete matrix;
        }
    }
```

```
// **************< FactoredDeinitialize >**************
// *   Purpose: Common function for de-initializing    *
// *                 factored                          *
// ****************************************************
void Factored::FactoredDeinitialize(void)
   {
   if(factored != 0)
      {
      delete factored[0];
      delete factored;
      }
   factored = 0;
   }
```

The constructors envisaged are similar to those analysed for the class Matrix, but with two exceptions: file constructors were not implemented and a copy-initializer constructor is constructed so that it flags an error if it is used.

Example:

```
FactoredGauss A; // default constructor
```

Example:

```
FactoredCrout A(2,2);
A(1,1) = 1.; A(1,2) = 2.; A(2,1) =3.; A(2,2) = 4.;
```

Example:

```
FactoredQR A(2,3,;
              1.,2.,3.,
              4.,5.,6.);
```

Example:

```
Matrix B(2,5,
         1.,2.,3.,60.,30.,
         4.,5.,6.,10.,50.);
MatrixGauss A(2,2,1,4,B);
```

In this last example, matrix A is initialized with a sub-matrix of B. The coefficient of matrix A are:

```
60.,30.,
10.,50.
```

Remember that the function `CommuteMatrixToFactored`, which transforms a normal `Matrix` into one which can access methods of linear algebra without causing the two matrices to co-exist, is an important alternative to a matrix constructor.

Access to Coefficients

If the variable `matrixStatus` in the object `matrix` has the value `AVAILABLE`, a number of operations can be carried out – in particular matrix coefficients, rows or columns can be modified or used.

Example of access to coefficients:

```
FactoredGauss A(5,5);
A(1,1)= 1.;
float x = A(1,1);
A.SetValue(2,3,55.);
x = A.GetValue(2,3);
```

The operator `[ ]` was not overloaded.
By not overloading it, I wanted to emphasize that access to the coefficients of a matrix of these classes has to be controlled.

The functions `SetRow`, `GetRow`, `SetColumn`, `GetColumn` are used to access rows and columns.

```
FactoredCrout A(3,3);
Vector v(3,1.,2.,3.);
A.SetRow(2,v);
A.SetColumn(3,v);
Vector w;
w = A.GetRow(2);
w = A.GetColumn(3);
```

As the classes `FactoredGauss`, `FactoredCrout`, `FactoredQR`, `FactoredLQ` are derived from `Factored`, they must not create their own dedicated functions for accessing data, because they exploit the function implemented in `Factored`.

If a matrix, even if it is `AVAILABLE`, has already been factorized and is used in one of the above functions that modify it, the variable `matrixStatus` is set equal to `MODIFIED`.

The user is not responsible for the correct sequential use of library functions. The object hides all operations from the user and automatically permits or prohibits access and is modified when necessary.

For example, have a look at the following sequence:

```
FactoredQR A(4,2,
                1.,2.,
                3.,4.,
                5.,6.,
                7.,8.);
Matrix Q;
A.GetMatrixQ(&Q); // calculate Q of A = QR
A(1,1) = 10.; // change A
Vector b(4,3.,2.,5.,6.);
Vector x;
Solve(A,b,&x); // must refactorize A
```

The matrix **Q** of the factorization **QR** is obtained with the function GetMatrixQ, as we shall see. Obviously, the matrix A has to be factorized to obtain this. A is then modified, so the previous factorization is incorrect for the new matrix. When the function Solve is used, the object A realizes it has been modified and performs another factorization.

By contrast, consider the following sequence:

```
FactoredQR A(4,2,
                1.,2.,
                3.,4.,
                5.,6.,
                7.,8.);
Matrix Q;
A.GetMatrixQ(&Q); // calculate Q di A = QR
Vector b(4,3.,2.,55.,6.);
Vector x;
Solve(A,b,&x); // does not have to refactorize A
```

In this example, the object A realizes it has not been modified and uses the previous factorization, when Solve is used.

Functions for Linear Algebra

A few functions relating to linear algebra problems were implemented in the class Factored that are common to all possible factorizations. So the user always has the same interface whatever the factorization used.

The following identifiers were overloaded for solving linear systems:

```
Solve
TransposeSolve
HyperSolve
```

Using the first function, Solve, linear systems can be solved either with a right-hand vector or matrix:

Ax = b
AX = B

The following variants were implemented:

```
Solve(A,b,&x);
Solve(A,&bx);
Solve(A,B,&X);
Solve(A,&BX);
Solve(&A,b,&x);
Solve(&A,&bx);
Solve(&A,B,&X);
Solve(&A,&BX);
```

The original matrix A, matrix, is saved in the first four versions and an auxiliary matrix, factored, is used in factorizing. The variable matrixStatus remains AVAILABLE and modifications to the matrix are permitted.
Example:

```
FactoredGauss A(2,2,
                5.,3.,
                2.,6.);;
Vector b(2,8.,8.),x;
Solve(A,b,&x);
x.Print("Solution of first system);
Matrix C(2,3,
            8.,16.,24.,
            8.,16.,24.);
Solve(A,&C);  // must not be re-factorized
    C.Print("Solution with several known terms");
double det = A.Determinant(); // OK does not refactorize
A(1,1)=9.;    // change A; possible because AVAILABLE
Solve(A,b,&x); // factorizes again
    x.Print("The solution changes");
det = A.Determinant(); // does not re-factorize
```

The original matrix A is overloaded with the coefficients the factorization requires in the last four versions of Solve. The matrix cannot be modified, but all functions that require factorization of the matrix can be used.
Example:

```
FactoredGauss A(2,2,5.,3.,2.,6.);
Vector b(2,8.,8.),x;
Solve(&A,b,&x);
```

```
x.Print("Solution first system");
Vector c(2,16.,16.);
Solve(&A,&c);   // must not refactorize
c.Print("Solution second system");
double det = A.Determinant(); // OK does not refactorize
A(1,1)=9.;   // try to modify: error
             // the program stops
```

The following functions:

```
TransposeSolve(A,b,&x);
TransposeSolve(A,&bx);
TransposeSolve(&A,b,&x);
TransposeSolve(&A,&bx);
```

solve a system with the matrix $\mathbf{A}^T$ as matrix of coefficients.

The implementation of these functions, for classes FactoredGauss and FactoredCrout only, are shown in file FACTPLR.CPP.

Example:

```
FactoredGauss A(2,2,5.,3.,2.,6.);
Vector b(2,7.,9.),x;
TransposeSolve(&A,b,&x);
x.Print("Solution with transposed matrix");
```

The functions:

```
HyperSolve(A,b,&x);
HyperSolve(A,&bx);
```

solve the system iteratively and thereby improve its solution.

Here, we have to make another brief digression into the field of numerical analysis.

If the system below is solved numerically:

$$\mathbf{Ax = b}$$

a solution $\mathbf{x'}$ that approximates the true solution is obtained. If $\mathbf{d}$ is the error committed, the following can be written:

$$\mathbf{A(x' + d) = b}$$
$$\mathbf{A\,d = b - Ax'}$$

from which the correction **d** can be deduced and then applied to **x'** to obtain a tentative second solution **x"** and so on. Two conditions have to be satisfied for the procedure to be successful.

(1)   The system must not be too ill-conditioned.

(2)   The residual **b** – **Ax'** has to be calculated with greater accuracy than in the solution of the system.

> The most important point to highlight here is that each of the functions Solve, TransposeSolve and HyperSolve uses a virtual function, which permits the compiler to choose the appropriate method in the derived class.

The following functions were defined as *virtual pure* functions (equal to zero) in the class Factored.

```
// ============================================================
// *********    Functions for linear algebra    ***********
// ============================================================
// For each factorization PLR, Gauss, Qr, SVD
virtual void Factorization(void) = 0;
virtual void SpecificInitialize(void) = 0;
virtual void SpecificDeinitialize(void) = 0;
virtual void Solution(const Vector &b,Vector *x) = 0;
virtual void Solution(Vector *bx) = 0;
virtual void TransposeSolution
         (const Vector &b,Vector *x) = 0;
virtual void TransposeSolution(Vector *bx) = 0;
virtual void Solution(const Matrix &B,Matrix *X) = 0;
virtual void Solution(Matrix *BX) = 0;
virtual float Condition(void) = 0;
virtual double DeterminantEvaluation(void) = 0;
```

Here, virtual functions and the derivation of classes makes polymorphism possible and these functions can make full use of it. In this sense, they are the keystone of the above implementation.

For example, look at how Solve is implemented in a version which modifies neither matrix A nor vector b:

```
// ********************< Solve >********************
// * Purpose: Solves a linear system for a vector    *
// * Description: Matrix A is saved                   *
// *              the solution replaces x             *
// * Example: Solve(A,b,&x);                          *
// ****************************************************
void Solve(Factored &A,const Vector &b,Vector *x)
```

```
      {
    if(b.Size() != A.numRows)
       Error("%s%s%sSolve",
       Factored::ERROR,ERR_CHECK_DIMENSION,ERR_FUNCTION);
    A.PrepSolve();
    if(b.WhoAmI() == x->WhoAmI())
       A.Solution(x);
    else
       A.Solution(b,x);
    }
```

Note that

```
  if(b.WhoAmI() == x->WhoAmI())
```

is used to ensure that vector **b** is different from the vector in which the solution is placed.

The function PrepSolve is called first, then the correct version of Solution. PrepSolve checks the state of the matrix and, if necessary, proceeds to factorize:

```
// ******************< PrepSolve >********************
// *   Purpose: Prepares for factorizing             *
// *   Description: factored and matrix are          *
// *                independent                      *
// ****************************************************
void Factored::PrepSolve(void)
   {
   if(factorizationStatus == UNFACTORED &&
      matrixStatus == DESTROYED)
         Error("%s%s%sPrepOnlySolve",
         Factored::ERROR,
         Factored::ERR_DESTROYED,ERR_FUNCTION);
   else if(factorizationStatus == UNFACTORED &&
           matrixStatus == AVAILABLE)
       {
       FactoredInitialize();
       SpecificInitialize();
       Factorization();
       factorizationStatus = FACTORED;
       }
   else if(factorizationStatus == FACTORED &&
           matrixStatus == MODIFIED)
```

```
        {
        memcpy(factored[0],matrix[0],size*sizeof(float));
        Factorization();
        matrixStatus = AVAILABLE;
        }
    }
```

The way this function works can be broken up into three parts:

(1)   The matrix may be unusable. If it is, an error is flagged and the calculations are interrupted.

(2)   The matrix has yet to be factorized and so preparations are made for this to happen. The function `FactoredInitialize` is called and it initializes the auxiliary matrix `factored`. This function is common to all factorizations. The other two functions, `SpecificInitialize` and `Factorization` are *virtual* to the class `Factored`. Consequently, the corresponding derived class functions, which are using the function `Solve`, should be used.

(3)   The matrix has already been factorized and modified, in which case the auxiliary matrix and the portion dependent on the class do not need to be initialized. But copying the matrix and another factorization must go ahead.

The procedure is similar when you do not want the original matrix to be saved. The implementation is as below, in cases where the right-hand side vector and the solution vector are overloaded.

```
// *********************< Solve >*********************
// *   Purpose: Solves a linear system for a vector      *
// *   Description: The matrix A is factorized           *
// *                    the solution substitutes bx      *
// *   Example: Solve(&A,&bx);                           *
// ****************************************************
void Solve(Factored *A,Vector *bx)
    {
    if(bx->Size() != A->numRows)
        Error("%s%s%sOnlySolve",
        Factored::ERROR,
        ERR_CHECK_DIMENSION,ERR_FUNCTION);
     A->PrepOnlySolve();
    A->Solution(bx);
    }
```

```
// ******************< PrepOnlySolve >******************
// *  Purpose: prepares for factorization               *
// *  Description: The matrix factored is overloaded     *
// *                  onto matrix                        *
// *****************************************************
void Factored::PrepOnlySolve(void)
   {
   if(factorizationStatus == UNFACTORED &&
      matrixStatus == DESTROYED)
        Error("%s%s%sPrepOnlySolve",
        Factored::ERROR,
        Factored::ERR_DESTROYED,ERR_FUNCTION);
   else if(factorizationStatus == UNFACTORED &&
           matrixStatus == AVAILABLE)
      {
      Norm();
      factored = matrix;
      matrix = 0;
      factorizationStatus = FACTORED;
      matrixStatus = DESTROYED;
      SpecificInitialize();
      Factorization();
      }
   else if(factorizationStatus == FACTORED &&
           matrixStatus == MODIFIED)
      {   // factorized and modified
      Norm();
      FactoredDeinitialize();
      factored = matrix;
      matrix = 0;
      matrixStatus = DESTROYED;
      Factorization();
      }
   else if(factorizationStatus == FACTORED &&
           matrixStatus == AVAILABLE)
      {   // factorized con PrepSolve
      if(matrix != 0)  // frees matrix
         {
          delete matrix[0];
          delete matrix;
         }
      matrix = 0;
      matrixStatus = DESTROYED;
      }
   }
```

How the function PrepOnlySolve works can conceptually be broken up into four parts.

(1)   The matrix's accessibility is checked.

(2)   matrix's storage is used for factorizing. Before the original matrix is destroyed by overloading onto it the coefficients of the factorization, the function Norm, which, if necessary, is subsequently used to calculate the condition number, has to be called.

(3)   When the matrix has been factorized and later modified, the factorized matrix is de-initialized, factored's storage is freed and then matrix's storage is used for another factorization.

(4)   The matrix has been factorized but not modified, in which case matrix's storage needs only to be freed and an indication given that it has been destroyed.

The functions TransposeSolve are similar to Solve except for the fact that they call the virtual function TransposeSolution instead of Solution.

But the implementation of HyperSolve is more complex:

```
// *******************< HyperSolve >*******************
// *   Purpose: Solves a linear system for a vector      *
// *            with iterative improvement of solution   *
// *   Description: Matrix A is saved                     *
// *                solution replaces bx                  *
// *   Example: HyperSolveSolve(A,&bx);                   *
// *****************************************************
void HyperSolve(Factored &A,Vector *bx)
   {
   const int NITER = 10;
   float **mat = A.matrix;
   Vector b = *bx;
   Vector x(A.numColumns);
   Vector r(A.numRows);
   Solve(A,bx);
   x = *bx;
   double delx;
   float normdxOld;
   for(int iter =1;iter <= NITER;iter++)
      {
      for(int i=1;i<=A.numRows;i++)
         {
         delx = b[i];
         for(int j = 1;j <= A.numColumns;j++)
            delx -= mat[i][j] * (*bx)[j];
```

```
            r[i] = Control(delx);
            }
    *bx = r;
    Solve(A,bx);
    float normdx = bx->NormI();
    float normx = x.NormI();
    if(iter == 1)
        {
         normdxOld = normx;
         if(normdx > .5*normx)break;
        }
    else if(normdx >= normdxOld)break;
    normdxOld = normdx;
    x += *bx;
    *bx = x;
    if(normdx < 10.*MACH_EPS*normx)break;
    }
}
```

The function uses function Solve iteratively and ensures that the norm of the corrections to be made to the solution continues to decrease to the precision bound of the computer.

The other implemented functions, which were valid in all factorizations, are:

```
double Determinant(void);
char Singular(void); // 1 if singular 0 if not singular
void Inverse(Matrix *inv);
Matrix Inverse(void);
float ConditionNumber(void);
```

They can be called by any object of the four derived classes, in whatever order and without a system having had to be solved with one of the Solve functions.

The first function is used to calculate the matrix's determinant. I must again stress that this number is practically of almost no interest in modern algebra.

Example:

```
FactoredGauss A(2,2,1.,2.,3.,4.);
double det = A.Determinant();
```

The second function is needed to find out if there were serious problems during factorization. If the function return is equal to 1 the matrix is probably singular and if it is equal to 0 it is probably not.

Example:

```
FactoredGauss A(2,2,1.,2.,3.,4.);
if(A.Singular() == 1)
    Message("\nSingular matrix\n");
```

```
else
    Message("\nNon-singular matrix\n");
```

Even when this index is equal to zero there is no guarantee of having obtained a good solution to the system. There may be a non-singular but very ill-conditioned system for which the solution proves imprecise.

The inverse matrix can be evaluated in the form demonstrated by using the following functions:

```
FactoredGauss A(2,2,1.,2.,3.,4.);
Matrix inv1.inv2;
A.Inverse(&inv1);  // this version better
inv2 = A.Inverse();
```

Remember never to invert a matrix unless it is specifically required. When an inverse matrix appears in a formula, there is always a better, more efficient and more accurate alternative that does not require matrix inversion.

The condition number can be estimated with the last function.

This index is much more meaningful than the value of a determinant and has replaced it.

Example:

```
FactoredGauss A(2,2,1.,2.,3.,4.);
float cond = A.ConditionNumber();
```

The condition number for the classes under consideration can be calculated only if the matrix is squared.

The subject of calculating condition numbers merits a brief digression.

The condition number of a matrix **A**, is defined as the ratio between the value of one of its norms with that of its inverse matrix's norms.

Which norm is used is not important, because all lead to a value of the condition number that has the same order of magnitude – and that is sufficient.

The problem is that to calculate an inverse matrix norm, the matrix has to be inverted. This triples the calculation time needed to solve systems.

Matrix inversion can be avoided, yet a good estimate of the condition number could still be provided if one of the factorizations that we looked at is known. Here is not the place to go into the subject in any more depth, but it is important to stress that the condition number can be calculated with minimum effort.

15.4 The Class `FactoredPLR`

The class `FactoredPLR` is derived from the class `Factored` and is used as a base class for two classes `FactoredGauss` and `FactoredCrout`. In fact, the two classes share many characteristics that can be developed in their mother class, `FactoredPLR`.

This, too, is an *abstract* class because the function `Factorization` is a *pure virtual* function. Factorization algorithms can only be implemented in classes derived from it.

The class adds some quantities to those which are common to all classes derived from `Factored`:

```
int *indx;
int signd;
```

The first pointer is used to store the rows interchanging during factorization. The second is used to calculate the determinant with the correct sign.

> Let me emphasize again the advantage of being able to hide from users all the quantities needed by the function the users are using, but of whose purpose they are unaware. For example, the vector where interchanges of rows should be stored is one of the auxiliary vectors which, in FORTRAN, must be passed with the correct dimensions to the dedicated SUBROUTINES for factorizing and solving systems.

Initializing and De-Initializing

> Remember that a derived class must redeclare its constructors; they are not inherited.

The implementation of constructors is such that full use can be made of the constructors in the class `Factored`.

By way of example, the implementation of two constructors is shown below:

```
// default constructor;
FactoredPLR(void)
: Factored(){FurtherInit();}

// constructor from Matrix
FactoredPLR(const Matrix &rval)
: Factored(rval){FurtherInit();}
```

The function FurtherInit is used to initialize the new quantities of the class to zero.

```
// ********************< FurtherInit >*******************
// *   Purpose: Ends initialization                      *
// *   Description: Adds specific elements               *
// ******************************************************
void FactoredPLR::FurtherInit(void)
   {
   signd = 0;
   indx = 0;
   }
```

When the matrix has to be factorized, the base class, Factored, creates the space that may be needed for factored and calls the virtual function SpecificInitialize which is dedicated to initializing the derived class's own quantities, in this case the variable indx:

```
// ****************< SpecificInitialize >***************
// *   Description: Adds specific elements               *
// ******************************************************
void FactoredPLR::SpecificInitialize(void)
   {
   if(numRows != numColumns)
      Error("%s%s%sSpecificInitialize",
      Factored::ERROR,
      ERR_CHECK_DIMENSION,ERR_FUNCTION);
   indx = new int[numRows + 1];
   if(!indx)
      Error("%s%s%sSpecificInitialize",
      Factored::ERROR,ERR_SPACE,ERR_FUNCTION);
   }
```

De-initialization must go on in the same way, but in the opposite direction.

15.5 The Class FactoredQRLQ

The class FactoredQRLQ is derived from the class Factored and is used as the base class for the two classes FactoredQR and FactoredLQ. This class adds some quantities to those common to all the classes derived from Factored:

```
int *indx;
float *dqr;   //for LQ and QR
float *bqr;   //for LQ and QR
```

As far as the problem of initialization and de-initialization is concerned, the same applies as for the class `FactoredPLR`.

15.6 The Classes `FactoredGauss` and `FactoredCrout`

The objects of these classes can be used to factorize a matrix in the form **PLR**.

> Methods of solving linear systems with this kind of factorization are in practice the fastest (for dense and non-structured matrices).

Until a few years ago, the Gaussian factorization method and those derived from it were not viewed in a very favourable light because it appeared that the accuracy of results declined for theoretical reasons. Subsequent studies re-evaluated the method, which should be considered as the *first choice* for *squared, dense, non-symmetrical and non-structured matrices*.

> The implementations for these classes accept only squared matrices. Class types **QR** or **LQ** have to be used for rectangular matrices.

15.7 The Classes `FactoredQR` and `FactoredLQ`

The objects of the class `FactoredQR` are recommended for dealing with matrices that have a greater number of rows than columns. Conversely, the objects of the class `FactoredLQ` are useful for matrices with a lower number of rows than columns.

Example:

```
FactoredQR F(4,2,
             1.,2.,
             3.,4.,
             5.,6.,
             7.,8.);
Vector x,b(4,3.1,7.2,10.8,15.);

    // the solution that minimizes
    // the sum of the square of the residuals
Solve(F,b,&x);
x.Print("solution");
```

```
FactoredLQ G(2,4,
              1.,2.,3.,4.,
              5.,6.,7.,8.);
Vector c(2,10.,20.);
Solve(G,c,&x); // Finds x with minimum _2 norm
x.Print("Solution");
```

When the number of rows is equal to the number of columns, the methods employed by these classes are slower in comparison with those of a **PLR**. Calculating times tend to double when large matrices are involved.

The advantages gained by using these classes are as follows:

(1)   The solution is a little less sensitive to ill-conditioned matrices. So, sometimes squared matrices are also advantageous.
(2)   Rectangular matrices can be dealt with.
(3)   The **Q** matrices that can be deduced by factorizing have important characteristics. For example, they are essential in problems of optimization with linked variables.

The functions `GetMatrixP`, `GetMatrixQ` and `GetMatrixR` were implemented to deduce the matrices **P**, **Q** and **R** which are important in the factorization:

PA = R
A = QR

The way the functions are used is simple:

```
FactoredQR A;
Matrix P,Q;
MatrixRight R;
....
A.GetMatrixP(&P);
A.GetMatrixQ(&Q);
A.GetMatrixR(&R);
```

As stated previously, the order in which they are called does not matter. If the matrix has already been factorized, a call to them smoothly uses the factorization. If not, factorization proceeds automatically.

One small detail for anyone interested in numerical implementations – the matrices **Q** or **P** are physically calculated only if this is specifically requested. If not, only those coefficients that are needed to solve systems are stored.

Since one of the most frequent uses of factorizing **QR** is linked to problems of regression or at least to solving over-determined systems, it is useful to be able to deduce the residuals of the equation:

r = Ax – b

If the system is over-determined, **QR** produces an estimate of the residuals as a sub-product of factorization.

There are two advantages to this.

(1)   Calculation time is shorter.

(2)   The residuals can be calculated, even if the original matrix has been destroyed because it was overloaded with coefficients of the factorization.

The function, `GetResiduals`, does what its name suggests and is used as follows:

```
FactoredQR A;
Vector r;
......
A.GetResiduals(&r);
```

15.8 Examples

Numerous examples of how the classes are used are shown in the following files: `EXGAUSS.CPP, EXCROUT.CPP, EXQR.CPP, EXLQ.CPP`.

Linear Regressions

Let's look at how a few problems relating to calculating a linear regression can be solved, to demonstrate the convenience of having a program library based on object-oriented programming.

 What must be emphasized is that the approach used to solve problems is different – objects are responsible for the functions that manipulate them.

First, let's look at calculating the variance V(y):

$$V(y) = f^T(F^TF)\text{-}1^f\sigma^2 = (R^{\text{-}T}\,f)^T(R^{\text{-}T}\,f)\sigma^2$$

The following program could be written:

```
FactoredQR F(5,3,      // define F
             1.,1.,1.,
             1.,2.,4.,
             1.,3.,9.,
             1.,4.,16.,
             1.,5.,25.);
Vector f(3,1.,2.,4.); // define f
float s2 = 1.e-4;     // variance s2
MatrixRight R; // define a MatrixRight

     // calculates the matrix R of F = QR
F.GetMatrixRight(&R);

Vector x; // define a Vector x

// solves RTx = f
TransposeSolve(R,f,&x);

     // calculates V(y)
float vy = Dot(x,x)*s2; // or x%x*s2;
```

As can be seen, the code is very easy to write and interpret.

Suppose you want to calculate the residuals of the model, given certain experimental values of the variable **y**:

```
Vector y(5,1.1,2.1,4.5,3.2,1.3); // define y
Vector b; // vector of the parameters
Solve(F,y,&b);   // calculates the parameters
Vector res; // vector for residuals
F.GetResiduals(&res); // calculates the residuals
```

You need not concern yourself about the order in which operations on object F are performed; it knows whether factorizing has taken place and it is still available.

If you want to calculate the mean square error of the model all that has to be written is:

```
float mse = res.Norm2();
mse = mse*mse/2.;
```

as it is the square of norm-2 of the residuals divided by the degrees of freedom, 5–3=2.

If you want to calculate the matrix of variance and co-variance of parameters:

$$V(\mathbf{b}) = (\mathbf{F^TF})^{-1} \sigma^2$$

it is advantageous to use the matrix **R** again instead of calculating $\mathbf{F^TF}$ and then inverting it:

$$V(b) = \mathbf{R^{-1}R^{-T}}\sigma^2$$

The program is:

```
Inverse(&R); // calculates inverse of MatrixRight R
MatrixSymm V;  / defines a MatrixSymm
ProductT(R,R,&V); // calculates RRT and places it in V
V *= s2;
```

Check on the Function `ConditionNumber`

In some circumstances, the condition number can be calculated theoretically and the technique used to obtain the estimate can be checked to see if it is satisfactory.

Remember that a value that has the same order of magnitude as the true value is all that needs to be obtained for it to be satisfactory.

Take the matrix below as the first example:

$$A = \begin{vmatrix} 11 + a & 10 + a & 14 + a \\ 12 + a & 11 + a & -13 + a \\ 14 + a & 13 + a & -66 + a \end{vmatrix}$$

Its condition number is $(3a + 35)(166a + 1843)$.
If $a = 50$ it is 1876455.
Using Gauss factorization an estimate of 1445970 is obtained and by factorizing **QR** an estimate of 1316943.

Take the matrix below as a second example:

$$A = \begin{vmatrix} 1. & 1. + a \\ 1. - a & 1. \end{vmatrix}$$

The theoretical condition number is $(2. + a)(2. + a)/(a*a)$. If $a = .01$ it is 64618.
An estimate of 40201 is obtained by Gauss factorization and of 40180 by **QR** factorization.

Check on the function `HyperSolve`

The condition number of the matrix:

$$A = \begin{vmatrix} 11 + a & 10 + a & 14 + a \\ 12 + a & 11 + a & -13 + a \\ 14 + a & 13 + a & -66 + a \end{vmatrix}$$

if a = 50 is 1876455. Poor accuracy can be expected from a solution based on a system such as this. Taking the vector below as the right-hand side:

$$\mathbf{b} = \begin{vmatrix} 3a + 35 \\ 3a + 10 \\ 3a - 39 \end{vmatrix}$$

the theoretical solution is $\mathbf{x} = (1., 1., 1.)$.

Using Crout's method $\mathbf{x} = (0.98932, 1.0109, 1.0000)$ is obtained. The error committed is in the second decimal figure, as predicted by the value of the condition number and by the accuracy of the calculation ~ 1.e-8.

If the function HyperSolve is used in this case, the exact solution of the seventh decimal figure is obtained.

Factorization LQ

If the system is under-determined (that is, the number of equations is less that the number of unknowns), factorizing **LQ** gives the solution **x**, with the minimum value of the Euclidean norm.

For example consider the simple problem of a single equation in two unknowns:

$$x_1 + x_2 = 1$$

This is the equation for a straight line passing through the points:

$$(x_1 = 0, x_2 = 1)$$
$$(x_1 = 1, x_2 = 0)$$

There exists an infinity of pairs of values of x_1 and x_2 that satisfy an equation of this kind. By factorizing **LQ**:

```
FactoredLQ A(1,2,1.,1.);
Vector b(1,1.),x;
Solve(A,b,&x);
x.Print("Solution with LQ");
```

the solution obtained is $\mathbf{x} = (.5, .5)$ which is the solution that minimizes the norm of **x**, or that which is found on the straight line and is nearer than the origin of the axes.

This property is useful, for example, in applications of Newton's method for solving systems of non-linear equations when a row of the Jacobian is almost a linear combination of the others – the corrections δx which are obtained are those of the minimum norm. The danger of having abnormal corrections is therefore reduced.

Summary

E come quei che con lena affannata
uscito fuor dal pelago alla riva
si volge all'acqua perigliosa e guata...

Just as a swimmer, still with panting breath,
now safe upon the shore, out of the deep
might turn for one last look at the dangerous waters, . . .

Dante, *Inferno*, I

Interactions Between Classes

A complex program may contain several classes which interact with one another. The most appropriate implementation should be chosen for the situation in hand. The choice is often evident, but sometimes you have to spend long periods of time on planning, frequently rethinking parts of the program or making changes, even quite substantial ones, to it.

Two classes can be made to interact in one of three different ways. By:

(1)   making classes friends of each other;
(2)   using the composition technique, that is, by using a class object in the definition of another class;
(3)   deriving one class from another.

Chapter 12 provided many examples of the first technique. The various classes for defining matrices and vectors can access each others' private data and thereby reduce calculation times for implemented operations.

 Using the technique of making classes friends of one another is a good idea, if, for whatever reason, you want to maintain the independence of the two classes, particularly when they do not stand in any logical relation to each other.

For example, a class designed to manage a video screen has no point of contact with another class designed for solving a numeric problem. But it can be useful to make them `friends` to improve the efficiency of whatever task they are expected to perform.

> Efficiency in calculation times should always be considered in classes intended for solving numerical problems. Sometimes, you have to forego deriving one class from another so that you can write optimally efficient codes.

For example, the class `Vector` had everything that was required for the class `Matrix` to deduce it. But there would have been a penalty in terms of calculation time, since vectors have to be treated as matrices with only one column.

Instead, using a class common to `Matrix` has to be looked at as a serious possible alternative, where matrices with a special structure are involved (Right, Left and Symmetric). In fact, addition, subtraction, saving and copying are identical for all classes, once all matrices have been stored as a single vector.

In Chapter 13, the composition technique was adopted for defining the classes of sparse matrices, and `struct Element` was used in defining the `class MatrixSparse`. In this case, a true object is *not* used in the composition.

> You should bear in mind that every time a class is defined using an object of another class, the alternative of *deriving* one class from the other should be seriously considered.
> Composition may instead be useful when affinity between the two objects is poor or non-existent, in which case one object uses the other.

Finally, examples of deriving classes for linear algebra were provided in Chapter 15.

You may wonder when it is best to derive one class form another.

> *Deriving* one class from another must be seriously considered, if the two objects' classes have at least one of the following characteristics.
>
> (1)   many features in common
> (2)   only a few differences between them
> (3)   an hierarchical relationship
> (4)   a relationship involving different degrees of abstraction.

Object-Oriented Programming

Let's have another look at some of the basic concepts of object-oriented programming.

Functions are the *basic blocks* that are used to build programs in procedural programming, whereas *objects* are used in object-oriented programming. An object should be thought of as a kind of *mini-program*; and it is much more than a simple function. When an object is defined, it performs a certain number of tasks with its constructor, as if it were a normal program. But it is much more than a normal program. It can interact with other objects, that is, with other mini-programs. And such mini-programs can perform other tasks when they leave scope or when they are dynamically de-initialized by the `new` and `delete` operators. During their lifetime, objects communicate with the rest of the program, and, using the appropriate interface, with other objects. Functions are used inside objects to manipulate variables and the objects themselves. Everything that characterizes objects (functions, variable and objects) is *encapsulated* in objects and *hidden* from the user, who can communicate with objects only across an interface which has been prepared by whoever implemented the class of which the object is a specimen.

The main advantages to be gained from using objects instead of functions, as is done in procedural programming, are as follows.

(1) An object is always aware of the tasks it is performing and it can, as a result, check whether certain tasks can be performed. It can also take decisions by itself.

(2) Users are not required to be aware of the tasks performed inside the object, when they call it across its interface.

(3) Functions encapsulated inside objects can be optimized in terms of calculation times, because the object, not the user, is allowed to use them and objects know when they can be used correctly, because they know the history of the data that is being sent to them.

The advantages listed so far stem from the two characteristics that we looked at first – *encapsulation* of functions with data and data *hiding* of both inside objects.

The other two pillars of object-oriented programming are *deriving* classes and *polymorphism*.

Deriving one class from another has the following advantages.

(1) It is possible to define classes using existing codes for a similar class, or a class with a different hierarchical order. It saves a considerable amount of programming time.

(2) It reinforces the opportunities offered by encapsulation and data hiding.

(3) Genuine *polymorphism* can be achieved by using *virtual* functions.

We have followed the evolution of the concept of *polymorphism* throughout the book.

(1) We began with a crude, but most important form of polymorphism – overloading function identifiers.

(2)   Then we encountered overloading operators, a more interesting form of polymorphism.

(3)   Finally, it developed into its most mature form – object-oriented programming linked to the idea of virtual functions and deriving classes.

Polymorphism confers the following advantages.

(1)   Codes are easier to read and write.
(2)   Programs can be written more quickly.
(3)   Large tranches of existing code can be used without correction and re-compilation.
(4)   Classes can be derived from other classes, the source code of which is not at hand.
(5)   The capacity to extend a class can be dramatically boosted.

The four concepts of *data hiding*, *encapsulation*, *derivation* and *polymorphism* are all packed tightly into one single concept – the *object*.

We see the real world as being made up of objects. Functions and data are essential for carrying out calculations.

We have to adapt our way of thinking to the demands of the computer when we are using procedural languages.
But when we are using object-oriented programming we seek to adapt the language of the computer to our way of thinking.

E quindi uscimmo a riveder le stelle.

And we came out once more to see the stars.

Dante, Inferno, **XXXIV**

Bibliography

N. Barkakati, *The Waite Group Turbo C++ Bible*, SAMS (1990)

P. A. Darnell, P.E. Margolis, *Software Engineering in C*, Springer-Verlag (1988)

B. Eckel, *Using C++*, Osborne McGraw-Hill (1989)

M. A. Ellis, B. Stroustrup, *The Annotated C++ Reference Manual*, Addison-Wesley (1990)

B. Flamig, *Turbo C++. A Self-Teaching Guide*, John Wiley (1991)

T. L. Hansen, *The C++ Answer Book*, Addison-Wesley (1990)

S. R. Ladd, *C++ Techniques & Applications*, M&T Books (1990)

S. B. Lippman, *C++ Primer*, AT&T Laboratories (1989)

J. S. Shapiro, *A C++ Toolkit*, Prentice Hall (1991)

J. D. Smith, *Reusability and Software Construction: C and C++*, John Wiley & Sons (1990)

B. Stroustrup, *The C++ Programming Language*, Second Edition, Addison-Wesley (1991)

K. Weiskamp, B. Flamig, *The Complete C++ Primer*, Academic Press (1990)

R. Winder, *Developing C++ Software*, John Wiley & Sons (1991)

Index